Wedemeyer Reports!

As the United States stands poised "on the brink" of war with Red China and the U.S.S.R., General Wedemeyer delivers a devastating indictment of the Grand Strategy of World War II —strategy which inevitably set the stage for today's world crisis.

In an expert revaluation, Wedemeyer, a top military strategist, has dared to open the Pandora's box of World War II high command and diplomacy. Powers and personalities emerge in arresting new perspectives as Wedemeyer bares official correspondence and conversations, secret meetings and agreements which foreshadowed the Allied invasion of Europe, the war in the Pacific, and American postwar policy in Asia.

WEDEMEYER REPORTS! is also an objective, dispassionate record of self-examination, spanning a tumultuous period. Detailed with accuracy and candor, it is destined to stir up a storm of controversy from the Pentagon to distant political capitals of the world.

Illuminating the report are candid close-ups of great wartime figures; revealing sidelights on the pre-Pearl Harbor newsbreak of General Wedemeyer's "Victory Program" and his subsequent investigation by the FBI; the momentous trip to London in April, 1942, with Marshall and Hopkins; and the postponement of OPERATION BOLERO (the proposed invasion of Europe in 1943) to OVERLORD in 1944. Perhaps most revealing of all are the disquieting facts behind his famous Wedemeyer Report on China and the Acheson-Truman White Paper which followed.

Condemning a score of tactical and diplomatic errors in World War II strategy—from Churchill's plan for "closing the ring" on Germany to our own bankrupt postwar Asian policy— this logical, documented report by a topflight strategist, commander of American troops in the China Theater and Chief of Staff to Chiang-Kai-shek, makes a profound and exciting contribution to modern history.

The Devin-Adair Company *Publishers*
23 East 26th St.; New York, N.Y. 10010

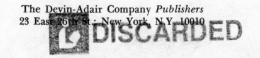

GENERAL ALBERT C. WEDEMEYER

WEDEMEYER

REPORTS!

THE DEVIN-ADAIR COMPANY

NEW YORK

For
Mr. Thomas A. O'Hara
and
The late Dr. Merrill Moore

"Our God and soldiers we alike adore
Ev'n at the brink of danger: not before;
After deliverance, both alike requited,
Our gods forgotten, and our soldiers slighted."

—FRANCIS QUARLES

FOREWORD

"The Second World War," says historian Walter Millis, "was administered." Since administration presupposes a comprehensive plan, this, as I take it, means that special efforts had to be made to see the war whole. As a war planner in Washington from 1940 into 1943 I was intimately involved in an attempt to see the war whole—and even after I had moved on to Asia, where I served successively on Lord Louis Mountbatten's staff in India and as U.S. commander in the China Theater, I was still close to the problems of adapting Grand Strategy to a conflict of global dimensions.

It was inevitable, then, that the subject of Grand Strategy should predominate in this book. I was not deprived of my own share of war experience from close up, but my most strenuous battles were those of the mind—of trying, as we in Washington's planning echelons saw it, to establish a correct and meaningful Grand Strategy which would have resulted in a fruitful peace and a decent postwar world.

There were many obstacles in the way of developing a meaningful strategy, of assuring that our abundant means, material and spiritual, would be used to achieve worthy human ends. First, there was the pervasive influence of the Communists, who had their own plans for utilizing the war as a springboard to world domination. Second, there was the obstinacy of that grand old man, Winston Churchill, who, as we soldiers felt, could never reconcile his own concepts of Grand Strategy with sound military decisions. Because we *had* to contend with the machinations of Stalin on the one hand and with the bulldog tenacity of Churchill on the other, this book has had to be harsh in some of its personal assessments. But I hope I have made it plain that none of my judgments is personal in the ordinary connotation of the word.

My acknowledgements of aid in maturing a point of view would, if set down here, go back far into my past and take up all too many pages. But I wish especially to thank the late George Creel, Woodrow Wilson's World War I Administrator of War Information, for many hours of sage conversation and advice. I wish also to thank John Chamberlain for editorial aid in reducing the manuscript to manageable proportions, and Freda Utley for editorial help. Further thanks must go to Alice M. Miller, who has been in charge of the files of the Army's War Plans Division for many years; to the personnel of the Military History Division of the U.S. Army, Colonel Douglas G. Gilbert and Israel Wice; to Sherrod East and Wilbur J. Nigh from the National Archives and Records Service; to the Army's Record Section; to Elaine Hill; and to Elaine Mauser, Katherine Moore, and Edna Moore for help in preparing the manuscript for the press. Finally, I owe more than I can express to all the members of my family who have patiently borne with me the trials and tribulations of a neophyte author. My friend, C. D. Batchelor, the distinguished artist, has provided illustrations for this book as well as advice and inspiration.

I am conscious that I have not paid a deserved tribute to scores of comrades-in-arms who worked with me in Washington, India, and the China Theater. I hope to make amends later for this in a book devoted especially to the Far East.

A. C. W.

CONTENTS

WEDEMEYER REPORTS!

CHAPTER I

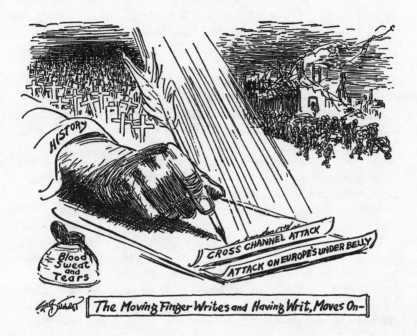

The Moving Finger Writes and Having Writ, Moves On—

PRELUDE TO WAR

PEARL HARBOR brought an abrupt and inconclusive end to the Great Debate between the interventionists and the isolationists. There could no longer be any question whether to fight or not to fight, once America had been attacked. We were now, willy-nilly, engaged in combat in the Pacific, and Germany, by declaring war on us in support of her Japanese ally, shut off any opposition to our intervention in the European struggle. The America Firsters henceforth joined in the war effort as ardently as the Britain Firsters and the Russia Firsters. The fact that Japan's attack had been deliberately provoked was obscured by the disaster at Pearl Harbor and by the

1

subsequent loss of the Philippines, where the American garrison was regarded as expendable by an Administration bent on getting us into the European war by the back door. The noninterventionists, together with those who realized that Communist Russia constituted at least as great a menace as Nazi Germany, henceforth held their peace although well aware that President Roosevelt had maneuvered us into the war by his patently unneutral actions against Germany and the final ultimatum to Japan. Whatever one's views on the origins of the war, we now had to go all out to win, and leave the debate to the historians of the future.

Today, seeing the wreckage of the hopes which led America to mobilize her great industrial strength for total victory and to send her sons to fight and die again in foreign wars, despite President Roosevelt's repeated assurances that they would never be called upon to do so, one should examine how and why the United States became involved in a war which was to result in the extension of totalitarian tyranny over vaster regions of the world than Hitler ever dreamed of conquering.

Thanks to the publication of many biographies and memoirs by leading actors in the most tragic drama of our time, and also to the revelations to be found in published documents from American, British, and German state archives, facts which were only dimly perceived by noninterventionists in the fateful years preceding Pearl Harbor are now revealed to all who read or care to inform themselves. Yet, although the results of the Second World War have proven far more harmful to our security, there has as yet been no era of "debunking" such as followed the 1914–18 war. In the twenties, the public on both sides of the Atlantic was disillusioned concerning the origins, causes, and consequences of that conflict by a flood of books, articles, and speeches exposing the facts which contradicted wartime propaganda. Within less than a decade the myth of sole German "war guilt" had been shattered, the real causes of the war uncovered, and the evil consequences of the punitive Versailles Peace Treaty recognized. But today, many years after the fighting ended only to be succeeded by the cold war with our former "gallant ally," the Union of Soviet Socialist Republics, there has been no comparable probing into the real causes of the war or general recognition that the present perilous world situation is largely of our own making.

Few will even admit that the Soviet colossus would not now bestride nearly half the world had the United States kept out of the war, at least until Soviet Russia and Nazi Germany had exhausted each other. If we had followed the policy advocated by ex-President Hoover, Senator Taft, and other patriotic Americans, we probably would have stood aside until our intervention could enforce a just, and therefore enduring, peace instead of giving unconditional aid to Communist Russia. And if, after we became involved in the war, Roosevelt and Churchill had not sought to obliterate Germany, which was tantamount to destroying power equilibrium on the Continent, we might not have fought in vain.

Our objective should have been maintenance of the Monroe Doctrine and the restoration of a balance of power in Europe and the Far East. The same holds true for England, whose national interest, far from requiring the annihilation of her temporary enemies, was irretrievably injured by a "victory" which immensely enhanced Soviet Russian territory, power, and influence. It is indeed one of the great ironies of history that Winston Churchill, who had proclaimed that he had not become the King's First Minister "in order to preside over the liquidation of the British Empire," pursued policies which hastened Britain's decline to her present status of a second-rate power. In none of his books has he ever recognized either his own or Roosevelt's responsibility for the disastrous outcome of the war. Yet in the preface to his history of the Second World War he writes:

> The human tragedy reaches its climax in the fact that after all the exertions and sacrifices of hundreds of millions of people and of the victories of the Righteous Cause, we have still not found Peace or Security, and that *we lie in the grip of even worse perils than those we have surmounted.* [Italics added.]

Churchill indeed seems to lack either the wisdom to recognize his mistakes or the greatness to admit them and say *mea culpa.*

It is indeed strange that Churchill, who belonged by birth and tradition to the long line of British statesmen who had made England the greatest power in the world by intelligent strategy in peace and war, reveals himself as lacking their wisdom and statecraft. Instead of seeking to re-establish the balance of power in Europe, which had been the constant objective of British policy for more than three hundred years, he sought the destruction of Germany and thus gave Russia an opportunity to dominate Europe. Churchill's folly in disregarding the precepts of his forebears and letting his passions sublimate his reason was matched by Roosevelt's disregard of George Washington's advice to his successors in the conduct of United States policy. In his "Farewell Address," Washington said:

> In the execution of such a plan, nothing is more essential than that permanent, inveterate antipathies against particular nations, and passionate attachments for others, should be excluded; and that, in place of them, just and amicable feelings towards all should be cultivated. The Nation which indulges towards another an habitual hatred or an habitual fondness is in some degree a slave. It is a slave to its animosity or to its affection, either of which is sufficient to lead it astray from its duty and its interest. . . . The peace often . . . of Nations has been the victim.
>
> . . . Sympathy for the favorite Nations, facilitating the illusion of an imaginary common interest in cases where no real common interest exists, and infusing into one the enmities of the other, betrays the former into a participation in the quarrels and wars of the latter, without adequate inducement or justification. . . .

This and other wise precepts of the Founding Fathers of the Republic which have stood the test of time were ignored by Roosevelt who, like the dictator he so passionately hated, directed U.S. policy on the personal level and imagined that Stalin was, or could be induced to become, "his friend," and Soviet Russia a permanent ally.

There is little doubt that a majority of the American people, remembering the broken promises of the 1914 war, desired to keep out of the Second World War which they instinctively, or by reason of past experience, realized could not lead to any better results and might well prove more disastrous. It was made clear both by Roosevelt's campaign promises and by the support given to Charles Lindbergh and others who forewarned of the disastrous consequences which would ensue from their engagement in yet another "Crusade" that they wanted to follow George Washington's too often neglected advice.

A generation born or brought up in the debunking era of the

twenties and thirties wanted no part in another world holocaust. The First World War had resulted in the establishment of Communist tyranny in Russia. The punitive peace which followed had stunted the growth of democracy in Germany and eventually led to the destruction of the Weimar Republic and the establishment of Nazi tyranny in Germany. The Versailles Treaty had also converted Eastern Europe into a hodgepodge of unviable small states whose peoples were worse off, and enjoyed less liberty and opportunity, than under the Austro-Hungarian Empire which Wilsonian principles had split up into antagonistic parts. And who would say that these peoples enjoyed any advantage and were not endangering their own existence by being utilized by France for the purpose of "containing" Germany? A second war "to make the world safe for democracy" was unlikely to lead to any better results and might prove disastrous to Western civilization.

Today it would seem almost certain that the policy advocated by American noninterventionists would have been more beneficial to Britain as well as to the rest of the world than that of the powerful Anglophiles and other interventionists. In a famous speech which brought opprobrium on his head, Lindbergh said on April 23, 1941:

> I have said before, and I will say again, that I believe it will be a tragedy to the entire world if the British Empire collapses. This is one of the main reasons why I opposed this war before it was declared and why I have constantly advocated a negotiated peace. I did not feel that England and France had a reasonable chance of winning. France has now been defeated; and, despite the propaganda and confusion of recent months, it is now obvious that England is losing the war. I believe this is realized even by the British Government. But they have one last desperate plan remaining. They hope that they may be able to persuade us to send another American Expeditionary Force to Europe, and to share with England militarily, as well as financially, the fiasco of this war.
>
> I do not blame England for this hope, or for asking for our assistance. But we now know that she declared a war under circumstances which led to the defeat of every nation that sided with her from Poland to Greece. We know that in the desperation of war England promised to all those nations armed assistance that she could not send. We know that she

misinformed them, as she has misinformed us, concerning her state of preparation, her military strength, and the progress of the war.

Following Germany's attack on Russia, those who knew something about communism foresaw that American intervention would in all probability result in creating what Churchill recognized too late as "worse perils." For instance, Professor Nicholas Spykman of Yale wrote in a book published shortly after Pearl Harbor (*America's Strategy in World Politics: The United States and the Balance of Power*) that the annihilation of Germany and Japan would open Europe to Soviet domination and observed: "A Russian State from the Urals to the North Sea can be no great improvement over a German State from the North Sea to the Urals."

Ex-President Herbert Hoover was among those who had the wisdom and foresight to realize that our aid to Communist Russia would have disastrous consequences. In June, 1941, when Britain was comparatively safe from German invasion thanks to Hitler's attack on Russia, he said (as recalled in his broadcast August 10, 1954) that "the gargantuan jest of all history would be our giving aid to the Soviet Government." He urged that America should allow the two dictators to exhaust each other and prophesied that the result of our assistance would be "to spread communism over the world." Whereas, if we stood aside the time would come when we could bring "lasting peace to the world."

President Roosevelt was undeterred by this and other prophetic voices. He was determined to get the United States into the war by one means or another in spite of the reluctance or positive refusal of the American people to become involved.

Step by step from the Lend-Lease Act to the Atlantic Conference in August, 1941, the President had resorted to both open and covert acts contravening the international laws which circumscribe the action permissible to neutral powers and directly contrary to the intent of Congress and the American people. Acts "short of war" taken to help Britain were succeeded by belligerent action when secret orders were given to the Atlantic fleet on August 25, 1941, to attack and destroy German and Italian "hostile forces." This order came two weeks after the Atlantic Conference, at which Roosevelt had said to Churchill, "I may never declare war; I may make war.

If I were to ask Congress to declare war, they might argue about it for three months." Following the *Greer* incident in which an American destroyer fired on a German submarine, the President on September 11 made his shoot-on-sight speech in which he called the Nazi submarines and raiders "rattlesnakes": said that "when you see a rattlesnake poised to strike you do not wait until he has struck before you crush him," and stated that henceforth "if German or Italian vessels of war enter the waters the protection of which is necessary to American defense, they will do so at their own peril."

Thus we should have been openly involved in the war months before Pearl Harbor had it not been for Hitler's evident determination not to be provoked by our belligerent acts into declaring war on us. Count Ciano in his diaries, published after the war, wrote that the Germans had "firmly decided to do nothing which will accelerate or cause America's entry into the war."

Roosevelt had carried Congress along with him in his unneutral actions by conjuring up the bogey of an anticipated attack on America. We now know, thanks to exhaustive examination of the German secret archives at the time of the Nuremberg trials, that there never was any plan of attack on the United States. On the contrary, the tons of documents examined prove that Hitler was all along intent on avoiding war with the United States. He did not declare war on us until compelled to do so by his alliance with Japan.

In the words of the eminent British military historian, Major General J. F. C. Fuller, writing in *A Military History of the Western World* (p. 629), in 1956:

> The second American crusade ended even more disastrously than the first, and this time the *agent provocateur* was not the German Kaiser but the American President, whose abhorrence of National Socialism and craving for power precipitated his people into the European conflict and so again made it world-wide. From the captured German archives there is no evidence to support the President's claims that Hitler contemplated an offensive against the Western Hemisphere, and until America entered the war there is abundant evidence that this was the one thing he wished to avert.

Extreme provocation having failed to induce Germany to make war on us, and there being no prospect of Congress declaring war because of the determination of the great majority of the American people not to become active belligerents, Roosevelt turned his eyes to the Pacific. It could be that Japan would show less restraint, since it was possible to exert diplomatic and economic pressures that would practically compel her to make war on us. She was too far committed to retreat without endangering her national existence, and we offered her no possibility of a compromise that would enable her to retire from her untenable position without losing face.

On July 26, 1941, the President had decreed economic sanctions against Japan which, had they been imposed at the outset of the Sino-Japanese war, might have saved China but could no longer bring her any benefit. Sanctions were now being imposed, not in order to help China, but to provoke Japan to attack, and thus resolve the President's dilemma of how to get us into the war to maintain British power.

In his account of the Atlantic Conference (*The Grand Alliance*, 1950, page 446), Churchill reproduced a telegram he sent home on August 12, 1941:

> We have laid special stress on the warning to Japan which constitutes the teeth of the President's communication. One would always fear State Department trying to tone it down; but President has promised definitely to use the hard language.

Again, in a message to Menzies, the Australian Prime Minister, Churchill stated that "the President promised me to give the warning to Japan in the terms agreed to . . . You should note that the President's warning covers an attack upon Russia . . ." No doubt because Australia would be endangered by war with Japan, Churchill erroneously reassured her Prime Minister that this ultimatum to Japan would cause her to "lie quiet for a while."

That this was not the purpose was clearly revealed by Roosevelt when he said, on November 25, that he thought Japan would attack us by the following Monday. Later Stimson put it this way: the question was how we could "maneuver the Japanese into the position of firing the first shot but allowing no danger to ourselves."

It proved impossible for the President and his closest associates to fool all of the American people all of the time they were engaged in maneuvering us into war. But Franklin D. Roosevelt, the proclaimed champion of democracy, was as successful as any dictator could have been in keeping Congress and the public in ignorance of his secret commitments to Britain—commitments which flouted the will and wishes of the voters who had re-elected him only after he had assured them he would keep us out of war. Indeed there are few more flagrant examples of cynical disregard of the will of the people than that revealed in Roosevelt's personal correspondence with Churchill, as revealed in the latter's books. This correspondence and Churchill's own account of his talks with Harry Hopkins, whom he describes as "the main prop and animator" of the American President, prove beyond doubt that as early as January, 1941, Roosevelt had concluded what amounted to a secret alliance with Britain committing America to war.

On January 10, 1941, Harry Hopkins, who Churchill had been informed was "the closest confidant and personal agent of the President," arrived at 10 Downing Street and "with gleaming eye and quiet constrained passion" told the British Prime Minister:

> The President is determined that we shall win the war together. Make no mistake about it.
> He has sent me here to tell you that at all costs and by all means he will carry you through, no matter what happens to him—there is nothing that he will not do so far as he has human power.

There sat Harry Hopkins, Churchill writes in *The Grand Alliance,* "absolutely glowing with refined comprehension of the Cause." This "Cause," as Hopkins told Churchill on behalf of Roosevelt, was to be "the defeat, ruin and slaughter of Hitler, to the exclusion of all other purposes, loyalties or aims." Thus did the President of the United States through the mouth of Harry Hopkins renounce adherence to the Constitution of the United States and repudiate his pledged word to the American people to keep them out of foreign wars for the sake of an aim he conceived to be higher, namely the "slaughter" of Hitler.

The previous December, secret joint staff conversations with the British had begun and the policy resulting in the Victory Program launched. The question, as Admiral Stark said, was no longer "whether" we should enter the war but "when." On January 10, 1941, Roosevelt asked Congress to pass the Lend-Lease Act, by which it in effect surrendered to the President its constitutional right to declare war. Subsequently Roosevelt, again in Admiral Stark's words, viewed the United States as being in the European war "except officially." But he could not make it official, at least until he could provoke Germany or Japan to shoot first.

My own opposition to premature or unconditional American intervention may have had its genesis in my historical studies and my family background. But it was mainly due to what I had learned in Germany about both Communism and Nazism. Most Americans of the period (aptly described by Eugene Lyons as "The Red Decade") had been given little or no opportunity to learn the facts about communism and Soviet Russia. But in 1936–38 I had spent two years studying at the German War College and had there been exposed to constant propaganda about the Bolshevik menace. Beneath the propaganda I discerned a great deal of truth about Communist aims, practices, and methods unknown or ignored in America until recently. I had also come to see Germany in a different light from most of my contemporaries. Not that I approved of the Nazi regime or condoned its brutalities, but I realized that Hitler had come to power as a result of the treatment of Germany after the First World War, and that his hold over the German people was due to their desperate search for a way out of the economic chaos and misery which had been their lot during the last years of the Weimar Republic. However much one disapproved of Hitler's methods, the feeling of the German people that he had raised them out of the abyss was real. He had gained his power by giving work and hope to the millions who had been unemployed, and he had made Germany too strong to be contemptuously ignored or repressed as she had been from 1918 onward.

Moreover, I was convinced that the German search for *Lebensraum* did not menace the Western World to anything like the same degree as the world-wide Communist conspiracy centered in Moscow. Germany's *Drang nach Osten*—drive to the East—was a national movement to win "living space," meaning sources of raw materials and markets. It was caused by the same compulsions as the drive to empire, "the blind amphibious instinct" of her British cousins in previous centuries. However reprehensible the German national aim might seem to Americans whose forefathers had wrested half a continent from the Indians, the Spanish, and the Mexicans, or to the British who had conquered an empire "upon which the sun never set," and however greatly one was revolted by Hitler's treatment of Jews and his arrogant bullying of small neighboring nations, one was compelled by knowledge of the record and the facts of Germany's situation to understand the dynamic force of self-preservation which underlay the Nazi revolution.

The Western World, meaning mainly France and England, had denied justice, self-respect, and the opportunity to earn a living by hard work to the defeated Germans so long as they were "peace-loving and democratic" under the Weimar Republic. Overburdened psychologically and politically by the "war guilt" clauses of the Versailles Treaty, crushed by the huge reparations demands of the victors and then, after a brief interlude of artificial prosperity founded on loans from abroad, finally ruined by the world economic crisis that began in 1929, the Weimar Republic had been destroyed by the fanatical nationalists who were the full-grown offspring of the dragon seeds planted after the First World War.

It has been said that the greatest harm results not from not knowing but from believing "what just ain't so." Few Americans have had time or opportunity to acquire more knowledge of European or world history than they gleaned from school or college textbooks or from superficial or prejudiced articles by popular journalists. It was hardly surprising that so many of them were easily led by propaganda to believe that Germans are the most belligerent of peoples. The fact that history belies this contention mattered little to those who wanted to make us fear and hate the Germans in order to get us into war and who regarded the destruction of Germany and Japan as our paramount, or only, war aim. Conversely, it was no trick at all to make them believe that since Communist Russia was Germany's enemy she must be our friend. Hence the ruin of the hopes for which so many fought and died and the fact that to-day there is a real and present danger to the Republic far greater than Nazi Germany ever constituted except in the fevered imagination of Roosevelt and his speech-writers.

It did not require any prolonged study of history to learn how false was the popular image of Germany as the most aggressive of nations and recurrent disturber of the peace. Nor did a glance at the map bear out the contention that either Britain or France had been peace-loving. If so, one might ask, how had it come about that they ruled over so great a part of the earth?

Nations and peoples have been aggressive or "peace-loving" at various periods in their history according to their circumstances. Britain, from the days of Elizabeth I to the end of the nineteenth century, had fought innumerable wars all over the globe for trade and profit or for territories to colonize or exploit, with such success that prior to the Second World War the 40 million people of the British Isles governed some 450 million subject peoples in Asia and Africa. Germany and Italy, countries which did not win national unity until the second half of the nineteenth century, had meanwhile accumulated few colonies and, coming late into the race, found little left to conquer. They had joined in the "scramble for Africa" at the end of the nineteenth century but had not acquired territories comparable to the huge colonies and protectorates which Britain and France had already conquered or subdued by force or threats. Moreover, during the half century which followed the defeat of Napoleon and the end of France's centuries-old effort to dominate Europe, Prussia was the only important state in Europe which waged no wars. While the other German states were also at peace with the world, Russia fought Persia and Turkey; England and France fought Russia in the Crimean War, besides waging "colonial" wars in Africa and Asia. Hence the untruth of the widely propagated myth that "the Germans" were the most aggressive of Western nations, which softened up the American people's opposition to involvement in Europe's "interminable wars."

Winston Churchill leaves a reader no doubt as to Roosevelt's determination to involve the U.S. in the war. He writes in *The Grand Alliance* that although the President was "more reserved" than the Prime Minister in their close personal correspondence, which went on for two years before Pearl Harbor, the latter "knew very well where he stood and what he wanted." Roosevelt, Churchill continued, "was aloft, august, at the head of a mighty neutral Power, which he desired above all things to bring into the fight for freedom. But he could not as yet see how to do it." The President and his trusted friends, Churchill further states, had "writhed under the restraints of Congress" which kept America at least nominally neutral. Thus, says Churchill, the Japanese attack upon the United States was "a vast simplification of their problems and their duty.

How can we wonder that they regard the actual form of the attack, or even its scale, as incomparably less important than the fact that the whole American nation would be united for its own safety in a righteous cause as never before?" Churchill also notes that they knew "the full and immediate purpose of their enemy." This must be taken to mean that, thanks to the breaking of the Japanese code, Roosevelt, Admiral Stark, and presumably also General Marshall, were forewarned of the Japanese attack scheduled for December 7. Indeed, naval officer Murphy summoned by Senator Homer Ferguson to a hearing on Pearl Harbor is witness to the fact that the Japanese war message was read by Roosevelt and Hopkins in his presence on the night of December 6 in the White House. When Hopkins urged preventive action, Roosevelt said no, a democracy must make a good record and wait.

When the first news of Japan's attack was received, Churchill was at Chequers with Ambassador Winant and Averell Harriman. He notes that "one might almost have thought that the two Americans had been delivered of a long pain." As for Churchill himself, he "went to bed that night to sleep the sleep of the saved and thankful."

In the debunking postwar era of the twenties it was generally recognized that Germany's "war guilt" was a one-sided conception, and that the fundamental cause of the war had been Anglo-German industrial and trade rivalry. As John Maynard Keynes wrote in his famous book, *The Economic Consequences of the Peace,* England had fought to destroy a trade rival as in each preceding century.

Just as President Roosevelt spurred us on to war by raising false fears concerning our security, so back in 1910 during the British election campaign Mr. Balfour, leader of the Conservative opposition, tried to win by telling the electors that England was in danger —as Winston Churchill, then a liberal, said at the time, "to raise a panic without reason, a policy of trying to raise ill-will between two nations without cause."

That Balfour did not look with disfavor on the idea of provoking war with Germany is indicated by a conversation between him and U.S. Ambassador Henry White, who was sent by the State Department to London from Italy to confer at a time when the Anglo-German trade war was at its height. As recorded by the American historian, Allan Nevins, in his book *Henry White, Thirty Years of American Diplomacy,* the conversation was as follows:

Balfour (somewhat lightly): "We are probably fools not to
find a reason for declaring war on Germany before she
builds too many ships and takes away our trade."

White: "You are a very high-minded man in private life.
How can you possibly contemplate anything so politically
immoral as provoking a war against a harmless nation
which has as good a right to a navy as you have? If you
wish to compete with German trade, work harder."

Balfour: "That would mean lowering our standard of living.
Perhaps it would be simpler for us to have a war."

White: "I am shocked that you of all men should enunciate
such principles."

Balfour (again lightly): "Is it a question of right or wrong?
Maybe it is just a question of keeping our supremacy."

The eminent British military historian, Major General J. F. C.
Fuller, remarks with reference to this recorded conversation that its
interest does not lie simply in the evidence it affords of Balfour's
unprincipled cynicism. Its significance lies in the fact that "the Industrial Revolution had led to the establishment of an economic
struggle for existence in which self-preservation dictated a return
to the ways of the jungle. The primeval struggle between man and
beast had been replaced by the industrial struggle between nation
and nation in which all competitors were beasts."

All that I had ever learned in my studies of history, the centuries
of bloody struggle in Europe up to and including World War I, and
the conditions or circumstances leading up to the conflagration just
ignited in Europe, caused me to oppose an untimely American intervention in World War II. However, as a professional soldier, it was
not within the sphere of my responsibility under our type of government to make decisions concerning war or peace. It was my job to
anticipate developments and continuously make plans so that my
country would be prepared for any contingency which fate, politicians, or power-drunk leaders might precipitate.

Thus I became the Victory Program planner of a war I did not
want. Once engaged in my assigned task, I devoted all my energies
to working up a plan calculated to bring our enemies to their knees
in the shortest possible time and in a way that would leave us in an
advantageous position at the peace table to work for a world in
which America would be menaced no more.

CHAPTER II

THE CURTAIN ASCENDS

DECEMBER 5, 1941, is a date I am unlikely ever to forget. Entering my office in the Munitions Building at 7:30 A.M. on that Friday two days before Pearl Harbor, I sensed at once an atmosphere of excitement. Officers were milling around and there was a buzz of conversation which ceased abruptly as my secretary, in visible agitation, handed me a copy of the Washington *Times-Herald*. The room was silent and all eyes were fixed upon me as I read the screaming banner headlines:

F.D.R.'S WAR PLANS

And in somewhat smaller type below:

GOAL IS 10 MILLION ARMED MEN; HALF TO FIGHT IN AEF

PROPOSED LAND DRIVE BY JULY 1, 1943, TO SMASH NAZIS

With mounting anxiety, I scanned the report, published under the by-line of Chicago *Tribune* correspondent Chesly Manly, which began:

> Confidential report prepared by the Joint Army and Navy high command by direction of President Roosevelt calls for American expeditionary forces aggregating five million men for a final land offensive against Germany and her satellites. It contemplates total armed forces of 10,045,658 men. It is a

15

blueprint for total war on a scale unprecedented in at least two oceans and three continents, Europe, Africa, and Asia.

As I read on, it became all too clear that the Chicago *Tribune* correspondent had published an exact reproduction of the most important parts of the Victory Program, on which I had been working day and night for the past several months. Information pertaining to the Victory Program was the most zealously guarded secret in the War Department. Dramatically described by correspondent Manly as "an astounding document which represents decisions and commitments affecting the destinies of peoples throughout the civilized world," the Administration's secret war plan was now revealed to the world.

I could not have been more appalled and astounded if a bomb had been dropped on Washington. Revelation of the program to mobilize the Army and Navy on an unprecedented scale and detailed plans for their employment overseas against Germany and Japan were political dynamite. Here was irrefutable evidence that American intervention in the war was planned and imminent, and that President Roosevelt's promises to keep us out of war were only campaign oratory. And I myself was the officer responsible for the security and absolute secrecy of the Victory Program, revelation of which might even precipitate American participation in the war.

On July 9, 1941, the President had directed Secretary of War Stimson and Secretary of the Navy Knox to draw up an estimate of the "over-all production requirements required to defeat our potential enemies." Stimson, who had been instructed to co-ordinate the Army and Navy estimates, sent the Presidential directive along to the Army Chief of Staff, General George Catlett Marshall, who in turn promptly turned it over to Brigadier General Leonard T. Gerow, Chief of the War Plans Division. This was the division of the General Staff charged with the continuing responsibility of drawing up plans for any and every contingency affecting the national security.

The actual responsibility had devolved on me, then a major in the War Plans Division, brought there a few months before from command of troops at Fort Benning. Thus, by a procedure reminiscent of a famous baseball combination—passing the ball with lightning speed from Tinker to Evers to Chance—the job of drawing up the Victory Program had been tossed from Stimson to Marshall to Gerow to Wedemeyer. Although the procedure was normal, the task was more than usually challenging, since a war plan of global dimensions had never before been attempted. It meant traveling on uncharted seas without a compass toward a fatal Shangri-la, and with only the stars to guide us, since no national aims or strategic objectives were given us. General Gerow had, however, assured me that the various agencies in the War Department would be directed to assist me, and that I was authorized to contact other government departments to obtain the information required. He had stressed above all the need for utmost secrecy. This was all too obvious since the public as a whole still had faith in President Roosevelt's promises to keep us out of war, and the Gallup polls had revealed that the great majority of voters were opposed to U.S. intervention.

The Administration's war preparations and its unneutral actions, calculated to provoke the Axis powers to declare war on us, had been glibly explained as measures designed to keep us out of war by strengthening Britain and Russia. Our own military build-up was similarly represented as necessary to deter aggression against the United States, its island possessions, and the Western Hemisphere.

Our "war aims," as now revealed, were not confined to "the final destruction of the Nazi tyranny," as pledged in the Atlantic Charter. As Chesly Manly wrote:

> The official report also explodes some of the other popular myths that have been most sedulously fostered by administration spokesmen and war propagandists generally.
>
> For instance, it scorns the popular notion that this is a war to overthrow Hitler and the Nazi regime rather than a war against the German people, in the following words:
>
> > "It is believed the overthrow of the Nazi regime by action of the German people is unlikely in the near future, and will not occur until Germany is upon the point of military defeat. Even though a new regime were to be established it is not at all certain that such a regime would agree to peace terms acceptable to the United States."

While there were ample historical precedents for the drawing up of plans for every possible contingency affecting the security of the United States, President Roosevelt tried to curdle our blood by talking about Nazi plans to invade South America from Dakar in Africa, when in fact there never was any such menace. Hitler had neither threatened nor planned to attack the Western Hemisphere. Nor is it easy to believe that the President himself or any of his advisers actually believed that the U.S. was in danger of being so attacked. Roosevelt knew that the only way he could fulfill his secret commitments to Churchill to get us into the war, without openly dishonoring his pledges to the American people to keep us out, was by provoking Germany or Japan to attack. In the memoranda of the Atlantic Conference conversations among President Roosevelt, Churchill, Sir Alexander Cadogan, Harry Hopkins, and Sumner Welles (Part 4, pages 1784–92), Roosevelt said that he would assume responsibility for letting the Japanese know that if they moved southward, "various steps would have to be taken by the United States notwithstanding the President's realization that the taking of such further measures might result in war between the United States and Japan." When Sumner Welles suggested that the U.S. must essay a wider role than that of policeman of the Southwest Pacific and should stand ready to repel any Japanese thrust "against China, against the Soviet Union, or against the British Dominions or British colonies, or the colonies of the Netherlands in the Southern Pacific area," Churchill and Roosevelt concurred. However, the President apparently felt that this should remain a secret understanding. Churchill later reported to the British Parliament (January 27, 1942) that the Atlantic Conference gave him increasing assurance that the U.S., "even if not herself attacked," would come to a war in the Far East, and that if Japan were to run amok in the Pacific, "we shall not fight alone." Meanwhile the President had instructed the Secretaries of War and Navy to prepare secretly for all-out war and the mobilization of all American resources for the defeat of Germany and Japan. Hence the Victory Program now dramatically revealed by the Chicago *Tribune* and Washington *Times-Herald.*

When Mr. Roosevelt's friends were confronted with the fact that plans, now revealed, contemplated sending millions of American boys to far-flung battle areas, primarily in Europe, they replied that if we must fight, it would be better to fight on foreign soil than on our own. Better a war in Europe than a possible German advance through Spain or Italy to Africa, on down to Dakar, and then across the Atlantic to South America. Assuming that the Germans did reach Brazil, the fact was glossed over that they would be farther away from the U.S. than if they had remained in Europe. The Germans or Italians simply could not mount an effective force to attack our homeland from bases in South America; they could not even reach the Panama Canal without passing through our region of strength in the Caribbean Sea. Their necessarily long supply lines would be entirely at the mercy of our Navy and Air Force. So while the President was creating a hobgoblin, our military leaders were actually not alarmed, for they realized that any Nazi military effort in Latin America would be relatively harmless, certainly not decisive.

Any military man, or anyone versed in military science, would recognize at once that such an advance by the Germans was preposterous. Although dramatic, it was a false description of German capabilities—and, as we learned later, even intentions. But many trusting souls accepted this blown-up threat to our homeland and were ready and willing to accept Roosevelt's alternative, an expedition to Europe. Very few people in government paid serious attention to the patriotic endeavors of staunch defenders of the principle of no involvement in European wars. However, several members of Congress as well as a handful of courageous private citizens pointed out that the Germans had not been able to span twenty-two miles across the English Channel even with the support of a devastating bomber attack. But Roosevelt and his followers (suddenly including the Communists after June 22, 1941) insisted that the Germans could and would span thousands of miles of water—the Mediterranean and the Atlantic Ocean, establish an effective invasion force in South America, fight through hundreds of miles of impenetrable jungles in Brazil and Central America, and finally invade the United States.

It is interesting to note that no military man publicly exposed this Roosevelt fear-strategy for the fraud that it was. But they did realize that we Americans would have to prepare to defeat Germany by actually coming to grips with and annihilating her air and ground forces and thus breaking her will to fight. This, in turn, meant that a large American expeditionary force would be required to fight in Europe. The specific operations necessary to accomplish the defeat of the Axis powers obviously could not be predicted at the time (summer of 1941).

As accurate an estimate as possible had to be made of the general scheme of maneuver and the strength and composition of the American armed forces needed to defeat Germany, Italy, and Japan. Requirements for all military forces in terms of training, equipment, armament, vehicles, shipping, planes, and thousands of other items had to be made available to implementing agencies as soon as possible. These necessitated, in turn, a study of America's potential production capacity as well as careful calculations concerning the manpower which could be drafted into the armed services without militating against the continued operation of our internal economy and administration (including essential communications, transportation, industry, hospitals, law enforcement, and utilities across the country).

We had to envisage the broad scheme of maneuver for the employment of our forces, including the time and place of prospective employment, so that priorities could be established for the various categories of requirements: cargo ships, steel helmets, four-engine bombers, rifles, binoculars, tanks, blankets, and the myriad of other items required to equip, train, transport, and maintain a huge modern fighting force in far-flung combat zones.

It was readily apparent that American industry would have to expand its productive capacity enormously in order to provide not only the equipment and transportation for military forces deployed for the defense of the United States, its outlying possessions, and bases selected for the defense of our country and the Western Hemisphere, but also for American task forces which would be dispatched to areas of prospective combat; and finally to provide essential supplies to Allied powers committed to the policy of stopping Nazi aggression.

The Army part of the Victory Program was prepared under my direct supervision, and the Army Air Force collaborated in providing the estimates specifically pertaining to that arm. The Navy part was prepared in the Navy Department and copies were furnished to me and to Colonel William Scobey, the Army Secretary of the Joint Board. Before the Victory Program was produced in booklet form, five typewritten draft copies of the complete Army (with Air Force) estimate were assembled and distributed as follows:

One copy to Secretary of War (Stimson).
One copy to Assistant Secretary of War (McCloy).
One copy to Chief of Staff (Marshall).
One copy to Chief of War Plans Division (Gerow).
One copy retained as work copy in my office (Wedemeyer).

All copies were numbered and registered, for this was the most secret undertaking in Washington at that time. In spite of the precautions that were taken, we now were confronted with an alarming situation—an obvious breakdown of rigid security measures. I was profoundly disturbed when the chief of my division, General Gerow, informed me that an investigation by the FBI had been ordered by the President. I knew that I had not divulged information pertaining to the Victory Program or any other secret matter to unauthorized persons; but working under the stress of a war-imminent situation, I could not be certain that I had never neglected to exercise proper precautions. There was never any doubt in my mind that as soon as my country was at war, I would give unstinted and loyal support to the decisions of higher authority. Under the mental anguish and pressure of the FBI investigation, this inner conviction enabled me to carry on my assigned duties.

General Gerow was sympathetic and assured me of his complete confidence. He expressed conviction that the responsibility for this serious breach of security would not be found in the War Plans Division. The attitude of my loyal chief was in direct contrast to that which I experienced a few hours later in the office of the Assistant Secretary of War, John J. McCloy. He had only recently joined Mr. Stimson's staff as Assistant Secretary, occupying a sumptuous room with a big mahogany desk and the national colors as well as the Assistant Secretary's flag resplendent in the far corner. When a new civilian official arrived in any government bureau, everyone made evaluations of him, either consciously or subconsciously. Some of my associates thought McCloy was inordinately ambitious, would invariably agree with higher authorities, but would assert himself and swing his weight around in contacts with subordinates. I stood at attention for he did not suggest that I sit down, and I listened to his veiled insinuation: "Wedemeyer, there's blood on the fingers of the man who leaked the information about our war plans."

CHAPTER III

INVESTIGATED BY THE FBI

A SHORT TIME AFTER I had returned to my office, two FBI agents arrived. Edward Tamm, second in command of that efficient organization, asked if I had any idea how the breach of security had occurred. He also questioned me about the method by which I had provided for the security of the copies of the Victory Program and all papers pertaining thereto. Mr. Tamm was so courteous as to be disarming, but I sensed that his suspicions centered around me, or at least that he suspected a member of my staff. He was accompanied by Joseph Genau who, I was informed, would be in direct charge of the investigation. Mr. Genau proved to be a capable investigator as well as a thorough gentleman. It was obvious that the FBI agents were mainly interested at this initial meeting in evaluating my sincerity and sense of responsibility. They were obviously observing me closely for anything they could detect in my demeanor which might suggest guilt. I did have what might be called a vicarious sense of guilt because I was not sympathetic with the "war party" groups in the Administration; and later in the investigation I frankly told Mr. Genau that I did not agree with those who felt our security was jeopardized and that we should go into the war, at least at that time.

During the initial questioning, however, my main concern was lest I might have been careless at some time during the many days and nights on which I had worked on the Victory Program. During the succeeding days, in addition to holding myself available for intermittent examination and providing information to the FBI agents concerning members of my staff and others with whom I had contact during the preparation of the program, I carried on my usual duties as a member of the War Plans Division of the General Staff.

The FBI was assisted in the investigation by representatives of G-2 of the Army General Staff. On December 9, Mr. Tamm, Colonel J. T. Bissell, and Captain Lowell J. Bradford, of Military Intelligence, questioned me. Excerpts from the report submitted by these gentlemen indicate the suspicion under which I was held:

> After completion of the Army portion, Colonel Wedemeyer * stated that five copies were typed and the air force data integrated with the ground forces. Both General Gerow and General Marshall approved them. One copy was submitted to Colonel William P. Scobey, who was Secretary of the Joint Army-Navy Board which formulates and distributes war plans prepared by the Army and Navy. It was Colonel Wedemeyer's understanding that Colonel Scobey arranged to have stencils cut to make additional copies. Colonel Wedemeyer further testified that Secretary Stimson had the original copy which was taken to the President by the Secretary. He stated that he recalled assisting Secretary Stimson put the Number 1 copy of this plan into his brief case late in the evening of September 10th. . . .
>
> Here Colonel Wedemeyer crossed himself up to a certain degree because later under questioning by Colonel Bissell and Mr. Tamm he stated that it was the 25th of September when he gave Secretary Stimson a copy for the White House whereas previously he had stated categorically that it was on September 10th. Colonel Wedemeyer again insisted that the copy he referred to was a purely Army study until the Joint Board received the Navy study and integrated the two. This doesn't make sense because Mr. Stimson would not take over a half-prepared document for Mr. Roosevelt to peruse and perhaps this is why Colonel Wedemeyer changed his date from September 10th to September 25th to allow the Navy time to get their study in. Colonel Wedemeyer stated that to his knowledge no messengers handled the document between

---

* I was promoted to the rank of lieutenant colonel in December, 1941; to colonel in June, 1942; to brigadier general in July, 1942; to major general in September, 1943; to lieutenant general in January, 1945; to general in 1953.

any of its routing points and while so stating he recalled that he sent five copies to the Chief Clerk for mimeographing.

The investigators also observed:

> Colonel Wedemeyer was very ill at ease during this interview and several times fell back upon the old adage that "I could not remember" and seemed to be thinking up excuses for himself and his actions. As it was not until the middle of October 1941 that Colonel Scobey received instructions to finally assemble and produce the entire document, Colonel Wedemeyer becomes responsible for any leakage up to that date.

I certainly was ill at ease although I had nothing to conceal. The atmosphere of suspicion was compounded by an anonymous letter addressed to the Secretary of War and shown to me by General Marshall:

Washington, D.C.
December 8, 1941

DEAR SECRETARY:

I feel it my duty to acquaint you with the following:

Everyone knowing them knows the situation and were aghast at the vital positions assigned these men: 1) the Defense Commission and the latter *War Plans*. General Embick * openly condemns Britain responsible for Germany's actions and condones all they have done as natural, is thoroughly in sympathy with Japan, and his son-in-law, Major Wedemeyer, who spent several years in Germany, thinks and says Hitler is a saviour and after America is taken over by the people and National Socialism is established here, the present injustices in government will be swept away.

These are certainly not trustworthy men to have on our Defense Commission and our War Plans and may account for the serious "leak" of last week. Surely the President or General Marshall should investigate these officers' real feelings. It is common knowledge in Washington.

Sincerely,
O.S.A.

* General Stanley D. Embick was the author's father-in-law. He was born in Pennsylvania of Scotch-German parentage; both sides of his family were early pioneers in this country, having settled here before the American Revolution. General Embick was graduated from West Point in 1899 and had a distinguished career in the Army.

Reading the record of the FBI investigation for the first time many years later I discovered with a sense of shock that some fellow officers who were good friends of mine had not been certain that I was not responsible for the leak. For instance I read that:

Colonel Scobey, wishing to go off the record, stated that there were quite a few divergent political opinions in the War Plans Division. Certain officers were actually of the opinion that the United States was messing around business with which it should have nothing to do, and several officers were members of the America First Organization while others were strongly sympathetic along that line. Colonel Scobey frankly stated that he believed that he was the Secretary of the Joint Board because of the fact that he believed that the United States should be in the war up to the hilt. Colonel Scobey did not say so in so many words but indicated that Colonel Wedemeyer was one of those officers he had previously described and there seemed to be a question of opinion between them. However, the contrary demands which were mentioned were only the differences of opinions as to the concept and the ultimate requirements necessary to defeat our political enemies and did not mean that there was a great variance of political opinion in the Joint Board.

Colonel Scobey and I have always been and remain the best of friends. I am sure that he had no intention of harming me in any way. Obviously I cannot make the same observation concerning the writer of the anonymous letter.

I was not a member of the America First Organization, although I was in accord with some of its objectives. I definitely did not believe we should meddle in the affairs of European countries or any others without a clear conception that our action was in the national interest. Our own country was not in imminent danger.

I had been trying the past several months to ascertain our national aims, and to discover whether there was any policy or agreement that might justify or compel our intervention in Europe. The Monroe Doctrine was one policy that could be clearly understood; however, no one could state seriously that Germany or Italy was planning or could possibly carry out territorial expansion in the Western Hemisphere, which would of course have been a violation of the Monroe Doctrine. After the Soviet Union and Germany (June 22,

1941) abrogated their roles of cynical collaborators and resumed their traditional roles of archenemies, it was my oft expressed conviction that the Western powers should remain as quiescent as the situation would permit while the two colossi chewed each other up. England, and possibly the United States, could then step in and exercise the historic role of arranging a balance of power, thus precluding the domination of Europe by either the Communists or Fascists.

Further on in the same investigation, Colonel Scobey testified about information concerning a proposal by the British and an agreement by the Americans at the Atlantic Conference to send American troops to Iceland that leaked and appeared in the press. Here is the report:

> Colonel Scobey discussed the Iceland leak and stated that he had completed a check on the Iceland copies. Representative Tinkham, General Westerwell and General Wood were Colonel Scobey's subjects for suspicion in so far as the Iceland leak was concerned. Colonel Scobey stated that several officers in the War Plans Division knew these last named gentlemen but they didn't care to mention any names, merely stating that the political opinions of those he had mentioned were similar to the opinions of those three gentlemen. Colonel Scobey believes firmly that the leak was from the five copies (carbon copies) and mentioned that he had a report from Colonel Wedemeyer which stated that there was no officer present when the stencils were mimeographed, and quoted Wedemeyer's report:
> "A clerk from the Chief Clerk's office remained and personally brought them back."

I was not familiar at that time with the Iceland leak. I did not personally know Representative Tinkham or General Westerwell, to whom Colonel Scobey referred. However, I knew and admired General Robert E. Wood and presumed Colonel Scobey was alluding to him, for he was an active member of the America First Organization. But I had not seen General Wood for more than a year. As I was a comparatively junior officer (lieutenant colonel on the General Staff) when this investigation was being conducted, and had only recently joined the War Plans Division, I seldom expressed my views on foreign policy except to persons whom I knew well and who I felt confident would interpret my remarks in the spirit intended, namely of seeking the appropriate courses of action in the best interests of our country.

On February 19, 1942, Mr. McCloy, the Assistant Secretary of War, was interviewed by Captain L. J. Bradford and Joseph A. Genau and said he thought that "the 'leak' got out of the War or Navy Departments and into the hands of perhaps some isolationist on Capitol Hill who supplied the information to Chesly Manly. He [McCloy] doesn't believe that the 'leak' came from any other government agency."

Major James H. Higgs, Office of the Chief of Air Corps, when asked whether "either officially or unofficially did this thing come to your ears before it came out in the papers?" had replied:

> If it did, I didn't pay any attention to it because, as I told you, when I saw that thing in the paper, my concept—I hate to put this on official record if it is an official record—I got the idea that it was a plant, that it wasn't a true program, that it wasn't anything so secretive. I thought it was a plant to do two things: first of all, to show the Axis Powers that we weren't kidding about this business and that we had the production going and that we were making a tremendous effort. The second reason was that from a political standpoint it was fine propaganda to let our own people know that we weren't sitting down here doing nothing.

In another interview with Major Higgs, Mr. Tamm of the FBI said:

> The allegation is made from some source that this plan was not handed by someone in the War Department direct to a newspaperman but that it went through channels on the basis of a personal liaison between someone rather prominent in the isolationist group who had connections in the War Department and other connections on the Hill or in newspaper circles. Naturally in an inquiry of this kind the name of Colonel Lindbergh comes into discussion and I wondered if you knew anything about Colonel Lindbergh's connections in the Air Corps—who he might have a business association with, what his associations were?

> Answer: . . . I don't know what his connections in the War Department are. I have heard gossip, you know, that there

was . . . that he knew a friend of Colonel Truman Smith's. I was never told anything about it.

Of course I had been wondering just what type of man Manly could be ever since I saw his by-line over the *Times-Herald* story on the morning of December 5, 1941. An officer, Lieutenant Hubert L. Allensworth, on duty with the Air Corps at the time, testified that he had known Mr. Manly for several months and that he had been at the latter's home on many occasions. He was asked the question during the course of the investigation: "Would you consider him [Manly] an isolationist or what?"

> Answer: I would consider him a representative of his newspaper. Let me say this. He seems to be violently opposed to communism and totalitarianism of every description, especially Nazism. I would classify him as a rugged individualist of the Herbert Hoover variety but with the strength of his convictions. This is my view of Chesly Manly. He will not lie or cheat. He is a typical Texan, from that part of the country where I live. He is the picture of courtesy and grace.

Should Manly have taken it upon himself to divulge the Victory Program in his newspaper? A valid justification for the revelation of the secret Victory Program in a news story was provided by Arthur Sears Henning's report to the *Chicago Tribune* Friday, December 5, 1941. Our war plans, said Mr. Henning, were known to the British and the Russians "and even to the Axis Powers, according to a German authority," but not to the American people.

Furthermore, a month or so *before* Chesly Manly's article appeared in the newspapers, Eugene S. Duffield, chief of the *Wall Street Journal* Washington Bureau, had written practically the same story. (See the *Wall Street Journal*, October 20, 1941). This newspaper is read by tens of thousands of Americans. It is therefore remarkable that Duffield's article, appearing in an outstanding, highly respected periodical, did not attract much attention. Here are some extracts:

> Sharpest and most revealing is the shadow cast by the "Victory Program." The newly evolved munitions schedule which Washington and London expect will beat Hitler . . .
> Director Knudsen of the Office of Production Management

first hinted at what is now called the "Victory Program" when he said that by mid-1943 65 percent of the nation's economy must be devoted to war. No percentage more than half that large had been mentioned officially before . . .

With the manpower of the Russian armies removed from the war, the question of raising an army to man the "Victory Program's" vast armaments faces Britain and the United States. Assistant Secretary of War McCloy has estimated German armed strength at 9 to 10 million men. Militarily, an attacking army must have a 50 percent to 100 percent superiority, according to experts here. An attacking army is contemplated. By its emphasis on tanks and ordnance, the "Victory Program" reveals that long-range bombing and ocean blockade no longer are counted on to subdue Germany. That Britain cannot raise more than a third of the necessary army is shown by parliamentary debates within the past two weeks. Raising of the rest of the force—an army far bigger than has been contemplated by anything but the "Victory Program"—may fall on the United States, taking one of every three men between the ages of 18 and 45.

This is by no means all that Duffield had to say on the subject. On October 29, 1941, the *Wall Street Journal* printed in full the text of a speech made by Duffield at a meeting of the Industrial Advertising Association of New York. He attributed the disclosure of the main outlines of the Victory Program to no less a person than President Roosevelt himself: "Last Friday morning," so the *Wall Street Journal* bureau chief told the ad men, "the President opened his press conference by disclosing that he was working on an enormously increased armament program." Furthermore, the President "promised to tell all about the new program in his message to Congress in January." The President's own words, Duffield continued, put "greatest stress on land armament"—tanks and guns. "May I suggest," said Duffield, "that this program, by its accent on tanks and guns, reveals for the first time that the governments of Britain and America recognize the necessity for an expeditionary force on the continent of Europe . . . Who will the troops be? . . . I think the 'Victory Program' gives a broad hint about who will use its weapons. How many men? The War Department says Germany has 9 to 10 million men under arms . . . That means an Allied army of 15 million men. England and the portions of the

Empire at war probably cannot furnish over 7 million men. Look around the world and guess where the rest are to come from."

This, in essence, is exactly what Manly wrote for *his* newspaper more than a month later. The big difference of course was that Manly quoted chapter and verse from the official Victory Program. There was no investigation of the *Wall Street Journal* for leaking secret information. Could it be that publicized secret information was considered a serious leak or a treasonable act only when it turned up in anti-Administration papers, for example, Colonel McCormick's?

I continued to be questioned from time to time by FBI representatives, principally Mr. Genau, who was meticulous in his search for evidence pertaining to the security provisions and the distribution or handling of each copy of the secret document. I learned later that he had checked my every move over a period of many years— my family, friends, and associates. I soon discovered that he was thoroughly acquainted with many incidents in my life which I had long forgotten. Gradually, with his prompting, my replies simply served to confirm or clarify what he already knew.

Here are a few of the more pertinent questions asked by the interrogators and my answers, jotted down roughly at the time of the FBI examination:

Question: Tell us about your parents and grandparents.

Answer: My fathers' parents were born in the vicinity of Hanover, Germany. His mother was of French Huguenot descent. After their marriage in Germany they came to this country in 1830 and settled in Atlanta, Georgia. Although Grandfather Wedemeyer left Germany to avoid compulsory military service, he fought throughout the Civil War on the Confederate side. Mother's parents were born in County Clare, Ireland. They came to the United States and lived originally in Alexandria, Virginia. They soon moved out west and settled in Nebraska. In contrast to my somewhat puritanical forebears on the Wedemeyer side, Mother's father, Michael F. Coady, was a kind and improvident Irishman. I always heard that he was a brilliant orator, generous to a fault, and on occasions a tippler. He fought in the Civil War, but on the Northern side.

I explained that my father, like many Americans of German descent, had no sentimental ties with Germany but tried to take an objective view of history. His parents did not even speak German at home and apparently had cut ties completely with the old country and adopted their new homeland with pride and patriotic fervor. I mention this because among my boyhood recollections I recall Father's friendly arguments with a neighbor, Doctor Colin H. Ross, who had previously been a British subject and had become a naturalized American citizen. The doctor, immediately prior to World War I, was vehement in his denunciation of Germany. He wanted to "whip the Kaiser" and to "remove the scourge of German aggression." He insisted that the warlike propensities of the German people were traditional, that they posed a continual threat to the peace of Europe; that the British were culturally closely akin to us, and through great sacrifice and skillful diplomacy they had maintained peace in the world.

Father calmly referred to historical evidence which cast serious doubt and at times refuted our neighbor's views that the Germans were the most belligerent of European peoples. He thought that most Germans were not by choice a martial people but in order to survive they had had to fight. History clearly records the attacks to which they were subjected again and again from all sides, and especially from the French. He mentioned the fact that from the time of Richelieu onward France had fought to establish the French frontier along the Rhine and also had constantly tried to keep Germany divided and thus impotent. He believed that the basic cause of the First World War was economic. He reviewed the development of the British Empire, starting back in the sixteenth century under Queen Elizabeth. The British, he maintained, expanded their domain, conquering or controlling vast areas which produced raw materials and created markets for their processed goods. England became the industrial nub of the world, the leading maritime power, a concomitant of naval power. Father traced briefly the industrial expansion of the Germans which followed about two hundred years later but which grew to such proportions, particularly during and after Bismarck's time, that it posed a definite threat to British commercial supremacy. The Germans understandably also sought colonies as sources of raw materials and as markets, exactly in the pattern of their neighbors across the Channel. But, as events proved, they were too late and diplomatically too clumsy.

Mr. Genau seemed interested in Father and then wanted to know where I had lived in this country. I told him that I was born and raised in Omaha, Nebraska, and lived there until I entered West Point. After graduation from the military academy in 1919, I served at Fort Benning, Georgia; the Philippines; Washington, D.C.; China; the Philippines again; Fort Leavenworth, Kansas; the German War College in Berlin; Fort Benning, Georgia, again; and back at Washington, D.C.

"While in Germany, did you form any particular friendships?" was the next question, to which I replied:

I knew and considered as friends many students at the German War College and also several of the instructors as well as a few civilians whom I met socially. I rented my apartment in Berlin from a member of the Nazi Party, Herr Gerhard Rossbach, but he was the only party member I knew at all well. The vast majority of my friends in Germany were military colleagues.

I told Mr. Genau that I was sent to Germany primarily to learn as much as possible concerning military tactics and techniques, but also to keep my eyes and ears open and try to acquire information about Nazism, the character of its leaders and objectives, as well as its psychological effect upon the German people. Incidentally, I also learned a great deal about the organization, the objectives, and the operations of communism, or, as the Germans preferred to call it, bolshevism. The Germans regarded Russia as their principal opponent and were constantly, in press and radio, revealing chapter and verse of Karl Marx as practiced by Lenin and Stalin. Naturally I tried to find out as much as possible about communism which even then I believed as dangerous to the free world as Nazism.

While residing in Germany, I was careful not to embarrass my German friends by discussing politics. Actually no member of the German Army, Air Force, or Navy was allowed to be a member of the Nazi Party. The officers with whom I was associated daily for approximately two years at the War College had been carefully selected for their character, abilities, and professional potentialities. They were intelligent and very earnest about their work. They had been admonished not to discuss politics. Even what might appear to be an innocuous remark against the regime might bring a severe reprimand or even imprisonment. There were other exchange students in the War College from Italy, Holland, Bulgaria, Turkey, Japan, Argentina, and China.

Among my friends in Germany I counted General Ludwig Beck, the Chief of the German General Staff. Prior to my departure for Germany in June, 1936, Lieutenant General Friedrich von Boetticher, the German military attaché in Washington, had written to General Beck concerning my prospective stay in that country. General Beck had been very kind to me, entertaining me informally at his home on several occasions.

Mr. Genau noted this with considerable interest and asked:

> Did you have any occasion to attend Nazi Party meetings while living in Germany?

> No [I answered], I did not. However, if I had been invited to a Nuremberg rally, I certainly would have accepted, not because of sympathetic leanings toward the Nazi movement but as a matter of curiosity and to observe the mass psychosis and unusual spectacle which had been described by friends who had attended Nazi rallies as spectators or guests.

> Question: Do you still carry on correspondence with any of your friends in Germany?

> Answer: When I first returned from Europe late in the fall of 1938, I received several communications from German friends, particularly those with whom I was associated in the German War College—both students and instructors. Such correspondence dwindled in 1939 with the advent of war. I presume most of my friends are at the front fighting. I received one very interesting letter from Germany after the war began from my former instructor at the German War College, now General Jodl.

> He described the advance into France in May, 1940, in considerable detail. I translated the letter and made it available to the G-2, military intelligence of the General Staff. That is the last communication I received from Germany.

Reverting to the Victory Program, Mr. Genau asked me what contacts I had made in fulfilling my task. I replied that in collecting the pertinent data I had of necessity had to explain the authority for, and the objectives of, the Victory Program to officials of the various government departments and agencies contacted but had stressed the vital need for absolute secrecy.

I had naturally assumed that the persons in responsible positions whom I consulted in various departments and bureaus were security-checked and fully understood their responsibility to maintain secrecy. No one individual, however, in those various government agencies had access to all of the data I collected or to a completed plan except my colleagues in the War Plans Division. In performing tasks connected with the preparation of each phase of the Victory Program, I turned over the drafted portions to a group of three senior officers of the War Plans Division, whom I dubbed the Murder Committee: Colonel Thomas Handy, Colonel Leven C. Allen, and Colonel Frank Kibler. They made corrections, deletions, and additions under the general supervision of Colonel Charles Bundy. When my best efforts were returned to me, sometimes there was little remaining; hence the opprobrium, Murder Committee. Actually I have often wished while writing this book that I might have access to their editing.

The completed Army program had been submitted on September 10, 1941, through my immediate boss, Colonel Bundy, to General Leonard Gerow, the Chief of War Plans Division. Copies of the Navy portion of the Victory Program were made available later. Finally all documents, maps, and charts of the Army and Navy were bound together for submission to the President on September 25, 1941. General Gerow then instructed me to turn over a copy of the Army program to Colonel William Scobey, the Secretary of the Joint Board, so that stencils could be cut and additional copies made.

As the investigation progressed I hoped that Mr. Genau would devote his time-consuming attention to one of the above-mentioned gentlemen. Instead, his line of questions continued in an area where I might be considered vulnerable:

Question: Did you have any contacts with a person or persons within the America First Organization?

Answer: Yes, I have several friends connected with that organization: Mrs. Taft, John T. Flynn, Senator Wheeler, and Colonel Lindbergh. I haven't seen them for some time because I've been too busy.

Question: Do the views expressed by members of the America First Organization meet with your approval?

Answer: In many ways, yes.

I had attended one meeting in the autumn of 1941 at the National Theater when Mrs. Taft and Senator La Follette spoke and, as I recall, John T. Flynn also made a brief talk. I wanted to give exact expression to my feelings on this subject, and told Mr. Genau repeatedly that I did not believe we should enter the war under existing circumstances.

My early thinking, influenced by Father in discussions at home before World War I, and confirmed by additional information obtained later through reading and discussions, had led me to believe that we were propagandized into World War I. Knowing about the concocted propaganda, both stories and photographs, which was used to create hatred against the German people during the 1914 war, I was naturally skeptical about the information then being disseminated by all of the belligerent nations.

Mr. Genau asked if I believed in totalitarian governments, and I assured him that I was unequivocally opposed to Fascism or any other form of dictatorship. I added that I believed bolshevism or communism to be a far greater menace to our country's security than Nazism or Fascism. There was ample evidence that Nazism was more localized as a national movement, whereas communism was a ruthless international conspiracy with the clearly stated objective of communizing the world.

Mr. Genau continued his gently insistent probing by asking if I had ever been in any kind of trouble either prior to or after entering the Army. The one thing I could recall was hardly serious. At the time of its occurrence in 1921, however, it had seemed all-important to me, a young officer just out of West Point. I had been reared in a sheltered atmosphere, followed up with an almost monastic life at West Point. My new-found freedom after graduation had tempted me to kick over the traces on occasion. In February, 1921, at Fort Benning, Georgia, I accompanied a friend to a club located in the nearby hospitable city of Columbus. This club was noted for its libations and good fellowship. We imbibed too freely and returned to Fort Benning in an uninhibited intoxicated condition, irresponsible and noisy. This was a heinous offense on an Army post, particularly during prohibition. I was not fast of foot or glib of speech when a senior officer appeared on the scene. "Hurrah for the twenty-ninth. I'm in it and damn proud of it," I shouted at the Colonel who stood before me barefooted and in his nightshirt. It was 2:00 A.M. when I profaned the hushed silence of the Army camp.

Charges were preferred against me for conduct unbecoming an officer and a gentleman. I pleaded guilty and was fined $50 a month for a period of six months and also was restricted to the post for a like period. With this disciplinary action so early on my record as an officer, I felt that my future in the Army was blighted. Feeling really depressed and hopeless about the future, at least in the military service, I submitted my resignation from the Army and applied for employment on a freighter operating between New Orleans and South America. The steamship company accepted my application. However, I was informed that an officer could not resign while under charges or sentence of court-martial; in other words, six months would have to expire before the authorities would consider my resignation. I had served only two months of my punishment when the commanding general, Paul B. Malone, appointed me on his staff as aide-de-camp. Fortunately, he was a wonderful individual who understood human fallibilities and the exuberance of young lieutenants. While approving unequivocally the discipline meted out to me, he advised that I should pitch in and learn all I possibly could about the Army and expressed his personal conviction that my future was assured in the Army or in any other profession I might follow.

His attitude caused me to accept philosophically my youthful and consequently greatly exaggerated feeling of disgrace. This was the only incident that had occurred in my service which resulted in disciplinary action.

At this point, Mr. Genau referred again to the anonymous letter:

> Could you give any reason why an individual would write such a letter to Secretary Stimson?

> Yes, I believe so, [I replied]. You already know about my course of instruction at the War College in Berlin. After my

return from Germany in the fall of 1938, I purchased a powerful short-wave radio and tuned in frequently to the Berlin broadcast to help retain a degree of facility in the language. Also, the situation in Europe was becoming increasingly tense and I found it interesting to hear the German broadcasts, presenting their biased views and affording me an opportunity to compare the reports of other countries in Europe, particularly those emanating from the B.B.C. in London.

Moreover, there had been some humorous incidents during my service in Germany, some of which might be interpreted as indicating pro-Nazism on my part by a malicious informant. For example, during the first year of instruction at the German War College, as I entered the school building the charwomen working on their hands and knees in the halls would invariably throw up their right arm, extended in the Nazi salute, and respectfully say, "Heil Hitler." At first I did not know what to do but finally decided to reply, and did so by heiling our own President in a similar salute, "Heil Roosevelt." Apparently this caused considerable amusement around the halls of the German school, for during the second year the charwomen, still scrubbing the floors, would greet me with the Nazi salute but would say, "Heil Roosevelt," to which I replied, "Heil Hitler."

I had never condoned or glossed over Nazi barbarities: the suppression of individual freedoms; the regimentation of mind, body, and spirit; the abuse of political nonconformists; the persecution of Jews; and the ruthless Nazi methods of asserting power. Shortly after my arrival in Berlin with my family, Colonel Gunther Lohmann, an officer in the German Air Force, called upon us, accompanied by his wife. They were close friends of Lieutenant General Friedrich von Boetticher, the German military attaché in Washington, who had written to the Lohmanns concerning our arrival in Berlin. A lasting and valued friendship developed. Colonel Lohmann was an instructor at the German War College so that I saw him almost daily. Frequently my wife and I spent an evening or a Sunday afternoon with the Lohmanns.

My last night in Berlin was spent with them. After the family dinner, the two children, a boy and girl, left to prepare their schoolwork. Colonel and Mrs. Lohmann and I had coffee and liqueur in the library. Finally she asked to be excused and I bade her good-by, noticing that she seemed to be emotionally upset. After she left he was obviously ill at ease, too. He referred to our enjoyable times together and emphasized how much our friendship meant to them. Finally he said, "There is something I must tell you: Maria and I feel that we should have done so long ago. We must tell you now that you are returning to the United States." In grave tones, almost in a whisper, he said, "Maria is a Jewess." Now I understood why they were so upset. He was finally unburdening what was to him a terrible load to carry in Hitler's Germany but to me, as to most Americans, wholly unimportant.

He looked at me steadily, searching for my reaction, and said, "I hope this will not affect our friendship." I told him that our friendship was based on mutuality of interest and respect as well as compatibility and that I had no religious or racial prejudices. It had never interested me, and in fact I didn't know, that Morgenthau, the Secretary of the Treasury in the U.S., was a Jew or that LaGuardia, the Mayor of New York, was half Jewish until I read about it in the Berlin newspapers. I made it clear that I had several good friends who were Jewish and that I accepted as loyal citizens of my country those who professed Judaism or any other religion. Lohmann commented that he had been told that there was a wave of anti-Semitism sweeping the United States—in fact the world. (Of course this was the Nazi propaganda to which all Germany and Western Europe were subjected at the time.) I said that I had no way of knowing about waves of anti-Semitism but I was not anti-Semitic or anti-Nordic any more than I could be anti-Irish, -Swedish, or -Russian. In so far as nationalities are concerned, I told him that I expected peoples to be loyal to and proud of their particular country. Actually I wouldn't respect them if they weren't. Lohmann then asked me if I would look after his children if it should develop that he could not do so. I assured him that I would do everything possible for them. He seemed greatly relieved and we shook hands warmly as we parted.

There were some aspects of the Third Reich which seemed good at the time—for example, the public works program; encouragement of the arts, music, and science; the building of roads and communications; and cultural opportunities such as travel abroad for underprivileged people at government expense. Also I rendered favorable reports to the U.S. War Department that German military tactics, training, and technique and development of new equipment were far superior to our own.

Many rather personal questions were asked by Mr. Genau and the military intelligence officer. For instance, they were curious about a deposit that I had made in the Riggs National Bank of Washington. I explained that a relative had died a year earlier in a state where one year is required to probate a will and that I had made the deposit about the time the breach of security had occurred. They asked about my connection with Mr. Chesly Manly and were obviously surprised when I told them that I had never heard of him prior to the morning of December 5 when I read the article about the Victory Program in the Washington *Times-Herald* under his by-line. Then the investigation turned to my connection or association with Colonel Truman Smith of the G-2 Division, General Staff, and Colonel Charles Lindbergh, both unjustifiably suspected of pro-Nazi leanings.

I first met Colonel Smith in Berlin [I told them]. He was serving as American military attaché while I was a student at the War College. Unfortunately while in Germany he was stricken with diabetes, and the medical authorities recommended his immediate retirement as physically unfit for active duty. However, General Marshall knew him both personally and professionally and, fully aware of his outstanding abilities, arranged to retain him on active duty. He served for several months in the G-2 Division where his fund of information and sound judgments pertaining to European countries, particularly Germany, were most helpful in the formulation of our policies and courses of action prior to and during the war.

General Marshall had been trying to compel certain incompetent officers to retire on physical grounds. One such incompetent in some manner learned that Truman Smith had been recommended for retirement by medical officers yet was retained on active duty. He broadcast this information with claims of favoritism and the Chief of Staff was compelled to approve Smith's retirement for physical disability incurred in line of duty in September of this year. This valuable, almost indispensable, officer is presently at his home in Fairfield, Connecticut.

(A few months later, Pearl Harbor was upon us and General Marshall personally telephoned Truman Smith and asked him to return again to active duty with the Army Intelligence Division. Colonel Smith returned at once to Washington, there to give unstintingly of time and effort in military intelligence.)

I continued to relate my personal evaluation of Colonel Truman Smith to the investigators:

> It is my conviction that had it not been for his poor health he would have been given positions of great responsibility.

I told Mr. Genau:

> There has been an unusual and certainly un-American form of persecution conducted by persons unknown against Colonel Smith since his return from service in Germany. These Gestapo tactics reached such a point that General Marshall arranged for Colonel Smith temporarily to leave Washington last summer. He and his loyal wife, Kay, visited us at Fort Benning incognito for a period of two weeks.

I have described Colonel Smith's experience in considerable detail because I feel that the American people should know that while their President was rightfully deriding the Gestapo methods of Nazi Germany, there were shadowy figures in our own country unjustly attacking an American of unquestioned loyalty. Furthermore, Colonel Smith requested an opportunity to confront his accusers but was never permitted to do so.

Mr. Genau also asked about my connections with another fine American, Colonel Lindbergh, concerning whom I replied:

> I first met him in Berlin when he visited the Truman Smiths back in 1938. After returning to the United States I saw Colonel Lindbergh only occasionally. He has contacted me a few times. I respect him and agree with many of his ideas concerning our entrance into the war.

I was asked when I last saw him and said:

> Approximately a month ago I saw Truman Smith and Lindbergh together.

My interrogators seemed to attach considerable significance to this meeting and asked a series of questions, to which I replied:

It was purely a social visit. We discussed the international situation, and I might add that on every occasion that I visited with Truman Smith or Charles Lindbergh we invariably discussed national and international problems.

Years later, in delving through official records of events during those hectic months immediately prior to Pearl Harbor, I discovered that my friendly reactions to the German people not connected with the Nazi movement and the favorable reports I had submitted concerning my experience and observations in Germany caused even some of my fellow officers and friends to consider me sympathetic to Nazism. Those who suspected my actions because of my German ancestry ignored the fact that many of our senior and most distinguished leaders in the military service had Germanic backgrounds: Krueger, Nimitz, Eichelberger, Ollendorf, Stratemeyer, Spaatz, and Eisenhower. I had perhaps at times been too outspoken or indiscreet in expressing my conviction that we should not become involved in the war. I accepted the fact that a situation might develop requiring our intervention. These frank revelations aroused considerable interest on the part of the interrogators and they repeatedly sought to elicit my views on isolationism. I said:

I do favor international co-operation—diplomatic, economic, and cultural, but I am opposed to the indiscriminate distribution of our military and economic resources. Assistance to other countries should be given on a reciprocal basis. We should avoid becoming involved in fratricidal or internecine struggles abroad, but hold ourselves in readiness to ease frictions and to promote sound economies and honorable peace.

Lofty words—impractical ideas because too idealistic! My diary records my forebodings after the United States was finally precipitated into the war. On January 1, 1942, I wrote:

The New Year promises much suffering and sacrifice, not only for Americans but for peoples all over the world. Conflicting ideologies, greed, leaders seeking power, groups striving to reach a higher standard of living, these contribute to the maelstrom involving chaos, destruction and barbarism throughout the world. We Americans are committing ourselves to the defeat of one ism with the clear prospect of creating an equally dangerous ism under another cloak. Our fine country, with its wonderful potentials for the role of stabilizer in a war-torn world, must be victorious in battle and at the peace table.

By this time I and the other officers in the War Plans Division were too busy trying to get the Victory Program into high gear to be any longer greatly concerned with the result of the investigation. My experience in this searching inquiry had, however, taught me something I should never forget: namely the danger of accepting circumstantial evidence, particularly in those nebulous areas involving interpretation of an individual's motives, his thinking processes, his sense of loyalty to principles and country, all of which are wrapped up with his innermost and private life. This was not to be my last experience with guilt by association, but it was then that I realized for the first time the seriousness of probing into and sometimes transgressing an individual's rights and dignity, prodding one's heart, searching one's mind, scrutinizing one's associations. I understood that suspicion had fallen on me because I had had so much to do with the Victory Program and pertinent secret documents. I accepted the fact that it was unavoidable, in fact necessary, to establish my unequivocal loyalty, certainly to the satisfaction of everyone with whom I was associated in the War Department.

This experience was to prove helpful to me as an individual when, years later, I had to cope with situations that involved the loyalty and ideology of other individuals.

Pearl Harbor on December 7 focused the attention of every American on the sacred duty of protecting our country. We all closed ranks—the America Firsters, the Anglophiles, the Francophiles, the Chinophiles, the One Worlders, the interventionists, the internationalists, the isolationists. No longer could there be, nor was there, dissension—no deviation or diffusion of purpose in the loyal and patriotic outpouring of our best efforts to insure an early victory.

The FBI investigation of the Victory Program leak continued, but public interest faded quickly. In the tremendous upheaval of the next four years the release of the secret document vanished from the news. My efforts to fix responsibility for this episode came to naught. I retain, however, vivid recollections of the Washington scene—the war-imminent climate, the progressive build-up by F.D.R. of valid reasons for entrance into the war, and the clever conditioning of the minds of people to soften the blow of any irrational act which would precipitate 135 million Americans into the European caldron of death and destruction.

CHAPTER IV

EDUCATION OF A STRATEGIST

It may well be asked, and I have often myself wondered, how and why it happened that I was given responsibilities in strategic planning. What prior experience, training, aptitude, or interest had brought me to the War Plans Division of the General Staff and caused me to be selected to work on the Victory Program?

It has been wisely said that one's character is one's fate. It may also be true that early influence and environment mold one's character, stimulate interest in this or that direction, and thus shape one's future course through life to a degree which one realizes only in retrospect.

Looking back at early influences which shaped my life, I realize that my father first awakened my avid interest in history, which has remained my favorite study and has provided background for strategic thinking. As I have already related, Father's discussions with friends prior to our entrance into the First World War concerning its origins and German guilt had stimulated my thinking, made me immune to crude and unscrupulous war propaganda, and encouraged me to study what that mellow ironist, the historian Gibbon, called "the record of the follies, crimes, and cruelties of mankind." Hence came my early interest not only in military but also in political, economic, and social history. I did much reading in my teens, although in general my formal education in Omaha's primary and

44

secondary schools had produced little tangible results on my academic record.

It was my father, a strict disciplinarian, who stimulated my intellectual development, although he never succeeded in making me apply myself diligently to school tasks. Like most normal, healthy boys, I wanted to be outdoors playing with other children. As I grew older I took an increasing interest in football and baseball and did only the minimum amount of study required of me. It was my wonderful mother who succeeded by her sympathy, understanding, and love in making me obey and behave and do enough schoolwork to get by.

Even at West Point I was a subtle resister, although when examinations approached I buckled down and did enough work to pass them. By that time I had a really passionate interest in baseball and pitched for the Army team. The coach was the old New York Giants' player, Hans Lobert, whom the cadets loved and respected. I played against many college players who went on to become well-known professionals—for example, Lou Gehrig of Columbia University and Frankie Frisch, the "Fordham flash." To this day I carry a scar on my ankle from one of Frisch's flying spikes.

The United States Military Academy had a lasting effect upon me, as I believe it does upon every young man who experiences its carefully supervised physical, mental, and spiritual training. Aside from technical instruction, the cadet is taught the importance of discipline, humility, and respect for others regardless of economic or social status. West Point training inculcates a sense of honor and personal integrity which in my judgment are the invisible guaranty of America's future. Among my West Point classmates who distinguished themselves in later years were Al Gruenther, who became Eisenhower's chief of staff and finally Supreme Allied Commander in Europe; "Nuts" McAuliffe, who resolutely refused to surrender to the Nazis at Bastogne; and Nate Twining, who became Chairman of the Joint Chiefs of Staff. Those of us who were given the chance to prove ourselves cannot, however, but remember with sadness friends and associates of our youth. There were many officers in the regular service, National Guard, and reserves who were outstanding, yet did not attain high rank or world renown simply because their true value or real potential was not observed or appreciated by someone in position to give them greater responsibilities and rank.

After graduation from West Point my class traveled in Europe for a few months. During this trip I saw the dislocations and destruction wrought by war and visited the hallowed ground where row upon row of white crosses stood as silent reminders of bravery, sacrifice, and devotion to country. I began to be somewhat less preoccupied with my own comfort and security and more concerned about others. I adopted a more serious approach to life slowly, almost unconsciously. I read a lot and studied voluntarily, not to pass formal examinations but to satisfy a rapidly expanding curiosity. There was much joy in discovering unusual characters, sharing their exciting experiences, and acquiring a broader view of life from books.

It was, however, only later that I started to mature. The Spartan environment of my early Army career encouraged my private study and reading. My first station in the military service, Fort Benning, Georgia, was located in an isolated area about twelve miles south of the city of Columbus. The site had just been selected (1919) for the infantry school. Personnel, administrators, faculty, students, and some equipment were moved in before appropriate facilities had been made available. There were no permanent structures, no roads, no sidewalks, and only limited utilities. It was a truly primitive existence.

We Fort Benning "pioneers" soon discovered that creature comforts were not a prerequisite of effective work or enjoyment of life. All officers and enlisted men caught the spirit of the frontier and enthusiastically joined in the tasks which we were called upon to perform. We all lived in tents. A pyramidal tent, 14 feet by 14 feet, was my castle. Ablution and toilet facilities were as primitive as those of medieval castles. The few opportunities for recreation in the evenings included a weekly dance at the officers' club and a crowded silent movie. I had no car—and a car was practically a "must" if one were to date a Georgia belle. Bachelors were forty-deep on the doorsteps of the limited number of local eligible girls. Many junior officers devoted their leisure hours to sports in the daytime and the Victrola, cards, and reading in the evening. Civilian families in the nearby communities of Georgia and Alabama, particularly in Columbus, opened their hearts and their homes to military personnel, resulting in many valued and lasting friendships, and—I might add—marriages.

Having no car, I was immobilized, so I remained perforce in my tent and spent my evenings, for the most part, reading books, playing popular tunes on my violin, or listening to classical music on my phonograph. Occasionally a friend would take me to the city as on the ill-fated evening that I have mentioned.

Practically all of my pre-1941 service in the Army was in the lower ranks. My West Point class had been submerged in the post–World War I promotion list so that we remained in the lowly rank of lieutenant for seventeen years and then in that of captain for several years more. I had only just been promoted to the rank of major when I reported in 1940 for duty in the Office of the Chief of Infantry, Washington, D.C. When one is far down the ladder in any organization, be it military, civic, or industrial, responsibilities are limited and opportunities few. However, I had been fortunate in receiving several interesting assignments both in the U.S. and overseas in the Philippines, China, and Europe.

There were welcome opportunities as the years rolled along to pick up information about politics, economics, history, and diplomacy. Anywhere on the globe life can be fascinating and rewarding if one has a sympathetic understanding and interest in humanity. I came to recognize man's fallibility, especially my own, as well as to appreciate his noble qualities; and learned that regardless of race, color, social or economic status, and religious or political convictions, the same defects and the same fine qualities are to be found everywhere.

After my service at Fort Benning, I spent most of the next ten years in the Philippines and China, with a short tour in Washington intervening. Duty in Tientsin, China, was particularly educational. Both the officers and their wives were encouraged to study Mandarin—the spoken language of the North and the official and literary language of all China. We sweated for six days each week until we could pass a satisfactory test. Our teacher knew no English; his method was to point to an object, name it, and make us repeat the name after him. We *really* learned by ear. At the time of my Tientsin experience, war lords were contending for northern China, and the Kuomintang was just coming to the fore as the great power in the South determined to unite, modernize, and strengthen the ancient Kingdom of Cathay. It was important to know some spoken Chinese if only to say to a contending war lord's soldier, "Don't shoot; I'm an American," or "Come with me and I will give you some food."

My days at Tientsin and my two tours of duty in the Philippines gave me some insight into the ferment that was just about to shake the Orient.

In 1925, on Corregidor, I married Dade Embick, whom I had met traveling with her parents on the boat going from San Francisco to the Philippines. A year later my first son, Albert, was born in Washington, and in 1928 my second and last son.

On my return home I was assigned as a student to the Command and General Staff School, located at Fort Leavenworth, Kansas. The course of instruction lasted two years (1934–36). During the first year we were taught the tactics and techniques of military units up to and including a reinforced division. In addition we learned the tactical and technical handling of all weapons and services in the infantry division, including tanks, artillery, signal communications, engineering, and motor transport. Instruction included methods of supply and movements by motor, rail, and water.

Military history was an important and, for most students, enjoyable feature of the first-year course. Some of the school problems were solved on maps, and others were applied to nearby terrain appropriate to the type of maneuver the school wanted to simulate. Everyone worked hard. Even more important, although class standings were divulged only to the War Department, each student knew that the quality of his work would strongly influence his future in the service.

Between the first and second year of instruction students were given what was ostensibly a vacation; however, on return to the school, each was required to submit a thesis on a military subject or a translation of something pertaining to a historically important military operation that had been recorded only in a foreign language. I elected to translate a French historical record of World War I fighting in the vicinity of Belfort Gap. If I had known in advance that I would be sent to the German War College after graduation from Leavenworth, I would naturally have undertaken a translation from the German instead. But it was only during my second year at Leavenworth that I was told I was being considered for this assignment. The Assistant Commandant had noted on my official record that I had studied German. I explained that my instruction in that language was limited to two years in high school and that I had forgotten practically all I ever learned. However, I expressed interest in the assignment and agreed to study German with a private tutor. One of my West Point classmates, then Captain Harlan N. Hartness, had been sent to the German War College the previous year after completing the two-year course at Leavenworth. I wrote and asked him about the German school, living conditions in Berlin, and schools for American children. His reply was enthusiastic and he urged me to accept the detail if offered.

The second-year course at Leavenworth involved instruction in handling large units—for example, corps and armies. We were also required to study military history, including the campaigns of Frederick the Great, Napoleon, Caesar, Philip of Macedon, and Alexander. The principal campaigns of the American Civil War and of World War I were analyzed in detail. Instruction was also given pertaining to other military services—the Navy and Air Force.

At Leavenworth I had furthered my education in advanced military science. But my real education as a strategist, using the word in its broadest connotation, began during my two years of study at the German War College, 1936–38. This was my most professionally remunerative assignment and, no doubt, the principal reason why I was assigned to the War Plans Division of the General Staff in Washington early in 1941.

At the Kriegs Akademie not only was I given a chance to study new tactics of mechanized warfare and air power, subsequently to be employed with such devastating results by the Germans in the early stages of World War II, but I also acquired a deeper and broader understanding of international affairs and of the true, basic causes of world tensions and conflict. Thanks to my assignment in Germany, I was afforded an opportunity to acquire a broad concept of strategy embracing political, economic, and psychological means for the attainment of war aims, in place of the narrower concept of strictly military science which I had studied at Leavenworth.

I arrived in Berlin on July 2, 1936, just in time to witness some of the events of the Olympic games. With the summer in Europe still before me, I had almost three months during which I could improve my German, which was far from good, in fact *schrecklich* (terrible)!

During my two years' service in Germany, I traveled extensively as part of my assigned duties at the War College, for recreation, and to satisfy a thirst for knowledge about Europe. The U.S. Government had made a reciprocal arrangement in 1935 with the Defense Department of Germany for an exchange of students, the exchange being limited to one from each country for each class. Actually the Germans did not choose to send a student to our school. They were too busy in 1936 making preparations for war and consequently were striving to train in Germany as many students as possible for command and staff duties. It was suggested tactfully that the Germans did not think very highly of the U.S. course of instruction at Leavenworth.

The German War College was located in a rather unattractive industrial area, the Moabit district of Berlin; but instruction facilities were excellent—including modern, well-equipped study halls, map rooms, lecture rooms, library, and gymnasium. Having just completed two years at Fort Leavenworth, I was constantly drawing comparisons. Most of all I was impressed by German methods and the quality of instruction. The German pedagogy and curriculum were, in my judgment, superior to our own.

At Leavenworth the instruction had been much more theoretical. Furthermore, instructors were not so well qualified or trained as those at the German War College. Just before I left Leavenworth in June, 1936, Colonel Burt, the Assistant Commandant, called in members of my class to obtain their views about the curriculum and instruction. With some trepidation I told Colonel Burt that I felt I had learned a great deal at Leavenworth "in spite of the poor instruction." Fortunately he recognized that I was endeavoring to offer constructive criticism. With his encouragement I explained that there were only a few instructors at Leavenworth who were really well-equipped to teach. The remainder were mediocre. I told him that I felt sure they had the knowledge but lacked the ability to impart information to others or had not been trained in this art.

He asked me how I accounted for this. I suggested that the instructors were probably assigned to Leavenworth because of friendship with someone already on the faculty. I had heard that members of the faculty were asked at the end of each school year by the

Commandant or Assistant Commandant to recommend an officer's name for assignment as an instructor. Too often, in making recommendations, an individual's golf-playing ability or his comradeship was the main criterion, not his professional knowledge or ability to teach.

At the German War College, instructors definitely knew how to impart their knowledge. They were thoroughly grounded in all tactical and technical principles of the German Army. There wasn't a day that passed in the classroom when students didn't have practical work to master. The instructor would assign a problem involving a large unit—for example, a division or a corps. He would then designate a student to act as the commander, others as staff officers, or as observers prepared to criticize plans and actions. Every student had a definite role to play either in issuing orders or in interpreting them, which required him to make tactical and technical decisions. These procedures went on every day at the German War College, an unconscious rebuke to Leavenworth where the solution of problems had been highly theoretical.

The history course at the German War College was also extremely interesting and well conducted. The great geopolitician, Haushofer, talked to the class several times, dwelling principally on higher-level strategy. He explained the "heartland" theory and discussed the principles enunciated by Clausewitz, Von der Goltz, and du Picq. The Germans, in analyzing military history, did not study the American Civil War, whereas in England officers were required to study the tactics and techniques of both the Confederate and Northern armies. (I discovered later that many British officers—and especially Prime Minister Churchill—knew as much as, or more than, most American officers about our Civil War.) The Germans stressed the campaigns of Frederick the Great, Napoleon, Caesar, Alexander, and Philip of Macedon. World War I tactics were studied and references made, of course, to American participation in that war.

I might add that mention of the United States, while not derogatory, emphasized that our overpowering production capabilities were the decisive factor in the war. We had built ships faster than German submarines could sink them. The references to American production were in line with Hindenburg's remark about our "pitiless industry." There was never the least suggestion that tactical skill or strategic judgment was evident among American military leaders.

When we studied a campaign of Frederick the Great or of Napoleon, we generally went to the area where the battle had been fought. The military history instructor reviewed the situation, analyzed dispositions and tactical decisions, and injected interesting anecdotes. We also visited World War I battlefields, in particular Tannenberg in East Prussia. Hindenburg and Ludendorff—supported gallantly by von François—were depicted as a fortuitous combination: Hindenburg, stoic, unemotional and solid; Ludendorff, the brilliant tactician; von François, dash, *élan*, boldness, courage. These three generals reached the heights at Tannenberg, overcoming superior numbers of Russians. Together, Hindenburg, Ludendorff, and von François provided a modern example of the principle of annihilation.

My principal instructor the first year was Ferdinand Jodl, brother of the World War II Colonel General Alfred Jodl, who was later to be condemned at Nuremberg as a war criminal. Major Jodl, who conducted the course in tactics and techniques the entire year, was outstanding as a teacher. Other instructors were assigned to such special subjects as Supply and Evacuation, Signal Communications, Air Power, Armored Units, and Artillery.

Between the first and second year at the German War College, instead of recreation, the students were sent "to troops." They served in a command or staff position, putting into practice what they learned in theory at the War College. Toward the end of each summer they reported to large units in order to participate in autumn maneuvers. In this manner students obtained thoroughly practical training.

The second-year course began on October 1. Instruction included the handling of larger units in combat, i.e., army, corps, etc. The broader subject of grand strategy was introduced. The importance of geography, demography, climate, temperament of the people, political structure, and economics was emphasized in a series of thought-provoking lectures.

Prior to going to Germany I had read a fascinating account of the heartland theory by Sir Halford MacKinder, the British "geopolitical" thinker, who had speculated on the importance of controlling the Eurasian heartland if one aspired to control the world.

The Germans had taken Sir Halford for their very own, and their eminent strategist, Haushofer, had proceeded to improve upon him. The heartland consisted of enough of Eastern Europe to preclude an attack from the East, if and when one were thinking of turning one's attention to the West. Sir Halford's idea was that control of Eurasia and Africa, the "World Island," would enable a continental military empire to outflank the oceans. This, in popular parlance, would put America and Australia in the hole.

Bismarck's own way of speaking of the heartland was to say, "The master of Bohemia is the master of Europe." Bohemia is, of course, a part of Czechoslovakia. One of the map problems given while I was a student in Berlin involved a hypothetical attack against Czechoslovakia. Later, it developed that the problem was not so hypothetical. The school solution was in fact very similar to the operations which were actually executed about a year later when the Germans quickly overran their neighbors to the south.

My two years in Germany led to valued friendships. Many of my closest friends among the German officers were to be implicated in the tragically abortive plot to kill Hitler in July, 1944. (This subject is dealt with in a later chapter. Here I shall only record that it was their uniform hope that Nazi control of their country could be broken and a negotiated peace with the Western Allies effected.)

One of my German acquaintances was a confirmed Nazi, Herr Gerhard Rossbach, from whom I rented a furnished apartment located at Konstantzerstrasse 56 in the Wilmersdorf section of Berlin. I was informed that Rossbach was intimately connected with the Nazi movement. A so-called Front Fighter, Rossbach had fought in Poland against the Communists after World War I. He was a close friend of Captain Roehm, the leader of the Nazi Brownshirts (SA). Some of Hitler's close associates wanted to kill Rossbach as an accomplice of Roehm, charging him with conniving to seize power from Hitler. However, Hitler spared his life for unknown reasons, and relations between the two when I was residing in Berlin were apparently quite amicable. Rossbach had a picture of Hitler, draped with a Nazi flag, prominently displayed in my apartment. I promptly replaced Hitler's picture and the Nazi flag with a picture of President Roosevelt and an American flag.

Herr Rossbach once invited me to a party where I met several top Nazis—Hess, Goebbels, Goering, Ley, Bohrmann, and many others. It was readily apparent, even to the most casual observer, that Goebbels was a dynamo with a brain. He held a diploma from a Jesuit school in the Rhine Valley—he being the only prominent Nazi who had graduated from a university. His mind was a veritable idea factory; he was an ideal man for public relations and propaganda. Even among his intimate contacts his character was considered shifty and unscrupulous.

Rudolf Hess impressed me as being stolid, not overly intelligent, and superficially a gentleman. The son of a German foreign service officer, he had lived in Egypt as a boy and spoke both Arabic and French. My conversation with him was casual. When he fled to Scotland by plane during the war in an effort to bring about a *rapprochement* between British and Germans, many people in Germany felt his motives were honest and constructive. What Hess proposed to the British may never be revealed, but the effort in any event was bound to prove abortive.

Field Marshal Goering gave the impression of being jovial and an ebullient extrovert. He wore colorful uniforms on the two occasions that I saw him, a white field marshal's uniform with a great number of impressive decorations. He seemed to revel in pomp and display, but even his associates considered him gauche and heavyminded.

While at the War College I was in daily contact with many German officers, both students and instructors. My class consisted of approximately 120 German officers of captain rank who averaged about thirty-five years of age. There were nine officer students from foreign nations—two from China, two from Argentina, and one each from Bulgaria, Italy, Japan, Turkey, and the United States. The class was divided into study groups consisting of from fifteen to eighteen officers each. In my study group (*Hörsaal*) there was one other foreign officer beside myself, a Captain Rudolfo Fasano of the Italian Army. He was an attractive individual, who spoke German much better than I and studied diligently.

My classmates and instructors were at all times friendly; a few were particularly helpful. A German classmate, Fritz Berendsen, who sat next to me during the two years of school, was ever ready to help me. I shall never forget the language hurdles he helped me take. The first time I heard the instructor use the term "*Hinhaltenderwiderstand*" I was in mild shock and by the time I had interpreted the word (simply "delaying action"), he had not delayed one bit and I lost a sentence or paragraph—hence some of the instruction was gone. There were other German officers whom I also remember favorably; however, the vast majority were killed in the war. Berendsen today is a respected and effective member of Parliament in the new German Reich. He speaks English quite well and is happily married to a very charming woman. They have three children, and I am godfather to his daughter.

Wessel Freitag von Loringhoven was also a close and valued friend. He was an active member of the anti-Hitler group, and after the abortive July 20, 1944, attempt to kill the Fuehrer, von Loringhoven was shot by the Nazis.

There were others with whom I corresponded after my return to the United States before World War II, including Colonel and Mrs. Lohmann, whom I have mentioned earlier. After the war I learned that Lohmann was compelled by the Nazi regime to obtain a legal separation from his Jewish wife. Their devotion and loyalty to each other was so great that immediately after the war they were remarried.

Claus von Stauffenberg was another member of my class for whom I had great admiration and respect. Later, he became deeply involved in the anti-Hitler group. I was not assigned to the same study group with Captain von Stauffenberg; however, we were often together after school hours and I enjoyed visiting with him. He spoke fairly good English. I was impressed by his broad knowledge and understanding of developments at home and abroad. He was a handsome man, with fine chiseled features, dark brown hair, clear blue eyes, and a strong chin.

The von Stauffenbergs were a highly respected Catholic family from Swabia in Bavaria. As a colonel, Claus von Stauffenberg was to gain distinction in World War II fighting with General Rommel in North Africa, where he lost his right eye, his right hand, and two fingers of his left hand. He was decorated for outstanding bravery and proved to be an inspiring leader in combat. Because of his crippling wounds, he was returned to Berlin to serve on the General Staff of the Home Forces. In this assignment his considerable talents as an organizer were put to good use. He was also to have favorable opportunities to plan the overthrow of Hitler and his despised henchmen. Von Stauffenberg's lovely wife, Nina, was also descended from a fine old German family. Exceedingly pretty, vivacious, and intelligent, she was a delightful hostess. The von Stauffenbergs entertained modestly; it was apparent that tact and purpose motivated the selection of guests, and their parties were interesting, provocative, and entertaining.

Von Stauffenberg's outlook on life, his curiosity, and vision happened to be much greater than that of the average officer of the German Army—or perhaps of any other army, including our own. He had many outside intellectual interests—music, literature, poetry, art, and the sciences. He knew much about the problems and policies of foreign countries, including America. Stephen George, the poet and prophet of a new spiritual awakening, took von Stauffenberg into his circle. Von Stauffenberg memorized most of his friend's poetry which he enjoyed quoting at parties. He was not always discreet in expressing his contempt for the Nazis or for Hitler, but he was so greatly liked and admired that no one betrayed him. Selflessness, courage, and tenacity, combined with unusual professional abilities and a strongly practical Christianity, were to make him a key figure in the bomb plot. Everyone in the resistance movement recognized and respected von Stauffenberg's outstanding courage, character, and ability.

As will become evident in a later chapter, suspicions had apparently been aroused among the Nazi hierarchy through prior attempts to kill Hitler. Therefore, every precaution had to be taken. Von Stauffenberg enjoyed a position of trust. From time to time he was required to attend staff meetings on the highest level in order to give Hitler and key staff officers résumé of the situation pertaining to the Home Forces. Von Stauffenberg thus had no difficulty in arranging to travel from Berlin to whatever place high-level meetings were held. This provided an ideal opportunity to carry out any plans that he might care to make in connection with the resistance movement.

As a guest of the German Government I was careful never to allude to Hitler or any other political leaders. I avoided political discussions with all Germans, military or civilian. They for their part were correct at all times in their attitude toward me, but it was subtly revealed that the professional military men disapproved of Hitler and the Nazi Party.

There would be veiled statements, sometimes hints which would indicate shame, disgust, or displeasure with the Nazis. I never let on that I noticed them. However, it was not a great surprise to me that Captain Claus von Stauffenberg was to be involved in a plot to kill the leader of the German Government. Nor was it a shock to learn that General Ludwig Beck and Captain Wessel Freitag von Loringhoven were deeply committed to an anti-Hitler movement. I had met General Beck shortly after my arrival in Berlin in 1936. At the time I knew him only as a dedicated individual with a firm sense of honorable military tradition. Observing his finer sensibilities and his great loyalty to Germany, I could readily understand why he ultimately decided to make any sacrifice, including his life, to remove Hitler from power.

Each spring a ski trip (*Skireise*) was arranged for the students of the War College accompanied by the instructors as a phase of instruction and training. The first spring (1937) my class went to the vicinity of Krummhübel, southeast of Dresden close to the Czech border. We spent a delightful two weeks skiing in the mountains close to the frontier. This was my first experience on skiis. I was far from proficient but enjoyed trying to learn the rudiments of a wonderful sport. While on these trips students were required to solve terrain problems involving application of tactical and technical principles taught at the school.

On March 12, 1938, Nazi troops marched into Austria. This was termed the *Anschluss* (Annexation). I was skiing at that time with my classmates along the Austrian border. We were billeted at Obersdorf and were scheduled to have a terrain problem when my German classmates left the skiing site unceremoniously—in fact, I did not miss them until I reported at the prescribed assembly point on the ski course at 8:00 A.M. Eventually my instructor (Major Koch) arrived and informed me that orders had been received by all German officers to proceed elsewhere. He did not amplify and of course I didn't inquire. It was a curious experience—the evening before in good camaraderie, arms linked, drinking wine and singing songs; this morning an ominous secrecy, a charged atmosphere. Could it be war? Living in Germany at this particular time one had mixed feelings, almost always tension, occasionally an exciting eruption of some kind. I wondered what had happened to cut short the ski trip which had at least one more week to go. Major Koch politely suggested that I could remain at Obersdorf if I so desired or I could return to my residence in Berlin. I told him that I would visit my two sons who were in school near Montreux, Switzerland.

As soon as I crossed the border into Switzerland, I learned from excited passengers on the train that the Germans were marching into Austria. I remained only a short time at Gai Matin, my boys' school located in the Alps, then flew to Vienna in order to observe the Nazi troops as they goosestepped between rows of excited people. The Viennese, who were outwardly exultant, cheered lustily. But I wondered. Somehow the Viennese cheers sounded unnatural, lacking in spontaneity. It soon became apparent that many Germans prominent in civilian life as well as a large number of military men were greatly concerned about Hitler's hunches, his dangerously provocative moves on the international chessboard.

From the very beginning of the Nazi movement, but particularly when Hitler and his henchmen seized power in Germany, there was a dignified but inarticulate resistance or disapproval among the officers of the Army. Though Hindenburg had become somewhat senile, he remained deservedly the symbol of decency and honor to all Germans. The professional officer corps and businessmen in Germany resented Nazi treatment of the hero of Tannenberg.

The feeling against Hitler and the Nazi movement was not overtly strong within the ranks of the military at the time I was in Germany. In the first place, Hitler had somewhat ingratiated himself with professional military men by refusing to integrate into the Army the quasi-military Brownshirts (*Sturmabteilung*). The Brownshirts were war veterans, political followers and, by and large, flag wavers who enjoyed military pomp and ceremony. (Professional military men were not permitted to join any political organization, including the National Socialist Democrat Party.) It was quietly rumored that the senior military men initially harbored the illusion that they could handle "the little corporal."

The first serious portent of revolt appeared when top military men firmly opposed the Fuehrer's aggressive policies, which they realized must lead to war. Unplanned and unheralded, anti-Hitler sentiments began to assume tangible form, and many of Germany's outstanding military leaders expressed increased concern to each other and to key civilians in government and in business.

Colonel General Ludwig Beck, Chief of the German General Staff, was a symbol of such opposition, an unflinching anti-Nazi. He had no sympathy whatsoever for the policies and actions of the Nazi political or economic philosophy. Nor did he admire or respect Hitler. Nothing that General Beck ever said during my residence in Germany revealed this attitude to me, but his feelings were known to a few intimate colleagues. He opposed the Nazi policies of aggrandizement, and the German annexation of Austria caused him to protest strongly to Hitler. General Beck then pointed out that a policy of aggression and ruthless conquest would unavoidably lead to a catastrophic war, one which would involve all of Europe. He urged Hitler to pursue a policy of peaceful cooperation with neighboring states. *Der Fuehrer* arrogantly ignored General Beck's warning and refused to acknowledge his Chief of Staff's courteous but firm admonition.

When the Czechoslovakian crisis was reaching an explosive point in the summer of 1938, General Beck requested an interview with the German Chancellor. During the course of the discussion, Hitler made no attempt to deny his intention to annex Czechoslovakia. He frankly admitted his determination to go forward, to acquire Czechoslovakia, using force of arms as and if necessary. Paradoxically, Hitler emphasized that he was not aiming at war. Beck was not satisfied. He demanded definite guarantees, but Hitler indignantly refused, declaring, "The armed forces are an instrument of politics. I shall allot the Army its task when the right moment has come. The Army has to fulfill its assigned task and is not to argue whether it is right or wrong."

General Beck calmly replied, "This is a point of view which I cannot accept. As Chief of the General Staff, I am not prepared to take the responsibility for orders which I do not approve." Beck immediately tendered his written resignation, but Hitler tried to circumvent his Chief of Staff by avoiding all reference to the matter. However, General Beck was adamant. He never again visited the Chief of Staff's office in the Ministry of War nor did he perform any duties of that post. Only in this manner could he compel Hitler to acknowledge his resignation as Chief of the German General Staff.

General Beck was the antithesis of the Allied propagandists' picture of the German General Staff officer. He spoke in a quiet, modulated tone. He was calm and composed. When he made a statement, it was expressed in deliberate, well-considered phrases—

sentence by sentence, building up the thought that he wished to convey in an intelligent, concise manner. He had definite ideas concerning international relations and recognized the potentially explosive situation in Central Europe. He had an uncanny grasp of the political, economic, and psychological factors which so strongly influenced European developments. Furthermore, he was thoroughly familiar with the military capabilities and limitations of each European nation. Steeped in the tradition of the German professional officer, he was disciplined, knowledgeable, courageous. He was a student of Clausewitz and Von der Goltz but equally conversant with the teachings of Spengler, du Picq, and Sun Tzu. He foresaw the German collapse in Russia long before Stalingrad, and he also predicted the manner in which war in the West would turn against Hitler. To intimate friends he said that an Anglo-American cross-Channel operation would succeed because of the overwhelming power of the Anglo-American Air Force supporting the invasion forces on sea and land.

During my German War College period I could hardly foresee the political mistakes that would lead Hitler to a fateful Armageddon. Not knowing Hitler's character from close up, I lacked General Beck's prescience on this score. But assuredly I recognized that the Nazi leaders were preparing for war.

It was Colonel Truman Smith, who was then the military attaché at the U.S. Embassy in Berlin, who kept me informed of the startling growth of the Nazi war machine. Smith was not a West Point man but a graduate of Yale University, where he had been captain of the water polo team and a classmate of Archibald MacLeish and Dean Acheson. After a distinguished career in World War I, Smith had become one of the Army's foremost intelligence experts. He kept abreast of new developments, new weapons, and new techniques and tactics. His reports to Washington from Berlin were brilliant summaries of the strength, composition, deployments, and combat capabilities of German military and quasi-military units.

I like to think that some of Truman Smith's shrewdness and knowledge rubbed off on me during my German War College period. It was his penchant for handing out the truth "with the bark on" that made some people uncomfortable. On one occasion, at a reception in Berlin given by Ambassador Dodd, I had the opportunity to watch Truman Smith in action. We were talking together when Ambassador Dodd passed us and remarked facetiously, "What are you two soldiers doing, hatching up a war?" Whereupon Colonel Smith politely and smilingly replied, "Oh no, Mr. Ambassador, you diplomats hatch up wars, we soldiers fight them." I thought this is a deserved rebuke to soft-headedness in high place. Ambassador Dodd was certainly not the man to take the measure of the Nazis.

Truman Smith's most effective intelligence exploit in Berlin was the source of considerable misunderstanding: it involved Colonel Lindbergh. Noting that Lindbergh was visiting in London, Smith invited the Lone Eagle to come to Berlin. He had a feeling that Lindbergh would be able to get information about the Nazi *Luftwaffe* from Reich Air Marshal Goering and World War I ace Udet that no other foreigner had been able to acquire.

It worked out as Smith had foreseen. Lindbergh was shown the Heinkel plant near Oranienburg and given every opportunity to examine the equipment there. Moreover, his questions concerning German air developments were answered unequivocally. It was obvious that the Germans were fully prepared for war, especially in the application of air power. The reason for Lindbergh's trip to Germany was well known to the political authorities in Washington. Yet, instead of gratitude from their countrymen, all that Smith and Lindbergh received for their brilliant exploit in warning Washington of the extent of Nazi power was obloquy from a clique which wished to play down German capabilities.

After my return to America from two years at the German War College, I was asked to compare my experiences there with my previous tour of duty at our own staff college at Fort Leavenworth. My 100-page report concerned not only the organization and functioning of the German War College but also went into the new German concepts of warfare involving the use of armored divisions, airborne divisions, and antitank units, none of which existed at that time in the United States. I had personally reported to the Chief of Staff, General Craig, and subsequently to the various divisions of the General Staff, and I had been disillusioned by the superficiality and nonmilitary type of questions put to me. I had been asked all sorts of questions about Hitler's peculiarities, the Nazi persecution of Jews, and about Goebbels and Goering's love life, but almost nothing pertaining to strategy, or German capabilities, military training, and organization.

General Marshall, as Chief of War Plans, was a gratifying exception. He had read my report carefully. When I went in to see him he had a copy on his desk. We discussed Germany for several hours. He then asked me to lunch and afterward continued our conversation through the afternoon. He showed more interest than I could have imagined possible, and we were very drawn to each other. I believe this first meeting resulted in my assignment to war planning duties a year or so later.

At any rate, I felt that Marshall thought well of me. On one occasion he took a hastily written memorandum and said to his aide, "Here, take this to that long-legged major in War Plans and have him fix it up. He seems to know how to write." Marshall did not know that I had been the author of the memorandum he considered poorly written. The aide knew that I had prepared the initial version but dutifully kept mum and returned the paper to me with the amused comment, "The Chief thinks this is terrible and wants you to fix it up." I rearranged the written material slightly—added a number of polysyllabic words—but did not change the basic ideas, for I felt they were sound. Later, when the Chief had read the revised paper, he remarked to the aide, "Now, you see, that's the way it should be written."

CHAPTER V

THE VICTORY PROGRAM

THE PURPOSE of the Victory Program, as we have seen, was to provide the Administration with the data and estimates it required for the mobilization of manpower, industry, and transport for the defeat of our "potential enemies." This proved to be a stupendous task. It was not the product of a particular individual or agency. I happened to be the officer responsible for the groundwork—conjuring up national objectives and the broad scheme of maneuver and estimating forces in terms of major military units.

There were many questions which had to be firmly answered before production could be geared to the realities of war. Where, for example, would our forces be fighting? How many ships for cargo and personnel would be required to move and maintain military forces in the areas of prospective employment? How many airplanes of various types would be necessary to gain undisputed control of the air over our land and sea operations? How many planes would be required to reconnoiter and give warning of enemy submarines, enemy planes, enemy dispositions? What could be done to effect an economic blockade of the enemy territory and what types of forces would be required to do it? How rapidly should we induct men into the military services, insuring that equipment, training facilities, and transportation would be available so that they could effectively participate in scheduled combat operations?

In planning a military program of such magnitude, one begins by asking most of the questions posed by a journalist when he is trying to construct for himself a good newspaper "lead." The journalist asks: "who, what, where, how, when, and why?" The "who" to the military planner is, of course, the assumed enemy and allies, complete with an estimate of their intentions and capabilities. The "what" is the type of victory envisaged, whether it be limited or total, or whether it be based on maneuver and assault or on "bleeding" and blockade. The "where" and the "when" are obviously important to what might be called the flow-chart of men and equipment. The "how," or the "with what," must be assembled or created, for no end can be accomplished without first creating the means.

The most important question of all, I found almost impossible to have answered satisfactorily, namely: what kind of conditions do we wish to create and maintain at home and abroad in the process of fighting and crushing militarily the Germans, Italians, and Japanese? Surely I thought we are not going to repeat our experience of World War I—kill—destroy—disrupt—then woo back our former enemies and rehabilitate war-stricken areas and—most tragic of all—permit negotiations at the peace table that will inevitably lead to even greater future dangers to peace, justice, and decency among nations. It was inconceivable to me that we should again fail at the outset to declare our determination to create certain conditions—political, economic, territorial, and social—that definitely would preclude continued tyranny. I was convinced that the American people did not want to supplant Nazism by communism. This, however, was something for the "Summit" to settle; lacking clarity on the point, I had for the moment to make shift with the nebulous.

Tackling the Victory Program on less exalted levels, I was necessarily swamped with literally hundreds of subsidiary questions which might facilitate a determination of the big answers. Military operations on a global scale involve not only the military forces that are to be deployed in consonance with a broad scheme of maneuver; they include different types of transportation—hundreds of ships readily available to move military units and equipment to the areas of contemplated operations.

It should be pointed out that a commander actually leading a military expedition or task force into combat has nothing to do with these preparatory steps. His job is to be aware of the tactical and technical capabilities of his assigned force as well as the obstacles, weather, terrain, the morale and effectiveness of his own troops, and then most important of all—the enemy. These are the factors that can interfere with or contribute to the accomplishment of his assigned combat mission.

The Victory Program was neither a strategic nor a tactical plan, yet many of the accepted principles of strategy and basic elements of tactics were inherently part of the framework within which production requirements were ultimately estimated. Elsewhere national aims are discussed and they, of course, should be the basis for our strategy *in peacetime* when we employ political, economic, and psychological resources as the key weapons in protecting American interests; or *in wartime* when we use our military in conjunction with political, economic, and psychological forces. The Victory Program was never static. As the months went by, adjustments were attuned to an ever-increasing productive capacity, to new scientific or technical developments, and to the demands created in far-flung combat areas. Long before Pearl Harbor, American industry raced against time to fill the urgent orders of the French, British, Chinese, and (after June 1941) the Russians.

British representatives, military and civilian, had been swarming about in Washington, visiting various offices and bureaus, sometimes openly, sometimes surreptitiously, giving advice and offering assistance before we got into the war—in fact several months before Pearl Harbor. Not only were they endeavoring to accelerate their own production throughout the British Commonwealth but they were urging us to step up our production of munitions of war. By January of 1941 they were discussing military plans of possible mutual co-operation with our senior military officials. It was considered only a matter of time before the United States would be a full-fledged belligerent. Those of us working on the Victory Program in midsummer 1941 recognized the importance of maintaining and improving bases in the British Isles and in the British-controlled areas of the Near East. We also foresaw the probability of needing bases elsewhere—in the Scandinavian peninsula, the Iberian peninsula, or along the African littoral. In estimating the number and type of military units we would require, we studied the strength and composition of the potential enemy armies, navies, and air forces as well as those of our allies. The generally accepted ratio of strength between an attacker and a defender would run anywhere from two-to-one to four-to-one, depending upon the terrain, the morale and combat effectiveness of the forces involved, and the ability to maintain the forces logistically. Estimating with any degree of accuracy an enemy's military potential is always very difficult, for there are many intangibles involved. But accepting the G-2 intelligence estimates of the number of Axis divisions that would be available in 1943, namely 400 divisions, we on the Allied side would by traditional rule of thumb require 800 or more divisions.

The British and other members of the Commonwealth could provide approximately 100 of these, so theoretically we would have to raise 700 divisions from other sources. The World War II division averaged in combat strength about 15,000, but that same number would be involved in maintaining and supporting the division in combat from home base to front lines on the battlefield. Planners called the total, namely 30,000, the division slice, which was used in all computations. Allowing about 30,000 men per division, we would have required more than 20 million men in uniform if we were to enjoy at least a two-to-one ratio in division strength. According to manpower studies we couldn't take that many men from our over-all population and still operate a wartime economy, including communications, transportation facilities, and the essential installations for public health and safety. But our wonderful body of scientists—patriotic, selfless men of the caliber of Karl Compton, Vannevar Bush, and Ernest Lawrence, and many other dedicated men in the pure and applied sciences—had introduced methods, weapons, and machines to conserve or replace manpower. We counted on our advanced weapons systems—technical prowess and stupendous production capabilities—to enable us to win the war with a total of approximately ten million Americans under arms. We couldn't be strong everywhere. Neither could the enemy. So we adopted the sound strategic principle of concentrating rapidly at decisive points. In the opening stages of World War II, air power with its great flexibility of employment, unmatched mobility, and terrific destructive power proved to be the decisive weapon. We thought that considering these factors: the scientists, mass production techniques, concentrating for decisive blows, and the exploitation of air power (sea and land based), would more than compensate for our over-all numerical inferiority in divisions.

The Victory Program envisaged an expeditionary force of ap-

THE VICTORY PROGRAM / 67

proximately five million, and an over-all total of almost eight and a half million in uniform in ground, air, and service units. To maintain logistically five million men in the European theater of operations would require about seven million tons of shipping. This would mean a fleet of a thousand vessels. The Maritime Commission informed me that it would take two years to build such a fleet. However, we estimated that it would take at least two years to generate the combat and service forces for the Army and Army Air Force contemplated in the program. This meant that we would phase the mobilization, equipping, and training of military forces so that appropriate units would be ready for deployment overseas in combat areas as the necessary cargo and personnel shipping became available.

In retrospect, the broad scheme of maneuver envisaged and the estimates of forces, ground and air, required to implement it held up surprisingly well. I recall that when I first submitted a draft to G-3 (Operations and Training Division of the General Staff) concerning the number of men needed for the various units, the then Chief of that important division was startled. He predicted that we would never be able to mobilize such a force and that it would not receive approval. He was certain that we couldn't possibly get together the approximately eight and a half million soldiers and aviators, organize them into major combat units with supporting and service elements, equip and train them, and finally move them to and maintain them on battlefields in far-flung areas as scheduled in the program. The timing and the magnitude of the job were beyond his imagination or grasp.

G-4 (Supplies and Transportation Division) was also flabbergasted, but the Chief, Brigadier General Ray Moses, expressed his determination to make a good try. He questioned the ability of U.S. production facilities to provide the tremendous volume of equipment needed for such a large army and air force. In fact, all of the supply agencies, including the Office of Production Management and the Munitions Allocation Board, had serious misgivings. One officer, reported to the Army logistics expert, Brigadier General (later Lieut. General) Henry Aurand, that the material required for the Victory Program "could not be produced before the year 2050." Of course he was proved wrong and so were those who likewise expressed, not opposition, but their honest conviction that the munitions and shipping goals simply could not be met on schedule and in the quantities established in the program.

Meantime the heads of state were directing their attention to global strategy. In August, 1941, they held an historic meeting at sea, off Argentia, Newfoundland, known as the Atlantic Conference. Roosevelt and Churchill seemed to be in complete accord concerning the mutual steps that would be taken against the Nazis. The chiefs of state made secret war agreements and also issued the lofty-principled Atlantic Charter which was to be more honored in the breach than in the observance.

Although the civilian chiefs were basking in mutual admiration, military men of the two countries were far from agreement. Americans had serious differences with their British counterparts. The British had presented a series of memoranda, one of which, "General Strategy Review by British Chiefs of Staff," was submitted to several officers in the War Plans Division for comment. It seemed that we all opposed the British ideas of coalition warfare, though our reasons were varied. One basic idea, which the American planners emphasized, was that if and when the United States intervened in the war we must not only make certain of victory, but we must not delay in achieving that victory. It is important to recall that at this time (summer of 1941) the best available intelligence reports predicted that the Nazi hordes would quickly overrun Russia in the pattern of Poland, Norway, and France. Obviously we would have to strike hard and fast if we were to take advantage of the fact that the bulk of the Germans were deeply and irretrievably committed to the Eastern Front. The comments by the War Plans officers are of considerable interest.

One outstanding officer, Colonel (later Major General) Frank Kibler, said: "There is no cause for optimism as to a British victory." He criticized severely the British idea of assigning to the United States the protection of the British Empire. "We ought," he said, "to retain our freedom of action until we have forces to undertake worthwhile operations in the war."

Another War Plans officer, whose judgment and abilities were highly respected, then Colonel (later Major General) Leven C. Allen, pointed out that U.S. strength was not sufficiently developed to make an impression on military operations. He argued that Germany should be combatted with economic force and that "the position as a non-belligerent seems most suited to our existing situation."

I submitted the following comments to my immediate Chief, Colonel Bundy. Emphasizing the defeatist attitude of the British paper, I stated that more of the British Commonwealth's own resources should be employed. I suggested that we give assurance of American determination to assist in every possible way short of war, but that the British should recognize that "we must not become an active belligerent until we have created the means by which we can accomplish our national objectives." I recommended that our political leaders should also recognize this. The military historian, Mark Watson, in his book, *U. S. Army in World War II—The Chief of Staff Pre-War Plans and Preparations* (pages 406-7), comments on my statement as follows: "The realistic attitude of this officer with regard to the Army's potentialities was founded on intensive studies of previous weeks which led to the monumental Victory Plan of which he was the principal author."

One point which stood out in the British paper was adherence to the long-established policy of adroitly organizing other peoples to do the fighting necessary to sustain a mighty empire. I did not blame the British one iota, but as an American I felt then, and with even greater conviction feel now, that we could learn a good deal from their long history.

From the outset General Marshall and practically everyone on his staff realized that the Lend-Lease program, which had been placed by President Roosevelt outside the control of the military establishment, hampered, if it did not positively stymie, all U.S. military planning. Again and again, both before and after our involvement in the Second World War, General Marshall, his staff, and in particular those of us working in the War Plans Division, realized that American interests were being jeopardized by President Roosevelt's policy of extending all possible aid to any nation fighting "those foes which the United States also recognized as enemies." We military planners or strategists of victory had no political power. We could only make suggestions. President Roosevelt was the final arbiter and his coterie of advisers, in particular Harry Hopkins, had final authority concerning the allocation of war matériel as it flowed in ever increasing quantities from American factories. Congress had no power to control the mushrooming wartime agencies. Harry Hopkins, Judge Rosenman, Averell Harriman, and others through their friendship with the President made fateful decisions or exerted strong influence although they had no knowledge or experience in the field of strategy.

We in the War Plans Division similarly had no voice as compared with that of the representatives of foreign countries, in particular Britain and Russia, who were dealing direct with the "Palace Guard" in their demands for urgent deliveries of munitions and Lend-Lease aid. It soon became obvious that we must have some way of procuring armament and equipment for our own forces, then being mobilized, if U.S. production were not to be given away to all and sundry claimants on our bounty.

Early in 1941 Under Secretary of War Patterson had expressed his concern at the lack of a system of allocation of equipment to our own and foreign forces based on clearly stated national aims providing a basis for a global American strategy. So long as every claimant for Lend-Lease could swallow up American products, our own U.S. forces and any American-planned strategy for victory could never be implemented. Accordingly, Patterson sent a memorandum to the Secretary of War urgently requesting a clear-cut directive based on our accepted strategy and the American and Allied forces required to implement it.

Armed with this memorandum, Secretary of War Stimson was able to get prompt action at the White House. In all likelihood the Patterson memorandum gave rise to the President's directive in July, 1941, which resulted in the Victory Program.

Conferences continued to be held, some at the instigation of Under Secretary Patterson and some suggested by his able assistant, General Jimmy Burns. Also, within the War Plans Division there were continuous studies and discussions designed to accomplish effective co-ordination between producers and users—in other words, between industry and the military services. Colonel Bundy prepared a memorandum for the head of the War Plans Division (General Gerow), pointing out the great confusion that existed concerning the needs of our own armed forces, and also the requirements for the Allies, the British and the Russians, and for Lend-Lease recipients in general. This memorandum said: "The situation is extremely confused and confusion will reign until an agency for formulating a policy based on all strategic plans is designated."

Seeking joint action, General Gerow sent a copy of Colonel Bundy's memorandum to his opposite number in the Navy War Plans Division. When nothing came out of the Navy's examination of this memorandum, General Marshall was alerted. He decided to act, and act he did in publishing the following instructions to the War Plans Division of the Army:

> We are continually receiving suggestions as to increases and changes in armament, bombers, etc. along with suggestions of a more far-reaching nature. To provide a base of departure for meeting these proposals we should have a more clear-cut strategic estimate of our situation from a ground, air, and naval viewpoint. With such an estimate kept up to date, the various organizational, tactical and strategical questions which are constantly arising could be answered with more consistency than at present.
>
> Please contact other divisions of the War Department General Staff and take the necessary steps to have an estimate prepared to be submitted to me in the rough. It should be brief. Appendices can be added at a later date to support the various statements. The initial paper could be utilized as a basis for obtaining the views of other departments. Then we could revamp the estimates.
>
> G.C.M.

There were many discussions and conferences during the summer of 1941 concerning the co-ordination of our production, and despite Under Secretary of War Patterson's excellent memorandum prepared early in April, it was July 9 before the President's directive (see Appendix) was received. This precipitated action and the military services began their studies, formulating global strategic plans and the estimates of forces and equipment necessary to make the plans a reality. In other words, production requirements could now be estimated as to type, quantity, and priority *in consonance with agreed strategy*.

General Burns, Patterson's Chief of Staff, was a frequent visitor at the White House, and one might guess that he was highly instrumental in getting action because of his important role in Lend-Lease matters. He had had considerable experience as a professional ordnance officer with industry, and he knew that action had to be taken quickly. Harry Hopkins, as head supervisor for Lend-Lease, was closely associated with Burns, so one can easily surmise how the directive from the President to the Secretaries of War and Navy had its genesis. It was not until September 25, 1941, that the White House succeeded in obtaining a combined statement of our Army and Navy requirements, a statement which Mr. Knudsen and his industrialists had been begging for ever since the Office of Production Management (OPM) had been organized.

I had already done some work on bringing projected military operations into line with production requirements. General Gerow had assigned that type of work to me back in May, 1941. One of my initial requests was directed to G-2, the Intelligence Division of the General Staff, asking for a complete estimate of capabilities of each of the combatant nations. Then I directed a memorandum to G-4 for information about shipping and munitions. On June 3 a memorandum was circulated to all chiefs of Staff divisions and of the arms and services outlining the information that I would require in preparing a global strategic estimate. There were necessarily certain assumptions embodied in the memorandum that was sent around (see page 183, note 39, *U. S. Army in World War II: Strategic Planning for Coalition Warfare 1941–42*, by Matloff and Snell.) One assumption was that July 1, 1943, was the earliest date that the United States armed forces could be fully mobilized, trained, and equipped for extensive operations. A second assumption was that we would be participating in the war under the broad scheme of maneuver visualized in Rainbow Plan 5 for limited operations in Europe or the Far East. Also, the memorandum pointed out that the War Plans Division would integrate the information provided by the other General Staff divisions concerning the combatant nations' capabilities, intentions, and limitations. Such information could be combined with data about the basis for conscripting troops, about shipping, munitions requirements, and munitions production.

I was working along these lines when General Gerow examined the draft which was completed early in July. He felt that it needed further development, and he pointed out in a memorandum to General Marshall that:

> The estimate is based upon a more or less nebulous national policy, in that the extent to which our Government intends to commit itself with reference to the defeat of the Axis powers has not as yet been clearly defined. An effort

has been made to reconcile the spirit of the various official pronouncements and laws with their literal and legal interpretations.

The time element is vital in strategic planning. To insure timely and effective exploitation of our war potential a careful coordination is necessary to provide and maintain munitions for a rapidly expanding military force. The lag between plan and execution is considerable, and makes necessary a clearly defined national policy for guidance in future planning.

General Marshall referred the draft estimate to General Embick and to the Navy for comment. There is no record of General Embick's oral comment but I discussed the memorandum with him. He made many excellent criticisms, and I was in the process of embodying his ideas in a new draft when I was directed to prepare the Victory Program for the Army as required by the President's directive of July 9.

One of Secretary Stimson's assistants, Mr. McCloy, did not understand our method of calculation, which was to begin with men before going on to matériel. He objected that the President's instructions had been for the Army and Navy to provide information on the "over-all production requirements required to defeat our potential enemies."

In his memorandum McCloy remarked to General Gerow that he would be "very much interested in seeing how your method of 'first figuring the number of soldiers that it will require to defeat the Axis powers and from such figures determining the number of weapons that are necessary' jibes with the method outlined in the enclosed." General Gerow showed me McCloy's memorandum, and asked me to draft a reply because, as he expressed it, our civilian friends might think that the war could be won solely on the production line. I prepared a draft memorandum, which he changed slightly to read as follows:

> We must first evolve a strategic concept of how to defeat our potential enemies and then determine the major military units (Air, Navy, and Ground) required to carry out the strategic operations.
> It would be unwise to assume that we can defeat Germany by simply outproducing her. One hundred thousand airplanes

would be of little value to us if these airplanes could not be used because of lack of trained personnel, lack of operating airdromes in the theater, and lack of shipping to maintain the air squadrons in the theater. Wars are won on sound strategy implemented by well-trained forces which are adequately and effectively equipped.

Ours was in fact a task whose complexity and importance were not realized until the program was completed on September 25, 1941.

I visited a number of government departments and obtained available data concerning the nation's total able-bodied manpower. Then I was given estimates of the total number required by industry. These data were provided by departmental statisticians and by other agencies. I asked the Navy how many men would be required for naval forces personnel. The first estimate was 1,300,000, which proved far from the mark. Actually the Navy required almost twice that number before war's end.

In addition to my fact-finding forays in various government agencies, I studied the ratio between soldiers and civilians in various other countries. Experience tables showed that in wartime in most countries military personnel seldom exceeded 10 per cent of the population. In other words, if a country's male population was 50,000,000, the military forces under emergency conditions usually amounted to 5,000,000. The U.S. population in 1941 was around 135,000,000; so if the situation required a maximum military mobilization we could safely put approximately 13,500,000 in uniform if it were necessary. This would still leave enough able-bodied men and women to carry on the needed activities in the country, including those required for an expanded war economy. My figures were predicated, of course, upon using women and older men in many industries. General Burns has been quoted as saying that the mobilization potential was set at 8 per cent of the population (*U. S. Army in World War II: Global Logistics and Strategy*, page 131). Actually we set the potential at 10 per cent, on the basis of the studies made.

Knowing that the Navy estimated it would require 1,500,000 men, that would leave approximately 12,000,000 for the Army and the Air Force. Step-by-step computations resulted in a fairly accurate estimate for the Victory Program, which was finally approved and implemented. The total requirements in the program as prepared in 1941 were 8,795,658 men for the Army, including the Air Force. Wartime records show that the actual peak strength reached for air and ground forces amounted to 8,291,336 on May 31, 1945.

While having some success in estimating the manpower requirements, I made several serious mistakes in determining the composition of the wartime Army. For example, I estimated far too many motorized divisions. My original purpose was to have several armored corps consisting of two armored divisions and one motorized division each, so that in combat the two armored divisions could crush the resistance in leading the attack, cracking the nut as it were. Then the motorized division was supposed to follow through and hold the ground taken from the enemy. Actually we mobilized only one motorized division in 1944 instead of the fifty-one that I had recommended in the original Victory Program. It was soon realized that a large number of motor vehicles would stifle mobility on the battlefield and the real fighting elements of the division would be unable to function properly. Besides, motor vehicles would be vulnerable to hostile air attack while on the move. In lieu of a large number of motorized divisions it was decided to maintain motor pools consisting of standard truck companies. When it was desired to move troops and equipment, the required amount of motor transport would be made available, and after completion of the move the trucks would be returned promptly to a pool available for other movements.

I also had estimated too many divisions initially. As a matter of fact, I figured on approximately 200, predominantly with armor. We ended up with about 110 divisions. The influence of my training at the German War College was apparent in making the recommendations concerning the composition of the wartime Army, for I had recommended ten airborne and ten mountain divisions. The requirement in service forces which I estimated proved insufficient, due to my failure fully to understand the logistic problems imposed by long lines of communication.

The computations of requirements by the Air Force were undertaken in General Arnold's office under the direct supervision of a group of brilliant air officers, Colonel (later General) Larry Kuter, Colonel (later Lieutenant General) Hal George, Colonel Ken Walker (later killed in action, awarded Congressional Medal of Honor), and Major Hayward Hansel (later Major General). These men did an outstanding job, and their data were integrated with the ground forces requirements I had compiled.

There were many subsequent adjustments found necessary in the Victory Program. These were handled by Colonel Jay McKelvie (later Major General) of Army War Plans Division, who was placed in charge of the program when I was assigned to other duties. McKelvie displayed sound professional knowledge in making changes in consonance with operational requirements and production schedules.

Unfortunately we mobilized some technical personnel too quickly. For example, surgeons who were sorely needed in civilian communities were performing nonprofessional duties for interminable periods of time in the jungles of Louisiana. This was one of the many unintentional and unfortunate mix-ups experienced when one is striving to integrate and co-ordinate the activation of thousands of units involving millions of men. The intent, of course, was to minimize lost motion and the dissipation of specialists like doctors, engineers, scientists, etc. In this repect I failed in some glaring instances.

CHAPTER VI

GRAND STRATEGY

Planned strategy was not his strong card. He preferred to work by intuition and by impulse . . . He was never good at looking at all the implications of any course he favored. In fact he frequently refused to look at them.

This characterization of Winston Churchill as a war leader (by Field Marshal Alan Brooke, Britain's wartime Chief of Staff) could be applied equally to President Roosevelt. The Allies won the war; but since the Anglo-American leaders did not know and did not even try to determine what they were fighting for, the crushing military defeat of Germany and Japan raised up new and more dangerous enemies.

Stalin, on the contrary, had other objectives in addition to destroying Nazi Germany. He knew that vacuums would be created during the course of the titanic struggle with its widespread killing and destruction; and he was determined to be in a position at war's end to achieve definite political, economic, and psychological objectives. Because he was intent not simply on victory but on creating favorable conditions for the realization of Communist aims throughout the Balkans and Western Europe, he emerged as the only real victor of the war.

Our gravest weakness, and one which continues in our present cold war with Communist tyranny, was a lack of concrete, definite, and realizable aims of sound strategy.

77

In spite of the bitter lessons of our past failures to formulate aims worth fighting for, we still seem only to know what we are against, not what we are for. We Americans react to danger bravely enough, but without foresight. Instead of seizing and maintaining the initiative, which could be ours—assuming that we had both vision and understanding—we simply react blindly and emotionally to the stimuli of actual or imaginary dangers.

Three and a half centuries before Christ, the great Athenian orator Demosthenes chided the people of his city, soon to be conquered by Macedon, for following a day-to-day policy of expediency. His words are relevant to our own case:

> Shame on you Athenians for not wishing to understand that in war one must not allow oneself to be at the command of events. You Athenians are the strongest of all the Greeks in ships, cavalry, and revenue. But you don't make the best of them. You make war like a barbarian when he wrestles—if he suffers a blow, he immediately puts his hand to it. If he is struck again, he puts his hand there. But he has not the skill to evade his antagonist, nor does he think of parrying the blow. You likewise, if you hear that Philip has attacked the Chaeronea, you send help there. If he is at Thermopylae, you run there. If he turns aside, you follow him to right or left as if you were acting on his orders. Never a fixed plan, never any precautions. You wait for bad news before you act.

Like the Athenians in their decline following the Golden Age of Pericles—or Churchill while the sun began to set on the British Empire—we Americans failed, and are still failing, to examine all the implications of various courses of action. Grand strategy has not been our forte. Despite ample evidence that power gravitates with awesome inevitability toward those who use it readily and effectively, we seem to wait for bad news before we act.

Does anyone really know today what we are trying to do in the Far East, in Latin America, in the Middle East? Do we have any real strategy in our conflict with the Soviet Union or any aim beyond containment or sporadic resistance here and there to her direct or indirect aggression?

I do not pretend to any greater wisdom than my contemporaries in the Army or in civilian positions of responsibility. But since boyhood I had taken more than an ordinary interest in history, and I had also learned that valuable lessons concerning our successes or failures were to be found in many excellent books written by diplomats, scholars, and military leaders after World War I. I often discussed the Versailles Treaty and the League of Nations with my father-in-law, General Stanley D. Embick, who had been present at the 1918 Paris Peace Conference as Chief of Staff to Woodrow Wilson's scholarly assistant, General Tasker H. Bliss. Together we had analyzed the reasons why the Versailles Treaty—far from securing lasting peace—had instead prepared the way for the Second World War. My friend, the late George Creel, who had been a confidant of Woodrow Wilson, and his principal adviser during World War I on public information matters, contributed much to my knowledge concerning the intrigues, machinations, and shortsighted national aims that motivated the representatives of Britain, France, and Italy.

The greatest incentive, however, to my thinking about the elements of a viable strategy was, as I have already mentioned, my assignment to the German War College in Berlin. There I was not only given an opportunity to absorb the teachings of eminent instructors in military history, but was also taught to consider the influence on strategy of geography, psychology, demography, economics, and politics.

In Nazi Germany I also realized the tremendous power of propaganda, the conditioning of people's minds by way of pictures and radio along with the printed word. While science had been improving our means of killing human beings and destroying their works, it had also sharpened and diversified weapons for the distortion or murder of ideas in the battle for the mind. The Nazis and the Communists had recognized the ever-increasing importance of propaganda—the modern methods of influencing the thinking of people in accomplishing strategic aims both in peace and war.

Back at Fort Benning, while training and conducting tactical maneuvers, I continued to reflect on my War College instruction and the impressions that I had received in Germany. Later, when I was ordered to Washington and finally assigned to the General Staff in the war-planning agencies, my earlier embryonic concepts of Grand Strategy had begun to crystallize.

I often talked over my ideas of strategy with friends in the service, particularly with my associates in the War Plans Division, but also with a British officer, Brigadier Vivian Dykes, who represented the British Army planning agencies. He had been temporarily assigned living accommodations at Fort Myer, in Virginia, where I also had my quarters. I saw him frequently in the evenings when he would visit my quarters and have dinner informally with me and my family; and we soon became close friends. Dykes was a well-read and cultivated gentleman who had traveled widely and acquired a *savoir-faire* that was both disarming and attractive. As we became better acquainted, our exchange of views became more and more uninhibited, at times brutally frank. He epitomized British thinking concerning international events, and I hoped that I was expressing accurately America's real interests in the global war.

During the course of our long, friendly, and fruitful discussions, Dykes and I examined the various classical and dictionary or textbook definitions of strategy, which I criticized as far too narrow as well as outdated.

Clausewitz defined strategy as "The use of battles in furtherance of the war." The Merriam-Webster dictionary called it: "The science and art of employing the armed strength of a belligerent power to secure the object of war"; and the Oxford dictionary described it as: "The art of so moving or disposing troops or ships as to impose upon the enemy the place and time and conditions for fighting preferred by one's self."

Some years later the Harvard military historian, Samuel Eliot Morison, in an excellent little book called *Strategy and Compromise*, wrote that the word "aircraft" should now follow "ships" in the Oxford dictionary's definition, and himself described strategy as: "The art of defeating the enemy in the most economical and expeditious manner." To me, it seems that in our modern age a far wider and ampler reformulation is required.

Morison in this same book writes: "Tactics means the moving of military and air forces in actual contact with the enemy." Dykes and I agreed that the lay mind was constantly confusing tactics and strategy. I then asked him for his definition of strategy, and he made suggestions which closely resembled Clausewitz's famous dictum that war is the extension of politics by other means.

We consulted many texts and recognized authorities. A conventional distinction between strategy and tactics stated that "Strategy comprises all the operations embraced in the theater of war in general," while "Tactics are the maneuvers of an army on the day of battle —its combats, its concentration, and the diverse formations used to lead the troops to the attack." Von der Goltz * offered the following: "As a rule, *strategy* concerns itself with those large-scale measures which serve to bring the forces into play at the decisive point under the most favorable conditions possible," whereas "*Tactics* relates to what is done in the engagement itself. *Strategy* might be called the science of generalship while *tactics* is that of handling troops."

The elder (Count Helmut Karl Bernhardt) von Moltke, Chief of the Imperial German Staff and a disciple of Clausewitz, had written: "Tactics is a system of makeshifts. It is more than a science; it is the application of science to practical affairs. It is carrying through an originally conceived plan under a constantly shifting set of circumstances. Strategy furnishes tactics with the opportunity to strike and with the prospect of success through its conduct of the armies and of their concentration on the field of battle."

These definitions seemed to me all too limited. They took no account of the factors which are equally important in determining the outcome of wars and the fate of nations, seeking either to preserve their territorial integrity and economic stability, or to increase their living space, resources, and influence. In our complex modern world, in which the dividing line between military and economic, scientific, technological, political, and psychological factors has almost disappeared, I thought that a far broader concept of strategy was essential to survival. Just before leaving for the Casablanca Conference, I tried out on Brigadier Dykes a concept of strategy which, many years later, I was to present to a National War College audience. "Grand Strategy," I said, "is the art and science of employing all of a nation's resources to accomplish objectives defined by national policy."

Grand Strategy, as I then pointed out, is an art because it deals with many imponderables, intangibles, and human emotions; and it is a science because many factors in strategy demand a concern

---

* A field marshal and prominent German soldier who wrote two excellent books on military subjects, *On Military Leadership* and *The Conduct of War,* both widely read shortly before World War I.

with accuracy of measurements and computation which can be determined with scientific exactitude—for example, distances, space, speeds, etc.

In my definition I referred to resources. I had in mind all of the resources—human, material, and spiritual—available within a country. For convenience I would place them in four broad categories normally found in varying degrees in any modern nation, to wit: political, economic, psychological, and military resources. These four categories actually constitute the four principal weapons or tools of national policy. If the first three categories are used intelligently and in a timely manner—that is, if they are employed in consonance with a co-ordinated plan—it might make unnecessary the employment of military force, the fourth category, in the classical, naked manner. Political resources include treaties and pacts, with friendly nations; economic resources include reciprocal trade agreements and embargoes or blockades; psychological resources include overt and covert propaganda; military resources include the armed might of a nation.

So, as I argued with Brigadier Dykes and have continued to argue ever since, dictionary definitions of strategy are too restricted and have been increasingly outmoded. The term Grand Strategy should be introduced to convey the broader meaning. In fact, I doubt that old definitions of strategy were ever fully descriptive or explanatory. All the other definitions that I have been able to uncover invariably place undue emphasis on the military. Admiral Morison, for instance, bases his newest definition on the premise of fighting. We should have a term available that will not only conjure up in one's mind military resources and wars; it should with equal or even greater emphasis comprehend ideas about political resources, economic strength, and psychological advantages, and the continuous world-wide struggle involving their employment.

History records a continuing struggle between individuals, armed hordes, kingdoms, nations, empires, and federations for political, economic, or psychological advantage. In the earliest medieval period the aims or objectives of people were simple, generally limited to food, land, booty, and shelter. Later, when knighthood came into flower with colorful tournaments, battles and even extensive crusades were fought, partly for glory and ideals. During these eras emphasis was placed on the use of force, physical strength, courage, and agility. But increasingly, as wily rulers, unscrupulous tyrants, and even respected leaders, discovered the effectiveness of economic force (such as denying an opponent food or essential supplies) or psychological force (such as the use of propaganda to condition people's minds through the use of truth, deception, or subversion), we find military force used less frequently, or only when the other means had failed to accomplish the desired purpose.

Inasmuch as modern objectives of nations in the international arena have been essentially aimed at gaining territorial advantage—including sources of important raw materials and markets, and concomitantly the acquisition of power—the grand strategy of nations has been marked by the widespread use of political, economic, and psychological weapons.

As Sir John Dill told me later, Dykes regarded me as a most "unorthodox" and "unusual" military man because of my concern over such things as economics and propaganda. (On our trip together to the Far East immediately after Casablanca, Sir John evinced great interest in my views on strategy. In the evenings we often discussed the importance of agreed Allied objectives as well as the co-ordinated use of all our resources in support of the military operations in order to accomplish our aims.) Neither Dill nor Dykes ever insulted my intelligence by calling me anti-British; they both had the good grace to realize that just as they were pro-British, so was I pro-American. In our discussions I often praised the younger William Pitt, England's Prime Minister in the Napoleonic period, as my ideal of a national leader. Pitt nursed the British through the years of the Napoleonic struggle with a minimum wastage of British blood and treasure. Cleverly, he had let other people bleed Napoleon. When the British put money or men into the struggle, it was always at a decisive point and the objects of intervention were always precisely laid down. I told Dykes that I wished the U.S. had acted in World War I as Pitt's England had acted in the 1800–1815 period. I did not blame the British in the least for trying to get the U.S. to carry the ball for them in 1914–18, and now again in 1941. The only time I bridled was when Britishers acted as if no other nation had the right to take a leaf from the book of William Pitt the Younger.

When Dykes mentioned that the British Navy was the principal barrier in keeping the Nazis from America's doorstep, I begged leave to differ. In the first place, the United States had its own Navy, qualitatively and quantitatively stronger than the Royal Navy; in the second, the Nazis could hardly vault the oceans without first building terrific aircraft carrier power of their own. In reviving memories of Jefferson's remark that the U.S. might under certain circumstances have to "marry" itself to the British fleet, Dykes was leaning toward propagandistic oversimplification. In Jefferson's and Madison's day, the U.S. had the merest beginnings of a Navy—not enough, in fact, to keep the British from landing and burning our capital, Washington. But that was more than a hundred years ago, in an era when sailing vessels, which were not tied to fuel bases, could go anywhere without worrying about the logistics of coal or oil.

The loss of the British Fleet in the event of Nazi victory, which Dykes casually (but not seriously) introduced into our discussions, was a popular subject for the journalistic pundits of the moment. But there was little likelihood that the British Navy would surrender even if the Nazis were to invade the British Isles successfully. Some ships would assuredly go down fighting, in the finest British tradition. The remainder would, of honor-based necessity, escape to the West, to Australia and Canada.

I admitted to Dykes that, since public opinion and views were by and large an outgrowth of common experience and similar environment of people, the Anglo-Saxon nations would tend to stand together in any deep crisis. But this did not give Britain the right to demand blank checks from Washington.

As science has increased the efficiency of the means of killing and destroying, another dangerous weapon has kept pace with changes in technology. At first this second development seemed innocuous, like the income tax when it was legislated in 1913. No one then dreamed that the income tax would end in the near-confiscation of property and personal wealth of individuals in this country. Likewise, when radio, television, and motion pictures came into being, dramatically conveying images and ideas all over the world, it did not immediately occur to people that they might have to learn to resist the propaganda of friend as well as foe, and to spread their own. Verbal and imagistic stimuli are today so pervasive and violent that the public opinion of the vast majority of people—not only in our own country but in all others—is conditioned or determined by propaganda. We live in an age of propaganda.

George Creel, the dynamic Director of the Committee on Public Information in World War I, often said to me: "Bayonets and bullets will not kill convictions, but a good idea expressed in an apt and timely manner may silence the guns." Creel explained at considerable length that the purpose of propaganda is to reach and influence the minds of the masses of people with a simply stated message, a message which would justify your actions, sell your product, and win fanatic support for your ideas. He maintained that the British author Sir Gilbert Parker was the most skillful propagandist of World War I. Sir Gilbert had been placed in charge of all English propaganda as it related to the United States. He had a splendid organization and used all the finesse which his British schooling and cultural background could provide. He had representatives throughout the United States with instructions to test public opinion in order to determine where pro-British sentiment was strong and where anti-war sentiment was organized and vociferous. He carefully avoided using Britishers to make direct representation. His method was to put words into the mouths of pro-British Americans on Park Avenue, on Wall Street, in the labor unions, in the schools, in government bureaus, in the banking industry, in the shipping industry, and among sports celebrities. Sir Gilbert flooded the United States with clever propaganda, which unquestionably was a strong influence for public acceptance of our ultimate entrance into the war on the side of the Allies.

One can appreciate immediately the importance of propaganda as a tool of Grand Strategy. If propaganda is used in conjunction with the political and economic tools mentioned previously, in an intelligent and co-ordinated manner, it may be possible to accomplish national aims without resorting to the fourth tool, the military. Thus international problems could be solved by *constructive*, peaceful negotiations and agreements in lieu of *destructive* wars. Certainly this is the goal of all civilized peoples.

CHAPTER VII

PROPAGANDA AND WAR AIMS

IN THE PRECEDING CHAPTER I have considered the four tools which must be used for the accomplishment of our national goals. In some areas of the world and under some circumstances, greater emphasis should be placed on political means; in others, on the economic; in others, on the psychological or the propaganda weapon; and as a last resort, the military. Neglect, misuse, or abuse of any one of them can be disastrous, will certainly delay victory, and may render it worthless. The four should always be continually used in peace and war.

Of these four weapons available for the attainment of national aims, propaganda is perhaps the most dangerous to handle because it is a double-edged sword. Or to use another metaphor, propaganda or psychological warfare based on lies and designed to arouse man's worst passions can be like poison gas which endangers whoever employs it against an enemy.

When the Second World War began, the use of propaganda was frowned upon by many of our leaders, both civilian and military. They did not recognize that propaganda is not always malicious lies, nor is it necessarily used for improper or destructive purposes. In other words, one shouldn't put all propaganda in the same category. The suspicion and general aversion which the word aroused was no doubt due to the experience of the American people during the days leading up to World War I, when stories of terrible German atrocities were made up out of whole cloth.

Propaganda is nothing more than salesmanship, at which Americans are supposed to be very good. Why, then, shouldn't Americans sell American ideas and ideals, using the same ingenuity and accepted skills which Madison Avenue has developed in selling a thousand products?

There has of course always been competition of ideas and ideals. Though electronics has given a new dimension to propaganda, even in Christ's time there were rival or competing propagandists. It was difficult for people then, as now, to distinguish and choose between true and false propaganda. Much depends on whether or not acceptance of an emotionally colored plea is in consonance with one's own objectives or aims in life.

The question of freedom of the press, freedom of expression, is often discussed in our country, and we like to feel that there are no restrictions whatsoever on those freedoms. So long as the average citizen knows that he is getting information which is not censored, and so long as we know that the propagandist is not resorting to unethical methods to win converts, I think we are on very safe ground and that a free society will be preserved.

However, we must learn to demand a high standard of performance from the press; and our public officials must not be stampeded when small, purposeful groups succeed in capturing key positions in journalism. At one time in World War II, the Communists, using fellow-traveler "transmission belts" with superior skill, had the initiative—in fact, the almost undisputed control of information media. For example, some correspondents in China, duped by a singular view that Mao Tse-tung was closer to Thomas Jefferson than to Lenin or Stalin, systematically passed along a most superficial and indefensible view of China's troubles. They could see that the Kuomintang was often corrupt, but they missed the bigger point that Mao Tse-tung was ideologically committed to the practice of mass murder. Publishers in America may have known better than their correspondents, but in some instances it was more than a publisher's life was worth to fire a reporter who accepted the prevailing line about China.

Similarly, during the war it was regarded as positively unpatriotic, or at least in very bad taste, to voice dislike and distrust of our

"gallant ally," the Union of Soviet Socialist Republics, or to denounce the tyranny of "good old Uncle Joe" Stalin. Naturally, the
press affected Washington's political judgments as well as the views
of most of the American people, and so tended to color official policies that were based on those judgments.

It was by false propaganda that a strongly emotional warlike attitude was gradually engendered in this nation prior to World War I
and World War II. The vast majority of Americans, however, did
not really know in 1917 why they were called upon to fight. They
were told we were fighting to make the world safe for democracy.
Later, in World War II, they were told of the Four Freedoms. Not
one of those high-sounding objectives was attained. We followed an
inane cycle of killing and destroying; then of wooing our enemies
and rehabilitating the areas devastated by war; then paradoxically
preparing with former enemies as staunch allies to oppose former
friends as hated enemies.

In 1941 American military men knew that while a Nazi victory
in Europe might entail large-scale increases in our military and
naval outlay, nevertheless the danger of an invasion by Nazi military forces was very remote. So the British propagandists took
another tack. They understood American susceptibility to moral
issues, how easily we could be aroused emotionally concerning any
"do good" campaign. Hence a new specter was conjured up, that if
the Nazis won in Europe, the philosophy of Hitler and his unscrupulous henchmen would infiltrate throughout America. I cannot
think so badly of my countrymen as to believe this could ever have
happened.

About two weeks after the attack on Pearl Harbor, Prime Minister
Churchill arrived in Washington with a large staff. He had previously dispatched his Foreign Secretary, Mr. Anthony Eden, to Russia. Stalin, who had has own blueprint for Europe (as a matter of
fact, the Communist blueprint took in the whole world), knew exactly what he was fighting for. Even at that time the Soviet dictator
had in mind the division of Germany into small states. He planned
to annex the Baltic States and Bessarabia, and to force Finland to
work for Soviet Russia. He insisted that the so-called Curzon Line
should be the future Soviet-Polish frontier, and he pressed for its
recognition by the British as early as 1941. These were some of the

indications of the practical strategic sense of the Russian Generalissimo Stalin.

One looks in vain for any comparable projected thinking or preparing for war's end on the part of Churchill or Roosevelt. At the conference held in Washington between the American and British representatives, a new organization was adopted to facilitate co-operation and co-ordination by the respective staffs. This was known as the Combined Chiefs of Staff—a committee which included senior representatives of the three services, Army, Navy, and Air Force, of each government. The Russians never had representation on the Combined Chiefs of Staff, and I doubt seriously that they had any interest in it, except as a vehicle to obtain ever-increasing quantities of military supplies and equipment.

The Combined Chiefs of Staff worked within the limitations of the Oxford Dictionary definition of strategy. But sound and victorious strategy can never be devised unless a clearly defined aim or objective is laid down to provide purpose and direction. One can destroy an enemy or break his will to resist by military victories. But in Grand Strategy one must look beyond the military victory. Churchill was a defective strategist when, in answer to the question, "What is our aim?" he told the House of Commons on May 13, 1940: "I can answer in one word: Victory—victory at all costs."

In pursuing victory at all costs, Churchill would not allow anyone else to question his confusion of means and aims. In the formulation of policies and plans for coalition war, France and the members of the British Commonwealth outside of England were not permitted to participate actively. This was a source of resentment, particularly in Canada and Australia and, to an even greater extent, among some of the French leaders, notably General Charles de Gaulle. Both France and the Dominions felt entitled to full representation in Allied councils. But Winston Churchill was determined to be the supreme architect of Allied strategy. He maintained that it was sufficient merely to keep the other members of the Commonwealth and other Allies informed. There wasn't much the Canadians and Australians could do about this. In contacts with Americans they surreptitiously expressed their dissatisfaction; but no one among us, even though sympathetic, could tactfully support their claim to sit in on the conferences.

Americans regarded war as a game which one simply strives with all one's might to win. Churchill's forensic utterances were useful in nerving up his followers, but his lack of any clearly defined aims beyond "killing Germans" and "total victory at all costs" was incredibly superficial, indeed tragic. War is a grim and earnest business and is judged by its results. One cannot achieve any purpose worth the terrible sacrifice of blood and treasure, as well as the demoralization experienced by victors and vanquished alike, if war is engaged in either as a game or a crusade against a mythical "power of darkness" symbolized by the person of the enemy. War can only be justified as a last resort to attain concrete, clearly envisaged, legitimate or vital national aims which have been proved unrealizable by any other means. As the Romans said, war is the final argument of states, *ultima ratio regum*. Long before Clausewitz pronounced his famous dictum that "War is the extension of political processes by the employment of military force," the Chinese philosopher, Sun Tzu—who lived about 500 B.C.—wrote: "To fight and conquer in all your battles is not supreme excellence. Supreme excellence consists in breaking the enemy's resistance without fighting."

Some truths are indeed so self-evident that in the course of human experience they have been perceived by wise men in all ages. Today these truths should be more apparent than in past generations, thanks to the lessons taught us in our lifetime by two world wars in which the Americans made supreme sacrifices in blood and treasure, not in order to implement a policy but as a result of the lack of one.

War is, or should be, the last means resorted to for the accomplishment of an aim. It cannot be a substitute for a policy, yet Roosevelt and Churchill—as well as the other Western "architects of victory"—seem to have regarded it as such. They confused means with ends, substituting total victory for a policy. They demanded the unconditional surrender of our enemies instead of defining civilized war aims and seeking to attain them at the least possible cost and with due regard to our future security vis-à-vis our temporary and reluctant ally, the Soviet Union.

Without a clearly defined political objective, war is but aimless or senseless slaughter. This fact is understood by every military man with any pretensions to professional knowledge. Winston Churchill, correctly described by his own Chief of Staff as no strategist, but as acting on intuition and impulse without regard for the implications or consequences of the courses he favored, waged war more like an Indian chieftain from the Arizona Territory intent upon obtaining the largest possible number of enemy scalps.

To Americans who have been taught to believe that Churchill was a great statesman, this last judgment may seem exaggerated or totally unwarranted. But Winston Churchill's own pronouncements and those of his closest friends and military advisers are witness to its accuracy. As one example among many of what can justly be described as the British Prime Minister's lust for blood, I cite here the evidence presented by Brigadier Fitzroy MacLean, who was sent on a mission to Marshal Tito during the war. In his book, *Eastern Approaches,* Brigadier MacLean recalls that the years he had spent in the Soviet Union had made him wary of the Communist menace. Realizing that Tito and his followers aimed at the establishment of a Communist regime closely linked to Moscow, MacLean told Churchill he was concerned that British policy in Yugoslavia would lead to this outcome. Churchill replied that no consideration of "long-term policy" should divert MacLean from his task of "simply finding out who was killing the most Germans and suggesting means by which we could help them to kill more."

In order to kill a maximum number of Germans, Winston Churchill dismissed politics or policy as a "secondary consideration," and on this and many other occasions said that there were "no lengths of violence to which we would not go" in order to achieve his objective. How much wiser as well as civilized was the ancient Chinese strategist Sun Tzu when he said, "In the practical art of war, the best thing of all is to take the enemy's country whole. To shatter and destroy it is not so profitable. So too it is better to capture a regiment, a detachment or a company entire than to annihilate them."

Our own leaders were just as vehement as our British cousins in proclaiming that slaughter of the enemy was a primary aim of the war. And it was Roosevelt, not Churchill, who formulated the demand for unconditional surrender.

To will or decide upon death and suffering for millions of human beings for the sole purpose of annihilating an enemy is immoral and uncivilized, and can only result in evil consequences. Conducting war in such a manner can only lead us back to barbarism. It can be even more injurious to those who win the military victory than to the vanquished. Because we had no definite aim beyond the destruction of Germany and the defeat of Japan, we were prepared "to take the aid of the Devil himself," as Churchill said when he consummated an Anglo-Russian alliance in 1941. Because we fought to win a military victory regardless of the consequences, we failed to bring about the better conditions which might have justified our resort to war.

After slaying one dragon, we found ourselves confronted in 1945 with a bigger and a more dangerous one. Having wanted to win at any cost, we insured the emergence of a more hostile, menacing, predatory power than Nazi Germany, one which has enslaved more people than we "liberated." This fact became obvious when, only three years after her defeat, we started to resurrect the Germany we had sworn to destroy. We needed this Germany as our partner in the defense of Europe against our former ally, the Soviet Union.

The huge and menacing power of the Communists, from the Elbe to the Yalu, now confronts the United States with a much greater and more present danger than any other we have experienced since the birth of our republic. The irony of it all is that the Soviet empire is largely one of our own creation. We first gave impetus to the growth of this outlaw power by recognizing and granting diplomatic status to the Soviet Union in 1933. None of the Soviet promises, gentlemen's agreements, or diplomatic overtures have been honored; since 1933 there has been a continuous repudiation of promises and treaties. The most flagrant violation, as reported by J. Edgar Hoover in his book, *Masters of Deceit* (1958), includes the penetration of our more sensitive government activities, labor unions, and educational fields with subversive propaganda countering every idea and ideal our founding fathers admonished us to protect. Second, had it not been for President Roosevelt's insistence on the unconditional surrender of our enemies as the chief war aim, we need not have given unconditional aid to Communist Russia. We were fearful during the war that Stalin might make a separate peace with Germany. Actually we know now—and should have known then —that Stalin could never have induced Hitler to make a separate peace with Russia. He was simply holding the idea over our heads and blackmailing us to give him more aid.

Twice in our generation America has intervened with her incomparable might to insure victory for the friendly nations in Europe. On both occasions we helped win the war only to find that our victory was barren or had generated worse evils than those we sought to destroy. These tragic results were due to the lack of reliable, realistic war aims. We had no Grand Strategy designed either to insure our own security by removing or diminishing the causes of war or to advance the cause of freedom with which we are identified. Instead, we permitted the perversion of our basic ideals by an unscrupulous ally, the Soviet Union. We lost compassion and objectivity in analyzing the situation, owing in large part to the pressures engendered by people whose hearts were controlling their minds, whose passions and emotions were understandably stirred to a high pitch by the experiences of their loved ones and friends at the hands of ruthless, cruel dictators. And also because we poisoned ourselves with our own propaganda and let the Communist serpent we took to our bosom envenom our minds and distort our ideals.

President Wilson can at least be credited with having endeavored to insure a just and lasting peace by his proclamation of the Fourteen Points toward the close of World War I. But he was not strong enough politically at home and diplomatically abroad to prevent Britain's Lloyd George, Italy's Orlando, and France's Clemenceau from dictating a punitive peace settlement which only served to aggravate the frictions, inequities, and rivalries which had led to war in the past. President Roosevelt, insofar as he had any plans, wanted a punitive peace to be enforced by the Big Three. By insisting upon unconditional surrender in lieu of realistic and humane peace terms, we ourselves enhanced the power of Stalin in Europe and Asia.

Reviewing history over the past half century, it would seem that policywise, whether in peace or war, we have floundered in unknown seas or muddled through with no clear idea of the direction in which we wished to steer the American ship of state. Instead of charting a clear course toward a secure haven, we let the sails jibe as the winds blew. We had no compass and ran the risk of foundering on the rocks of deceit, of greed, or aggression, while hoping to steer a course by the stars to the land of El Dorado.

Illusory visions of a perfect world to be won by a crusade have served only to prevent America from utilizing her vast material resources, and the energy and dedication of her people to liberty, for the attainment of a realizable objective consonant with our national interest and the ideals we cherish. By pursuing the will-o'-the-wisp of an entire world free from the curse of Adam, we forego our opportunity of making parts of it a little more like the Garden of Eden.

As I view the situation today, and as I also saw it very clearly in 1941 when, as a member of the first U.S. strategic planning group, I was involved in military plans for the defeat of Germany and Japan, we should have decided what we hoped to accomplish by war before becoming involved. We ought to have defined our war aims clearly and obtained a firm agreement with our Allies concerning the conditions which we wished to establish by crushing Nazi Germany, Fascist Italy, and the war lords in Japan.

With vivid memories of 1919 and 1945 etched deeply in heart and mind, if we are again involved in concerted action with other nations I would insist that we refuse henceforward to join with allies unless we can reach firm agreement as to the conditions of the joining. Our aims in World War I and World War II should have been consonant with our national interest, traditions, and principles. Instead, we were completely unaware of what we might or should accomplish by the mobilization of our tremendous economic capacity, our armed strength, and our spiritual forces beyond insuring Anglo-Russian victories.

"Make the world safe for democracy," "Revenge Pearl Harbor," "The Four Freedoms," and other slogans used during the First and Second World Wars were high-sounding phrases calculated to arouse patriotic fervor. They did not in themselves constitute tangible strategic objectives. Nor could they serve as guideposts to an equitable peace settlement. No plans, no preparations, were made for the vital role we were assuming in the international arena—the role of world leadership. Thus, although we emerged from the Second World War with the most powerful fighting machine the world has ever known, we lost the peace.

We had no American conditions of peace. Instead of carrying out a policy by military means, we had used the means as ends in themselves. We failed to realize that unconditional surrender and the annihilation of German power would result in a tremendous vacuum in Central Europe into which the Communist power and ideas would flow unless firmly checked by American concepts of equity and democracy. These, in turn, needed to be supported by our great military and spiritual forces.

Stalin, the wily, was prepared long before the war's end to move into the vacuum. He quickly took advantage of his unchallenged military power to extend the frontiers and to spread the influence of the Soviet world Communist conspiracy throughout both war-weary Eastern Europe and China. This never should have happened. It would not have happened if we had not given Soviet Russia billions of dollars of military and economic aid without firm and concrete agreement concerning war aims and postwar objectives. It would not have happened if we had not refrained in the closing stages of the war from utilizing our paramount military power to fulfill Western promises to the liberated peoples. Instead, even after Stalin started breaking the agreements he had been making, we held our armies back from Berlin, Prague, and Vienna in order to let the Red Army take over with its political commissars and establish a reign of terror.

To sum up, it is only too obvious today that our strategic planning should have been oriented toward denying to the Soviet Union the opportunities which she used so promptly and effectively to extend her frontiers and her power.

Our failure to use political, economic, and psychological means in co-ordination with military operations during the war also prolonged its duration and caused the loss of many more American lives than need have been sacrificed. Our failure so strengthened Stalin's hand that he alone gained from the war and took every trick at the peace table. Our demand for unconditional surrender naturally increased the enemy's will to resist and forced even Hitler's worst enemies to continue fighting to save their country. The courage of despair imbued the German armed forces with a heroic spirit until the very end. As wise old Sun Tzu declared, "Soldiers when in desperate straits lose the sense of fear. If there is no place of refuge, they will stand firm. If they are in the heart of a hostile country, they will show a stubborn front. If there is no help for it, they will fight hard." This Chinese sage also wrote, "Do not press a desperate foe too hard."

The Western Allies, by refusing to use the political and psychological instruments of strategy, and by committing themselves to defeat Germany solely by military means, gave Soviet Russia the initiative which should all along have been ours. This happened despite the fact that Chamberlain at the outset had proclaimed Britain was "not fighting against you, the German people, but against a tyrannous and forsworn regime." No attempt was made by the Western Allies to divide the Germans by offering Hitler's enemies decent terms of peace—this in spite of the fact that British and American intelligence agents were aware that Hitler was faced with the opposition of men holding some of the highest appointments in the Army, Navy, and Civil Service. Instead of encouraging the anti-Hitler Germans, we forced all Germans to fight to the last under a regime most of them hated. They had no alternative.

The British military writer, Major General J. F. C. Fuller, agrees that the proclamation of unconditional surrender "by its emphasis on a war of annihilation bereft the Western Allies' cause of a sane war aim." We tied our hands and gave Stalin the political initiative. At the same time we strengthened Hitler's hold over Europe as well as over his own people, who had no choice but to fight to the last. All the Continental nations desperately feared Communist Russia. By proclaiming the defense of Fortress Europe against the Communist hordes to the east, the Nazis won renewed strength through support among many of the peoples they had subjected. In January, 1943, at the very moment when Western strategic prospects were brightest, thanks to our hard-won supremacy in the air, the triumph over the submarine menace, and the Russian resurgence at Stalingrad, we annulled the prospect of winning a real victory by the Casablanca call for unconditional surrender.

It was only at the eleventh hour that Winston Churchill began to take cognizance of the postwar balance of power. In the last stage of the war he began to stress the political desirability of reaching Berlin with our own armies before the Russians could get there. By this time, however, the American Chiefs of Staff were running the show. Their leaders, Roosevelt and Truman, had ordered them to smash Germany's armed forces and to adhere to the agreements made with Stalin despite the fact that he had already broken them in Poland. The hour had come and gone. It was already too late.

CHAPTER VIII

TO LONDON WITH HOPKINS
AND MARSHALL

On April Fool's Day, 1942, I was informed that I would accompany the Chief of Staff, General Marshall, on a highly secret mission and would be absent from Washington for approximately two weeks. I was then the junior Army member of the Joint Staff Planners, whose principal duty was to prepare strategic plans for consideration by the Joint Chiefs of Staff. I assumed that the mission was related to the two plans for European operations, BOLERO and ROUNDUP, which had been presented by the Joint Staff Planners to the JCS, approved by them and finally also by the President.

The BOLERO plan envisaged the concentration in the British Isles of more than a million men. Air and naval operations against the enemy were to be intensified in order to neutralize or destroy his defense forces and installations. It was estimated that this preparatory phase (BOLERO) could be completed by midsummer, 1943, when the plan to invade the continent of Europe (code name ROUNDUP, later changed to OVERLORD) would be put into operation.

My assumptions were confirmed when General Marshall informed me that I was to be his aide-de-camp and that my principal task would be to assist him in the presentation of U.S. plans for the cross-Channel operation, and to provide supporting data based on the studies and analyses made within the planning agencies in Washington during the previous few months. Marshall and I were to leave for England on April 4. He instructed me not to reveal my destination or purpose, but simply to tell my family and friends that I would be absent on a routine mission.

Marshall's efficient and likable personal aide, Major (later Brigadier General) Frank McCarthy, provided more details and the Adjutant General issued appropriate secret orders. All references to the mission—telephone calls, radios, cablegrams, correspondence, and documents—would be identified by the word MODICUM. Inasmuch as secrecy was essential, fictitious names were assigned to the members of the party as follows:

Mr. Harry Hopkins to be known as Mr. A. H. Hones.
General George C. Marshall to be known as Mr. C. G. Mell.
Commander James R. Fulton to be known as Mr. A. L. Foss.
Colonel H. A. Craig to be known as J. H. Case.
Lt. Colonel A. C. Wedemeyer to be known as J. E. White.

Colonel Craig (later Lieutenant General), an Army Air Force officer of exceptional ability, was assigned responsibility for all flight arrangements to and from England. We were all admonished to wear civilian clothes in order to maintain secrecy concerning the flight.

On the night of April 3, Colonel Craig and I motored to Baltimore, where we were met by a Pan American Airlines representative, who informed us concerning arrangements for the trip and the location of the Boeing B-14 type flying boat in which our mission was to cross the Atlantic. After a few hours' sleep in a hotel we hurried down to the pier where the Clipper was moored. There we met Captain Gray, the Pan American pilot in charge of the flight, and the other members of an eleven-man crew. It was now 6:15 A.M. An official car drove up with General Marshall, Harry Hopkins, and Commander Fulton.

Luggage was soon put aboard the luxurious flying boat, which provided ample accommodations for the five of us. I did not understand why we required such a large crew. Also, I was surprised to see General Marshall in uniform. After we boarded the plane, I mentioned that McCarthy (his aide) had cautioned me to wear civilian clothes. Marshall was amused and remarked that possibly McCarthy had so instructed him but he had forgotten.

Marshall then told me that Harry Hopkins had been in poor health and that President Roosevelt hoped all of us would protect him as much as possible—not only against arduous experiences incident to the trip but against his own nature, for he had a penchant for driving himself too hard. Commander Fulton, an outstanding doctor and Hopkins' personal physician, was lent by the Navy and turned out to be a delightful traveling companion.

The giant flying boat taxied out into the middle of Chesapeake Bay for take-off. The propellers whirred and we skimmed rapidly along, before soaring into the air like a huge albatross. Soon we were flying over the Atlantic, winging our way to Bermuda, 750 miles away. About halfway along the route, the Number 2 engine dropped out. However, we continued with three motors functioning perfectly and arrived over Bermuda at 12:30 P.M.

While circling to land, I noted the gorgeous azure-blue waters washing the irregular and rocky shoreline of the group of tiny islands below. Many sailboats and launches were visible as well as beautiful homes and an inviting golf course.

We were met at the pier on Darrell Island by Admiral James of the U.S. Navy and by the aide of the British Governor General of Bermuda. After being transported to the Belmont Manor Hotel, where the accommodations were excellent, Craig and I took the two pouches in which I was carrying secret documents to the office of the American Consulate at Bermuda for safekeeping during our stopover. In the evening the entire MODICUM party went to the Governor General's palace for dinner.

The Governor General, Lord Knollys (pronounced Noles) was a dignified and experienced Foreign Office representative. He and Lady Knollys were most gracious and had won many friends in his important diplomatic post. During the conversation at dinner, which was mainly concerned with sporting and social events, jokes were made about the secrecy of our mission. Apparently everyone on the island knew exactly who we all were, and precisely why we were going to England.

Some concern was expressed concerning the danger we had incurred when our second motor went dead. Colonel Craig explained to our British hosts that our Clipper was designed to fly on only two motors, so that there had been no real danger when it dropped only one of its four engines. Nonetheless, no chances were being taken. The captain of our luxurious Clipper had radioed Pan American headquarters in New York for delivery of another motor, and for a reserve plane to enable the American VIPs to resume their flight to London on schedule.

The original flight plan had called for early departure on Easter Sunday, provided that weather reports were favorable. But to allow time for the installation of the replacement motor on our plane, our departure was postponed to Monday.

When he discovered that the MODICUM party would be in Bermuda for another twenty-four hours at least, the Governor General invited General Marshall to read the Second Lesson at the Easter services in the local English church. It is a tradition in the territories of the British Empire and the Commonwealth to ask the senior civil official to read the First Lesson and the senior military personage present to read the Second Lesson at the Easter Sunday service.

I was delighted that my chief was so honored and decided to find out what chapter and verses in the Bible he would be required to read. Lieutenant Giles, the Governor General's aide, phoned early on Easter Sunday to tell me that General Marshall would be expected to read Chapter 1, Verses 1-8, in the Book of Revelation. Hastily I thumbed these pages and saw that there were no difficult Biblical terms to pronounce.

Harry Hopkins, still in a dressing gown, dropped in and suggested that we all assemble in Marshall's sitting room for breakfast. While we were lingering over a final cup of coffee, I announced that I had learned through the kindness of the Governor General's aide the passages in the Bible which General Marshall would be expected to read at the Easter service.

I produced the Bible. The General was most appreciative. He commented, "I will read the Second Lesson and all of you be prepared to criticize." After hearing him we were all satisfied that he would give a good account of himself in the church a few hours later.

Unfortunately, I had misunderstood the information given by Lord Knollys' aide. Instead of Verses 1-8, the General was expected to read Verses 1-18. By the time I discovered this, we were all seated in pews well up in the front of the church. My chief was too far away for me to warn him that there were some tongue-twisting geographical terms in those additional ten verses. I suffered through the rest of the service on tenterhooks, but Marshall made a gallant attempt to run the verbal blockade and managed to get through the eighteen verses with undulating effect. One word apparently struck a responsive chord, and he almost shouted "Philadelphia."

As we were filing out of church after the services, an elderly lady rushed up and embraced General Marshall, exclaiming how proud she was to be an American on this occasion. Ecstatically she emphasized that she too was from Philadelphia.

General and Mrs. Strong had invited the MODICUM party to luncheon. Excusing myself, I proceeded instead to the Consul General's office, where I studied the material relating to war plans. Mr. Beck, the Consul General, dropped by and extended an invitation to cocktails at his home later that day.

I had lunch alone at a small restaurant near the Consulate before returning to work. Shortly before 5:00 P.M. I took a launch and went down to see our Clipper. Captain Gray was aboard and told me that the engine had been changed and that everything was set for our take-off to London. I returned to the hotel, where I received a telephone message from Colonel Craig announcing that our departure had been postponed another twenty-four hours by authorities in the U.K. No reason was given. Craig conjectured that it might be weather. Harry Hopkins thought the delay was due to security reasons.

At the party at the American Consul General's home that evening practically all officialdom and socialdom on the island were present. Our mission had certainly been rightly named MODICUM in view of the minimum of secrecy concerning it evidenced in Bermuda.

Next day, while General Marshall and Harry Hopkins went fishing, I also relaxed and accompanied Colonel Craig and Dr. Fulton on a shopping expedition and tour in Hamilton. Afterward General Strong explained the projected defense plans of Bermuda and described the purpose of the new installations under construction. These included a modern airfield with appropriate operational and maintenance buildings. The construction of this important air installation was under the direction of Colonel White, U.S. Army Engineers, and was being paid for by the United States. This was my first experience with wartime construction in out-of-the-way places, but "paid for by the United States" became a familiar refrain in the years to follow.

After this sightseeing, I returned to the hotel at about 6:00 P.M., where I met Harry Hopkins, proud and happy because of all the big and little fish he had caught. General Marshall had not caught a single fish.

Brigadier McConneghy of the British Army phoned several times. He wanted to show the party his motion pictures of Bermuda. We were all agreed that there is nothing so boring as amateur films. We did not want to be discourteous nor to offend a well-intentioned British brigadier, so I was elected to tell him the fib that the General and Harry had gone out and were not available.

A short time later we were all standing in front of the hotel when up drove Brigadier McConneghy. This was my second blooper and, as in church the day before, I wished that I could do a vanishing act. Harry Hopkins carried it off very well. He said we had just returned from an appointment and were about to leave for another. That evening the MODICUM party had dinner quietly together, enjoying Harry's fish, which were prepared in a most delectable manner by the hotel chef. Weather reports from England indicated everything was okay for departure at 6:30 A.M. the following day, Tuesday.

Back at the hotel in Bermuda the MODICUM group talked over our local experiences until about 11 P.M. I was becoming restless. A phone call shortly after midnight explained that all arrangements were firm for scheduled departure, and the British Overseas Airline official had arranged for our transportation from the hotel to the pier where the Clipper was tied up. I slept about three hours, got up at 4 A.M., ate breakfast, packed my belongings, went to Hamilton, and picked up the pouches at the Consul General's office before taking a small launch to Darrell Island. At the pier to bid us *bon voyage* was a contingent of American and British officials, including Brigadier General Strong, Consul General Beck, Captain Jones, and the Governor General's aides. We were told by the pilot that we had a straight over-water stretch of 3,000 miles, or about twenty hours' flying time, ahead of us. Our ship weighed gross 88,000 pounds, carrying 5,300 gallons of gas. Actually the weight exceeded the authorized limit by about 4,000 pounds. In flight the ship consumed about 200 gallons an hour.

The take-off was uneventful and a short time after gaining altitude the plane was driving through a front which caused considerable turbulence. After three hours of lurching, creaking, and generally rough going, suddenly the airway seemed to smooth out. That evening we went to bed in comfortable berths, every bit as large as those found in the most luxurious Pullman cars of American railroads. At first I was unable to sleep. Before drifting off, I read several papers pertaining to American views on Allied strategy.

At 6:00 A.M. I was awakened by Harry Hopkins telling me to look out the window. We were off Ireland, and Harry said that we would soon land, since we were following a direct course to Loch Erne. Without circling for the usual survey of the landing, the pilot skimmed along the surface of the beautiful lake, taxiing to a gentle stop at the pier of the seaplane base. We breakfasted with officials of the base while our baggage was transferred to a landplane at an adjoining airfield. Soon we were again aloft, now in an eight-seater transport, with ample room for the five of us and for the two or three officials of the Royal Air Force who accompanied us.

On our way to London we were escorted by fighters, which appeared off each wing and to the rear immediately after we took off. As we crossed the Irish Sea, we saw a convoy moving northward, well protected by destroyer escorts and also overhead air cover. Gradually we were being exposed to the grim realities of war—the constant fear of attack, the careful preparations to hit back.

The MODICUM mission landed at Hendon Airfield near London at 1:00 P.M. on April 8. There was a delegation of high government officials at the airport, including the Prime Minister and senior members of the British Chiefs of Staff. After brief but warm welcomes, we were whisked off to Claridge's in the heart of London.

My room at Claridge's was next to General Marshall's sitting room. Harry Hopkins was down the corridor, with Dr. Fulton in close proximity. Colonel Craig was in a room next to mine. General Marshall suggested that I could take the remainder of the afternoon and evening to look up old friends, and asked me to drop by when I returned to the hotel later in the evening. We would then discuss plans and review the material which I had brought along.

The blackout of the huge sprawling city was remarkably effective. To a newcomer it was rather disconcerting, but one quickly adjusted to barely perceptible traffic lights, to an occasional bump by another pedestrian, to double doors and black-draped windows. Evidence of past bombing raids was present everywhere. Colonel Homer Case took me on a brief tour of the bomb-damaged areas. We also examined the antiaircraft units in Hyde Park. One or two were manned by women, and I was told there was great rivalry between them as to the number of enemy planes shot down. I returned to the hotel at 9:30 P.M. and arranged the planning papers for General Marshall's perusal. He joined me in his sitting room at 10:00 P.M., and we discussed the various steps by which we should present our plans and the supporting data.

The following day (Thursday, April 9) I was awakened early by a valet. He helped arrange my clothes and also ordered breakfast, which consisted of two slices of very stringy bacon, mushrooms which seemed tough, toast, and execrable coffee. I missed my orange juice, egg, and large cup of American coffee.

The nucleus of the American senior command headquarters in the British Isles had already been established in London. The senior officer was Major General Chaney of the Air Force. His Chief of Staff, Brigadier General (later General) Charles L. Bolte, was an old friend of mine.

At 10:00 A.M. Generals Marshall and Chaney and I went to the British War Cabinet offices for our initial conference. We were greeted by the British representatives: Sir Alan Brooke, British Chief of Staff; Sir Dudley Pound, First Sea Lord; Sir Charles Portal, Air Chief Marshal; Admiral Mountbatten, Chief of Combined Operations; Sir Hastings Ismay, Secretary to the Cabinet; and Brigadier General L. C. Hollis, member of the British Secretariat. Also present, on the American side, were Rear Admiral Ghormley, the senior U.S. naval officer in London; and Brigadier General Robert A. McClure, the military attaché at our Embassy. After an exchange of pleasantries, including an expression of warm welcome by Sir Alan Brooke, General Marshall made a few introductory remarks concerning the strategic situation as the Americans envisaged it. He outlined in a broad way our proposals for Allied operations in the European area during the remainder of 1942 and on through 1943. General Brooke made a few comments in reply and was followed by Admiral Mountbatten, Sir Charles Portal, and Sir Dudley Pound.

I recall vividly this initial joust with the British concerning definitive plans for a cross-Channel operation, for it was the forerunner of many discussions, with the Americans always keeping uppermost in mind the basic idea of concentrating and making a decisive effort against the heartland of the enemy. The British, on the other hand, kept returning to a concept of scatterization or periphery-pecking, with a view to wearing down the enemy, weakening him to a point which would permit almost unimpeded or undisputed invasion of Fortress Europe by our forces.

The British Chief of Staff, Sir Alan Brooke, talked in low measured tones and was cautious as he commented upon the American concept as described by Marshall. The British were masters in negotiations—particularly were they adept in the use of phrases or words which were capable of more than one meaning or interpretation. Here was the setting, with all the trappings of a classical Machiavellian scene. I am not suggesting that the will to deceive was a personal characteristic of any of the participants. But when matters of the state were involved, our British opposite numbers had elastic scruples. To skirt the facts for King and Country was justified in the consciences of these British gentlemen. Lest I be considered prejudiced, I quote from Sir Arthur Bryant's *The Turn of the Tide* (page 282):

> To the Prime Minister, even the disaster that had befallen the American Navy [Pearl Harbor] seemed of far less consequence than the fact that the United States was now ranged on Britain's side. . . . Then at a Chief of Staff meeting next day (December 8, 1941) someone continued to advocate the same cautious approach to America that had seemed politic when her intervention was in doubt. He answered with a wicked leer in his eye: "Oh! That is the way we talked to her while we were wooing her; now that she is in the harem, we talk to her quite differently."

There was no expressed opposition to Marshall's ideas at this first meeting—just polite suggestions that there might be difficulties in undertaking this task or that. What I witnessed was the British power of diplomatic finesse in its finest hour, a power that had been developed over centuries of successful international intrigue, cajolery, and tacit compulsions. I recall speculating at the time on its ultimate efficacy. It is true, I thought, that the sun never sets on the British Empire. But neither does the dove of peace. Moreover, the wings of justice had constantly been clipped as British influence and possessions were increased all over the world.

I reflected upon the history of the British as I sat watching those senior military leaders carefully parrying, sidestepping, and avoiding a head-on collision at this stage of the scheduled conferences. Certainly the British were in a desperate situation. However, there was nothing in their demeanor to reveal concern or doubt about final victory. I reviewed in my mind the terrible ordeal that they had experienced since giving the fatal guarantee to Poland after first permitting Hitler to seize the dominating highlands of Bohemia. I could not help but feel that if Castlereagh, Palmerston, Pitt, or Disraeli had been in power a few years earlier, when Hitler was arrogantly calling the tune to which he expected European nations to dance, there would have been no surrender of the Rhineland or the Czech Army. The guarantee to Poland would have been predicated on an all-around defensible Allied position, or it would not have been given at all. Assuming a strong Hitler, a Disraeli or a Pitt would have bided his time. He would have made certain that the British followed their historic policy of preserving the balance of power in Europe by remaining out of the conflagration initially. Later, when the two colossí—Soviet Russia and Germany—had chewed each other up until both were practically destroyed, British legions would once again have marched through the fields of Flanders and on eastward to exercise the decisive role.

This was my first experience with those trained negotiators who had a great tradition and were familiar hands at using the intimidation of latent force or resorting to subtle deals, doing anything and everything to protect and extend British interests. Throughout English history those interests had generally been linked to the fostering of trade. Although we had become partners for an identical purpose—to defeat the Germans, the Italians, and the Japanese— I felt that we must realize that the British had certain ulterior motives or national aims to satisfy. We Americans, who were adolescents in the international field, had no clear-cut conception of our own national interest. We wanted to crush our enemies militarily— make the world safe for democracy—and protect the Four Freedoms. But, I reflected once again as I watched the British Chiefs of Staff in action, we had no definitive national aims.

We were very much in the position of being in a football contest, going all-out to win the game, and then with victory achieved, proposing only to return home to celebrate the victory. We were just that naïve. We did not seem to understand that in fighting wars with the Germans and Italians in Europe, and with the Japanese in the Far East, we should in the process strive to create the conditions which would bring a realistic and enduring peace.

All of these ideas went through my mind as I listened to the thrusts and parries of the conferees. Finally the meeting broke up around noon and we were invited to have luncheon with the British, as guests of Sir Alan Brooke.

During that morning's meeting I also had a good opportunity to size up the British as individuals. I surmised that Brooke would be a source of future trouble for my chief, General Marshall. I sensed in Brooke a quick, incisive mind. He was an articulate individual, sensitive; one who would nibble away to gain his ends, meanwhile skillfully avoiding the necessity of coming to grips frontally with a basic issue. Over the following months this initial impression was many times confirmed by many fellow Americans, and even by a few Britishers.

A note quoted from Sir Alan Brooke's diary, as edited by Sir Arthur Bryant in *The Turn of the Tide* (page 428), is revealing of Brooke's pertinacity in continually getting his way: "A very trying week, but it is satisfactory to feel that we have got just what we wanted out of U.S. Chiefs . . ."

Sir Dudley Pound was a typical British officer of the Royal Navy —a gentleman, courteous, a twinkle in his clear blue eyes, small in stature, large in his grasp of humanity, and at times rather taciturn. He gave the impression of not following closely the subject matter, but when asked to comment he proved to be mentally alert and completely in the picture.

Sir Charles Portal had an unusual face—large nose and high forehead. He seldom raised his eyes. When he spoke, it was evident that he used considerable care in choosing his words. He had a great capacity for the formulation and expression of logical ideas. There was never a tinge of resentment or smugness about him, and he seemed to weigh the other person's viewpoint in an intelligent and sympathetic manner without weakening his own position. In subsequent meetings I decided that Sir Charles was a notch above the other members of the British military hierarchy so far as character and all-around intellectual capacity were concerned.

At first blush, Sir Hastings Ismay appeared to be what we in America would call a "smoothie." He had a talent for ingratiating himself, and he obviously enjoyed the aura which surrounded his position of proximity to Prime Minister Churchill. I thought that he was insincere—a man without real convictions and incapable of reaching sound conclusions. Sir Hastings seemed cast in the role of Mr. Fix-It, of spreading oil on troubled waters, of alleviating difficult situations for the P.M. and for all of the senior officials in their relations with one another.

I was right about Sir Hastings' penchant for smoothing over difficulties for his colleagues in the British Government. But I was totally wrong and did him grave injustice in my initial impression that he was superficial. As I got to know him better, I learned that he made use of his charming personality, even to the extent of resorting to double-talk or flattery, but invariably when it served a constructive purpose. My final opinion of the man was that he would never stoop to duplicity when the chips were down. Further, he had moral courage and could exercise it when the occasion demanded.

Mountbatten was by all odds the most colorful on the British Chiefs of Staff level. He was charming, tactful, a conscious gallant knight in shining armor, handsome, bemedaled, with a tremendous amount of self-assurance. Because of his youthfulness, which was emphasized by his appearance, it was obvious that the older officers did not defer readily to his views. They were careful, however, to give him a semblance of courteous attention. After all, he was a cousin of the King and, no doubt about it, a great favorite of the Prime Minister. Later on, far across the world in Asia, I was to come to know and respect Mountbatten as a conscientious, energetic Allied commander.

Of the Britishers in lesser roles of the Secretariat, Brigadier Ian Jacobs and Brigadier Hollis of the British Marines were a wonderful pair of observers and performed exceptionally well in scheduling and recording important discussions and decisions.

In describing various key figures, both political and military, with whom I have been associated, I have tried to give objective and accurate characterizations. Many of the descriptions of leaders one reads in books about the war remind me of photographs; they seem flat and lacking in an appreciation of angles and facets. More like a sketcher, I have made an effort to go around men and to penetrate their motives, seeking to determine what makes an individual tick. While not describing people as many have visualized them, nevertheless I have made every effort to present faithfully my own reactions and observations in a dispassionate, sometimes necessarily unflattering way. When someone has performed an outstanding act or has given notable evidence of intelligence, courage, or perspicacity, I have tried to give due credit. And when shortcomings or human fallibilities have been revealed, I have endeavored to indicate them with the same degree of accuracy.

When we assembled at the Savoy Hotel for General Brooke's luncheon, General Marshall asked me to visit the Combined Operations Headquarters, which had recently been organized under Admiral Mountbatten. Marshall himself could not accept Mountbatten's invitation because he wanted to rest before his appointment later with Churchill. Marshall cautioned me that Mounbatten was enthusiastic about some gadgets the British had under development. He suggested that I make no commitments but be prepared to give him a complete résumé later.

I reported to the Combined Operations Headquarters that afternoon and was ushered into a room by Mountbatten. The Admiral explained that his organization comprised outstanding officers and enlisted men of the three services: Army, Navy, and Air Force. These men not only conducted experiments in the techniques of amphibious warfare, commando raids, and other limited-objective and unorthodox operations, but they were also interested in developing appropriate equipment for use in such activities.

Mountbatten introduced me to his key men: young admirals, generals, and air marshals. They impressed me favorably; obviously they were all enthusiastic about the new organization.

The Admiral then explained that closer co-ordination in planning operations was brought about by getting all of his men under one roof. He suggested that we Americans adopt a similar approach and even invited us to send young officers of captain and major rank in the three services to work with British Combined Operations in order to learn their new techniques, particularly in amphibious warfare. I told Mountbatten that I would recommend favorable consideration to my Chief of Staff.

After tea the meeting broke up. Mountbatten insisted that I remain; he wanted me to meet another group of individuals, which included a civilian inventor, a certain Professor Pike. This unusual character was professorial in appearance—tall, thin, cadaverous, with a neatly trimmed goatee. He shambled in and sat loosely in his chair as he prepared to explain an idea which Admiral Mountbatten had termed a most important secret. So hush-hush was his project that only a limited number of persons were being told about it, and the name of every individual to whom it had been so far revealed was carefully kept in a book under lock and key. The book was brought in and I was required to sign my name before Professor Pike launched forth on the nature of his idea.

Briefly, his proposal was to build a vehicle that would traverse ice, water, bog, peat, and the steppes of Russia—in other words, a universal vehicle that would not be slowed down or immobilized no matter how difficult the terrain or how mushy the surface. Actually, we did later undertake the manufacture of a few of the proposed vehicles. Professor Pike visited the United States often, getting in the hair of our production people and usually ending up in my office asking for sympathy and assistance.

It should not be construed from my experience with Pike that either he or the Combined Operations Headquarters was wasting their diversified military and scientific talents. There is no doubt that Combined Operations, under both Mountbatten and, later, Major General Robert Laycock, performed a great service. The organization was responsible for the development of many valuable—although ofttimes weird—contraptions in connection with amphibious operations. Many important innovations in modern warfare were developed and introduced by this splendid organization.

CHAPTER IX

PRESENTING AMERICAN STRATEGY
IN LONDON

I RETURNED to the hotel at 6 o'clock. Brigadier General Robert A. McClure was awaiting me, also Doc Fulton, who was indulging himself with a whisky and soda. We all accompanied General Marshall to the American officers' mess, which was operated by Colonel George Barnes as Headquarters Commandant. At this time there were about 130 American officers on duty in England. Some of them were in the U.S. Forces British Isles, which was General Chaney's group. The remainder were under General McClure, our military attaché at the U.S. Embassy.

At the officers' mess I saw briefly Colonels Dahlquist, Griner, Simms, Stice, Matejka, McClellan, and Barker. All of these men distinguished themselves later in positions of high rank and great responsibility. In the evening I talked to General Marshall for a couple of hours. Marshall was amused by my description of Admiral Mountbatten and his Combined Operations. He agreed, however, that we might detail a few officers to this group as observers, and that we should invite Professor Pike to discuss his weird contraption with our Inventors Council and with our people in production.

On Friday, April 10, I accompanied Colonel Craig and Commander Fulton to the American mess for breakfast. While it hardly seemed right, with the British being on such short rations, the breakfast in the American mess was not very different from what I would have had at home. There were ample quantities of bacon and eggs and really excellent coffee. I felt guilty about every mouthful; it seemed odd, in fact stupid, that we should establish and maintain such a mess of plenty in the midst of all-encompassing austerity.

After breakfast I was to have my first go-round with the British Joint Staff Planners. General Marshall had suggested that Colonel Barker, who had just reported to General Chaney's staff as a planner, accompany me to conferences in London. Marshall felt that he should be thoroughly familiar with the BOLERO and ROUNDUP plans. I had never met Colonel (later Major General) Raymond Barker before. He was a field artilleryman, and as time passed our acquaintance quickly ripened into friendship. I found him to be intelligent and extremely hard-working. The conference room was located far below Whitehall in a bombproofed, electrically lit, and air-conditioned room. After traversing a network of tunnels and displaying my pass to security police, I met with the British planners.

I was presented to Brigadier Stewart, representing the British Army; Captain Charles Lambe, the Royal Navy; and Air Commodore Elliot, the RAF. These officers comprised the first team of British Joint Staff planners. Then there was a second echelon of planners present, also representing the three services. This echelon included Lieutenant Colonel Cobb of the Army, Group Captain Dawson of the RAF, and Commander Norfolk of the Royal Navy. Finally there was a Mr. C. A. Scott, who represented the Foreign Office.

The presence of the British Foreign Office representative at this military planners' meeting confirmed what I had been taught in Germany when I was a student there: that political, economic and military experts should combine their thinking and planning for the military security and economic stability of a nation. I had often urged that our own State Department policies be thoroughly integrated with our military planning.

The British planners were attentive as I presented the BOLERO and ROUNDUP plans. It was obvious that they had already received considerable briefing from their chiefs. I suppose that their representatives in Washington, with whom I had talked at length

about BOLERO and ROUNDUP, had sent reports back to London
to give some indication of the strategic thinking in America.

The subject, then, was already warmed up. This led to lively and
constructive arguments, centering around the availability of formations or combat units as envisaged in the plan. Shipping and landing
craft were emphasized as two items which might be in short supply,
although I reassured my British opposites that the American production chiefs had carefully analyzed the implications of the plans
and had given President Roosevelt complete assurance that all the
requirements including shipping and landing craft for the execution
of BOLERO and ROUNDUP would be available at the times and
places stipulated. The Americans assumed, of course, full British
co-operation in all preparatory phases, including assistance from
British production facilities.

We discussed, in exploratory fashion, the idea of Anglo-American
forces occupying Western Europe. This question was brought up
by Captain Lambe of the Royal Navy. Although I sensed that I
would be getting on dangerous ground if I frankly discussed communism or even suggested that it was an even greater danger than
Nazism, I did in a veiled way bring out that it would be advantageous to occupy Europe with Anglo-American forces as far east
as possible at war's end. I also suggested the importance of controlling the disposition of the Balkans. Once again I expounded the
heartland theory. All listeners seemed to be in accord, at least in
principle, with the idea of decisive action against the critical areas
and vital installations of the enemy. Concern was however expressed about British interests in India, Africa, and the Middle
East, including the importance of the lines of communications to
those areas. Everyone spoke courteously and cautiously about the
various points raised. The conference was conducted in an atmosphere of friendly co-operation. The Foreign Office representative
listened closely but made no comments on strategy; the exploratory character of the conference was maintained.

Later, when I reported my experience with the British planners
to General Marshall, he heard me through and seemed optimistic.
Yet, for reasons inexplicable at the time, I had misgivings. Not
enough questions had been asked concerning the step-by-step preparation for the cross-Channel operation in 1943. Too often the
British would introduce the idea of conducting interim operations

in order to provide combat experience for the troops and to harass the enemy and keep him off balance. How many times I was to hear such suggestions in my subsequent discussions with the British!

Barker and I returned to the hotel for lunch at about 1 o'clock. In the afternoon I accompanied General Ira Eaker on a visit to the American Bomber Command Headquarters. This was an unusual and instructive experience. All the important command installations were underground, as were the focal points of communication. I met Air Marshal Harris and his charming wife. The Marshal was known as "Bomber" Harris and was recognized in many circles as the British exponent of the Douhet theory of relying for victory on all-out destruction from the air.

I asked Bomber Harris how he accounted for the victory in the Battle of Britain. Eaker had told him that my Berlin experience had given me some familiarity with German tactics. Harris said that the RAF had little difficulty in coping with the heavy bomber attacks launched by the *Luftwaffe* for the simple reason that the Germans provided no protection for their bombers. Eaker said something about "sitting ducks" and Harris nodded assent. The German bombers even lacked appropriate armor. Harris added that if the Germans had had a sufficient number of bombers to carry on for a few more days—say a week longer—they might have destroyed London. The SEA LION operation might then have been undertaken with a successful canopy of German air protecting the invading forces.

I had tea at Harris' home and met several staff officers of the British Bomber Headquarters as well as a few American officers. The British automobile-racer Cobb, who established many speed records on the salt flats in Utah, was present. He said he had much enjoyed his stay in the U.S. in preparation for his trials. He was impressed with the Mormon Tabernacle at Salt Lake City as well as with the religious beliefs of the members of the Mormon Church.

While in England I also had visits with American pilots at several bomber bases. Ira Eaker took me to see a famous exclusive girls' school called Wycombe Abbey, which he had selected for his future American bomber headquarters. It seemed a shame to force this fine school to close down, but throughout the British Isles every interest and activity yielded uncomplainingly, at least on the surface, to the demands of the military.

I inspected the installation with Ira. It was well equipped and a lovely place. I met several of the teachers, staid and proper ladies who successfully concealed their great sorrow.

In driving around to various installations, Eaker gave much evidence of his enthusiasm for his job. He had a real pride in his command. He asked me to draw comparisons between two bomber units that we visited. In the first, the Colonel was a happy-go-lucky fellow, sloppy and unmilitary in appearance and action. On the apron of his unit's area, where planes were being serviced, tools were thrown around indiscriminately. There was very little attention paid to military discipline or courtesy.

We then motored to another bomber command. The contrast was most noticeable. Everywhere there was evidence of organization and order: every tool was in place on a painted outline of its shape. The outlines had been provided so that the mechanic would automatically return tools to their proper place after use. The men were smart in appearance and saluted snappily. The Colonel was serious, industrious, and alert. He had a thorough grasp of his entire command and held a tight rein, yet not an irritating one.

After visiting these two bomber commands, Ira Eaker asked me if I had noticed the contrast. I told him I most certainly had. Eaker said the difference in their combat records was really remarkable. The bomber command which had such excellent discipline and order had experienced far fewer losses in flying over hostile territory, and the morale of its men was excellent. In the other command not only were the losses in combat excessive at times but the morale of the men was not always good—in spite of the fact that the Colonel was an easygoing, lovable man who was visibly proud of his unit and certainly interested in its welfare.

I spent that evening with General Eaker and his staff. The following morning we had breakfast at the RAF Club. I saw many British women in uniform and was told that they were much more efficient and better disciplined than the men. I was informed, confidentially, that class or social distinction was maintained in connection with assignments given to members of the WAFs. For example, the daughter of a member of Parliament would be assigned to a unit comprising girls whose fathers were similarly placed on the social ladder. All of these girls, however, were required to perform KP and other arduous duties. The hardships and dangers endured by British women during the war revealed a sense of duty, adaptability, and sheer courage that would do credit to the finest military organization.

General Marshall, Harry Hopkins, and I had been invited by Winston Churchill to spend the week end at Chequers, the country place of British Prime Ministers. Driving there on Saturday morning I saw many buildings which had been effectively camouflaged. Among the other security measures I noted were the large spikes set up in fields to prevent enemy planes or gliders from landing; pill-boxes at road junctions; and road blocks around which one had to drive with care. We also drove past an airdrome manned by Polish pilots who had volunteered to fight for the restoration of freedom to their countrymen.

When I arrived at Chequers, General Marshall and Harry Hopkins were already there. After an evening dinner the group gathered informally in a large living room. Historic crests, flags, and weapons were displayed attractively around the walls. The ceiling was high and beamed. At one end of the room there was a huge fireplace with a fire burning brightly. The Prime Minister was at his happy best in this environment. The whisky flowed freely along with entertaining conversation, mostly about the American Civil War and World War I. There were few references to the meetings concerning current strategy. Everyone seemed to be in a jovial mood.

Chequers was built very much on the pattern of Elizabethan houses, with a ground plan resembling the letter "E." It was three stories high and contained twenty-five or thirty rooms. Though the sitting room was huge, the bedrooms were small; at least the one to which I was assigned was hardly commodious; and the bed itself was not particularly comfortable, a very old bed. Most of the furniture in the house was Victorian. Striking portraits of various British leaders, both political and military, hung in the many rooms. Extensive grounds and lovely gardens, some formal and others rather hit-or-miss, surrounded the house. There was also a maze which I tried with difficulty to negotiate.

On the Sunday morning following our most interesting evening with the Prime Minister, I arose early and walked through the gardens. The Prime Minister, coming down the front steps, said, "Good morning, Wedemeyer, how did you sleep?" I answered, "Good morning, Mr. Prime Minister, I slept very well, thank you. I have been admiring your beautiful flowers." "Well," he said, "let's go to the root house and see what Harry brought me. You know, I received a box from him."

In order to explain the mortification which awaited me, I must relate that on our last day in Bermuda Hopkins had asked me to arrange to have two crates of fresh vegetables put aboard our Clipper. Because the Nazi submarine blockade had made fresh vegetables and citrus fruits very scarce in England, he wanted to give one crate to the Prime Minister, and had suggested that General Marshall present the other one to Sir Alan Brooke.

In proper Army fashion I had passed the buck by phoning a major in the Quartermaster Corps, and telling him to have two crates of fresh vegetables delivered to the wharf on Darrell Island the following morning at 5 o'clock. He in his turn, of course, passed my order on to a captain, the captain to a lieutenant, and the lieutenant to a sergeant. The sergeant presumably ordered some sleepy and wholly uninterested private to handle the matter. Two sizable crates were at the pier in the morning, and I carefully supervised their loading aboard the Clipper, without having the least idea what they contained.

As I walked along with Churchill, Hopkins and Marshall joined us. At the root house, which was an underground place used as storage for vegetables and other perishable articles, the yard man carefully pried open the crate as Churchill watched to see what precious gift had been brought him from America. To my dismay and acute embarrassment it contained only Brussels sprouts—one vegetable in abundant supply in the British Isles.

Churchill started to laugh and soon everyone joined in, including myself. I was mortified, but this last blooper of mine was a good joke —the equivalent of carrying coals to Newcastle.

That Sunday I returned to London to resume discussions with the British Staff planners. The British side was represented by Colonel Stanley, the Secretary for Colonies; Brigadier McNab; Group Captain Groom; Colonel Cobb; Wing Commander Allinson; Lieutenant Colonel Greaves; Captain Hewes-Hallett; and Major Carver. Again we had a thoroughgoing discussion of BOLERO and ROUNDUP. I was favorably impressed by Colonel Stanley, with whom I had lunch that day and on several other occasions. He was a tall man, with a shock of white hair and a kindly face. He had been a Member of Parliament and was a reserve officer, and I was interested in hearing his views concerning the future of the British Colonial Empire as well as his estimate of the political and military situation. Among the British planners at this session Captain Hewes-Hallett stood out. He had one of the most alert minds I encountered during the whole course of the war.

That evening I had dinner with Bob McClure and Commander Fulton at Claridge's. Later I visited Mr. and Mrs. Brooke, in the West End of London, taking them three eggs and a pound of sugar for which small gift they were unduly grateful. They were the British parents of Frau von Templehof, whose husband had been a classmate of mine at the German War College in Berlin. The Brookes were very worried about their daughter, knowing that an increasing number of bombers were raining death and destruction on German towns.

Next day I remained in conference until late in the afternoon with the British planners. The discussions were lively and constructive and devoid of any violent differences. The British were particularly interested in the logistic factors connected with our plans. Colonel Stanley presided.

At 5:00 P.M., I returned to Claridge's and we began preparing a report for General Marshall based on the notes I had made. I hoped to have it ready for him by the time he returned from Chequers.

At my conference with General Marshall on Monday, April 13, we exchanged notes concerning our experiences and impressions in our discussions with the British. Marshall's talks with Churchill had convinced him that the British had adopted in principle the BOLERO and ROUNDUP plans. The Prime Minister had told him that there was to be a meeting of the Defense Cabinet to decide on final action on the evening of April 14.

That morning I attended a briefing at the British War Office where an excellent appreciation of the enemy situation was presented. British intelligence experts explained enemy capabilities along the coast and also gave their estimates of possible redistribution of enemy forces should an attack be made on the Continent.

These British intelligence estimates were very much like our own. It was obvious that British and American intelligence people were continuously exchanging information. At 11:00 A.M., conferences with the British Joint Staff Planners were resumed, and later I lunched with Colonel Stanley at the Turf Club.

In my contacts with the British the contrast between them and the Germans was forcibly brought home to me. The Germans were without peer in the military field—disciplined, thoroughly trained in tactics, and ahead of anyone else in the adaptation for military use of scientific and technological developments. But they were stupid or inept in the field of diplomacy where the British excelled. The British were courageous in combat, but could not compare with the Germans as tacticians or strategists in the narrow military definition of the words. But they were superb diplomats and negotiators —clever, persuasive, and subtle. Their superiority in these fields as compared with the clumsy fumbling of the Germans, who never seemed to learn how to win friends and influence people, would bring victory to the British. They might lose all the battles but they would win the war; or, at least, they would have won it had they not come up against that master of duplicity Generalissimo Stalin, not only the dictator of "all the Russias" but the master of the Communist network which encircled the globe.

After dinner on the evening of April 13 the British planners reassembled and I joined them in the War Room. They had obviously received instructions from the top to elicit as much information as possible, not only concerning the way we Americans envisaged landing on the shores of France but also as to our conception of the manner in which a lodgment could be extended and exploited. During this meeting we developed, through questions and answers, the broad scheme of maneuver which had often been discussed in the planning agencies back in the United States. On this occasion I mentioned for the first time the importance of a diversionary effort coming up from southern France through the open Rhone Valley (which in 1944 was to become the ANVIL operation). The British comments in the closing minutes of the conference might be summed up as agreement that the tactical concept seemed sound, but doubt as to availability of the appropriate means to carry out the operation in the time envisaged.

One British officer, Captain Hewes-Hallett, brought up the so-called soft underbelly concept of operations. He referred to it as penetration from the south. I said that we had examined the European area meticulously for every possible point or area of ingress, starting at the Scandinavian Cap, then along the Peninsula and across to the Low Countries, along the coast of France, around the Iberian Peninsula, then Southern France, Italy, and Greece, to Turkey and the Bosporus. I told the group that an invasion from the Adriatic Sea, using the Ljubljana Gap into Austria and Hungary, had been ruled out by the American planners because it did not offer as many advantages to the invading forces as the one we had termed ROUNDUP—a crossing of the English Channel into France. The configuration of the terrain, lack of ports, poor communications, lack of air and naval bases made the Balkans hazardous if not impossible. The "soft underbelly," save for Southern France around the port of Marseille, was in reality a hard and bristling spine. (See Chapter 17.)

It should be noted at this point that the philosophy, or general strategic thinking, of the British up to the time of Pearl Harbor had been shaped by their meager resources. The British were short of shipping, aircraft, tanks, and trained military formations in all three services. Consequently, they could not think in terms of concentrating a large force for a decisive blow and still maintain a semblance of defense to prevent the enemy from making damaging sorties around the Empire's perimeter, or even a definite advance on such strategic focal points of communication as Gibraltar and Cairo. This accounts for the Prime Minister's insistence on deploying his forces in widespread indecisive areas. Possessing an active mind and vivid imagination, Churchill at various times conjured up, or strongly supported, nit-picking operations—a landing on the Norwegian coast, in the Dodecanese in the eastern Mediterranean, in Greece, on the North Africa coast, in the Canary Islands, at Dakar, and at Madagascar. He was constantly looking for places to employ his limited forces in some wonderful periphery-pecking operation which he imagined would weaken the enemy without calling upon Britain to go all-out for a decisive blow.

Now that the vast resources, the great war-making potential, of the U.S. had been made available, the British were faced with a sudden wrench in their strategical frame of reference. They still tended to think in terms of protecting their Empire lines of communication. Although the thought of concentrating for a major and decisive blow against the enemy was appealing and the professional military men readily agreed to it in principle, they wanted to push peripheral strategies at the same time. This was what produced the hesitancy to accept the American plan that I sensed at all of the conferences in London in April, 1942.

There were pleasant interchanges when I bade the British planners good-by. I expressed the hope that they would soon visit America in order to meet their opposite numbers in U.S. planning agencies. I had been particularly impressed with the three senior staff planners—Captain Charles Lambe of the Royal Navy, Group Captain Bill Elliot of the RAF, and Brigadier Stewart of the British Army.

Walking back to the hotel after the final meeting with the British, Colonel Ray Barker told me that he had just received a radiogram ordering him back to the States. He was enjoying his work in London; and was surprised at his orders to return so soon, having arrived only two weeks earlier. He also said he was going to be promoted to brigadier general. He asked if I thought General Marshall would object to his flying back with us in the Clipper. I told him I would ask the General and let him know.

Later, when I spoke to General Marshall about Barker, he reacted very unfavorably. Perhaps I did not explain the situation as clearly or tactfully as I might have. Marshall said, "He can go home, but not with us! So he wants to be a general, does he?" I thought Marshall had misunderstood what I had said, so at the risk of making him even angrier not only with Barker but with me, I explained that Barker, far from asking to be sent home, had expressed surprise that he had received orders to return.

Marshall never expressed his regrets for his outburst but still refused to take Barker with us. Many months later I was gratified to learn that Barker got back to the States and was given his promotion. He ended up the war with a fine record and with two stars on his shoulders. To this day I do not know how to account for General Marshall's peculiar reaction. He may have been tired or disappointed about something. I never could break the barrier with Marshall in incidents like this. After the General had had time to reflect upon the whole thing, it seemed to me he might have acknowledged that he had been hasty or out of sorts. But he didn't.

In all my contacts with Marshall I found him as a rule coolly impersonal, with little humor. He could laugh, but he never gave evidence of a deep-seated pleasure in life. I know of many acts of kindness and thoughtfulness on his part, and I myself had reason to be grateful to him for having given me the opportunity to prove my worth as a planner, but he kept everyone at arm's length. It was typical of him that no one I know, with the exception of General Stilwell, ever called him by his Christian name or was on terms of even the beginnings of familiarity with George Catlett Marshall.

On Tuesday, April 14, I was feeling fortunate that Uncle Sam was footing my bills. Though breakfast consisted of porridge, toast, coffee, and no fruit, the prices listed were high enough. Later, Marshall asked me to accompany him that evening to a scheduled meeting of the War Cabinet and British Chiefs of Staff; he wanted me to be prepared to explain any phase of our plans, and to bring with me pertinent documents and data. He also instructed me to make notes covering salient points which I thought he should emphasize.

This meeting was scheduled for 10:00 P.M. I invited Homer Case and Bob McClure to an early dinner at Claridge's. Doc Fulton came in to join us. When I left at 9:30 to accompany Marshall and Hopkins to Whitehall, I asked them all to wait for my return.

The next morning, Wednesday, April 15, I had another long conference with Marshall. He went over the planning situation as he viewed it and seemed quite confident that BOLERO was well on the way, although there was some doubt as to the full or unqualified acceptance of ROUNDUP.

In an informal talk I'd had with Captain Lambe and Air Group Captain Elliot, we had all seemed to agree that it was important for Anglo-American resources to be concentrated for a decisive effort against the enemy. Therefore, BOLERO had been recognized as sound procedure. But they had not been as emphatic as I about avoiding side shows or diversionary efforts that might militate against an early execution of the ROUNDUP plan. I told General Marshall that I considered their attitude an ill omen.

Toward the close of our London visit Marshall had luncheon with the King. After his return to the hotel he called me in to talk over his impressions. Harry Hopkins joined us for a short chat and asked me to accompany him to Parliament where he was scheduled to make an address to that august body. We drove off together. Our British chauffeur, Miss Duncan, had been an ambulance driver throughout the 1941 blitz; she told us first-hand stories about the destruction and chaos as we drove along through the bombed areas of London. The buildings near St. Paul's Cathedral were badly mauled, but the church itself was practically undamaged. There was a lot of destruction around Charing Cross; the Temple area was badly hit, and in some places whole blocks had been destroyed.

At the entrance to Parliament we were met by Sir Percival Harris and the Honorable Mr. Wakefield, who escorted us to the historic chamber of the "Mother of Parliaments." I sat on a bench alongside M.P.s. Anthony Eden and other notables were present; in fact, Eden sat directly opposite me. The old wooden seats run lengthwise along the sides of the high-ceilinged room. Harry Hopkins was introduced by Sir Percival Harris and was warmly welcomed by poundings on the shelves in front of the pewlike seats by the members. I did likewise but in a self-conscious manner. Hopkins appeared nervous at first, but gradually warmed to his subject. As he described the rapidly expanding war production of the U.S., he was cheered more and more frequently. His address was punctuated by "Hear, hear—hear, hear" and the rapping of knuckles on desks.

Unfortunately, in this first address ever given by an American before the "Mother of Parliaments," Hopkins talked more in the manner of a newspaper correspondent giving tidbits of information concerning the great, or of a salesman extolling wares, than as a statesman seeking to solidify the Anglo-American alliance in defense of the free world.

He regaled his audience with a humorous account of an incident that had occurred during Winston Churchill's visit to Washington in December. The British Prime Minister, attired in a nightshirt and in bare feet, had knocked on the door of Hopkins' room in the White House, and without waiting for a reply, had barged in. It so happened that Mrs. Roosevelt, who had been away when Churchill arrived in Washington, had also informally dropped in to visit Harry Hopkins in his bedroom, as was her custom when she wanted to discuss experiences, politics, programs, and policies with her powerful protégé. This to the considerable embarrassment of them all; for the British Prime Minister, barefooted and in his nightshirt, had met the First Lady for the first time.

I also felt embarrassed when I listened to Hopkins giving an exaggerated account of the huge U.S. production capacity which would insure a quick victory. His audience shouted, "Hear, hear," and pounded the shelves in front of their seats. But I knew that Hopkins was exaggerating the pace of American production, and I noted that Anthony Eden was shielding his face with his hand so that his smirk would not be visible.

On our way back to Claridge's, Hopkins asked me for my opinion of the British reaction to his speech. It was hard to conceal my feelings. Looking straight ahead as we drove along, I told him that the repeated cheering should assure him that his message was favorably received. Harry was intuitive—a highly sensitive and extremely vain man. What should one do under such circumstances, tell the truth or skirt the issue?

Homer Case drove me down to visit the Tower of London, where the Beefeaters, garbed in the same costumes as in Tudor times, guarded the heart of the city. The crown jewels had been removed at the beginning of the war, but there were many other interesting relics to see. The Germans had made only unsuccessful bombing runs on Tower Bridge and other bridges across the Thames, as also on the historic Tower of London. Some bombs had struck in close proximity, but no direct hits had been made.

After dining together at the American officers' mess, we walked about Hyde Park. It was very dark, of course, with a complete blackout. Yet there were clusters of people here and there listening to stump speakers on various subjects—religion, social problems, and so on. Here was freedom of speech in England at its best. As we sauntered along we inadvertently walked into a forbidden area— an antiaircraft position. A British sentry challenged us smartly but we had no difficulty in establishing our identity.

There were numerous barrage balloons bouncing around and forming eerie silhouettes in the sky. Searchlights occasionally shot powerful beams across the heavens, seeking out enemy planes.

Later that night, Bob McClure picked me up at Claridge's and took me to Waterloo railroad station to board the Prime Minister's special train. Winston Churchill, George Marshall, Colonel Sterling, General Ismay, Commander Thompson, Captain Brown, General McClure, Lord Cherwell, and Brigadier Bourne were in the party. It was a short train trip but afforded an opportunity to sleep quietly away from wartime London. When we awakened the following morning, we were in the vicinity of the training grounds of Ascot. Here we witnessed excellent demonstrations by British infantry units, tanks, and artillery, and exercises involving close-support techniques by the Royal Air Force. We went back to London in the evening and began preparations for the return trip to the U.S.

The following morning, General Marshall and Harry Hopkins had a last-minute conference with the Prime Minister. Homer Case brought over some presents for my two boys and for his wife. We left for Hendon Airport at 2:30 P.M. and boarded the Flamingo transport plane provided by the RAF. Our London mission had been completed. There remained the momentous business of changing ROUNDUP and BOLERO from blueprint to reality.

CHAPTER X

STRATAGEMS IN LIEU OF STRATEGY

On SATURDAY, April 18, the MODICUM party, with hearty fare-wells and Godspeed from Churchill and the British Chiefs of Staff at the London airport, flew in an RAF plane to North Ireland for a brief inspection visit of the American troops and installations there; and thence to Stranraer, an amphibious plane base, on the West Coast of Scotland. We boarded the Pan-American Clipper which was awaiting our arrival, and were soon airborne on a non-stop flight to LaGuardia seaplane base in New York. On the flight home I had several informative and important talks with Harry Hopkins, General Marshall, and Sir Dudley Pound, the British Sea Lord, who accompanied us. In these informal discussions I gave free rein to my view that it was vitally important that Anglo-American forces should get to Europe as fast as possible with "the mostest men," in order to prevent the Communists from winning control of the European heartland. We all agreed that 1942 would be the critical year. Future history was likely to be determined by the course of events during the next several months. The war could be lost by the Axis powers if they failed to crush the Russians. A Nazi breakdown in Russia would result in a prolonged struggle in which the process of attrition would work inevitably toward German-Japanese defeat.

When I mentioned Japan, Hopkins asked me what I thought the Japanese might do during the next few months. I replied that Japan was capable of consolidating her position in the Southwest Pacific merely by maintaining strategically situated bases which would allow her to exploit important economic resources. With her position secure in the Southwest Pacific, Japan would be able to launch a vigorous offensive against the Soviet, with a view to seizing the area east of Lake Baikal.

This operation would in all probability be co-ordinated with German advances in Russia. If successful, the last remaining immediate threat to the Japanese citadel would be removed, and Japan would be free to establish her "co-prosperity sphere" in the Far East.

I expressed the opinion that this would constitute Japan's maximum capabilities. The Axis powers, as I saw it, must recognize the strategic implications of Western industrial resources, which were only now being converted to full war production. The German and Japanese high commands would undoubtedly exploit their present military superiority and initiative to attain limited objectives in European and East Asia. These would provide further security for their respective positions in the world, both economically and militarily.

I told Harry Hopkins and General Marshall that, despite the recent Soviet reports of Red Army successes, the Russian situation remained an enigma to me. I felt that an accurate evaluation of conditions on the Eastern Front was hardly possible at this time. Perhaps Russia's strength had been greatly underestimated, both by our own military authorities and by the Germans. A true test of the Soviet Union's capacity to resist would probably come in the fall or winter. Maneuver seemed to be denied to the Germans whenever they encountered severe cold, snow, or mud in Russia. Toward the close of the 1941–42 winter it had become obvious that the Nazi armies were seeking a period of stabilization in the Eastern Theater.

Hopkins asked if I thought there would be any breakup inside the Nazi Party. I said there had been so many Nazi successes that deterioration was unlikely at the moment. Both the military and civilians in Germany were now convinced that their leader possessed unusual powers. So far as one could see, the Germans were united behind Hitler.

I was, however, hopeful that the German people would become dispirited if they were confronted in 1942–43 with the prospect of another winter of inconclusive fighting in Russia. What if they were to see their territorial gains slipping from their grasp? How would they react to the continued toll of German lives and the loss of more and more equipment? The German people must soon realize that seesaw warfare in Russia would not bring the era of prosperity and peace so long promised by Nazi leaders.

Assuming that the Eastern Front was the key to the military situation and perhaps to the entire future of the world, General Marshall speculated about Axis capabilities in Russia. I hazarded the view that there were two situations which could develop. First, the Germans might attempt stabilization along the present front in Russia, meanwhile turning to vigorous offensive operations against the Allies in the Mediterranean–Middle East area. Concurrently, the Japanese might try to push west through India in order to effect a junction with their European allies. But if the front were stabilized in Russia, the Soviet Union would have an opportunity to reconstitute its forces in rear areas and expand its industries behind the Ural Mountains.

The other possibility was that the Germans might make an all-out effort against the Russians in order to destroy the Red armies. Such destruction would take care of the Russians for four or five years. With a breathing space guaranteed, the Germans could make good use of the Ukraine, the Donets Basin, and the Caucasus. Meanwhile the Japanese might attempt to stabilize the military situation in the Southwest Pacific while exploiting the economic resources of that region. With the Russian armies destroyed in Europe, the Japanese could take the Siberian Maritime Provinces without much trouble.

General Marshall thought that if the Germans were successful in stabilizing the Russian front and driving deeply into the Middle East, this would precipitate a disintegration of the British Empire. It would necessarily interdict the lines of communication between Australia and the British Isles, and India and Egypt would be prey to the Axis. I pointed out that if the Axis were to divert men and matériel to a Middle East–Indian Ocean campaign, Japan's own position would be dangerously overextended. There would be terrible logistic problems. Japan, I felt, must seize the Siberian Maritime Provinces before daring to try for a junction with the Germans in the Middle East.

In my opinion, the Japanese lacked the capabilities of doing both things at once. If Japan were to move on India, she would lose her opportunity to secure her position militarily by seizing the Siberian maritime region.

General Marshall then brought up another supposition. If the Axis were to crush Russia militarily, this would remove the most immediate threat to its combined power for several years to come. Germany and Japan would be in a position militarily and economically to consolidate their respective positions in Europe and the Far East. Ample military forces would be released to extend Axis control through Northwest Africa, the Iberian Peninsula, the Mediterranean, and the Middle East, and to maintain an effective junction with the Japanese in India. Under such circumstances the Axis might be able to establish so effective a blockade around the British Isles as to compel capitulation. Japan would be so strengthened militarily and economically that her defeat would be rendered extremely difficult, even prohibitive.

If our evaluations were reasonably sound, it was obvious that the Allies must bend every effort to prevent the defeat of Russia. The problem as I saw it was to determine the most effective and timely aid we could give to the Soviet Union, not to produce a thundering Russian victory but to keep the Germans engaged until our own weight in the war had proved decisive. Hopkins asked me to outline the steps which might most effectively assist the Russians in 1942. He took out his pen and made notes on a pad as I talked. First, I mentioned delivery, with due regard to our own and British requirements, of appropriate war munitions to the Red Army. Next, the creation of a diversion which would compel withdrawal of the maximum number of German air and ground units from the Russian front. The British and Americans could do this by launching as strong an air offensive as possible against the Continent. A preliminary diversionary landing in France (SLEDGEHAMMER) might prove necessary, even though it could hardly succeed in sticking in 1942. There was no doubt that we could launch increasingly strong offensive air operations from the British Isles, thus serving to reduce enemy air strength over the Eastern Front.

It was now quite late, and General Marshall suggested that we go to bed. Harry Hopkins was profuse in his appreciation of what I had said. Just as we were breaking up he turned to Marshall and asked, "Could Colonel Wedemeyer come to my office from time to time and brief me on these matters?"

Marshall agreeing, Harry said, "Well, I will have my secretary call his and make appointments." Marshall then qualified his permission by saying, "Of course, Harry, the information he would be giving you would be highly classified and shouldn't be given to anyone else." Harry Hopkins assured General Marshall that he would treat the information as confidential. On that note we broke up. Hopkins and Marshall went to bed, and after some more conversation with Sir Dudley Pound I followed them.

We had luxurious berths which the attendant had already made up, and in very short order I was fast asleep. When I was awakened by some air turbulence that our ship was experiencing, I could hear Admiral Pound snoring above the din of the motors. Finally I fell back to sleep again. When I awakened the next time, I was told that we were making good progress toward LaGuardia Field. The British had double daylight, so there was a seven-hour difference in time. It was about 9 o'clock in the morning when we arrived at LaGuardia and were met by the Pan-American officials. Even at that hour there was a goodly supply of liquor and hors d'oeuvres. We stuck to coffee before boarding an Air Force plane for Bolling Field, where we put down without difficulty.

General Marshall asked me to prepare notes on the trip and give them to him so that he could give "Hap" Arnold and others on his staff a run-down. He also asked me to report to his office with suggestions for stepping up production and answering the various questions that the British had raised.

Soon after our return to the United States my doubts concerning wholehearted British support of our plans were given substance. I had been assured by Marshall that the British Cabinet and the Prime Minister had given their complete and unequivocal assent to the implementation of the BOLERO-ROUNDUP concept of Allied strategy. Marshall had first been told confidentially on April 12 by the Prime Minister that the British would approve the American plan. On the 14th of April formal approval had been given in London, and Marshall had dispatched a radiogram to the War Department and Secretary of War Stimson conveying the heartening information. In voicing his approval, Churchill in his usual dramatic style spoke of "two nations marching ahead in the noble brotherhood of arms."

The cross-Channel strategy had received President Roosevelt's blessing before he sent MODICUM to London. Our visit to England was quickly followed by that of the new Chief of War Plans, Brigadier General Dwight D. Eisenhower, whose task was to arrange for prompt joint planning organization for BOLERO between the British and ourselves. Eisenhower was accompanied by Generals Arnold, Somervell, and Mark Clark. While in London, they discussed British and American planning activities with General Chaney. To the British Chiefs of Staff Eisenhower stressed American views concerning command organization for the cross-Channel operation, ROUNDUP. He was particularly opposed to command by committees. The need, he said, was for one responsible leader with full authority over all three service elements.

Eisenhower later reported:

> It is quite apparent that the question of high command is the one that is bothering the British very much, and some agreement in principle will have to be reached at an early stage. No one thought it was necessary at that time [May, 1942] to name a Supreme Commander for ROUNDUP. However, as far as SLEDGEHAMMER was concerned, it had already been decided that such an emergency operation, if conducted in 1942, would be under British command.

Something in the British attitude, a faint but definitely perceptible lack of enthusiasm for the cross-Channel concept, disturbed Eisenhower. He had received a distinct impression that the British were skeptical about an operation in 1942, such as SLEDGEHAMMER. So were the Americans, but SLEDGEHAMMER was to be executed only under dire emergency conditions.

On June 3, after his return stateside, Eisenhower reported: "Our own people are able but it is necessary to get a punch behind the job or we'll never be ready by the Spring of 1943 to attack. We must get going."

A week or so later, General Marshall, recognizing the necessity for a dynamic approach to the preparations for BOLERO-ROUNDUP decided to appoint Eisenhower as the permanent head of a new

United States command organization in London, the European Theater of Operations for the U.S. Army, known as ETOUSA.

As I settled down to my Washington work in May, I quickly sensed that the British were up to something. As Marshall put it, they seemed to have agreed in London to our planning concepts with their tongues in their cheeks. They continued to be unduly fecund with new ideas which hacked away at our own concept of concentration as envisaged in the BOLERO plan. A sense of emergency would be associated with each effort on the part of the British to divert our resources and our men to other areas that held little promise of contributing to decisive results, but which would contribute to British prestige and greater security of the lines of communications connecting up their far-flung Empire.

As "Marshall's planner" and as a personal believer in the principle of going for the enemy's jugular vein, I was continually called upon to challenge British periphery-pecking concepts of strategy. The reader, and I am sure some of my British counterparts, might understandably gain the impression that I was an Anglophobe, or at least hypercritical of everything British. The contrary is true: I have always had the highest admiration for the British both as individuals and as a wonderful people. With their backs to the wall, the British are marvelous. They were "all for one and one for all" at Dunkirk and after. But the "one" in question was Churchill—and Churchill, as Marshall and I were both to discover, was a glorious leader and a magnificent English worthy with lamentable deficiencies as a strategist. England could hardly have lived through 1940 and 1941 without the rallying symbol of Winston Churchill and his wonderful oratory. But, after 1941, the problem was to restrain the pseudo strategist in Churchill while giving him full scope as an inspirational political leader.

With their ingrained habit of assuming authority, born of centuries of domination, the British naturally expected Washington to defer to whatever strategy was decided upon by their own military and civilian chiefs. Sir Alan Brooke, the British Chief of Staff, did not have a very high opinion of the American military leaders' knowledge or ability. He thought we lacked experience and couldn't be expected to evolve sound strategical concepts.

This attitude was a trifle odd, not to say presumptuous, for in 1941 the British themselves had had very little experience in offensive strategical maneuver. After all, they had been rapidly driven off the Continent in 1940; and from then on they had had little opportunity except in the air and on the sea to gain the experience Sir Alan Brooke talked about. The RAF wrote a glorious epic in the Battle of Britain, and the British Navy had already proved its ingenuity in developing new weapon systems and techniques to cope with the submarine menace. But the British Army, aside from the small forces engaged in North Africa, was surely no more combat-effective than our own.

I understood the British efforts to run the war on their own terms: they had the long-term prestige and trade advantages of their great Commonwealth of Nations in mind. The British were courageous, industrious, enthusiastic, and extremely effective as allies just so long as their own interests were not jeopardized. As an American, however, I felt that we should deal with our allies as equals. We also had our own national interest to protect; and as I saw it, it was certainly to the interest of Americans to adopt a strategy of concentration for decisive operations, decisive not only in a military sense but also in a political sense.

The defect of Churchill as a strategist for World War II was inherent in his islander's psychology. He held to the historic concept of Britain, the "tight little isle," covering up for magnificent home defense and meanwhile relying on judicious statecraft, the Royal Navy, and limited military thrusts at fortuitously opportune moments to win the day abroad. Then, too, he had been conditioned by his experience in World War I. He had witnessed the agonizing stalemate of the trenches. Like all Englishmen of his generation, he had vivid memories of the casualties of the Somme. Hoping to break the Western stalemate and bring the appalling casualties to an end, he had tried the back door at the Dardanelles, through which he sought unsuccessfully to effect a junction with the armies of the Czar. Whether this strategy of trying to effect a gigantic encirclement could ever have succeeded is still subject to debate; certainly it would have demanded a logistical miracle to supply a British Army committed to fighting its way into Central Europe via the Balkans.

Regardless of such questions, however, it was perfectly obvious that 1941–42 was not 1914–18, and Churchill should have realized it. In the era of fast armored vehicles, big bombers and swift fighter planes, trench warfare on the 1914–18 model was *démodé,* to say the least. Willy-nilly, a battle for the North European plain would be decided by maneuver, not by toe-to-toe slogging in the mud. Moreover, the new weapons of modern war made our fighting forces even more dependent on logistics than they had been in 1914–18. To train and assemble appropriate forces for a knockout blow against the Germans required unimpeded supply lines to and from a close-up base. As General Marshall felt (and this keen student of logistics had his own memories of 1914–18), this meant that the decisive campaign must be fought on the North European plain, with England serving as the close-up base and with necessary supplies moving through such ports as Le Havre, Cherbourg, and Antwerp, with ample dock facilities.

With his historically conditioned dread of fighting in Northern France, Churchill missed the point that a modern war of movement against the Nazis mounted from the underside of Europe, either through Italy or the Balkans, would present almost insurmountable logistic problems. There was no soft underbelly there. With the single exception of Marseille, there were no big ports capable of sustaining more than two or three divisions. Because of his prejudices Churchill began to distort the BOLERO-ROUNDUP-SLEDGE-HAMMER concepts even before they had been firmly accepted. The Churchill tactic was to emphasize the impracticability of SLEDGE-HAMMER—the plan to stage an emergency landing on the Cotentin Peninsula or elsewhere in 1942 if such an expedition seemed necessary to stave off a Russian collapse. Churchill took SLEDGEHAMMER out of its context almost shamelessly, using the obvious arguments against it to discredit any and all planning for an invasion of Northern France.

To this day Churchill's distortion of the over-all plans for 1942–43 continues to color the works of the memoirists. Practically all of the reports that I have read, emanating from British sources primarily, would indicate that the Americans were determined to launch an invasion of the European fortress in 1942. Actually this was never the case, at least in the framework of the over-all scheme of maneuver envisaged. The Americans felt that it was necessary to have a plan (SLEDGEHAMMER) to send emergency forces across the Channel and thus create a diversion, recognizing that possibly this expedition might be a sacrificial venture. It was always empha-

sized that such a maneuver would not be undertaken except under
the direct circumstances—for example, should the Russians indicate
that they would have to surrender if we did not do something desperate right away.

American officials and planners knew that we did not have sufficient resources to enter the fortress of Europe for keeps in 1942.
They knew it quite as well as their British opposites. Nevertheless,
Sir Alan Brooke, in Sir Arthur Bryant's *The Turn of the Tide*, gives
the impression that Marshall advocated an invasion in 1942. He
fails to add Marshall's opinion that such an invasion would be justified only under extreme emergency conditions. America, says
Brooke, overestimated her abilities and capabilities. But Marshall
never thought we could be capable of a full-scale invasion in 1942.

Actually Americans continued to advance the idea of SLEDGE-
HAMMER simply to restrain wild diversionary efforts proposed by
the British Prime Minister, none of which could accomplish decisive results for the Allied cause.

My premonitions of a British retreat from the April MODICUM
decision were sharpened by some conversations with my Fort Myer
neighbor, Brigadier Vivian Dykes. Together, in leisurely sessions
over a nightcap, we went over every facet of the problem presented
by the cryptic British reaction to our London visit. Dykes was constantly getting communications from his London friends, and I think
he was conveying as much as he thought he reasonably could to me
in discussing the most important points. These discussions led to my
conviction that the British were determined to undertake preliminary operations prior to ROUNDUP, either in Norway or in the
Mediterranean area, which might definitely prevent the execution
of ROUNDUP in 1943; certainly such an operation would be weakened if we acceded to their ideas of conducting operations along the
North Coast of Africa, in Scandinavia, or as far east as Syria.

I had exhausted my supply of ideas in talking to Marshall and
Hopkins on the MODICUM trip. Repeating the basic concepts after
my return to Washington, I noted that some of my colleagues in
the War Plans Division were weakening in their support of BO-
LERO-ROUNDUP. As we shall see, one of the strong arguments
used by the Prime Minister to break down the commitment to concentration for the cross-Channel invasion in 1943 was that he could
not politically support the idea of maintaining several million Tom-

mies in uniform for a whole year without using them somewhere against the enemy.

My answer to this argument was that a year of concentrated build-up would not be just a phase of *Sitzkrieg*. All through this interim period the British Navy would be engaged in tightening the blockade around Europe to deny the enemy sorely needed raw materials and supplies. The British Air Force, supplemented by the rapidly expanding American Air Force, was already pounding away with increasing intensity at important German industrial installations and communications. In the meantime the land forces were undergoing training and toughening exercises. They were also conducting raids along the northern coast of Europe to harass the enemy, thus obtaining combat experience.

I could see that I would have to do what I could within my own limitations to build up backfires against the growing conflagration which might consume both BOLERO and ROUNDUP, to say nothing of the emergency insurance features of SLEDGEHAMMER.

The nature of British second thoughts on BOLERO-ROUNDUP became obvious in early June with the arrival in Washington of Admiral Lord Louis Mountbatten. Lord Louis was closeted with Roosevelt for five hours. I understand that no American officer was present. It later developed that the subject of discussion was the BOLERO-ROUNDUP concept, particularly SLEDGEHAMMER. As I have said, when the MODICUM mission went to London, it had the thorough backing of F.D.R. Also the Secretary of War was firmly behind our strategy. Now we had an extremely articulate Britisher endeavoring to raise bogies about the hazards of a cross-Channel operation. Lord Louis had come to talk about the need for conducting preliminary operations to weaken the Germans prior to undertaking an invasion of Europe, ideas that had been expounded so forcefully and dramatically by the Prime Minister both before and subsequent to this time.

My good friend Brigadier Dykes gave me an inkling of what was in the wind at the White House. General Marshall also told me that the President had been talking to Mountbatten concerning the advantages and disadvantages of BOLERO and ROUNDUP. My concern was heightened by my great respect for Mountbatten's persuasiveness. After all, I had been exposed to his charm, plausibility, and enthusiasm when I was in London. I was not the only one who was impressed with Mountbatten's ability to sway opinions. On March 10, 1942, the British Chief of Staff Sir Alan Brooke made a notation as follows:

A long Chiefs of Staff meeting with Mountbatten attending for the first time. We discussed the problem of assistance to Russia by operations in France, either large raid or lodgement—decided only hope was to try to draw off air force from Russia and that for this purpose raid must be carried out on the Calais front. Now directed investigation to proceed further.

On March 28 Sir Alan continued:

Paget and Sholto Douglas were both there and Mountbatten. We were discussing ways and means of establishing a new western front. I had propounded clearly that a western British front to be of use must force the withdrawal of force from Russia, that it was impossible with the land force at our disposal to force the Germans to withdraw land forces from Russia, but that we might induce them to withdraw air forces. But to do this a landing must take place within our air umbrella, namely in the vicinity of Calais or Boulogne. Mountbatten was still hankering after a landing near Cherbourg, where proper air support is not possible. Finally, I think we convinced him sufficiently to make his visit to Chequers that evening safe.

Dickie's [Mountbatten] visits to Chequers were always dangerous moments and there was no knowing what discussions he might be led into and let us in for.

To judge from the foregoing, Mountbatten might logically have been expected to be an ardent supporter of a SLEDGEHAMMER operation against France in 1942. He was forever recommending large-scale raids or reconnaissance in force. Eventually he did undertake the famous Dieppe raid. This operation involved about five thousand men, mostly Canadians. Its aim was to elicit information about enemy dispositions, reactions, and installations, and to destroy military installations within working radius.

Unluckily, however, a German trawler ran into convoys bearing down on the French shore. The trawler alerted the enemy in time to give Mountbatten's commandos a disastrous welcome. Losses were staggeringly severe. The British operation caused the Germans to react in the air as well as on the ground, and the *Luftwaffe* took advantage of the opportunity to pound away. The Dieppe raid was a real failure in that it did not accomplish its purpose. It was not, however, in the same category as the proposed SLEDGEHAMMER, which would have committed a minimum of two divisions in an endeavor to secure a lodgment, thus compelling the Germans to take both air and ground action against our forces on a scale sufficiently great to pull planes and divisions from the Eastern Front.

The Dieppe raid, of course, was not to take place until August, whereas Mountbatten was talking to Roosevelt in June. But if the White House conversationalists had been able to foresee the fiasco that it was to be, it would have reinforced the arguments of the Prime Minister and his Chiefs of Staff as now expounded by the colorful and articulate Mountbatten. No matter what Mountbatten actually thought of his PM's notions, he would, as an Englishman, have given a good account of himself as an emissary when he enunciated them to our President.

Prior to Mountbatten's journey to Washington, the British had definitely stated their opposition to action "which might end in disaster and give the enemy an opportunity for glorification and our discomfiture." Thus, on the 28th of May, while Molotov was en route to the U.S. to discuss strategy as Stalin's representative, the British Government had already forwarded information to the effect that they had given Molotov no commitments; they had simply talked about the comparative advantages of operations in various places. In advising Roosevelt of Mountbatten's forthcoming visit, Churchill mentioned a possible foray against Norway. More significantly he said: "We must never let GYMNAST (North Africa) pass from our minds."

At the White House, Mountbatten discussed the possibility of JUPITER, as the Norway plan was called. He argued that control of the North Cape area would enable the Allies to secure the northern supply route to Murmansk. From a base near the North Cape we could operate both naval and air units to afford protection for our convoys running into the White Sea with supplies for the Soviet Union. Norway, however, proved to be the decoy duck to bring the North African campaign within shooting range. The objection to SLEDGEHAMMER, as Mountbatten put it to Roosevelt and Hopkins, was the presumed paucity of landing craft: with a necessarily limited landing force SLEDGEHAMMER would be at the mercy of the twenty-five German divisions stationed in France. In order to do anything at all with SLEDGEHAMMER, Cherbourg itself (or some other major port) would have to be seized. Otherwise, it would be impossible to support troops throughout a winter of containment in a small area. Lord Louis said it was completely out of the question to contemplate supplying a force over the open beaches.

Churchill's animus against SLEDGEHAMMER, as conveyed by the subtle Mountbatten, had its reportedly corrosive effect on Roosevelt's certainties about the whole principle of concentration on the invasion of Northern Europe. As Lord Louis said later, F.D.R. jumped from a thumbs-down attitude on SLEDGEHAMMER to doubts about the feasibility of sending any large number of troops to England for a BOLERO. Perhaps it would be more effective to detail six U.S. divisions to operations in North Africa or the Middle East.

I, of course, have no way of proving or disproving that the President made such statements, but I was present at many conferences and heard Roosevelt talk about BOLERO and ROUNDUP. It still seems a bit incredible that the President would be undercutting BOLERO to a foreign representative when he was definitely sold on an ultimate cross-Channel strategy. Roosevelt had had it frequently presented to him that the presence of American troops in the British Isles was needed not only for a Continental invasion but also to protect England in case of a possible Russian collapse. Moreover, troops in England were necessary to seize an opportunity to exploit a conjectural Nazi collapse, for it was already known that there were recalcitrants in Germany who were plotting to get Hitler out of power.

Whatever was actually said at the White House, it was obvious that Mountbatten was John the Baptist laying the groundwork for the great strategic evangelist, Winston Churchill, who arrived in America later on in June. It should not be forgotten that when Mountbatten was talking to Roosevelt and Hopkins there was no military planner present to ask appropriate questions of the Admiral and to develop in a professional manner the points which he raised.

Marshall and his staff now had to cope with British stratagems and I seriously doubt that the British ever had any intention of carrying out the American concept as envisaged in BOLERO-ROUNDUP or in SLEDGEHAMMER. Refusing to challenge us frontally, they carefully refrained from taking a strong position when Marshall and his assistants presented those plans in London in April. They must lay the groundwork for their own ideas in traditional diplomatic style. To circumvent the professional soldiers, they must shake the confidence of the political leaders in Washington. Never was there any mention of political or economic objectives; the reasons offered for weakening on BOLERO were always military, truly military. Presumably the military aspects of BOLERO might have been left to soldiers for handling in a sound manner. Insofar as I could determine, and I was far down the line, I was the only man in uniform who had broached the political aspects of the operations recommended. But I had been warned that political considerations were none of my business. It was paradoxical that I, a military man, had political objectives in view while the politicians, Churchill and Roosevelt, had narrowed their vision to purely military objectives. While political leaders were telling the soldiers how to win the war, soldiers were suggesting how to win the peace.

I knew it was the better part of discretion never to put in writing the political objective of denying Western Europe and the Balkans at war's end to our so-called ally, the Soviet Union, but had mentioned it several times to Marshall and Hopkins, hoping that they would convey that war aim to the President.

Sir John Kennedy, like General Handy in our own set-up, exercised over-all supervision of British war planning. As early as 1943 he was thinking ahead about postwar responsibilities—the Allied forces and areas to be assigned for occupational duties. The following quote from his excellent book, *The Business of War* (page 304), had a familiar ring; for I had experienced similar admonitions not to refer to the Russians in a critical sense or to the dangerous implications of communism:

> Another matter which we began to turn over in our minds was the strength of the forces which we should retain in peacetime. To me there seemed to be only one great power who could be regarded as the possible enemy: Russia. From this arose the question of what side Germany might take in a

future war if the Russians were to cling to their half of Germany after the war was over. These ideas were not communicated to the Cabinet at this time, but when it became known, a few months later, that we were thinking along these lines, we received a stern rebuke, and were told to desist from mentioning possible tension with Russia, or from taking Russia into our calculations as a potential enemy.

Anticipating the Prime Minister's visit, Marshall requested a memorandum detailing the reasons why the British GYMNAST plan for landings in North Africa would play hob with BOLERO-ROUNDUP. He asked me to draft this memorandum, inasmuch as I had accompanied him to London and was thoroughly conversant with his ideas concerning the disadvantages of scatterization as recommended by the British. There were several serious drawbacks to GYMNAST. To begin with, it assumed Franco's Spain would remain neutral and that the French would not react in anger. Secondly, the plan would tax Allied naval strength. These possibilities might have been accepted as calculated risks. But even if such risks could be taken in stride, it was obvious to all of us that GYMNAST would put off invasion of the North European plain for an indefinite period. As historian Samuel Eliot Morison was to say years later, the "ascending Mediterranean ladder" would "consume more of our forces than of the enemy's, and delay the cross-Channel operation at least a year—as indeed it did." The insincerity of the British about BOLERO-ROUNDUP was ultimately to be exposed long after the war, when Sir Alan Brooke (now Lord Alanbrooke) confessed that the promotion of GYMNAST was specifically designed to stall the cross-Channel invasion scheduled for 1943.

Prior to the arrival of Mr. Churchill, the President discussed GYMNAST with Secretary Stimson, who held with Marshall and the military staff that a defection from BOLERO would prove to be a snare. Stimson wrote an excellent memorandum in which he denounced any diversion from the strategy that had been agreed upon in April.

If anybody could have held Roosevelt to a steady course, that man would have been Stimson. I had disagreed with the Secretary about becoming implicated in a war on two widely separated fronts, Europe and the Far East, in the first place. But despite our initial differences I must pay heartfelt tribute to a man who refused to be

deflected from any course once he had been thoroughly convinced
that it was right. Stimson never kowtowed, never played politics. He
was the soul of honor.

In the afternoons during my early days in War Plans Division,
Mr. Stimson frequently arranged to have a few officers join him for
deck tennis at his lovely home on Woodley Road in Northwest
Washington. Since he had been an advocate of the strenuous life
dating back to Teddy Roosevelt's time, he needed his daily exercise. But he also used his exercise hour to become acquainted with
the officers in the War Plans Division. On several occasions his aide
phoned and asked me to be present. Luckily, I was often able
to accept.

After playing deck tennis—not too strenuously because of the
Secretary's advanced age—we would sit and talk on the porch and
have a drink. Stimson asked questions primarily concerning BO-
LERO and ROUNDUP, focusing on the reasons we had turned
away from the so-called soft-underbelly strategy. I had had several
contacts with our Secretary of War with reference to our strategy
when I was working on the Victory Program; in fact, my chief at
the time, General Gerow, had taken me to the Secretary's office
where I presented the ideas embodied in the Victory Program and
explained the strategic concept behind the program which visualized the employment of approximately eight and a half million men
in the Army and Army Air Force. But it was not until the informal
get-togethers on Woodley Road that I became convinced of Stimson's almost fanatic belief in the cross-Channel operation and in the
heartland theory. Stimson was determined to block any British or
Russian effort to scuttle American proposals for concentration of
means for employment in decisive operations against an area critical to the enemy.

I also discovered that the Secretary was aware of British intransi-
gence or duplicity whenever it cropped up. He seemed to understand that the loquacious PM would artfully approve American proposals while discussing them with military men, meanwhile taking
a different tack with Roosevelt. Stimson suspected that Churchill
used flattery, cajolery, and all the wily arts of an articulate politician to shake the confidence of F.D.R. in our strategy, while plant-
ing seeds for operations in the Mediterranean—even making the

President believe that he himself, as a great strategist, had fortuitously initiated the idea.

In addition to Secretary Stimson, Assistant Secretary of War Bob Lovett and Chief of the Army Air Force Hap Arnold, gave strong support to the concept of concentration. Brigadier General Pat Tansey of the Logistics Section, Operations Division, General Staff, was another man who labored for BOLERO. Pat Tansey was in constant contact with British opposite numbers pertaining to the allocation of munitions. British plans were of course readily reflected in their logistics requirements—shipping and various types of munitions, war materials drawn from American production. General Tansey kept me informed at all times concerning the logistical implications of British strategy. It was very early obvious to him, particularly (as he explained to me) in his discussions with his British friends who were representing British logistical agencies in Washington, that the British high command and British Prime Minister were determined to conduct operations in the Mediterranean, preferably North Africa, although there was a strong pull for Norway too.

Most of the members of the Strategy and Policy Group of Operations Division, having worked for many months on the two linked plans of BOLERO and ROUNDUP, were firmly convinced that it would be catastrophic if Allied strategy were changed. They felt as I did, that if the forces to be assembled in the British Isles were weakened by operations around the periphery, whether in the Mediterranean, in Syria, or in Norway, the war might drag on for years.

There was criticism offered at the time concerning the preparation of the BOLERO-ROUNDUP plans, criticism involving a consideration of the logistical factors. Some critics argued that American planners had not given sufficient consideration to the ability to equip and maintain, as well as to move, the great armies that were contemplated. But the criticism, we all felt, was misplaced. As I told the British planners in London, the logistical factors had been carefully gone over with the best available experts, both civilian and military, before our departure from Washington in April to present the plans to the British. The President had been assured by responsible officials in war production and manpower agencies and by experts in shipping and the manufacture of landing craft that all of these very important factors had been properly mulled over and analyzed. We thought we had convinced him that the program, as embodied in BOLERO-ROUNDUP, could be carried out.

None of this preparation was to avail, once Churchill put in his appearance late in June at Hyde Park, where he was closeted with Roosevelt and Harry Hopkins. The British Chiefs of Staff who had accompanied the PM to America were shunted on to Washington to confer with the American Chiefs. But what the Chiefs said to each other was largely meaningless, save as the conversations helped the British to get information for their Prime Minister's use.

Here, I felt, was a prime example of British cleverness in influencing American strategical decisions. The Prime Minister would work on Hopkins and Roosevelt. Meanwhile, the British military representatives would talk to their American opposites. They would be reinforced strongly by Sir John Dill, who had won the respect and admiration of the Americans to the point of gaining their complete confidence. In the course of discussions about strategy, the Americans would reveal their objections or affirmations concerning certain proposals. This information would be immediately transmitted by the British military to Mr. Churchill, who then would be in a position to work on Hopkins and Roosevelt—a clever trick and one that could have been worked both ways if Roosevelt and Hopkins had bothered to maintain the proper liaison. But they weren't interested. In this one-sided way American military opinion was conveyed to Roosevelt mostly through British eyes, ears, and expression. It was given the spin, the twist, which Churchill wished to impart to it.

At Hyde Park the PM took off from his distortion of SLEDGE-HAMMER-BOLERO-ROUNDUP. Suddenly SLEDGEHAMMER ceased to be a contingent desperation measure which was to be resorted to only in the case of imminent Russian collapse. In Churchill's mind it had become the action plan for a 1942 which must of necessity see action not only in the air but on the ground.

"No responsible British military authority," said the PM, "had so far been able to make a plan for September, 1942, which had any chance of success unless the Germans become utterly demoralized, of which there is no likelihood." Then, aggressively, Churchill closed in for the kill. Had the Americans a truly viable plan for SLEDGEHAMMER? "If so, what is it? What forces would be employed? At what points would they strike? . . . Who is the officer prepared to command the enterprise? What British forces and assistance are required?"

Then, as a mollifier, Churchill remarked that the British would be happy to welcome a viable SLEDGEHAMMER and "share to the full with their American comrades the risks and sacrifices." But if a SLEDGEHAMMER were to prove impracticable, "what else are we going to do? Can we afford to stand idle in the Atlantic Theater during the whole of 1942? Ought we not to be preparing within the structure of BOLERO some other operation . . . directly or indirectly to take some of the weight off Russia? It is in this setting and on this background that the operation GYMNAST should be studied."

It should be kept steadily in mind that no professional soldiers, either British or American, were present at Hyde Park; consequently, there was no one there to answer the rhetorical questions asked by the Prime Minister. However, I will venture a long-belated reply.

In the first instance, there was no reason why the British should have failed to make arrangements for a landing of six or eight divisions across the Channel in September, 1942, for, as the Prime Minister had previously stated to Roosevelt, they had agreed to do so. Admittedly, there was no American leader who considered such an operation would have any chance of success or even usefulness unless either one of two conditions were involved: (1) utter collapse from within on the Nazi front making it possible to go across the Channel with a small force and maintain ourselves in preparation for further advance; (2) the possibility that Russian resistance was on the verge of folding up, which would justify a sacrificial SLEDGEHAMMER. Under no other circumstances did any American suggest a 1942 cross-Channel landing.

When the PM asked if the Americans had a plan, what forces would be employed, what points they would strike, what landing craft and shipping were available, and so on, he was being a sophist. He knew very well that the forces to be employed would be those made available from British resources and American insofar as we had been able to ship them to the British Isles. They would strike at points selected by the responsible commander and his staff. As for the officer commanding the enterprise, it was clearly understood that if such an operation were undertaken the commander would be British. Churchill was right about a general shortage of landing craft, but there was every guarantee that there would be enough on hand for an emergency expedition by September of 1942. After all, we had plenty of landing craft for the North African invasion, which was staged just two months later. As for ready divisions, the British had thirty-four available in the British Isles by the summer of 1942. They could surely have spared six or eight if a desperation strike had been indicated.

The Prime Minister had said to Roosevelt, "But if a plan could not be found that offered a good chance of establishing a permanent lodgment on the Continent, the British Government is opposed to undertaking the operation at all; on the grounds that it would not help the Russians whatever in their plight, would compromise and expose to Nazi vengeance the French population involved, and would gravely delay the main operation in 1943." In this whole mishmash of assumed premises, not one was in accord with the emergency status of SLEDGEHAMMER. The PM avoided the main premise upon which SLEDGEHAMMER was based, namely to create a diversion. The question of permanent lodgment was beside the point. Nor could the PM have defended the statement that the operation would not help the Russians, whatever their plight. Nor could he have logically maintained that such an attempt would compromise and expose to Nazi vengeance the French population; Hitler wanted no more trouble with the French than was necessary. Nor could the PM have really believed that a SLEDGEHAMMER would gravely delay the main operation in 1943; actually, if successful in keeping the Russians in the war, it would have contributed to the operation in 1943. Furthermore, once we had set foot on the Continent, the American and British people would have insisted on an all-out effort to gain a permanent hold. Our direction would have been set and we would have concentrated our combined efforts on a common aim.

CHAPTER XI

"TORCH" BEGINS TO BURN

TODAY IT IS EASY to be critical of 1941–42 planning. However, one must not forget the atmosphere of those days. At that time (July, 1942) the best available intelligence estimates predicted that the Soviet Union might be knocked out of the war within a short time. The Nazis were making deep thrusts into Russia, capturing thousands of prisoners. If it were true that Russia was in mortal peril, it would be mandatory for us to establish a secure lodgment on the Continent as early as practicable. For a prostrate Russia would have enabled the Nazis to reverse their military juggernaut to the Western Front with a vengeance, leaving only a few divisions in the East to maintain order and to exploit their victory. In such a case the war in Europe probably would have ended in a stalemate. I don't think we could have been militarily defeated by the Nazis; but the struggle by the free nations against tyranny would have been made infinitely more difficult if the Nazis could have exploited the rich resources of the Ukraine, the Urals, and the Caucasus.

In Washington the Combined Chiefs of Staff were deciding against a revival of GYMNAST, a Northwest African invasion, even as Churchill was praising its possibilities in Hyde Park. The Combined Chiefs assembled in Washington produced a memorandum on the military situation for the consideration of the President and the Prime Minister. Their recommendations were against any considerable operation in the Atlantic Theater in 1942, unless the situation in Russia made it necessary or an exceptionally favorable opportunity presented itself. The Combined Chiefs were opposed to Channel Island operations, JUPITER (northern Norway), or any other peripheral operation that would divert attention from BOLERO. Any plan, however, would be preferable to undertaking GYMNAST, especially from the standpoint of dispersing base organization, lines of sea communications, and air strength.

What the Combined Chiefs had to say on this score never reached Hyde Park. There, before Churchill had finished, TORCH (as GYMNAST was shortly to be rebaptized) was already burning brightly. Viewed superficially, the news of the fall of Tobruk gave strong emotional appeal to Churchill's North African ideas. With the British intent upon maintaining their "lifeline of Empire," the importance of defending the Middle East loomed large in London. Everything in the headlines conspired in the Summer of 1942 to make the defense of Suez seem the natural be-all and end-all of British policy. There was the crisis in Egypt, where Rommel was threatening Cairo and Alexandria. Something had to be done, and quickly. Marshall offered to send immediately 300 M-4 tanks, 100 self-propelled 105-mm. guns, and 150 Americans trained to handle tanks and self-propelled artillery; also 4,000 Air Corps personnel. In carrying this offer out, Marshall remarked parenthetically that such assistance to the British in the Middle East would not affect the BOLERO-scheduled build-up of American forces in the United Kingdom. In the last weeks of June, just after Mr. Churchill and his party had returned to England, the British Eighth Army fell back and finally established a last line of defense at El Alamein, only 75 miles west of Alexandria.

The President was much concerned about the British reverses and asked the Joint Chiefs for an estimate as to what might happen if the Germans broke through to Cairo. He was told that the loss of Cairo and Alexandria would undoubtedly mean the loss of the entire Middle East. Suez would go, Cyprus would be isolated, and the rich oil-bearing regions would be prey to an advancing Rommel.

American intelligence experts estimated that the British Eighth Army would probably retreat to the south along the Nile into the Sudan. Marshall warned against an attempt to hold anything east of Suez if Egypt fell into Nazi hands. "A major effort in this region," he said, "would bleed us white." Better to ruin Suez for the Germans by blowing it up than undertake the impossible job of saving it by sending an army around the Cape of Good Hope. The Constantinople Convention insured passage of all ships under conditions of war or peace. Yet apparently we would have ignored this provision if it suited our convenience.

At the time of the retreat to El Alamein we were fortunate in having a shrewd military analyst, Colonel Bonner Fellers, in Cairo as military attaché. An ex-aide to General MacArthur in the Philippines and, in Marshall's words, "a very valuable observer," Fellers wrote eloquent reports which blistered the British desert war tactics and leadership. Fellers wanted the U.S. virtually to take over the African war, suggesting (among other things) that we bring in the 10th Air Force from India. When Tobruk fell, he redoubled both his warnings and repeated his recommendations. Although Marshall still insisted that large-scale Mediterranean operations would have no important bearing on the defeat of Hitler and would, as he stated, entail the liquidation of BOLERO, he weakened to the point of permitting the dispatch of planes to Egypt provided they came out of British allocations from our industry. Even though he disagreed profoundly with Fellers' recommendations on Middle East strategy, he recognized the seriousness of the situation when explaining to President Roosevelt that the loss of Egypt might allow the German and Japanese forces to join in the Indian Ocean.

At one point Marshall said:

> Agreements with the British that we made prior to Pearl Harbor have always assigned the Middle East as exclusively British responsibility: but we all do recognize the critical situation that prevails there and I have informed Sir John Dill that the War Department would assist in every practicable way to improve Middle East defenses . . .
>
> Of course the meat of the situation is the necessity of meeting our responsibilities in the Southwest Pacific, the reinforcement of Alaskan defenses, and above all the gathering of air power in England.

While the Near East was trembling in the balance, the Indian Ocean seemed menaced from the other side. The Japanese were advancing rapidly in Malaya, and their fleet was intermittently bombing Ceylon. Though the Americans were hanging on like limpets to BOLERO and arguing against any frittering away of means, Marshall perforce had to listen while the British built up the case that the Japanese had the capability of passing on through the Indian Ocean to join up with the Germans. The British even pictured the probable loss of Madagascar, to which they had sent a precautionary expedition in early May to seize a base at Diego Suárez. This was dissipation of means at its worst, when the heart of the German war effort was still in the Ruhr, and the Japanese were still faced with the problem of coping with the fast-recuperating Americans in the Pacific.

In April the Japanese sank two British cruisers, the *Dorchester* and the *Cornwall*, and an aircraft carrier, the *Hermes*, off the Malayan coast. The alarmed British asked at once for American help— aircraft carriers and heavy bombers to strengthen the defense of the Indian Theater. Admiral King expressed willingness to permit the aircraft carrier *Ranger* to ferry pursuit planes across the Atlantic to India, or at least to the West Coast of Africa, whence they could fly into India. These developments brought up conflicting claims on the air resources of the U.S. 10th Air Force, which had actually been assigned to General Stilwell for the purpose of supporting his operations. If the 10th Air Force were now diverted to support the British in the Indian Ocean, it would affect adversely Stilwell's campaign in Burma designed to relieve China.

The 10th Air Force was reinforced, and the British were authorized to call upon it if necessary; however, Stilwell still retained control.

While Churchill was threatening to subordinate or sabotage BOLERO by his revival of the North African GYMNAST plan, the cross-Channel strategy was also jeopardized by other demands on our resources. There were, for example, the Chinese. It was often said that T. V. Soong had pipelines to all U.S. Government bureaus; at any rate, he seemed well informed about the commitments our Government had made with Britain as well as with the Soviets. In May and June of 1942 the Chinese gave vent to their dissatisfaction with Western preoccupation with Europe and now particularly with the Middle East. A message from Chiang Kai-shek reached Soong, his representative in Washington, who hurried the message on to the President by way of Harry Hopkins. The Chinese complained that the disposition of American forces and, more important, the distribution of American munitions were worked out in close collaboration with the British but without consulting the Chinese. Moreover, little consideration was given to China in comparison to commitments to Stalin. The text of Chiang's telegram to T. V. Soong is poignantly revealing:

With what has been happening lately, I am afraid you could no longer avoid having a frank heart to heart talk with the President which I am sure he will not misunderstand. As you know, I have to fight continually against demoralizing doubts on the part of my officers who concluded that American attitude toward China is in essence no different from that held by other nations, that both in the all important matters of joint staff conferences and war supplies China is treated not as an equal like Britain and Russia but as a ward.

The President has consistently shown himself to be the one great friend of China and I may say on our part we have been loyally responsive. We have placed Chinese armies under American command and we have shown every readiness to support American policies, sometimes even against our own judgment. All that we have and all that we are we truly and unreservedly contribute to the cause of the united nations.

What a contrast this is to the attitude of the British and the Russians who whenever it concerns their own interests will not make concessions in the general interest so that to this day they will not concede to the United States the direction and the location of the Supreme Military Council. The result of this noncooperation is that there is in existence no organization to formulate and execute over-all strategy and every country looks to its own immediate interests so that the Axis is successfully imposing its grand strategy. What a difference there is between our attitude toward the United States and Britain and Russia.

If in the future the Anglo-American staff is not enlarged to include China and China is kept out of the Munitions Assignments Board, then China will be just a pawn in the game.

Gandhi told me when I visited India, "They will never voluntarily treat us Indians as equals. Why they do not even admit your country to their staff talks." If we are thus treated during the stress of war, what becomes our position at the peace conference. You must insist that we have our own stand and we have our own independent position to uphold.

T. V. Soong added a few points of his own. He concluded:

Finally the Generalissimo feels himself entirely out of touch with the main decisions of strategy which profoundly affect China's future. Whether an offensive will start from Australia, whether it is feasible to hold Burma, what steps are taken to protect the Indian Ocean route, what air force will be sent to India, Burma and China, and all these vital questions, his role [is that of an onlooker].

Down under, the Australians and the New Zealanders were also clamoring for help and were tangentially supported by Admiral King. A real discussion was precipitated by Admiral King's message to Marshall:

In my opinion the strength of the air forces planned to be sent to Australia, to the South Pacific and to the Hawaiian Islands is inadequate to implement surely and effectively the strategic concept on which the detailed plans are based.

While Admiral King did not contest the strategy of concentrating in England for a jugular-vein strike at Hitler, he did resist such concentration while the issue in the Pacific was still touch-and-go. He held that the needs in the Pacific, "although possibly smaller than those of Europe, were more urgent in point of time." King asked not only that the Army send heavy bombers to the South Pacific but also that the Pacific Theater as a whole be given priority over Europe and the Indian Ocean and Middle East theaters with regard to air and army units in general.

I have often speculated as to what might have developed if the United States after the Pearl Harbor tragedy had abandoned its agreed strategy with the British to defeat Germany first and had concentrated the bulk of its resources for the defeat of Japan. Psychologically this strategy would have been better understood and consequently more enthusiastically accepted by the majority of the American people.

At the time of Pearl Harbor the British had proved their ability to withstand the strong Nazi onslaught from the air, and the likelihood of a successful invasion, at least while the Germans lacked undisputed control of the air over the British Isles, was remote. But now, Hitler was busily engaged on the Eastern Front where he had concentrated the bulk of his air and ground forces with a view to crushing the Soviet Communists.

As I conjectured our deployments under these circumstances, we would immediately build up our air and naval forces in the Pacific, sending to the British Isles those resources not required in the operations against the Japanese. Gradually a formidable force, both air and ground, would be assembled in the British Isles to take advantage of a later opportunity to invade Fortress Europe. In the meantime Germany and Russia would continue to chew and mangle each other, and weaken their military strength as well as their war economies. These dispositions did not contemplate the dissipation of forces in nondecisive or subsidiary operations.

Importantly, greatly increased American resources would have been available to sustain the free government in China, not only to improve her military posture vis-à-vis Japan but also to strengthen the position of the National Government against the Communists. China would then not have been so exhausted and demoralized as to succumb to the Communists after the war.

Marshall's recommendation that we shift our main effort to the Pacific, if the British still insisted on diversions in the Mediterranean, brought him severe criticism. His detractors claimed that he pressured England to create a second front on the insistence of Communist Russia. Few were in better position than I to know that these criticisms were unjust. Marshall recommended an early cross-Channel operation because it was militarily sound to concentrate against the enemy when and where he was weak. With Hitler's legions tied down in a struggle to the death against the Russians, obviously the German Western Front could not be strongly defended.

In actual fact, the Administration in Washington was torn apart by the conflicting and urgent demands and requirements in all theaters of war. General Marshall's idea made sense and conformed to sound strategic principles. He felt that the British must be made to realize that if they refused to concentrate their then-limited resources along with ours for decisive effort in Europe, we should have no alternative but to conduct operations with a view to defeating Japan first. Senator Joe McCarthy, who popularized the idea that Marshall was a "second fronter" for sinister reasons, was absolutely wrong. From my own knowledge I can state categorically that the BOLERO-ROUNDUP conception was aimed at winning the war on preferential terms for the West. I was a member of the first joint strategic planning group which prepared the plan in January-February, 1942, and submitted it to the Joint Chiefs of Staff for approval in March the same year.

While Admiral King was emphasizing the Navy's point of view, the Australian Government and General MacArthur were bombarding Washington with fears that a large-scale Japanese attack on Australia was in the offing. Prime Minister Curtin had already asked Churchill for the return of the ANZACS from Egypt to defend Australia. Mr. Curtin also suggested the diversion to Australia of two British divisions that were about to be sent to India; that a British aircraft carrier be detailed to MacArthur's naval forces; and that shipping on the Australia-U.S. run be increased. Curtin tried to put a spin on the ball by adding that he was making his requests at the instance of MacArthur. Churchill flatly said no to the proposals; he insisted that India was in far greater danger than Australia.

In Washington it was considered quite natural that King, Curtin, and MacArthur should all join in making claims for the Pacific. But, after reviewing the whole situation bearing on the plan for concentrating in the British Isles, the staff observed:

> We are presented with a choice, which is: Do we intend to devote ourselves unreservedly to the idea of defeating the European Axis by concentrating our power in the eastern Atlantic, accepting calculated risks in all other theaters; or are we going to permit our resources to be distributed equally throughout the world and give up entirely the thought of decisive offensive action on our part?

Marshall added to the ideas prepared by his staff and came up with the following recommendation to the President:

> If the BOLERO project is not to be our primary consideration, I would recommend its complete abandonment. We must remember that this operation for 1942 depends primarily upon British forces and not our own. They have far more at stake than do we and are accepting very great

hazards to which our own risks are not comparable. They have accepted the BOLERO project with a firm understanding that it would be the prime objective of the United States. If such is not to be the case, the British should be formally notified that the recent London agreement must be cancelled. I present this question to you as Commander in Chief and request that you discuss the matter with Admiral King, General Arnold and me, and give us a formal directive for our future guidance.

Although Stimson had said, back in March, "The Middle East is the very last priority of all that are facing us, we have foreseen for months that the British would be howling for help here that we really should not give them, and I think now is the time to stand pat . . ." * It is understandable that, after the fall of Tobruk, Roosevelt should have felt concern about sustaining the British forces in Egypt. But limited help that would not detract from BOLERO and a full-out Anglo-American campaign in Northern Africa were two entirely different things. It was not mere help for Auchinleck against Rommel that Churchill was proposing at Hyde Park: it was a major military operation that would create a vacuum all its own in the western Mediterranean, drawing in men, matériel, and ships in such quantities as to make the ROUNDUP invasion of Northern Europe in 1943 a vain dream. TORCH would consume more than itself.

The President was as much impressed at Hyde Park with the Prime Minister's presentation of TORCH strategy as were the American military leaders in Washington with the British Chiefs of Staff's denial of GYMNAST's (now called TORCH) claims. Hopkins sent a dispatch from Hyde Park to Marshall and King, directing that they be prepared to discuss the following possibilities with the President, who would return to Washington shortly:

> On the assumption that the Russian Army will be hard-pressed and retreating in July, that the German forces are in August, first dangerously threatening Leningrad and Moscow, and second, have made a serious breakthrough on the southern front threatening the Caucasus.
> On the above assumptions, at what point or points can

* This memorandum was made by H.L.S. (Stimson) in his own handwriting, in pencil, on the memorandum prepared by the Chief of Staff for the President, dated 10 March 1942—"War Department Chief of Staff Army 381 War Plans."

(a) American ground forces prior to September 15, 1942, plan and execute an attack on German forces or in German-controlled areas which can compel the withdrawal of German forces from the Russian front; and (b) British forces in the same area or in a different area aid in the same objective?

The staff in War Plans Division immediately prepared memoranda covering the various points posed by the President's questions. On the first score, the staff called attention to the fact that in the original agreement, the purpose of which was to be prepared to conduct operations in 1942 (SLEDGEHAMMER) only under emergency conditions (the imminent capitulation of the Russians or the sudden crumbling of the Nazis), no detailed operational plan had been made because it was understood clearly by the British and Americans in April that the detailed plans would be made in London. However, the staff expressed its willingness to recommend operational procedures for meeting a sudden turn of events for better or worse on the Continent.

On June 21 the Prime Minister and General Marshall discussed this matter of future plans with Roosevelt at the White House. Harry Hopkins and the British Chief of Staff, Sir Alan Brooke, were both present, along with the Secretary to the British Cabinet, Major General Sir Hastings Ismay, who was Churchill's super-amanuensis. Despite Ismay's tactful mollifying efforts, the meeting was quite acrimonious. After tempers cooled, Ismay drafted a new outline for 1942–43 offensive operations, embodying the Prime Minister's ideas. This version, as presented for consideration by the American Chiefs was:

1. Plans and preparations for operations on the continent of Europe in 1943 on as large a scale as possible are to be pushed forward with all speed and energy. It is, however, essential that the United States and Great Britain should be prepared to act offensively in 1942.
2. Operations in Western Europe in 1942 would, if successful, yield greater political strategic gains than operations in any other theater. Plans and preparations for the operations in this theater are to be pressed forward with all possible speed, energy and ingenuity. The most resolute efforts must be made to overcome the obvious dangers

and difficulties of the enterprise. If a sound and sensible plan can be contrived, we should not hesitate to give effect to it. If on the other hand detailed examination shows that despite all efforts success is improbable, we must be ready with an alternative.

General Ismay then came in with the clincher, the alternative (in reality the substitute) for SLEDGEHAMMER:

3. Provided that political conditions are favorable, the best alternative in 1942 is operation GYMNAST. Accordingly the plans for this operation should be completed in all details as soon as possible. The forces to be employed in GYMNAST would in the main be found from BOLERO units which had not yet left United States.

It should be obvious that this final paragraph embodied quite different ideas from those agreed upon by all the professional military leaders, both British and American, who had worked so arduously on BOLERO-ROUNDUP.

The President continued to express views completely in consonance with Churchill's politically important phrase about "standing idle in 1942." There would be fall elections in the U.S.! Like many others at the time, the President did not take into consideration the great contribution which our rapidly expanding air and naval forces were already making toward weakening the Nazi war effort. Nor were the ground troops idle: multiple thousands were busy preparing bases from which air power with increasing loads of destruction was softening up the enemy. This preparatory phase was very much in the pattern of World War I days, when the Infantry would wait for hours, sometimes days, while the Artillery would hurl shells into the enemy positions and thus create favorable conditions for the Infantry assault. It was misleading to suggest that our troops would be "standing idle in 1942," but Roosevelt was often to be misled. And again, those fall elections!

Before the Ismay version had been formalized as an official document, the American planning staff commented on GYMNAST as follows:

The operation GYMNAST has been studied and restudied. Its advantages and disadvantages are well known. One of the greatest disadvantages is the fact that the operation, even should it be successful, may not and probably will not result in removing one German soldier, tank or plane from the Russian front.

The staff planners had already considered every possible type and location for Anglo-American operations in the European area. They had concluded that the concentration of American forces in the British Isles for a joint invasion across the Channel afforded the greatest opportunity to strike a decisive blow at the enemy. They had reaffirmed that only a cross-Channel invasion, carried out boldly and aggressively, could cause withdrawal of German forces from the Eastern Front. "Pin-prick" operations would obtain no worthwhile results, and would dissipate our means.

In retrospect, Churchill's ability to carry the day for GYMNAST —or TORCH—is amazing, given the weight of articulate military opinion against it. The American Chief of Naval Operations, Admiral King, argued valiantly against a North African operation in 1942. He did not want to open a subsidiary front which would absorb shipping and other vital resources needed for truly remunerative operations. An operation in North Africa would require the withdrawal of combat ships from the Pacific, thus increasing the risks already being accepted there. King expressed his suspicions concerning British intentions: "that in his opinion the British had never been in wholehearted accord with operations on the Continent as proposed by the U.S." He said to me privately, "The British will never go into Europe except behind a Scotch bagpipe band."

It was revealed, surprisingly by Sir Charles Little of the British Navy, representing Sir Dudley Pound, First Lord of the Admiralty, that his chief would agree with Admiral King in opposing GYM-NAST, since the naval situation in the Atlantic was already difficult enough without taking on new commitments. A précis of the British Chiefs of Staff attitude, as expressed in Washington in 1942, would indicate that most of them agreed with the objections to GYMNAST (TORCH) raised by the American Chiefs of Staff. In brief, the professionals were predominantly against the operation. Marshall summed it all up by saying: "Large-scale operations on the Continent in 1943 would clearly not be possible unless all efforts were concentrated now on their preparation. If we changed our plan now and opened up another front, we should probably achieve nothing."

When it became apparent that the chances for BOLERO-ROUNDUP were rapidly diminishing, Marshall proposed the alternative, as Eisenhower passed the word on to the British, of "turning our backs upon the eastern Atlantic and going full out as quickly as possible against Japan." On July 13, General Marshall asked his planners for a careful analysis of the implications of GYMNAST in terms of forces and shipping, and also the most favorable results that might be expected if the operation were successfully conducted. The following questions were included in his memorandum:

1. What is there in the outline of the Pacific plan prepared on Sunday, July 12, that might be compromised in favor of providing more means to the UK?
2. What would be the effect of the Pacific plan on allocation of landing craft? What has already gone to England? What can or should be sent to the Pacific, including Alaska?
3. What was the effect of the cut in the estimate of production for vehicles? Is that cut definite and final or could the situation be improved?
4. Are the landing craft already sent to England sufficient for commando operations?
5. If the British give us tonnage, can we afford to send them more divisions? If so, how many?
6. What changes in schedule of airplane deliveries would be effected by a change in the basic plan? Figure out on a time basis what the schedule of delivery of airplanes would be to England and to the Pacific area.

It was memoranda like this emanating from the facile mind of our Chief of Staff which caused the officers in my Strategy and Policy Group of OPD to spend many sleepless hours in the Pentagon. In this instance, Marshall wanted answers by Thursday morning, July 16. We went to work feverishly in conjunction with Somervell's logistics experts in the Services of Supply. But it quickly developed that President Roosevelt had ideas of his own. On July 14 the President sent word to Marshall that he did not approve the basic alternative and that he would confer with him Wednesday morning, July 15. Furthermore, he had definitely decided to send Marshall, King, and Harry Hopkins to London at once. On the afternoon of July 14, a meeting of the JCS was held. I made the following notes:

> It was indicated that unquestionably the President would require military operations in Africa. The relative merits of operations in Africa, particularly in northwest Africa and in the Middle East, were discussed. All agreed to the many arguments previously advanced among military men in the Army and Navy that operations in the Pacific would be the alternative if SLEDGEHAMMER or BOLERO were not accepted wholeheartedly by the British. However, there was a stated appreciation of the fact that apparently our political leader would require major military operations *this year in Africa.*

The first point that President Roosevelt made after his return to Washington from Hyde Park was that he opposed any idea of delivering an ultimatum to our allies, the British. He said it would be a serious strategic blunder to devote our effort to the defeat of Japan at this time, before our Navy had been built up. Curiously, he used the same objections to a Japanese campaign that we had been using against GYMNAST. It would not bring about the defeat of Germany. It would be uneconomical, a waste of power. Said Roosevelt:

> It is of the utmost importance that we appreciate that defeat of Japan does not defeat Germany and that American concentration against Japan this year or in 1943 increases the chance of completing German domination of Europe and Africa. On the other hand, it is obvious that the defeat of Germany or the holding of Germany in 1942 or in 1943 means probable eventual defeat of Germany in the European and African theaters and in the Near East. The defeat of Germany means the defeat of Japan, probably without firing a shot or losing a life.

In his instructions to Hopkins, Marshall, and King before they flew off to England, Roosevelt gave evidence of his own determination. Here was his admonition: "It is of the highest importance that U.S. ground troops be brought into action against the enemy in 1942."

The President outlined several operations for discussion in London: (1) proceed with SLEDGEHAMMER and stay in France if they can; (2) get all U.S. troops in action as quickly as possible; (3) proceed in all other theaters as now planned; (4) keep up aid to Russia but via Basra. These proposals were seemingly flexible, but the President knew what was in Churchill's mind.

As another alternative, the President proposed to the JCS: (1) abandon SLEDGEHAMMER for 1942; (2) slow up BOLERO in 1943 for the coming three months; (3) take all planes now headed from U.S. to England and reroute them to (a) the Middle East and Egypt, (b) Southwest Pacific, giving the majority to the Middle East and Egypt; (4) send five divisions to England slowly; (5) send five divisions to the Middle East fast; (6) speed up BOLERO preparations by October so that BOLERO-ROUNDUP will be ready April, 1943; (7) keep up aid to Russia but via Basra.

The American Joint Chiefs of Staff, accompanied by Harry Hopkins, arrived in London on July 18. There were conferences first with the resident Americans, Admiral Stark, General Eisenhower, and General Spaatz. The Americans worked hard to convince the British Chiefs of Staff that a SLEDGEHAMMER which had been worked out by Eisenhower's staff providing for a seizure of Cherbourg and the Cotentin Peninsula would achieve its effect of helping the Russians. But the British would have none of it. After hearing this, which surely did not surprise him, Roosevelt directed his representatives to agree on one of five alternatives (in order of preference):

1. A combined British-American operation against North Africa.

2. An American seizure of French Morocco.

3. Combined operations against northern Norway.

4. A reinforcement of Egypt.

5. A strengthening of Iran and the southern supply route to Russia.

Faced with such an array of unappetizing alternatives, Marshall and King swallowed all their previous hard words and went for GYMNAST (TORCH). Marshall now realized that a North African invasion was the only operation that would have the full support of both the President and the Prime Minister. He also realized that, for political reasons, a democratic nation at war must fight at least one major campaign a year. North Africa was preferable to the Middle East because it would not involve long lines of communications and would not require the integrating of expeditionary forces.

And, as the returning officials explained to Roosevelt, North Africa offered the most promising objective in case a dangerous weakening in Soviet resistance forced the Allies to abandon the build-up for a strong cross-Channel attack in 1943.

In accepting North Africa, Marshall and King could not resist one parting shot:

> Nothing developed in the discussions with the British clear through 22 July which changed our considered opinion that Great Britain is the only area from which the combined strength of united nations can be brought to bear against our principal enemy, Germany, so that no avoidable reduction in our preparation for ROUNDUP should be considered as long as there remains any reasonable possibility of its successful execution.

The British and Americans soon evolved the joint operational plan now called TORCH. The Chiefs of Staff agreed on the appointment of an American as over-all commander. When Hopkins asked Roosevelt for suggestions about the date for the invasion, the President sent word that the landing should be not later than October 30. Once again the national elections in the first week of November loomed prominently in F.D.R.'s initial step into the field of strategy. Politician that he was, Roosevelt recognized the great impetus that would be given to his Administration at the polls if he could greet voters with an announcement that a highly successful military operation had just been pulled off against the enemy.

When Roosevelt summoned Stimson, Admiral William D. Leahy, General Arnold, and General McNarney to give them an outline of developments in London, wise General McNarney reported at once to Marshall that the President's decision "had been reached before we arrived. There was no discussion as to the relative merits of his decision and the plan recommended." According to McNarney, the President said he "could see no reason why the withdrawal of a few troops in 1942 would prevent BOLERO in 1943."

Thus with Roosevelt supporting Churchill, TORCH had already been set. However, General Marshall, who still recognized the dangers of a diversion in the Mediterranean, said that he personally did not consider the decision to be irrevocable. He raised the old point, that a vote for TORCH meant the end of ROUNDUP. Obviously, he could not hope to prevent TORCH. But he did want to force a recognition of realities.

When Admiral King made one last attempt to call TORCH into question, Roosevelt showed impatience. On the evening of July 30 the President concluded the strategy deliberations started by Churchill in June. According to Harry Hopkins:

> The President stated very definitely that he as Commander in Chief had made the decision that TORCH would be undertaken at the earliest possible date. We considered that this operation was now our principal objective and the assembling of means to carry it out should take precedence over other operations as, for instance, BOLERO. He mentioned the desirability of sending a message immediately to the Prime Minister advising him that he, the President, as Commander in Chief, had made this decision and requested his agreement since we are now, as far as the record is concerned, committed to the provisions of CCS 94 [the paper number which the Combined Chiefs of Staff had been working on in London the past two weeks], which calls for the final decision to be made by September 15th.

The British planners proposed TORCH ground forces at ten or twelve divisions and proposed initial landings on a wide front in the Mediterranean, eastward at least as far as Algiers. The operation would be timed to secure the coast of Algeria and Tunisia before winter closed in on the Russian front. I should like to comment here that if twelve divisions could be assembled for North Africa in 1942, it at least argues convincingly that we could have assembled a sizable cross-Channel force for ROUNDUP in 1943. Back in Washington we were all very much put out. We had never given up hope that something would develop which would make TORCH unnecessary. We planners in the lower echelons more or less reflected General Marshall's own ideas. At one point Marshall said: "The decision to mount the operation has been made but it is still subject to the vicissitudes of war."

All of us felt with Marshall that the decision to invade North Africa was a radical change, practically a repudiation of the overall strategy that had been agreed to earlier by the British. We all foresaw that TORCH would open the door to continuing operations in the Mediterranean area. Knowing our disappointment and apprehensions, Sir John Dill, the British representative in Washington who kept his ear to the ground, wrote a note to Marshall:

> I am just a little disturbed about TORCH. For good or ill it has been accepted and therefore I feel that we should go at it with all possible enthusiasm and give it absolute priority. If we don't it won't succeed. From what our planners tell me, there are some of your people who feel that TORCH is not a good operation. That, of course, must be a matter of opinion, but those who are playing a part in mounting the operation must be entirely whole-hearted about it, or they cannot give it all the help it should have and overcome all the difficulties that will arise.

Sir John Dill ended his letter by saying: "All I aim to add is to insure that we all think alike—and enthusiastically."

Marshall talked to me about this letter, realizing that I was one of the persons to whom Sir John referred. I said that I felt it my duty as a planner to continue to examine the implications of TORCH. General Marshall replied that he agreed with Sir John, that the officers actually charged with executing TORCH must lend their complete support to the operation. However, Marshall went on to say there must also be absolute candor on the part of his planners. In short, Marshall told me that he was not particularly concerned with Dill's final plea that "all think alike—and enthusiastically." To Dill he said: "You may be assured that U.S. planners will enthusiastically and effectively support decisions made by the Commander in Chief."

I was having my own troubles with the British planners at this time. On one occasion I was apparently misquoted to Sir John Dill, who reported it to Marshall. I told Marshall that Dill's information was not correct. I received Marshall's permission to wire my room so that I could make a recording of conversations held with my British opposites in the future. From that time on, whenever I had occasion to discuss official matters of importance with any foreign representative, I could turn on a recording machine with my knee and catch everything that was said. On one occasion I played back a recorded discussion with the British planners for General Marshall, so that he could hear them making unreasonable demands, while using big names like Roosevelt and Hopkins to intimidate me or influence my action. Marshall was extremely interested and advised me to record all future discussions, which I gladly did. Later, when I explained to Sir John Dill what I had done, he was surprised, but sympathetic, too.

Sir John was a gentle genius at covering the waterfront in Washington for King and Country and for the ever present (in person or in spirit) Winston Churchill. During the critical war days he insinuated himself into the confidence of almost every important American. He had ways of learning about the most confidential and top-level discussions taking place. He enjoyed perhaps the most preferred position of any foreigner in our nation's capital. His diplomatic skill, tact, and calm philosophical manner were all disarming. I was always mindful of the fact that his first loyalty was to England. Although I admired and respected him, I tried never to forget for a moment that day and night his efforts were concentrated on furthering British interests. When British interests contravened American, I simply resisted Dill's maneuvers. Unfortunately there was no one in a high American position who seemed as alert to American self-interest as Dill was to British, except possibly Admiral King. On more than one occasion I got the impression that our top men were kowtowing and genuflecting to foreign representatives, both British and Russian. The attitude of "Give them everything, no questions asked" made the job difficult for dedicated men in the lower echelons who were doing their utmost to protect America's interests.

Dill kept the Prime Minister fully informed of his diplomatic maneuvers in the United States. He was a first-rate reporter of our feelings, as his message demonstrates:

15 July 42

FIELD MARSHALL DILL TO PRIME MINISTER

Marshall leaves for England with Harry Hopkins and King tomorrow evening.

Broadly, objections to GYMNAST are: (a) It would necessitate drawing naval forces from Pacific, particularly carriers, which are urgently required for operations U.S. have in hand there, and of which you are aware. (b) It would necessitate new line of sea communications, which they would have difficulty in maintaining together with other commitments. (c) To strike only at Casablanca, where landings are difficult and facilities for maintenance poor, would withdraw nothing from Russian front, and to strike inside Mediterranean, at, say, Algiers, and even Bizerta, would be too hazardous, particularly in view of ease with which Axis could cut communication through Straits of Gibraltar. (d) GYMNAST would build up into such a large commitment as to destroy any possibility of ROUNDUP in 1943.

Vague plans for action in Pacific have been put to [the] President . . .

All these activities would use up shipping at present earmarked for BOLERO, and would reduce the U.S. air forces sent to Britain by some two-thirds . . . It is quite clear that Pacific ventures can give no immediate relief to Russia, and will be slow to obtain anything decisive against Japan.

There is no doubt that Marshall is true to his first love, but he is convinced that there has been no real drive behind the European project. Meetings are held, discussions take place, and time slips by. Germany will never again be so occupied in the East as she is today, and if we do not take advantage of her present preoccupation we shall find ourselves faced with a Germany so strong in the West that no invasion of the Continent will be possible. We can then go on pummelling each other by air, but the possibility of a decision will have gone. Marshall feels, I believe, that if a great businessman were faced with pulling off this *coup* or going bankrupt he would strain every nerve to pull off the *coup*, and would probably succeed.

King's war is against the Japanese.

I have a feeling (based on nothing more than the American thought that the Pacific could be a substitute for BOLERO and the strong American desire to build up an army of seven million) that there are highly placed Americans who do not believe that anything better than a stalemate with Germany is possible.

May I suggest with all respect that you must convince your visitors that you are determined to beat the Germans, that you will strike them on the continent of Europe at the earliest possible moment even on a limited scale, and that anything which detracts from this main effort will receive no support from you at all? Marshall believes that your first love is GYMNAST, just as his is BOLERO, and that with the smallest provocation you always revert to your old love. Unless you can convince him of your unswerving devotion to BOLERO everything points to a complete reversal of our present agreed strategy and the withdrawal of America to a war of her own in the Pacific, leaving us with limited American assistance to make out as best we can against Germany.

I couldn't have presented the American position better if I had tried. One wonders where Dill got this information, which certainly would be considered classified.

The truly depressing thing about TORCH was that, even as it was being accepted, the danger of a junction of the Germans and the Japanese in the Indian Ocean had completely evaporated. The fall of Tobruk had been a momentary worry. But it was more than compensated for by the sudden weakening of the Japanese position in the Pacific. The American intelligence people had been able to intercept Japanese messages about concentrating a carrier force in the Central Pacific, either against Dutch Harbor in Alaska or against Midway. When it was finally determined that the strike would be against Midway, Marshall and King assembled a striking force of bombers in the Hawaiian Islands. Early in June these bombers had won the first clear American victory. For three days a struggle ensued between air and naval forces, and the American Navy won a gallant victory decided almost entirely by sea-based airpower. This reduced the Japanese superiority in aircraft carriers and was a turning point in the Pacific war. This victory coupled with the earlier success in the Coral Sea, meant that Japanese offensive capabilities in the Pacific had been reduced to nil. Furthermore, the threat to India and the Middle East had definitely been removed. The British could no longer logically play up such a threat as they had in the past in order to obtain resources from American production for their African ventures.

The die had been cast, however, before the full implications of Midway had dawned on the authors of TORCH. We were committed to North Africa. This might have been digested without danger to ROUNDUP; but our "feet were on the ladder," and North

Africa led to Sicily. One more rung on the ladder, and Sicily led to the Italian boot.

True, the campaigns in the Mediterranean "blooded" some of our divisions; but most of these continued to be used in Italy. The majority of the divisions which stormed the beaches in Normandy in 1944 with the *sang-froid* of veterans had no combat experience. True also, the capture of Tunisia and Sicily released shipping to the Atlantic which had hitherto been tied up by the demands of the long route to the East around the Cape of Good Hope. Nevertheless, I for one still think of the Mediterranean as a trap which prolonged the war in Europe by a year. It was a side show, and it cost many unnecessary lives.

CHAPTER XII

CASABLANCA

IN MANY WAYS CASABLANCA, the high-level conference held in French Morocco in January of 1943, was the "watershed" conference of the war.

It was here, in what had become a behind-the-lines setting made secure by the prodigious success of TORCH, that World War II became politicalized in an utterly irretrievable manner.

First, the decision was made to push the impetus of TORCH beyond its only legitimate strategic justification, which was to clear the Mediterranean and release Allied shipping for use in the Atlantic. Second, Casablanca gave official Anglo-American sanction to unconditional surrender, that most sterile of war aims.

Considered together, the decision to climb further rungs on the Mediterranean ladder and the promulgation of the doctrine of unconditional surrender almost certainly lengthened the war by a full year. Unconditional surrender meant that anti-Hitler Germans, the vast legion of the lukewarm, had no recourse but to fight to the end. The decision to invade Sicily (which was to lead insensibly to the further employment of Allied armies up the tortuous spine of Italy) inevitably sidetracked the main Normandy commitment, the really decisive operation, until 1944.

The Casablanca decisions were made without benefit of Stalin. But even though the Russians were not consulted, the strategy adopted by the Allied leaders played right into Soviet hands. Postponement of ROUNDUP meant that Anglo-American forces could hardly hope to beat the Russians into Central Europe. And unconditional surrender precluded the possibility that an anti-Hitler *coup* might be successfully staged in time to permit the Germans to lay down their arms in the West while the Russians were still considerably short of the Vistula River.

It is interesting to note that the head of the Soviet Union, Generalissimo Stalin, never had to lift a finger to make things come out his own way. He attended none of the early strategic confabulations of the Allied leaders. Long before the U.S. entered the war, Roosevelt and Churchill exchanged views and made commitments off the coast of Newfoundland aboard a battleship. A few months later, Pearl Harbor brought the two world leaders together in our nation's capital. In the interim there were many Anglo-American meetings to discuss the co-ordination of projected joint operations against the enemy. These conferences were held in London and Washington; they were attended by Army and Navy officers, by representatives of production and shipping agencies, and by political henchmen of the President. This did not involve the State Department, for Secretary Hull was excluded almost entirely from information pertaining to joint planning between British and Americans both before and after Pearl Harbor. The President had announced that he was his own State Department.

The United States had been at war for six months when the PM and his staff, making their second visit to Washington, assumed the strategic reins without appearing to do so. Henceforward, the virtuoso Churchill led the Anglo-American orchestra, although we furnished practically all of the instruments and most of the musicians.

TORCH was a wasteful side show. But it was, tactically speaking, a grand success. By December it was obvious that the leaders would have to meet to decide the next Allied step. The basic issues would soon stand out in bold relief. The question posed itself as follows: Should we stop operations now in the Mediterranean and continue with the strategy agreed to at an earlier date, assembling maximum strength in the British Isles with the idea of invading Northern Europe in 1943, or should we continue operations in the Mediterranean with the ultimate objective of invading the Balkans?

In the first week in December President Roosevelt broached another meeting on the highest level, with Stalin participating. Churchill suggested foregathering in Iceland but the President reacted in a humorous way, saying "I prefer a comfortable oasis to the raft at Tilsit." This bit of levity turned the attention of everybody toward a warmer clime, perhaps Cairo or some other location in Africa where the climate would be more moderate in December. Eventually Casablanca, on the west coast of French Morocco, was decided upon. Stalin was invited, but said he was too preoccupied to accept. His troops were locked in a fight to death or victory in what was to prove the most decisive battle of the war, Stalingrad. The Germans had penetrated deeply eastward toward Stalingrad and the Caucasus where they were fighting desperately against heavy odds. They had overextended their lines of communication. The weather was frigid and they faced a seemingly endless stream of reinforcements brought up by their adversaries who were used to the rigors of a Russian winter.

Our departure for Morocco was shrouded in secrecy, yet at a small dinner party two nights beforehand I overheard the able columnist of the Washington *Star*, Constantine Brown, telling a U.S. Senator that there would soon be a world conference in Casablanca. The Senator asked Brown where Casablanca was located. Brown, with a smile, suggested that the Senator ask me. I moved away but wondered of course about our security measures inasmuch as this conference would mark the first time that the President had been out of the United States since we entered the war. Incidentally, the Casablanca journey also marked the first time Roosevelt had flown since he had become President. Unfortunately, the Chairman of the Joint Chiefs of Staff, Admiral Leahy, was stricken with bronchitis and could not accompany the President.

With ample relevant planning data prepared by my fine staff, I went to the Washington airport on January 9. I traveled in Admiral King's plane along with General Somervell, Admiral C. M. Cooke (the Navy planner), and Commander Libbey, Admiral King's Flag Secretary. In General Marshall's plane were General Arnold and Sir John Dill; my good friend Brigadier Dykes; Colonel McCarthy, Marshall's aide-de-camp; and General Johnny Deane, the Secretary of the General Staff. The two planes flew direct to Borinquen Field, near the northwestern tip of Puerto Rico.

En route to Belém, Brazil, from Puerto Rico, I saw the Southern

Cross for the first time since I had left the Philippines nine years earlier. The trip was the first in his long seadog's life that had ever taken Admiral King across the Equator. This astonished me and, I think, everybody else aboard the plane. Our pilot, Captain Milo Campbell, turned over the controls to the Admiral as we crossed the "line," near one of the mouths of the Amazon. Each passenger was later presented with a certificate precisely as if we had crossed the Equator by water. We were now airborne members of the ancient order of shellbacks.

The flight from Puerto Rico to a spot on the hump of Brazil, near the mouth of the Para River, took only a few hours. We landed at a fine field near Belém. Approximately 250 officers and enlisted men of United States forces were stationed at the airfield where we spent the night. The air was sultry and reminded me of the Philippines. Admiral Cooke and I took a short hike into the Brazilian jungles adjoining the airfield. Brazilian troops were to be seen everywhere guarding the planes and maintenance facilities or manning the anti-aircraft guns and searchlights around the landing field. When we motored into the nearby town, Belém, the nine-mile route was entirely lined by troops. Instead of facing in toward the automobile, they faced the jungle with their backs toward us as we motored along. When one thought about it, this made sense for these soldiers were there to protect our President and an assailant would logically approach from the tropical undergrowth on either side of the road. In Belém, the people, buildings, and general atmosphere resembled Manila or the native city of Panama.

While motoring along, I asked the driver to stop the car for I saw a band of ants, literally trillions of these red insects, energetically moving in a column approximately two feet wide. *Rats, Lice and History*, that excellent book by Hans Zinsser, came to mind. Nazis, Communists, and history pre-empted my time and effort now. But many times since then I have recovered that sight—those ants which I am told consume everything in their path.

The next day we proceeded south to Natal before crossing the Atlantic at nighttime. Our take-off was about five minutes after that of General Marshall's plane, which we could see heading to the east. We were bound for Ascension Island in the middle of the Atlantic. I understood that about two hours out we would meet a plane carrying Patrick J. Hurley back to the U.S. from Russia and the Middle East.

Captain Campbell invited me forward to the control cabin. I sat for about three hours in the co-pilot's seat. It was a wonderful experience—a magic carpet hurtling through space at 200 miles an hour; 9,000 feet below, an ominous black sea; above, clear sky and brilliant stars.

Early in the morning on January 12, 1943, we landed in Africa. As we were approaching the coast, the pilot called my attention to several star shells, which might be coming up from a ship in distress. He explained that we could not investigate as German submarines often fired them hoping to decoy our planes into circling within range of their anti-aircraft guns. He reported that we had already lost several planes mysteriously, perhaps by such a ruse. The pilot was quite certain that this was a German submarine.

At Bathurst, Gambia, where we made our African landfall, we were met by American Brigadier General C. R. Smith, a highly competent airline executive who was on wartime assignment with the Air Transport Command. In a very short time he had established an effective organization throughout Africa. There were American guards all about, rehearsing, as I was told, security measures for the arrival of President Roosevelt. The natives appeared emaciated —unusually tall and skinny—but they carried themselves erect and their muscles gleamed through shiny ebony skin.

After breakfast in an officers' mess concealed in a niche of the jungle, we took off for Marrakech and Casablanca. As we flew northward we enjoyed a splendid view of Dakar and the Canary Islands. General Smith accompanied us and related many interesting experiences about the operation of a modern air transport service in Africa. Finally our plane swung in an easterly direction toward the Atlas Mountains, which looked very much like the Rockies with jagged, snow-capped peaks. We landed at Marrakech and were taken to a beautiful villa which belonged to an American, a Mrs. Moses Taylor. The building had carved cedar doors, gorgeous draperies, and exquisite furnishings, inlaid pearl everywhere, beautiful grounds and tropical flowers in a formal garden. My room had a large connecting bathroom, all tile inlaid, with a sunken tub effect, almost large enough for a swim. The American Vice Consul, Mr. Pender, took several members of our party on a tour of the city.

It was really fascinating to see—at times nauseating to smell. The women concealed their faces with veils, their bodies with flowing robes. The men wore the traditional fez. There was a sprinkling of Arabs in long white gowns. We visited the market, which is the meeting place for all classes of people. There were weird noises of magicians and entertainers; and there were odors that I had previously associated only with China. Churchill later referred to Marrakech as the "Paris of the Sahara."

This was a delightful interlude in the grim and sometimes prosaic business of planning the war. The following morning we hopped on to Casablanca, only an hour by plane to the north of Marrakech. The British and the American Chiefs of Staff and their planning staffs were lodged in the beautiful Anfa Hotel, a few miles south of the city. The PM and the President, along with close members of their respective entourages, occupied attractive villas in close proximity to the hotel. A temporary barbed-wire barricade shut off the entire area; there were guards everywhere.

The American Joint Chiefs met on Wednesday, January 13, in the afternoon, with Admiral Cooke present to help Admiral King. I was on hand to assist Generals Marshall and Arnold. I had already noted the presence of swarms of British officers of all ranks, representing the three services. There were several echelons of planners. Very early, it became apparent that Admiral Cooke and I, the sole representatives from the military planning agencies back in the States, were going to have a tough row to hoe. However, we believed thoroughly in our strategy, and we were so close in our thinking that we could in clear conscience support each other at all points. I believe we also had the full confidence of our chiefs. The unknown quantity was the President. Could Churchill continue to lead him down the garden path?

At the first meeting Admiral King outlined his ideas concerning global warfare. He thought that we Americans should present basic strategic concepts to the British in the hope of compelling a decision on emphasis and the allocation of resources as between Germany and Japan. While en route to Casablanca, Admiral King had talked to me and, at great length, to Admiral Cooke about the build-up of Allied forces in North Africa. What purpose, he asked, would be served if we were to continue operations in that area?

I told King that in my judgment we had already accomplished

the purpose of TORCH, namely to deny French North Africa to the Nazis and to drive out the enemy from Africa. We had already seized naval and air bases along the coast and were establishing additional facilities that could be used for protection of communications between Gibraltar and Cairo. Having done this, it was my conviction that we should cease to pour forces into the area. In fact, I added, these were the objectives of the TORCH operation as repeatedly stated by the British. We should return to our preparations for decisive operations against the Germans by assembling all possible means in the British Isles for an early cross-Channel onslaught. I was surprised when King asked if General Marshall agreed with those views. I assured him that he did, without any reservations whatsoever.

Was I right or wrong about sticking to the original American concept of concentration at the decisive point? I might say here that once TORCH had been pushed through to success it could have been absorbed into the larger pattern of BOLERO-ROUNDUP. Luckily, recalcitrant Franco would not permit the Germans to undertake operations in Spain to close the "defile" at Gibraltar. TORCH had restored relatively secure sea communications through the Mediterranean, thus releasing for other purposes much of the shipping that had been going 5,890 miles around the Cape of Good Hope instead of 2,200 miles through the Mediterranean. Allied troops and commanders had gained valuable battle experience and also training in amphibious operations. Moreover, pressure on Egypt had obviously been relieved.

All of these achievements were recognized and appreciated by the Americans. So far we had not prejudiced the cross-Channel operation scheduled for 1943. But the trouble, as I was soon to learn, was that the British had never had any intention of executing a major cross-Channel operation if they could avoid it. They were determined to strike at the so-called soft underbelly and penetrate the Balkans. They now started to argue that the Mediterranean lines of communication would be made much more secure if we established air bases on Sicily or Sardinia. The Americans held that we could easily neutralize the Italian boot and Sicily with our air and navy supremacy from bases that would now be available to us along the African littoral as a result of TORCH. We still hoped to execute ROUNDUP while the bulk of German forces were tied down by the Russians far to the east.

In most of the British accounts of the war, three "unknowns" are offered as justification for postponing the cross-Channel strategy to 1944. There was, first, the "unknown" of aviation—could Fortress Europe have been sufficiently softened by aerial bombardment for an invasion in mid-1943? Second, there was the question of availability of combat-tested, or blooded, troops. And third, there was the matter of landing craft.

It would have been difficult at Casablanca to anticipate appeals to the unknowns and refute them in advance. But the fact is that the thousands of planes that were diverted to Mediterranean and Pacific operations in 1942 and 1943 could have been used to pound Fortress Europe as contemplated in BOLERO—the preparatory, or preliminary, phase to ROUNDUP. As for the argument about blooded troops, it is significant that the vast majority of the divisions which took part in the initial OVERLORD landings in 1944 had no previous combat experience. The untested troops fought gallantly, very much like veterans, which is a tribute to those responsible for their training and to their valiant commanders.

The argument about landing craft is a little more difficult to counter. But as the war progressed I noticed a curious distribution of landing craft, personnel carriers, ships, and cargo vessels. I discovered in later years that the preponderance of personnel carriers, i.e., transports capable of being combat loaded (ATAs) and cargo ships capable of carrying combat loads (AKAs and LSTs), were out in the Pacific Theater in 1943. The majority of the LCIs (Infantry Landing Craft) were in the European Theater. After reviewing the BOLERO-OVERLORD concept for the invasion of Europe with responsible production officials, I was assured that the landing craft both by type and numbers would be available from American production by the summer of 1943; otherwise there would have been no justification for being a stickler for BOLERO-ROUNDUP.

Since, by 1943, a large number of personnel ships were in the Pacific, operating in an area which had been designated as defensive, it is obvious that we weren't concentrating for our original purpose. Now, why? I can't find anything in writing about this, but I did learn in conversations with our Naval officers, including Admiral King, that they were very dubious about British intentions in Europe; and some expressed the conviction that the British would persist in conducting periphery-pecking operations in the Mediterranean to improve their over-all Empire position. It was clearly in Admiral King's mind that the British hoped the Germans would be so weakened by the Russians, their own naval blockade, and the bomber offensive, that the Allies would eventually be able to land on the Continent without fighting for a lodgment. Inasmuch as this was King's assessment of British strategy, why wouldn't he be justified in diverting forces, including landing craft, to the Pacific where our forces were confronted by an aggressive enemy striving to consolidate his earlier gains?

Lamentably, it was not until the Cairo and Teheran Conferences in December, 1943, that OVERLORD was rebaptized and was granted top priority in the landing-craft schedule.

At Casablanca, back at the Anfa Hotel after our first session with the British, Admiral King forthrightly outlined his views on Allied strategy. He emphasized that only a slight proportion—my notes indicate that he mentioned 15 per cent—of our total resources was allocated at the time to holding the Japanese in the Pacific. In his judgment this was not enough to prevent Japan from consolidating the gains she had already made; indeed, she might pass over into dangerously offensive operations against Australia or India.

General Marshall's reaction to King's view on this score made complete sense. After their terrific mauling by Nimitz at Midway, the Japanese would no longer be able to conduct extensive operations. Under these circumstances, General Marshall felt that our submarines and combined Army and Navy air strikes could successfully restrict the Japanese and prevent them from consolidating their positions.

The following day at the Combined Chiefs of Staff meeting, Sir Alan Brooke opened by making a comprehensive review of the world situation. He pointed out that, in the judgment of the British, the Pacific enemy was definitely on the defensive, and more or less confirmed Marshall's concept of operations in that area. Continuing his résumé of British thinking, Sir Alan noted that Allied strategy was developing very favorably against the Germans and that it might be possible to achieve victory in the European Theater before the end of 1943. This was encouraging to all on the American side of the conference table, but he let the cat out of the bag a little later by saying we could "definitely" count on getting into Europe in 1944.

The British all felt that air operations against the fortress of Europe should be stepped up to maximum proportions. There was a difference of opinion about the merits of daylight bombing. Said Churchill, after talking things over with General Eaker:

> I put these points to Eaker who knew my view and was much troubled by it. He stated the case for the daylight fortress bomber with powerful earnestness and pointed out that immense preparations had already been made in England—the transfer of many squadrons from America, the piling up of men, materials etc. I pointed out in reply that here we were in the beginning of 1943, the Americans had been in the war for more than a year, they had all the time been building up their air power in England but so far they had not thrown a single bomb on Germany by their daylight methods except perhaps on one occasion when a very short raid was protected by British fighters. We had been led to believe at Washington the year before that in four or five months very heavy deliveries of bombs would be taking place by American aircraft but nothing had happened though an immense expenditure of resources had been made.

In Churchill's comment to Eaker, recalled in *The Hinge of Fate,* there was something sophistical, to say the least. It is perfectly true that American military authorities had estimated that American bombers would be operating with ever-increasing intensity against the Germans on the Continent beginning about the middle of 1942. But the Americans did not then know that there would be diversions, initiated by and insisted upon by the British, which would inevitably compel the dispatch of bombers, fighters, and related air effort into the Mediterranean.

Despite the disagreement over day and night bombing, it was reassuring to hear the British talk about air concentration against Germany. It was at this point, however, that Sir Alan Brooke chose to drop the big bombshell, aimed not at the Germans in Europe but at the American conferees at Casablanca. The bombshell was Sir Alan's stated conviction that continued operations in the Mediterranean offered the best chance of helping the Russians by compelling the Germans to dissipate their resources in the West. Specifically, Sir Alan Brooke suggested that we should do everything possible now to knock Italy out of the war and to persuade the Turks to come in on our side.

Anticipating General Marshall's objection to continued campaigns in the Mediterranean, Brooke very pointedly remarked that the operations visualized by the British would be limited in scope and would not interfere with the BOLERO-ROUNDUP concept. There would, he observed, be available for cross-Channel purposes twenty-two divisions in all, thirteen British and nine American. Sir Dudley Pound supplemented Sir Alan Brooke's remarks and expressed his concern about the protection of the convoys which were carrying supplies to our hard-pressed ally, the U.S.S.R. Sir Dudley referred to the German submarine activities in the Atlantic, emphasizing that the Allies must obtain both long-range air protection and additional escort vessels for the convoys. Sir Charles Portal agreed with Brooke that air operations should be conducted to compel the Germans to overextend their lines of communications and cause them to disperse their forces and their deployments of air units.

Our own Chiefs of Staff were not at all in accord with the British. But General Marshall's relationship with Roosevelt differed subtly from the relationship that existed between the British Chiefs and the Prime Minister. They had frequent, almost daily, access to their political leader, as well as to officials in all branches of the government, particularly the Foreign Office. Churchill would often make informal visits to the lower echelons responsible for the planning of strategy. Besides keeping close contact with them he studied military intelligence reports and thus kept himself informed of the military situation daily, even hourly.

This close informal contact between the political and military leadership in Britain made for unanimity of purpose and insured a united front whenever the Britishers marched off to conferences. They always knew in advance what they wanted. They had aims. Usually their aims could be related to Empire or their postwar position in the world of commerce. Every Britisher was fully informed and loyally supported the interests of the British Isles and the British Commonwealth, whatever and wherever they happened to be. Would that we in America had such an organization and leadership; and such a clear understanding of our aims!

The President, of course, was Commander in Chief of our military forces, and he did consult with his military advisers, primarily the Chiefs of Staff, from time to time. But he was surrounded by many drugstore strategists—Mr. Harry Hopkins, Judge Rosenman, "Pa" Watson, Averell Harriman. Having been exposed to service with the Navy as Assistant Secretary in World War I, Roosevelt, too, thought that he was something of a strategist. This made it difficult to obtain decisions based on carefully considered and professionally evaluated military plans and operations.

More dangerous than our loose organization was our lack of unanimity. We had no national agreement on the objectives for which we were fighting, no specifically American aims. There were, of course, the Four Freedoms. But these were extremely nebulous objectives upon which to base military strategy. Finally, we Americans were not closely knit in our negotiations and contacts with other nations. It was not at all unusual for Americans to differ in the presence of foreigners. This practically never happened with the British in peace or wartime. They always presented a united front; apparently their differences of opinion ended at the water's edge.

George Marshall answered the British in a tactful manner, pointing up areas of general agreement and tactfully noting points of difference. He emphasized the importance of keeping Russia in the war as an effective fighting force and of coping with the U-boat menace. But he said categorically that Americans looked with favor upon an early cross-Channel operation mainly because it offered the best chance of knocking Germany out of the war. He went on to speak of the shipping that could be saved by conducting such an operation, with supplies flowing directly to the Continent from the U.S.

At this point Marshall gave the floor to Admiral King, who referred at once to Sir Dudley Pound's description of the submarine menace. King felt that attention should be focused on the destruction of submarine pens. He also recommended bombing the assembling and building yards, the submarine production facilities, as well as the sea avenues that they had been using to attack our shipping. He expressed the view that the anti-submarine warfare of the Americans and British had not been well thought out; our anti-submarine measures were too sporadic.

Naturally, the Admiral expressed his fears that the Allies might, in their understandable concern with European preparations, allow the Japanese the opportunity to consolidate their gains. He felt strongly that it was not sufficient merely to maintain pressure against the Japanese. He maintained that more resources should be allotted to the Pacific area and that limited offensive operations should be undertaken. He also referred to RAVENOUS, the code name for operations in the Chindwin Valley of Burma. Because of his responsibility in the Pacific area, King had great interest in the launching of operations in Burma in order to bring assistance to the hard-pressed forces of Chiang Kai-shek. He reminded the conferees that the Chinese had been completely cut off by sea, and unless one supply line could be established into China, she might be forced out of the war. Hence the vital need for the execution of RAVENOUS in order to protect the air supply route over the Hump into China.

King visibly annoyed the British, and they shifted uneasily. In postwar reports and narratives King is often depicted as anti-British. Actually, he was simply pro-American in the same way that Churchill was pro-Empire. No one had greater integrity than Admiral King. He was not disagreeable save when the British seemed impossibly intransigent in pressing their own demands. At Casablanca he posed the specific question, "Who would be carrying the greatest burden in fighting Japan once Germany had been knocked out of the war?" He sensed, and I believe justifiably, that the British were lukewarm about operations in the Pacific, in the Indian Ocean, and even in Burma. They were certainly lukewarm about ANAKIM, which was the code name for full-scale operations to recapture Burma from the Japanese.

The British had tacitly agreed that the Pacific was primarily a U.S. strategic sphere. By the same token Americans had recognized the British primary interest in the Mediterranean. The European Theater alone had dual equality of interest, as was recognized in the concept of joint operations for BOLERO and ROUNDUP. The Americans who kept urging the 1943 execution of ROUNDUP were no more anti-British than the British who would have denied strength to the Pacific were anti-American.

On January 18, Prime Minister Churchill sent a message to the Deputy Prime Minister and War Cabinet concerning the progress of the Casablanca Conference, in which he said:

Admiral King, of course, considers the Pacific should be a first charge on all resources, and both American Army and Navy authorities are keen on . . . a large scale 'Anakim' [Burma] later in the year. General Marshall is also keen on this but otherwise his emphasis seemed to lie towards building up 'Roundup' or 'Sledgehammer' at the expense of the Mediterranean.

This, I must insist, is a manifestly unfair report concerning the attitude of Admiral King. Both at Casablanca and later at Cairo, King was the only high-ranking American who had the feeling that he was among his peers and entitled to rate the Pacific as being fully as important to America as the Mediterranean was to the British. His truly American position was reinforced by able assistants, Rear Admiral (later Admiral) Forrest Sherman and Rear Admiral (later Admiral) C. M. Cooke. King at no time argued that the Pacific should be a "first" charge on "all" resources, but he did rightfully present the irrefutable fact that a certain proportion of American resources must be directed to the Far East in order to preclude a situation developing there that would permit the Japanese to run rampant. Incidentally, if it hadn't been for the operations of the American Navy under Admiral King, the Japanese might have moved on India and toward the Mediterranean, both of which possibilities were on Mr. Churchill's mind at the time of TORCH.

CHAPTER XIII

UNCONDITIONAL SURRENDER

THE BRITISH interpreted our commitment to a "Europe first" concept to mean that they could make unlimited demands on U.S. production. If they had had their way, they would have taken so much of the war production of our expanding industries that there would have been practically nothing left over for the rehabilitation and expansion of our own military forces, particularly those of the Navy, for vital requirements in the Pacific. Among American military leaders there was complete unanimity that operations must be continued in the Southwest and mid-Pacific at least to keep the Japanese off balance and protect our lines of communication. Obviously, such operations would require appropriate reinforcements. If Admiral King had not insisted so forthrightly upon protecting our interests in the Pacific, the Japanese would unquestionably have consolidated and expanded the area under their control, thus making the problem of defeating them much more costly than it ultimately proved to be.

During the Casablanca discussions, King, as Chief of Naval Operations, was logically the man to carry the burden of presenting our views on the Pacific. He ought, however, to have received greater help from his colleagues. Frankly I was surprised that Admiral King's position was not reinforced by supporting statements on the part of Marshall and Arnold. Earlier, in the discussions among senior American leaders, King had unequivocally supported the broad strategic concept: namely, greater emphasis in the European Theater with a view to defeating Germany first. But he also maintained all along that America's security and strategic interests in the Pacific should not be entirely neglected.

Sir Alan Brooke, who did most of the talking for the British Joint Chiefs of Staff at Casablanca, was visibly disturbed and impatient with King's position. At one point when the British seemed particularly stuffy, Admiral Cooke turned to General Deane, the American Secretary taking notes at the meeting, and said, "Nuts." Sir John Dill, sitting across the table with his British colleagues, heard Cooke's remark and, realizing that Anglo-American tensions were becoming acute, skillfully performed his role of peacemaker. Appeasing and conciliating were his forte. He used his consummate diplomatic skill to win the confidence and co-operation of Marshall. To pour oil on ruffled feelings at this particular juncture at Casablanca, Dill whispered something to Brooke. The latter, apparently warned by Dill of a possible blow-up, made a move to adjourn, which prevented what might have been a more heated exchange.

In my judgment King was the strongest man on the U.S. Joint Chiefs of Staff. He had a keen, analytical mind. He was incisive and direct in his approach to the solution of a problem. He did not understand and could not engage in small talk. Perhaps he took himself too seriously, for he seemed outwardly to be devoid of humor. Years of military training had left their stamp—a rigidly self-disciplined man who did not ask anyone to conform to a strict code unless he himself within his own conscience knew that he was capable of performing in a similar manner. He never engaged in sarcasm and was completely selfless. If he had been a smoothie or a person given to double talk, he might easily have assuaged the hurt feelings of the British when he took a definite position against their efforts to commit practically everything to the Mediterranean.

Some weeks before Casablanca, General Marshall had expressed his fear that the British were still opposed to cross-Channel operations based on the British Isles. Now at Casablanca he told me the British were determined to conduct an operation against Sardinia and Corsica, from which they might conduct air and naval attacks against the Italian boot. I asked him about Sicily. He replied that they didn't seem so favorably inclined toward Sicily. I told the General I was convinced that the British were making every effort to draw us into the Balkans via Italy. I pointed to the map of Europe on the wall and stated the obvious to my chief; namely, that if our aim was primarily to improve the protection of the sea lanes through the Mediterranean, then Sicily was the most logical place to capture. If Italy was the objective, then we should go for Corsica or Sardinia. General Marshall agreed and said he could not yet fathom Roosevelt's attitude, but he knew the Prime Minister had been working on the President. Churchill kept reiterating that now we had driven the Germans from the African continent, we must not lose momentum, but should push on up the Italian boot, knock Italy out of the war, and get into the Middle East by persuading or intimidating Turkey to come in on our side.

I asked General Marshall how the British could justify a campaign to seize Corsica and Sardinia, and land in Italy when we all knew that if we undertook such operations it would weaken BOLERO and probably make ROUNDUP impossible. While agreeing that further Mediterranean thrusts would be a drain on resources needed for far more decisive operations from the United Kingdom, Marshall seemed to have little hope of preventing the British from having their way.

We had gone to Casablanca without an agreed or clearly defined position among the American Army and Navy representatives. Nor did President Roosevelt bring mature leadership to our own Joint Chiefs of Staff. While permitting them freedom to state their personal views, he seldom gave them any specific knowledge of his own plans and policies. So once again we had no assurance that the President would support our choice of concentration, and, on the military level, we were without agreement among ourselves as to how to convince the British of the danger of frittering away our combined resources on indecisive, limited operations.

Although it was difficult to prepare for Casablanca under these hit-or-miss conditions, the officers of the Strategy and Policy Group did their utmost to provide a broad range of planning data. This information, embodied in the "black books" we prepared, proved invaluable to me and to Marshall and also, I believe, to General Arnold.

On January 7 there had been a meeting at the White House with the President and the four Chiefs of Staff—Leahy, Marshall, Arnold, and King—with the Secretary of the Joint Chiefs of Staff, General Deane, attending. Marshall told me later that Roosevelt was sup-

porting BOLERO, but had also indicated that his mind was still
open concerning the relative merits of cross-Channel versus immediate Mediterranean operations. Marshall also informed me that
at this meeting there had been mentioned for the first time the
"unconditional surrender" formula which might be considered at
Casablanca. There had been no discussion by the military staff of
this fatal formula, first announced at the January 7, 1943, White
House conference. I differed strongly with General Marshall's and
the JCS's general unconcern with such political considerations as
war aims. In my judgment the military should always know the
political leaders' aims and policies. How else could they be prepared to recommend the operations necessary to achieve the objectives which the civilian leaders might have in mind?

At Casablanca, at a morning Chiefs of Staff meeting, General
Marshall again brought up the question, off the record, of unconditional surrender. General Deane had already expressed to me his
great concern. He was sound, intelligent, and completely honest—an
outstanding officer who deservedly enjoyed the confidence of everybody with whom he came in contact. Deane had come by my room
to ask what I thought of the idea. I told him that unconditional
surrender would unquestionably compel the Germans to fight to the
very last. This worried me, for I was confident that there were many
people in Germany—more than we were permitted to realize because
of anti-German as distinct from anti-Nazi propaganda—who wanted
to get rid of Hitler. Our demand for unconditional surrender would
only weld all of the Germans together. Deane feared that the idea
would be adopted regardless of its effect in prolonging the war and
of its disastrous long-term consequences in strengthening Soviet
power.

Learning (probably through Deane) that I had definite ideas on
the subject, Marshall asked me to express them briefly to the Chiefs
of Staff at the morning JCS meeting. This I proceeded to do with
great earnestness and considerable emphasis. I hoped that because
I had been in Germany, and was possibly better acquainted with
the situation there than the JCS members, my words would bear
weight.

An incident occurred after that morning JCS meeting which particularly endeared Marshall to me. We had been told to report to
the President's villa, where our pictures were to be taken with the

President. We were also invited for luncheon. While we were walking to the villa, I mentioned to General Marshall that I hoped he and the other members of the JCS did not feel that I had been disrespectful when I commented so strongly on unconditional surrender. The Chief of Staff halted in his tracks. "Wedemeyer," he said, "don't you ever fail to give me your unequivocal expression of views. You would do me a disservice if you did otherwise."

It made me feel very happy to hear this. Naturally it increased my already great respect and admiration for George Marshall.

I never did learn how unconditional surrender had been dealt with between the JCS and Roosevelt. The Chiefs expressed no views for the record and I can find nothing now. The only reference that I had was the notes I made and kept for myself. The next thing that happened was the announcement by the President, at a final press conference in Casablanca, that the Prime Minister and he had decided they would require unconditional surrender as the terms for cessation of hostilities.

Admiral Cooke and I were meeting from time to time with the British planners, every day in fact. We were constantly in demand by Britishers who wished to prove their unanimous and well-organized intention of continued operations in the Mediterranean. Admiral Cooke favored Sicily over Sardinia and Corsica. It was obvious to both Cooke and me that our chiefs, whether through acquiescence or compulsive gestures from the President, were going along with the British on a continuing Mediterranean campaign. I had a premonition that this would happen—in fact, I wondered if the President and the Prime Minister had not made the decision several days earlier. The military discussions may well have been merely a sop to the ego of the men in uniform.

It was obvious to all of us that none of the Mediterranean islands would create a second front for the Russians or divert Axis forces from the Eastern Front. Marshall understood this better than anyone. He could not, however, stand out against Roosevelt, his Commander in Chief, once a decision had been made at the summit. In his *The Business of War*, Major General Sir John Kennedy, Assistant Chief of the Imperial General Staff, surmises that it was Sir John Dill who made it easy for Marshall to complete a *volte-face*. "A profound friendship," says General Kennedy, "had grown up between him and Marshall; and although Dill took no part in the discussions, the two were constantly to be seen between the meetings, walking in the grounds in deep and earnest conversation . . . The fact that our point of view got across so often was largely due to Dill and the immense respect and affection which he inspired in Washington." In 1944, after Dill's death, Marshall said: "No one will ever take the place of Sir John; as far as I am concerned, he is irreplaceable."

The point to remember here is that we had no Dill of our own in London. Even had we had one, it is doubtful that he could have penetrated the *glacis* set up by the British conviction that their decisions were beyond argument. Kennedy admits that the Americans "had bigger ideas than ours, and more drive." But, he adds: "We had as yet no great respect for the quality of their staff work . . . We found the American officers, behind their hearty and friendly manner, extremely difficult to know; but, from the beginning, we all felt that Roosevelt and Marshall, in particular, were true friends of ours."

True friends, yes. But the British test of friendship was not always loyalty to one's own conceptions of the right thing to do for both parties. To the British—negotiating, arguing, and fighting in the international arena—the true friend might be the man who could be manipulated or enticed to see things as the British themselves saw them. There was no give and take between British and American planners. It was all "take" on their part, with the pattern established by centuries of negotiation and now symbolized by the voluble Mr. Churchill and the sensitive Sir Alan Brooke.

Brigadier General (later General) J. E. Hull and Colonel (later Major General) Charles Gailey, both of OPD, arrived on the fourth or fifth day of the conference and kindly pitched in and rendered valuable assistance to the one-man Army planning staff. I had been busy day and night, not getting more than three or four hours' sleep. I suggested to General Marshall that Hull and Gailey be put on the combined subcommittee which was appointed to draft the conclusions and set forth the major decisions of the conference for inclusion in a message to Stalin.

After considerable discussion, the conference gave formal approval to continuing Mediterranean operations. HUSKY (the code name chosen for the invasion of Sicily) was set in motion. Although the prospects for ROUNDUP in 1943 were becoming dimmer and dimmer, there was one concession to concentration: a high priority was given to the air offensive by Anglo-American bomber forces operating in the United Kingdom.

The target date for HUSKY landings was July 10, which gave us some six months to clean up in Tunisia and get set for the next step up the Mediterranean ladder which led nowhere. To shift the metaphor we were, in General Archibald Wavell's words, committed to killing an octopus by cutting off tentacle after tentacle. This was found to be a laborious business. Sir Alan Brooke took a lighter view of the matter, probably to mollify the Americans. At the January 18 meeting he had the temerity to state that Churchill, in discussing HUSKY with the British Chiefs of Staff, had urged that plans be made to undertake the establishment of a beachhead in northern France and that a commander be appointed and a fixed target date named. Sir Alan went on to explain that, while the Prime Minister had not favored a 1942 attempt at a lodgment on the French coast, *he now agreed that everything possible should be done to invade in 1943.* Sir Alan then let it slip that the PM was also interested in some operations at the extreme eastern end of the Mediterranean, to lure the Turks into war on the Allied side. Brooke mentioned the Dodecanese Islands. The American Joint Chiefs frowned on this proposal for still another operation in the Mediterranean.

Chiang Kai-shek had not been invited to Casablanca, nor had China's needs been given serious consideration. The Chinese had been fighting much longer and had suffered far more than any other people on our side, and had received only a trickle of American aid as compared with the massive and almost indiscriminate material support we had given to Britain and Russia. The Nationalist Government headed by Chiang Kai-shek had proved itself to be our most loyal and least demanding ally, by spurning the very tempting Japanese peace offers following Pearl Harbor—although Japan's subsequent rapid conquest of Hong Kong, Malaya, and Burma against little British resistance had rendered Free China's situation well-nigh desperate. Yet, thanks in large part to British influence on our thinking and strategy, China's role and China's claim for a voice in Allied counsels were disregarded. At Casablanca and subsequently, we surrendered to British demands which entailed the perversion of American strategy for the sake of preserving British imperial interests. We ignored the voice of China which, it must be admitted, was only feebly raised, thanks to Chiang's old-world, behind-the-scenes diplomacy which took little or no account of "democratic" means to influence public opinion. His reasonable attitude, of course, got him nowhere in a world where public relations, propaganda, or blackmail were the means adopted by other nations to secure the maximum American aid.

On the night of the 22nd of January, Marshall and I discussed our experiences with the British during the preceding days. He told me that next day the American and British Chiefs of Staff would be meeting with the President and Prime Minister to outline the combined report of the accomplishments of the conference. Marshall was worried about the submarine menace. If we didn't do something about it, neither HUSKY nor ROUNDUP would be successful. So Marshall was supporting King on this matter. I suggested that Marshall should reach the President before the meeting and bring up the question of China. Obviously it was important to maintain air bases in China to supplement our submarine attacks on Japanese shipping. We couldn't do much in the Pacific at that time, given our Germany-first strategy.

Before the Casablanca conference ended, General de Gaulle put in an appearance. Unlike Chiang Kai-shek, the leader of the Free French constantly challenged the right of Britain and the U.S. to make all the strategic and other decisions. Charles de Gaulle had always taken the position that France had a right to a seat at these high-level meetings. Churchill had violently objected. Argument over this was the cause of the initial rupture of their friendship. De Gaulle was offended by his exclusion, which he took to be an insult to France. Once he had displayed his mettle, the British with their inimitable skill in neutralizing or destroying anyone who would not go along with their views started gently denigrating de Gaulle by remarking that he was being "his usual difficult self." Similarly they had undermined and discredited Chiang Kai-shek.

When de Gaulle arrived at Casablanca, it was at once arranged that he should meet with Giraud. The object was to give the world some evidence of an amicable arrangement between the French factions. Giraud, who believed in utilizing Vichy Frenchmen if they defected, had his own ideas about the situation in France. Newspapermen and cameramen in droves were on hand to record the historic meeting of the two Frenchmen. It was at this point that President Roosevelt, with an eye to maximum effect, chose to make public his sensational but unconsidered statement concerning unconditional surrender.

There were some diversions for us at Casablanca. I inspected the battered hulk of the French battleship *Jean Bart*, which had been pounded by American naval shells and bombers on the 8th of November, when we were landing on the northwest coast of Africa (TORCH). Several smaller French naval vessels had been sunk during the engagement; one could see parts of their superstructure protruding from the water. Admiral Mountbatten took the Joint Chiefs and their staffs on an inspection tour of His Majesty's Ship *Bulolo*, a British merchant vessel which the Combined Operations staff had converted into a headquarters ship especially designed for amphibious operations. Admiral Mountbatten, always enthusiastic, had brought this ship down in order to provide communication facilities for the conference. Colonel (later Brigadier General) John Ratay, an old friend of mine and a gallant soldier, who had waded ashore with the initial assault waves, showed me various points at the Fedhala beaches where the Americans had infiltrated during the first hours of TORCH.

The night before the conference closed, General George S. Patton, Jr., who had commanded the forces landing at Casablanca, gave a dinner party. The President of the United States was present along with his son Elliott, who was on an Air Force photographic mission. Patton invited several officers attending the conference, including General Ed Hull, Admiral Cooke, and myself. The conversation was light and spirits gay. The President related many interesting anecdotes and an enjoyable evening was had by all.

On Sunday, January 24, the conference came to an end. I swallowed my disappointment about the decisions reached; but I felt there was no point in trying to mislead my superiors about my true feelings. Before leaving the scene, I wrote as follows to General Thomas T. Handy, the head of Operations Division: "We lost our shirts and are now committed to subterranean umbilicus operation in mid-summer." I was referring, of course, to the phrase often used by the Prime Minister, "the soft underbelly" of Europe.

There were several weaknesses in the planning work of the American staff: we lacked pre-prepared studies, and were forced to rely on memory. Our Army and Navy should have scrupulously avoided airing their differences in the presence of foreigners. The President should have been better briefed on the logic of our proposals. I felt depressed about our poor showing, as planning was my chief responsibility. In the same letter to Handy I said the story of the conference could be summed up, "We came, we listened, and we were conquered." I told Handy that General Marshall had done a magnificent job but that he had been almost entirely on his own. I felt I had not rendered him adequate help; but I had been faced with a large and well-organized British delegation. In expressing my admiration and envy at the way the British had handled the entire show, I commented as follows:

> They swarmed down upon us like locusts, with a plentiful supply of planners and various other assistants, with prepared plans to insure that they not only accomplished their purpose but did so in stride and with fair promise of continuing in the role of directing strategy the whole course of this war. I have the greatest admiration for them, as I indicated above; and if I were a Britisher, I would feel very proud. However, as an American, I wish that we might be more glib and better organized to cope with these super-negotiators. From a worm's eye viewpoint it was apparent that we were confronted by generations and generations of experience in committee work, in diplomacy, and in rationalizing points of view. They had us on the defensive practically all the time.

The wings of BOLERO and ROUNDUP had already been badly singed in the flames of TORCH. When, at Casablanca, the decision was reached to continue Mediterranean operations (HUSKY), I knew that a cross-Channel operation in 1943, in time to gain a decisive victory over Germany while denying the Soviet Communists a dominant position in Western Europe, was out.

CHAPTER XIV

AROUND THE WORLD IN WARTIME

FROM CASABLANCA I flew to Algiers with Marshall and Arnold. It was the beginning of what, to me, was a momentous trip which was to take me to virtually every active war zone save the Russian. Many American officers were to experience the close-up phases of warfare more intensively than I, but few were to have my opportunities to see the war whole. My experience in practically all the theaters in which we were involved convinced me more than ever that there was little virtue in fighting for every last goat track on the world's far edges. It was the power centers—such as the Ruhr, the oil supply line from the Indies to Japan—that counted.

Originally, Marshall and I had been told that we were to go on to Moscow to confer with Stalin and his staff, and we had equipped ourselves with winter flying clothes. But President Roosevelt received a message from Stalin at Casablanca saying that he could see no purpose in having Marshall and Wedemeyer visit the Soviet Union. The President therefore informed Marshall that he wished me instead to accompany Arnold and Somervell to the East. Sir John Dill would be with us. We would fly to Cairo; to the Middle East; thence to New Delhi, for a talk with the British and with Stilwell; and then on up to Chungking to explain the significance of the Casablanca decisions for the China Theater. My final mission was to continue on to Australia, where I was to explain to Douglas MacArthur the strategy adopted at Casablanca as it affected the Pacific.

Before I left Casablanca President Roosevelt and General Marshall warned me that when I talked to MacArthur in Brisbane I probably would not be able to get a word in edgewise for an hour. They told me to listen carefully and then convey the information which I had been sent to give.

Thus I became both a high-level and high-altitude courier. But interspersed with my conversations with key theater commanders were opportunities, which I willingly seized, to visit the remote and least-known theaters of war. My itinerary was to take me to Ceylon and India, Kunming and Chungking, and then across the northwest coast of Australia and south to Perth, to Fremantle, across Australia to Sydney, to Brisbane, up to Port Moresby, to the north coast of New Guinea and islands fiercely contested or fiercely held by our Marines, thence to New Caledonia, and to the Admiralties, to Hawaii, and back to the United States, landing in California and arriving home in Washington on March 10.

Like all fast-moving journeys, my two-month trip around the world left me floundering in a jumble of often-unrelated impressions. But I came to know certain landmarks, both geographical and human, which, in the light of later experience, were to become part of a more mature perspective.

How much, for example, should I have credited the gossip, picked up in Algiers, that General Eisenhower and Major General (later General) Bedell Smith could be counted on always to settle a dispute in favor of the British when it involved an American? Many old friends encountered in Algiers asked me if I thought that General Marshall knew about this, and some of them even asked me please to convey the information to him. The gossip came to me from so many people that it was obvious it represented a widely held view. Even some of the men who were most loyal to Eisenhower nevertheless felt that Ike was leaning over too far in favoring the British. Although I was skeptical for a time, I feared my friends were right when Eisenhower began to weaken in his support of the cross-Channel operation in 1943. He changed the number of divisions for OVERLORD from six to twelve, a sure sign he was losing faith in the American plan.

The strangest sensation in the midst of war was to come upon an idyllic Eden virtually next door to carnage. At Biskra, close to a bomber field, I visited a beautiful oasis—I think it was the one called the Garden of Allah. There were many small tents over trenches, which had been put up by the men. All about us were date palms, calm and peaceful and wonderful. Only a short distance away, in Tunisia, bitter fighting was going on as we flew across the war zone to Cairo. In Egypt I had my first glimpse of the sphinx and the pyramids, and was fascinated. But Arab poverty like that of China was enduring. King Farouk's palace stood out in contrast to the general poverty. In the evening I had dinner with Ambassador Alexander Kirk. He impressed me very favorably—a brilliant man, thoroughly aware of the political and economic situation in Europe and now very entertaining and interesting on the situation in the Middle East. He talked to me at length about Bonner Fellers, our Cairo military attaché. Kirk had a high regard for Fellers' ability as an intelligence officer but felt that he was overzealous in the performance of his duties in a way that unnecessarily antagonized the British.

From Cairo we flew to Haifa, passing over the Suez Canal. We could easily see the Great and Little Bitter Lakes, also Ismailia, the Gaza-Arabian Desert, and Tel Aviv, where we put down. There was considerable construction going on at Tel Aviv under an American engineer, Colonel Jacobs. He seemed very capable. Beautiful orange, lemon, and olive groves were everywhere.

Somervell and I motored over to Jerusalem—my first visit to the Holy City. We saw many camels, Arabs, donkeys, Jews in the undulating hilly country, which seemed rather sparsely settled and arid. We visited the Church of the Holy Sepulcher and had lunch at the King David Hotel. Then we motored back to Tel Aviv and along the littoral to Beirut, where Bill Somervell wanted to inspect the dock facilities. We talked to Colonel Duncan there, had dinner, and visited with the British port authorities to discuss the capacity of the port. Then we motored south to Haifa, where we arrived at 2:30 in the morning. We stopped at the Windsor Annex, a lovely hotel on Mount Carmel overlooking the sea.

From Haifa we flew eastward to Teheran in a heavy rain which could not obscure the Dead Sea, the River Jordan, or the Sea of Galilee. The terrain became mountainous and practically devoid of foliage; the soil seemed completely unproductive. On our arrival at the Persian capital we were met by Major General Donald H. Connolly, who was in charge of the flow of supplies to the Russians from the Persian Gulf.

Teheran, located on a high mountain-rimmed plateau, was filled with Russians. We had dinner at Don Connolly's in the evening. Four Russians were present: two colonels and two civilians. Ostensibly they were there to act as Russian Soviet representatives in connection with the flow of supplies. We talked about the battle of Stalingrad, and I learned for the first time how the German communications, which were long and overextended, had been attacked by the Russians from the north. The next day, when I went out to the airport to board my plane, the Russian guards did not want to let my car through. After some protest and a lot of jabbering, they were apparently satisfied that I was not Adolf Hitler and I was permitted to pass. We flew to Basra on the Persian Gulf, passing over very high mountains at an elevation of 17,000 feet.

When we reached the Basra area in the afternoon, we looked for a landing strip in a dense dust storm. The entire place was covered by clouds and one couldn't see the ground; it was like being suspended in a dust cloud. The pilot couldn't see any of the landing strips, so he had to fly to Baghdad, where we landed at Habdaniya, a Royal Air Force field. The next day we took off again for Basra, flying over a large body of Arab troops on camels. The first person I met in Basra was West Point classmate Brigadier General (later Major General) Don Shingler, who showed us the dock, rail, and boat facilities, and the truck and airplane assembly plants which were keeping Russia in the war. The temperature was 107 in the shade, and I didn't blame Don Shingler for wanting to get out of the place.

In Karachi, where we were met by Major General (later Lieutenant General) Raymond A. Wheeler, we received a radio message from General Marshall to proceed to India at once because conferences were scheduled with General Wavell and his staff.

General Stilwell arrived in New Delhi at 11 o'clock in the evening just after we flew in. I met him at his office at 9:30 the next morning, and we all went together to Wavell's headquarters at 10:30. Wavell and his staff struck me as old and lethargic. We discussed the Burma operations until noon and then had lunch in the hotel. In the afternoon I worked in my own room and went over the situation, as I understood it from the early morning conference, and made notes concerning my observations.

Here in New Delhi and a few days later in Chungking I had my first direct experience of the logistic and political problems, the wrangles, and animosities in the China-India-Burma Theater, where there was an acrimonious three- or four-cornered contest between the British, General Stilwell, the Chinese Nationalist Government, and Major General (later Lieutenant General) Claire Chennault. Until now I had regarded Stilwell as a romantic fighting man, and the best-informed U.S. officer on China. It would be a long while before I finally pierced his legend to discover his gullibility concerning the Communists and his prejudiced view of Chiang Kai-shek and the Nationalist Government of China, whose problems he never seemed to understand. But in New Delhi and China in 1943 I began to realize his weaknesses, his vanity, and his acute sense of public relations insofar as the press was concerned, as contrasted with his lack of diplomatic qualifications in his dealings both with the British and the Chinese. More shrewd than myself, Sir John Dill quickly took Stilwell's measure. At one point in our travels he sarcastically remarked, "I understand that General Stilwell does not like publicity." We had both observed that everywhere Stilwell went there was a newspaper correspondent or newspaper photographer present to catch him in brave poses: peering between leaves at the enemy, or snuggling close to a gun, always giving the appearance of being a field soldier, which was the role in which he so loved to be presented.

In New Delhi at my first meeting with him in 1943, Stilwell had held forth at length about British bluffing, saying that they had no intention of fighting in Burma to reopen a road to China or of carrying out any bold, aggressive operations against the Japanese. His dislike and scorn for the British equaled his contempt for Chiang Kai-shek and the Chinese Nationalist Government whom he likewise accused of refusing to fight. He was nevertheless determined to push forward in Burma with the Chinese divisions which had been trained and equipped in India. His confidence in the fighting qualities of Chinese soldiers, if only they were properly armed, adequately fed, and well led, stood out in marked contrast to his contempt for the Chinese Nationalist Government. Years later when I read Freda Utley's *Last Chance in China,* I realized how well she had described "Vinegar Joe," whom she had known in

Hankow in 1938 when he was the U.S. military attaché. As she wrote:

> In spite of his hatred of the British and all other imperialists, Vinegar Joe reminded me of the best type of British Indian Army officer who damned the Indian Nationalists but loved his Indian soldiers, just as Stilwell despised and hated the Chinese Nationalists but loved the Chinese "common man."

One of the main subjects at the conference in New Delhi was the amount of tonnage which could be transported over the Hump from India to China.

After the conference we flew on to China, accompanied by Stilwell. My impression of India as it disappeared below was dominated by the sacred cows and water buffaloes; but the land of poverty was forgotten with the sight of Mt. Everest rising in the Himalayas. At Kunming we were met by General Chennault, another man whom I was destined to see for a time through a haze of unwarranted preconceptions, some of them derogatory. In the evening at Kunming, Brigadier General Jerry Waters, General Stilwell, Colonel Edwin Sutherland, a West Point classmate and good friend, Sir John Dill, and I all had dinner together.

In Kunming I learned that "Hap" Arnold, who was crossing the Hump in another plane, had arrived at 3 o'clock in the morning after a long, dangerous trip in a B-17. He had passed over Kunming with a tremendous hundred-mile tail wind. The pilot had figured on many more hours and didn't realize he had traveled so fast.

Hap Arnold and I discussed the organization of U.S. air units in the India-Burma-China Theater. Arnold thought that General Chennault with his 14th Air Force should remain under Major General Clayton Bissell, who commanded the 10th Air Force in India, at least for administrative and logistical purposes. At that time I didn't know that Bissell and Chennault did not get along together. Bissell was Stilwell's air officer, and Chennault and Stilwell had been at loggerheads for a long time. Arnold wanted Chennault's 14th Air Force to be kept separate operationally from Bissell's command, and told me he had arranged to increase Hump tonnage to approximately 4,000 tons a month by allocating 140 transport planes to the route.

I spent part of February 5, 1943, which was the Chinese New Year and also my wedding anniversary, walking around Kunming with Sir John Dill. The weather was beautiful and the scenery lovely. After our walk, we again conferred with Generals Stilwell, Bissell, Chennault, and Arnold. Next day we took off for Chungking, 800 miles to the north, landing at about 4 o'clock in the afternoon on a small island in the Yangtze River. It was a foggy landing, made entirely by instruments. After descending from the plane we had to climb 366 steps up a steep hill to reach Chungking. Firecrackers, a symbol of the New Year, were exploding all about. We had dinner at Stilwell's. I went to bed in a cold hotel room which was made bearable by a little charcoal stove. When the stove went out I was very cold, with insufficient bedding. Finally I got up, put on some clothes, and went to visit Sir John Dill. I was worried about him because he had been in pain ever since we had gone horseback riding on a pigsticking expedition with Wavell in India. In Kunming, where we were billeted together, he had complained about terrible pains. Being unable to sleep, Dill had talked to me at length concerning Marshall, who had given him a a great deal of information about his own views and those of his staff members, thus enabling Dill to convey much important information to the British. I had recoiled on hearing this, seeing him for a moment as a sort of super-spy. But I could understand why anyone would love and admire Sir John Dill, since he had endearing personal qualities. I succeeded in getting a Chinese servant and building a little charcoal fire beside his bed. Such was my introduction to Chungking, the city I was to know so well in the last year of the war.

The next day, after a ride in a ricksha, I dropped in at Stilwell's office for further discussions concerning the implications of the Casablanca decisions. Once again Vinegar Joe told me the British definitely did not want to fight and were just making a show of it. He said that Generalissimo Chiang Kai-shek would not co-operate, that he was getting as much as he could out of the United States and doing the minimum toward winning the war against the Japanese. He said Chinese leaders were all convinced that now we

were in the war they could lie back on their oars and let us tow
their ship of state in the wake of our own.

After my discussion with General Stilwell I drove about the
place. What impressed me was the contrast between squalor and
deprivation and the smiling good nature of the Chinese, particularly the children. "Ding Hao," they would shout, with their thumbs
up. This was such a contrast to what I had experienced in India,
where everyone looked at the white man through eyes of burning
hatred. As I drove around in Chungking I saw many areas that had
been demolished by air bombing. The Japanese would come up
the Yangtze River, which was easy to follow from their air base
in Hankow, drop their bombs just about sundown, and then fly
back. Chennault explained that he had no Black Widow night
fighters and he asked Hap Arnold to send him some. The anti-
aircraft defense was very crude; the Chinese had no heavy anti-aircraft artillery. The largest were 30-caliber guns, which were scattered around the perimeter of the city. The air warning service
was very primitive. Fires would be lighted from hilltop to hilltop,
much as in the days of cavemen, or the early Indians in America.

I had lunch with Major Grinsdale of the British mission in
Chungking and the British ambassador, Sir Horace Seymour. After
lunch we went by ferry across the Yangtze and took a 20-mile drive
over on the south bank of the river to visit "the eagle nest," the
Generalissimo's place. The roads were winding and dangerous.
It was snowing, and the scenery was absolutely beautiful with the
snow festooning all of the foliage. We finally arrived at a group
of villas on a hilltop. It was still very cold. Lieutenant General
J. L. Huang, a Chinese who was a graduate of Vanderbilt University in Tennessee, was in charge of these hotels.

In Chungking it was our unwelcome task to inform Chiang Kai-
shek of the decisions made at the Casablanca conference. We endeavored to render them less disappointing to the Chinese by
announcing that the tonnage supplies over the Hump were to
be increased. The Generalissimo insisted that they must be increased to 10,000 tons a month by the fall in order to make it
possible for him to continue fighting the Japanese. He stipulated
that the Air Force in China be increased to 500 planes, either under
General Chennault or in actual Chinese air units. Chiang Kai-shek
summarized his several requests with carefully schooled conviction,

and added that if we did not agree China would not be able to go on with the war.

We told him that the question of logistical support and increased numbers of planes and personnel for the very large Hump tonnage he demanded would have to be carefully studied. The Generalissimo showed no interest whatever in the question of maintenance and supply. He simply reaffirmed his position, saying that he would like very much to have us present his request to President Roosevelt for decision.

On my return to Washington, I learned that Chiang was being supported at the White House in his demand for increased supplies. The President, on the recommendation of Harry Hopkins, had approved a separate air force to be set up under Chennault. Mr. Roosevelt had also given orders that additional transport planes be assigned to the Hump in order to reach the tonnage demanded by Chiang. Finally, the President promised that a total of 500 planes would be assigned to Chennault's air force. In order to insure maximum effective use of these planes, Major General Wheeler, who was now assigned to Stilwell's command, was instructed by the President to build airfields in Assam as rapidly as possible.

It was obvious that Stilwell was in for trouble on the Chennault issue. Chennault's aide-de-camp was Captain Joseph Alsop, who was a cousin of the President's; and who was also a close personal friend of T. V. Soong, the brother of Madame Chiang Kai-shek. Alsop knew Hopkins well from his days as a Washington political columnist and had access to other influential people in China and in Washington. This at least assured that Chiang's and Chennault's views were certain of a hearing at the White House.

Toward the end of April, 1943, Chennault and Stilwell were ordered back to the United States for consultation. General Marshall and Secretary of War Stimson had all along supported Stilwell in his difficulties with the British and with his air commander, Chennault. Stilwell was considered a hard-working individual, a good tactician, and first rate at training troops for combat. He was also known to be lacking in tact. Supposedly intolerant of intrigue, he had, like King John, his "little ways." On the other hand, there was some evidence that important Chinese had combined with Harry Hopkins to influence President Roosevelt in Chennault's favor. It was understandable that the President should be attracted by Chennault, who was a colorful and truly intrepid leader. With the help of his loyal and articulate aide, Captain Alsop, Chennault's daring exploits had been widely heralded. There was no doubt about his bravery and his qualities of leadership, which stood out during those terrible days in China when the "Flying Tigers" were practically holding on to box-kite tails to press their fight against the Japanese.

When, in April of 1943, Chennault and Stilwell arrived in Washington, following my return from my trip around the world, General Marshall allowed me to sit in his office while Stilwell discussed the problems of his theater. His description of Chiang Kai-shek remains etched in my memory although soon I was to realize how unjust, uninformed, and prejudiced it was. My notes confirm how he castigated the Chinese President as coolie class, arrogant, untrustworthy, and absolutely impossible to get along with.

When asked about Chennault, Stilwell said he didn't think Chennault was loyal to him. He accused Chennault of deliberately disobeying his instructions and carrying on intrigue with various Chinese officials, generals, or provincial war lords. Stilwell said that Chennault was sending small arms and other equipment to war lords, although he was specifically forbidden to do so. General Marshall referred to a magazine article which pointed up the bad relations between Stilwell and Chennault. Stilwell replied that this reflected Chennault's doings, and said, "There are many here in Washington, particularly around the President, and in high places in China who would be glad to have Chennault replace me as the American general in the area."

It was all too obvious that the relations between Stilwell and Chennault were hardly conducive to proper co-ordination and friendly co-operation. Chennault, whom I had met for the first time during my brief visit to China in 1943, looked the part of a fighter—a man of stocky build, leathery skin, piercing brown eyes, and a protruding chin that announced grit and extreme determination. He was, however, soft-spoken and amenable in his manner. As I questioned him about logistic problems in his theater, he spoke with conviction and expressed confidence in the success of his projected operations if given proper logistic support. He had an elaborate plan for the air interdiction of Japanese shipping along the China coast which, as he put it, would practically bring the Japanese to their knees. Finally, he hoped to establish satellite airfields and permanent bases in East China in order to carry on extensive operations against the Japanese home islands.

At no time did he mention difficulties with General Stilwell. He said he had talked to the President, who had invited him to write direct to the White House. Chennault's enthusiasm and confidence in his ability to stop the Japs with air power were infectious, and I could understand why the President had assured him that everything possible would be done to help him carry out his plans.

When I asked Chennault about the Generalissimo his reaction was poles apart from Stilwell's. In his estimation the Generalissimo was a great democratic leader, a devout Christian, and a man of absolute integrity, a real patriot. When I mentioned the Generalissimo's threat to stop fighting unless he received the support he had demanded when I was in Chungking earlier in the spring, Chennault said that Chiang would go on fighting in any event.

When I referred to the letters Joe Alsop was writing to friends in Washington, Chennault replied that the letters were on a strictly personal basis; that Alsop was just trying to help the war effort and was not trying to undermine anybody's authority, Stilwell's included. He again referred to the fact that he, Chennault, had been asked by the President to write direct any time he thought he had a problem.

In carrying out the President's instructions, the Hump tonnage was reallocated so that Chennault would receive 1,500 of the 4,000 tons flown into China each month. When General Marshall told Stilwell about this, Vinegar Joe promised to comply with the order but cautioned Marshall that there were maneuvers going on to put Chennault in command of both the 14th and 10th Air Forces, and he requested that an over-all air commander be appointed right away to forestall the intrigue going on in the White House and out in Chungking. Stilwell and Chennault stayed on in Washington to make presentations at the TRIDENT Conference, which took place early in May.

At Kunming, in 1943, Stilwell had emphasized to me the absolute necessity, as he put it, of having an American division or corps operate with RAMGAR forces (Chinese troops trained and equipped by Americans at Training Center located in Ramgar,

India). He needed them right away, and he also needed some mortars—the 60-mm. and the 3-inch types. Furthermore, he needed some amphibious equipment—alligators, jeeps, and tanks.

Leaving Kunming, our trip across the Hump was unusual inasmuch as it was clear most of the way. We could see plainly the deep canyons, the silver streams, the Salween and the Chindwin as well as the Irrawaddy Rivers. Over Dingan we turned south and followed the Brahmaputra to Calcutta, where we arrived at 2:30 in the afternoon. This is a large city, at the time the third largest in the British Empire. It was very warm. Lots of carabaos could be seen, and sacred cows wandered all over the street; there was even a sacred cow right at the entrance to the principal city bank. At the Great Eastern Hotel I basked in the sunshine for a while trying to shake a cold. At Calcutta I took my leave of Sir John Dill. I would be all alone for the remainder of my trip except for the two Air Force officers whom Arnold detailed to accompany me, Colonel (later Major General) Lewis R. Parker and Major (later Colonel) Frederick Wildman.

Ceylon is a beautiful island, but there wasn't much to detain me there. While waiting to take off for Australia I pitched for a British team in a baseball game against the Clipper plane crews that were scheduled to carry me on my way to northwestern Australia. When the weather reports remained pessimistic, I took part in a cricket match, this time playing with the Americans against the British. We got a trimming, even worse than the day before when the Americans beat my team at baseball. I had once played cricket in Tientsin, China, many years before, but my skill, if any, had departed.

It was ticklish business getting to Australia from Ceylon. The trip was 3,400 miles over water, and part of the time we had to go close to the Island of Java, which was occupied by the Japanese. There was always the possibility that they would come up and intercept us, for Clippers are slow and cumbersome. We planned to hit the Java stretch during the night hours. The pilots explained to me very carefully the point of no return, which was less than halfway out.

We crossed the Equator at about 2:30 in the afternoon, passing through many line squalls. Dinner on the plane was excellent, but I found it hard to relax. I walked back and forth like a tiger in a cage and read some of the papers I had taken to Casablanca.

Finally I retired at 10 o'clock. We were only three in a plane that was equipped to take care of forty. My berth was most comfortable. The pilot came back and told me that we had passed the point of no return, so it would be Australia tomorrow—or else.

We landed on the northwest coast of Australia at Exmouth Gulf, where we could see two U.S. destroyers. The Japanese had come in and bombed the place the day before; possibly they had gotten wind of my trip. We made a nice landing and drew up to a floating pier. The Navy officers were very helpful and explained that the two destroyers, as well as PBYs, had been there in case our plane came down. After refueling we took off for Perth, following along the western coast of Australia. Perth is a beautiful city, a terrific contrast to the unattractive country which stretched between it and Sydney, where we finally turned up the next day.

At Sydney I was extremely happy to be welcomed by Dick Marshall, an old friend of Corregidor days, now a Major General on MacArthur's staff. He was in command of all the SOS activities for MacArthur's area. Dick and I had lunch together. Sydney, a large, modern place with a gorgeous setting, reminded me very much of San Francisco. Dick Marshall had a beautiful set of quarters on the side of a hill overlooking the harbor.

From Sydney it was on to MacArthur's headquarters at Brisbane. On my arrival, Major General (later Lieutenant General) Richard Sutherland, Chief of Staff of MacArthur's Headquarters, told me there was to be a conference in Noumea between representatives of Halsey's and MacArthur's staffs; so I would have to wait and see MacArthur later, after he had finished with certain arrangements. I met Major General (later General) George C. Kenney, MacArthur's air general. Eventually I had a conference with MacArthur, Kenney, and Sutherland.

As I have already written, General Marshall at Casablanca told me that I would unquestionably have to listen to MacArthur's ideas of strategy before I could deliver my own message. Since I was supposed to tell General MacArthur about the strategy evolved at the Casablanca conference as it pertained to his command, there wasn't much encouraging news to pass on. Europe still had first call on Allied troops and matériel. I did, however, give him a run-down account of the discussions between the British and American Chiefs of Staff concerning continued strategy in the Mediterranean.

MacArthur asked about the Generalissimo and what was envisaged for the China-Burma-India area. I explained that because of the limited resources available, only restricted operations had been approved at Casablanca. These operations involved a convergence on the Mandalay plain by the Chinese under Stilwell's command and the British-Indian force under Wavell. I added that the U.S. Joint Chiefs of Staff were adamant in their determination to open a land route into China. It would be necessary, of course, to drive the Japanese out of northern Burma to permit the construction of a road, generally following the route from Ledo, Myitkyina, Lashio, and Kunming. I told the General that there were to be two pipelines paralleling the road in order to supply aviation fuel to the China Theater. I then related to the General that the Chinese officials were disappointed in the Casablanca decisions.

General MacArthur was much interested in the Chinese area and said the operations he envisaged would one day require effective air bases located on the mainland of China to support his drive back to the Philippines. This apparently stimulated his thinking and he didn't stop for at least an hour in giving me his personal views on global strategy. He was not at any time arrogant or disdainful in his stated objections to our strategy of defeating Germany first, but he obviously had given it considerable thought and was sure that we were going to lose our traditional position of great influence and respect throughout Asia if we did not quickly build up our strength and restore the confidence of Far East allies like the Filipinos and Chinese.

He asked many questions about the European plans and did not miss the opportunity to discuss cross-Channel vs. Mediterranean strategy. I was pleased to have the General confirm that if we must emphasize European operations we should concentrate our power for a decisive blow at a critical point. Together we looked at a map. I explained the reasons why we Americans had veered away from the southern barrier of Europe. Fully an hour went by. I had not noticed the time passing because I was so fascinated with the spectacle of MacArthur, full of vigor and confidence, pacing the floor and stopping to drive home a point, wielding his long cigarette holder like a baton.

MacArthur asked me to explain to General Marshall that the momentum which appeared to be the Prime Minister's major point about continued operations in the Mediterranean had an even greater application in the Southwest Pacific.

MacArthur questioned me as to how the President looked as well as requiring details of all he had said. He wanted to know about Churchill, Eisenhower, Giraud, de Gaulle, Marshall, King, Arnold, and Leahy. I told him that Leahy had not attended the Casablanca conference because he was ill.

The following day I flew to Port Moresby, on the south coast of New Guinea, an active war front. After arrival there we had an air alarm just about dark. All lights were out. The place by day was really lovely, very much like the Philippine Islands, mountainous with lots of tropical growth about. The ships in the harbor were all dispersed. There were several sunken ships about, indicating a reason for dispersal. I was awakened a couple of times during the night by air alarms; but the all-clear was sounded almost immediately, so it must have been unidentified planes flying over.

Dick Marshall's aide-de-camp, Captain Jones, was charged with taking me across the famous Owen Stanley Range. The route was by a dangerous pass, which could only be negotiated in the early morning before the severe winds came up. Despite the vaunted dangers we got through easily, carrying 5,000 pounds of freight, mostly steel airstrip matting. We flew over and circled the port being established at Orel Bay; then we passed over Buna battlefield and on to Dobruduba, where we landed at about 9 o'clock in the morning. Colonel (later Lieutenant General) Richard Lindsey of the War Plans Division was my companion. We were driven immediately to the 41st Division Headquarters, a secluded place in the jungle. The insects were thick in the swamps. There were many dead bodies still lying around and the stench was terrible. Everywhere we could see the wreckage of planes and tanks, and palm trees completely bare of leaves. After lunch we drove to the Buna area, where I saw many airplanes that had been destroyed. We returned in the evening to the 41st Division Headquarters and had a fine dinner. Fuzzy-Wuzzies were loafing all around the place; in New Guinea the wife carries the heavy loads and does all the work. I slept on a cot with no mattress and was kept awake by weird jungle noises. There was an air raid at 3:00 A.M., so this was the second rather sleepless night. The next day I slipped back through the pass over the Owen Stanley Range and then returned to Brisbane, where I bade MacArthur and his staff good-by.

We made a perfect flight to Espiritu Santo, where we landed at eight o'clock in the morning. There I saw Nate Twining, who had just been fished out of the water after his B-17 had gone down at sea. From Espiritu Santo I went on to Guadalcanal. I had a good visit with Lieutenant General (later General) Alexander Patch and Major General (later General) Joseph Collins, also with Colonel (later Major General) "Eddie" Seebree, a West Point classmate. I accompanied Seebree and Colonel (later Major General) Robert B. McClure on a tour of the Guadalcanal battle area. There were still some Japanese holed up on the island, but not many; the fighting had become rather desultory. The Marines, of course, got the credit for taking Guadalcanal, yet there was plenty of work still remaining to be done when the Army moved in and the Marines were evacuated to Townsville for rehabilitation. Both the Marines and the Army had done a creditable job.

After a somewhat sleepless night owing to bombings and a couple of plane crashes, Bob McClure and I drove over to Joe Collins' headquarters in a jeep and had breakfast with him and Brigadier General (later General) John Hodge. Then it was on to Noumea on New Caledonia for another conference. I went to visit Admiral Halsey aboard his ship, and we talked for over an hour. Then I had lunch with Lieutenant General "Miff" Harmon and had a good talk concerning his problems. He mentioned Patch's relief; he felt that Patch ought to get back, that he had been under terrific strain.

George Kenney, Dick Sutherland, and others soon arrived from MacArthur's headquarters. I said hello to them and good-by, for I was anxious to get on to Canton Atoll on my way to Honolulu. Flying conditions were favorable all the way, and it wasn't long before I was at Hickam Field. I slept soundly before waking up to visit with Admiral Chester Nimitz, Vice Admiral (later Admiral) Raymond A. Spruance, and others, including my old friend, Forrest Sherman. I went to the Young Hotel in Honolulu and got a haircut, then to the bank, and finally had lunch at the Fort Shafter Club.

Though I was not yet stateside on the mainland, I felt I was back in America. I had only a mere 2,400 miles to go to San Francisco, which I reached the next day.

As a fillip to my trip, I managed to stop off at Omaha, where I spent the night with my mother. We arrived at Omaha in a snowstorm and could hardly see the field. Fortuitously, the pilot of the plane which had brought me all the way from Perth, Australia, clear across the Pacific to Omaha had once been a pilot on a civilian airline in the Missouri Valley area, and he knew every twist and turn in the Omaha locale. The following day, after a good visit home, I was again at my desk in Washington.

CHAPTER XV

REFLECTIONS ON STRATEGY

DURING MY JOURNEY around the world I spent some two hundred hours aloft. This gave me time to reflect and make notes concerning our arguments with the British as well as to record my observations and impressions of people, places, and events along the course of my flight. I was unhappy about the showing I personally had made at Casablanca as strategic adviser to General Marshall. I felt that he had done a fine job but without much help from me. So I devoted many hours to making notes on the Casablanca conference —comparing the British organization and preparation for the conference with our own, and analyzing the effect of the major decisions reached on American plans for coalition warfare.

While I was reflecting on all these matters, the thought kept going through my mind that the British were concealing their objections to crossing the Channel in 1943 for fear that Admiral King would succeed in getting Roosevelt to shift the main U.S. effort to the Pacific. King recognized the British artifice; hence his efforts to get as much for the Pacific as he possibly could. There was no accepted rule for the allocation of resources and strengths in that theater of operations; hence Navy and Army were constantly resorting to step-by-step improvisation.

In my last talk with him after the Casablanca conference, Marshall had still adhered strongly to the BOLERO plan for the concentration of Allied forces in the United Kingdom, to be used in an attack on the enemy's center of power. But he now seemed more amenable to the allocation of increased quantities of resources to the Pacific. This would be fully justified if the British insisted on continuing operations in the Mediterranean Theater of war, for the Pacific was being starved thanks to our Germany-first strategy. Because of our surrender to British insistence on periphery-pecking operations in the Mediterranean, our Japan-last strategy had become indefensible.

Brigadier Dykes had dropped in one evening at my Anfa Hotel room in Casablanca and noted that I was depressed. I told him I felt that the British had drawn us into Mediterranean operations that would result in drain after drain, first with TORCH, and now with the prospect of HUSKY (Sicily) and then Italy. I said, "Your people have no intention of ever crossing the Channel." Dykes listened with sympathetic understanding, although he agreed with his countrymen that the HUSKY operation was necessary in order to protect shipping through the Mediterranean. Puffing at his pipe, he said: "There is no accounting for Winston." But he still maintained that the Prime Minister and the President had legitimate grounds for believing that they must not lose the attractive possibility of knocking Italy out of the war and bringing Turkey in. "There is no accounting for you Britishers," I said, as Dykes pulled hard at his meerschaum.

I insisted that our shipping could be protected from bases along the African littoral and maintained that Italy was a greater liability to the Nazis as an ally than she would be if she were knocked out entirely, or even if she were fighting on our side. I told Dykes that we should realize that the Russians might soon be moving westward and could be well into Western Europe and the Balkans before we could get there. Even if Russia had not been able to hold out at Stalingrad, it was militarily necessary and politically expedient for us to get into the Continent while the bulk of the Nazis were tied down far to the east. I have mentioned previously that we had been utterly frank in all our discussions. He knew why I was so intent on having Anglo-American forces occupy most of Europe, and he was completely in accord. I predicted that from here on out the Germans would be fighting on the defensive and would no longer have offensive capabilities of any great strength. Dykes, who had foresight as well as integrity, agreed, but only to the extent that Stalingrad would prove to be the smashing victory the Soviets claimed it to be.

This was indeed the turning point of the war. In the spring of 1943 the initiative was passing to the Allies; yet here we were, eighteen months after Pearl Harbor, still engaged in nondecisive operations on the fringe of the enemy citadel. Neither our air nor our ground forces were concentrated for a decisive effort. We had lost a grand opportunity to go across the Channel in 1943, striking at the heartland of the enemy to bring the war to a successful conclusion not only militarily but also politically. We fumbled a strategy that would have (1) saved human lives, both the enemy's and our own; and (2) permitted Anglo-American forces to overrun Europe, thus denying the opportunity to the Red Armies to advance as far west as their political commissars would undoubtedly urge them to go.

Dykes observed thoughtfully, "All we planners can do, Al, is serve up ideas and make recommendations to our masters." I longed for a leader on our side possessing the tenacity and persuasiveness of Churchill. Then we discussed the organization and functioning of the British planners. I mentioned that we had had no information that the British would bring so many staff planners to Casablanca. Finally, I suggested that in the future it would be helpful if he could always manage to tip me off about the direction of British thinking. In good humor I said that, since we were working for the same objective, I felt we should not withhold information from each other. Dykes agreed at once and told me that, within imposed limits, he would keep me informed of British views in the future. He mentioned Dill's own working arrangement with Marshall. Why, therefore, should not Dykes and I come to a similar arrangement?

Alas for the future, Dykes and I parted in North Africa never to see each other again. While in the Near East I received the sad news that my good British friend since Fort Myer days had been killed along with several others in a forced landing while on the way home to Britain. The British transport plane caught fire over the English Channel, just short of its destination.

One special item that I wished to investigate after Casablanca was the geographical distribution of our soldiers. When I eventually had this done by my planning group, I discovered that of approximately 500,000 United States troops abroad, there were 295,000 in the Mediterranean instead of the agreed-upon 185,000. There were 125,000 in the Pacific instead of the approved 80,000. And there were only 70,000 in the British Isles instead of the 250,000 that were supposed to be assembling there to prepare the cross-Channel push.

The movement of personnel to the Mediterranean and Far East naturally required supporting means such as shipping and landing craft. I was subsequently to be told again and again, even by friends who should have known better, that it would never have been possible to cross the Channel in 1943 because of a lack of landing craft. But we could easily have had the necessary landing craft in the U.K. if we had not dispersed them to other areas, for example, the Mediterranean. As a matter of record, large numbers of landing craft found their way out to the Pacific. As operations were increased in scope and intensity in that area, they dragged more and more matériel in their wakes.

In his *Crusade in Europe*, Eisenhower (page 278) implies that Churchill had long opposed the cross-Channel operation:

> On May 15 [1944, a few weeks before OVERLORD] a final conference was held at St. Paul's School under the supervision of SHAEF. . . . Every principal member of the British Chiefs of Staff and the War Cabinet attended, as did also the King of England and Allied generals by the score.
>
> Field Marshal Smuts came with his old friend Mr. Churchill. During the whole war I attended no other conference so packed with rank as this one. The purpose was to assure that any doubtful points of the earlier conferences would be ironed out and corrected. . . .
>
> This meeting gave us an opportunity to hear a word from both the King and the Prime Minister. The latter made one of his typical fighting speeches, in the course of which he used an expression that struck many of us, particularly the Americans, with peculiar force. He said, "Gentlemen, I am hardening toward this enterprise," meaning to us that, though he had long doubted its feasibility and had previously advocated its further postponement in favor of operations elsewhere, he had finally, at this late date, come to believe with the rest of us that this was the true course of action in order to achieve the victory.

Shortly after the decision to invade Sicily, I had written a letter to General Handy recommending that the United States carry out the operation with troops already available in the Mediterranean. This was adopted as a fundamental War Department goal. But Eisenhower shortly thereafter began to make demands for additional forces. The trend toward building up Allied resources in the Mediterranean continued. When the Germans capitulated in North Africa in May, 1943, the total strength of the Americans in the area was close to 400,000, which included well over 200,000 ground troops, 80,000 in the Air Force, and the remainder in service personnel. This reveals clearly the degree to which BOLERO-ROUNDUP resources had been siphoned off. As for the air offensive against Germany, it was not until March of 1943 that 100 bombers could be put into the air with any regularity. The Mediterranean created an irresistible pull on air as well as other resources.

On March 12, almost immediately after my return from my trip around the world, a meeting of representatives of General MacArthur and Admiral Nimitz was held in Washington. I was now thrown into the caldron of argument concerning the allocation of resources in the Pacific. Admiral Cooke and I, assisted by the Air Force Planner, Brigadier General (later Major General) Orville Anderson, met continuously with the MacArthur-Nimitz representatives. According to my own and Anderson's interpretation of the Casablanca decisions, a maximum concentration of bombers in Europe had already been ordered by the Joint Chiefs of Staff in order to intensify the bombardment of Germany. On the planning level we were not authorized to allocate additional resources to reinforce U.S. and Allied forces in the Pacific.

Our experience at Casablanca had proved that we must not accept British assurances that Sicily would mark the end of operations in the Mediterranean. Some of my British planning friends assured me that Allied air bases on Sicily and along the African littoral would secure the lines of communication from Gibraltar to Cairo. But I knew they could rationalize either side of a question and would do so if necessary to further their Mediterranean strategy. Hence I anticipated that they would not stop at Sicily but would insist upon operations against the Italian boot or a grab for Sardinia. I was even prepared to see the Prime Minister go rampant again and talk about the Dodecanese in the eastern Mediterranean. One simply could not foretell.

With the future so utterly conjectural, we decided, in preparing for the next-scheduled world conference (TRIDENT) to consider every possibility that might be conjured up by our Allies. By anticipating their proposals we might be prepared to hold the British within reasonable strategic bounds. We worked day and night, mulling over the advantages and disadvantages of various types of operations in the Mediterranean. Always we sought to assess their likely effect on our one key operation, the cross-Channel blow. We studied Sardinia, Corsica, Spain, Crete, the Dodecanese, the entire southern littoral of Europe, examining once again the terrain, the port facilities, the communications, and the availability of bases, both naval and air. During the course of these studies I found that some members of the Operations Division were no longer in complete agreement about discontinuing Mediterranean operations after Sicily.

Even General Eisenhower began to weaken. I recall vividly his message from Algiers to General Marshall:

> I personally have never wavered in my belief that the ROUNDUP conception is a correct one, but the time and assets required for building up a successful operation in that direction are such that we could not possibly undertake it while attempting, simultaneously, to keep the forces now in or coming into this theater [North Africa] operating usefully.

This message was referred to me for comment. I recall the misgivings I had, for I knew how the British Prime Minister was continually exerting pressure on Eisenhower, on Bedell Smith, and on others to shake their confidence in BOLERO-ROUNDUP. Eisenhower pointed out that the coastal defenses of Western Europe had been greatly strengthened during recent months, which was quite true. The number of German divisions had also been increased. But General Marshall continued to insist that a "decisive effort must be made against the continent from the United Kingdom sooner or later."

At the Joint Chiefs of Staff meeting on May 10 I suggested that they take the initiative at the forthcoming TRIDENT Conference by submitting our proposals to the British Chiefs of Staff at the first plenary session. My purpose, of course, was to insure that we did not repeat our experience at Casablanca when we spent practically all of our time considering proposals submitted by the British. The U.S. Joint Chiefs of Staff approved the idea.

Appearing before a Senate subcommittee, General Marshall had told the members that the British system of integrating policy-making agencies with the military was accomplished by close relationships between the Prime Minister, members of the War Cabinet, and the various military planning agencies.

As Senator Vandenberg was quoted later, in *The Private Papers of Senator Vandenberg:*

> In deciding joint questions with the British, he [Marshall] said we were always handicapped by the fact that when the British come to a conference with an idea, it is developed to the last degree. It has the completely integrated support of the British from Churchill down, including, frequently, a softening up of our own American situation through the activity of all the British Secretaries here in Washington. He said that this often puts us at a disadvantage.

We all felt the need of closer liaison with policy-making agencies. In a memorandum to General Marshall I suggested that we invite a State Department man to attend JCS meetings. Unfortunately my recommendation was not acted upon. Some of my colleagues objected that they could not be sure of the security of information if they shared it with civilian members of the government. I couldn't understand that. It seemed to me that putting a man into uniform didn't necessarily give him a new conscience. I was confident that State Department personnel could be as security-conscious as the military.

If our planning lacked liaison with the civilian policy-makers, we had the benefit of the Joint Strategic Survey Committee (JSSC), which was created in November of 1942 to advise the Joint Chiefs of Staff on long-range strategic planning. This high-level committee, composed of senior officers of sound military judgment and broad knowledge, included Lieutenant General Stanley D. Embick, former Chief of War Plans Division, and Deputy Chief of Staff of the Army; Major General Muir S. Fairchild, the Air Force representative; and Vice Admiral Russell Willson. This group met daily to consider the strategic implications of all long-range plans proposed by the Joint Staff Planners. It was an independent group of elder military statesmen operating directly under the Joint Chiefs of Staff to advise on broad questions of world strategy.

Despite the new high-level Survey Committee and a couple of lesser joint committees, our Joint Planners still continued to glean news of U.S. top policy through the British. Sir John Dill would often learn about a U.S. policy or decision from his own men in London; then he would pass the word on to Marshall, and Marshall would give it to me. On more than one occasion while discussing strategy with British planners in Washington, I was told by them that a certain U.S. policy had been changed. When I checked later, I would find that the Britishers were right. I disliked very much learning American policies through foreign representatives, even though they were friends and allies.

The Prime Minister arrived in Washington for the TRIDENT conference in May, 1943, accompanied by a large delegation armed with many studies and volumes of supporting data. This time I felt much more optimistic about our abilities to cope with the British. Our new staff committees, particularly the Joint War Planning Committee under Brigadier General William Bissell, had made strenuous efforts to get ready for the tussle. Everything hinged, of course, on the cross-Channel attack *vs.* Mediterranean strategy. Though we had given up on 1943, we believed that Roosevelt was fully committed to get a clear-cut decision from the British on a cross-Channel operation for early 1944.

Once more, however, we had to run the gauntlet of Churchillian oratory. Winston dwelt lovingly and repetitiously on the notion of sealing the doom of the German people by knocking out the Italians. He revealed his hand when he mentioned that an Italian collapse would yield ports and air bases necessary for operations against the Balkans. Artfully the Prime Minister conducted Roosevelt up the garden path leading north from the Mediterranean into Europe.

The arguments at the TRIDENT top-level conference in Washington narrowed down very quickly to the problem of post-HUSKY operations in the Mediterranean *vs.* more emphasis on BOLERO. The American position remained firm, with General Marshall playing the leading role. He continued to argue that a campaign in Italy would take men and shipping away from concentration in the United Kingdom for the cross-Channel attack. He suggested that air power alone might bring about the collapse of Italy. But the British wanted more. They brought up the suggestion of operations against the Dodecanese or Greece as a red herring to divert us. Since such operations would be even less decisive than an attack on Italy, we were induced to settle for the lesser waste of resources in the costly and time-consuming Italian campaign.

In summing up on May 14, Marshall said: "Mediterranean operations are highly speculative as far as ending the war is concerned. On the other hand, the British feel that Mediterranean operations will result in the demoralization and break-up of the Axis."

Disappointing and frustrating as the TRIDENT conference proved to be, we did at least succeed in obtaining a firm commitment from the British for the cross-Channel operation in 1944. To get this commitment we had had to accept continued operations in the Mediterranean that tied down a large proportion of our forces in an endeavor which contributed little to winning the war. However, we had at least obtained British approval for moving seven Allied divisions from the Mediterranean back to England for the big push. We had accomplished more than at Casablanca.

According to Maurice Matloff, a War Department historian, the TRIDENT conference posed a need for our planners to rethink ways and means of securing basic strategic objectives: How to deal with "current exigencies of the multi-front coalition war and still return to the principle of concentration for a major cross-Channel operation in which they still believed." He writes:

> The need to put over-all U.S. military planning on a firmer basis led General Wedemeyer, the Army planner, to sound what was to be a keynote of Army strategic thinking in the later war years. Pointing to the opportunism that had hitherto characterized British-American strategic planning, he stressed, at the close of April 1943, the need for "the adoption of a long-range concept for the defeat of the European Axis." Only upon the firm establishment of such a concept, he maintained, could long-range logistical planning be initiated. In the same spirit, Colonel Claude B. Ferenbaugh, head of the Operations Division, European Theater Section, emphasized the effects of the "lack of a definite and consistent long-range strategic concept of operations in the

European Theater." Its absence, he declared, prevents the formulation of "a sound plan both as regards troop bases and the types of equipment necessary for operations in the European or adjacent area."

The TRIDENT conference concluded with post-HUSKY operations left to Eisenhower for timing. The method of employing our forces against Italy with a view to knocking her out of the war would be decided by him, subject to the approval of the Combined Chiefs of Staff.

I was greatly pleased with the excellent quality of the work done by all our officers in dealing with the British during the two weeks of TRIDENT. The comments of the British Chiefs of Staff, particularly Sir Alan Brooke, indicate that they had discovered we now meant business in asserting our strategy. An excerpt from Brooke's papers is revealing:

> . . . as I was walking with Marshall and Dill to one of our meetings, Marshall said to me: "I find it hard even now not to look on your North African strategy with a jaundiced eye." I replied: "What strategy would you have preferred?" To which he answered "Cross-Channel operations for the liberation of France and advance on Germany; we should finish the war quicker." I remember replying: "Yes, probably, but not the way we hope to finish it!" . . .
>
> On top of it all, King has been gaining ground recently and was diverting more and more strength to the Pacific. Any attempts to unduly push our strategy on Marshall had a distinct tendency to drive him into King's Pacific camp. He even stated once or twice that, if our strategy was to be one of wasting our time in the Mediterranean, the American Forces might well be better employed in the Pacific. To me the strategy which I had advocated from the very start, and which was at last shaping so successfully, stood out clearer and clearer every day . . . My temporary inability to bring the Americans along with us filled me with depression, and at times almost with despair.

CHAPTER XVI

PATTON IN COMBAT

I FELT that TRIDENT was a job well done on the part of the rank and file in our planning agencies. But though I was happy over the outcome of this conference in May, 1953, I was physically exhausted. One morning as we were walking to work through Arlington Cemetery from our quarters at Fort Myer, General Marshall said to me, "You look tired starting out." I told him I had reached home at 2:00 A.M. "What time did you get home the night before that?" he asked. I said I had worked till midnight. "I think you should stop working such long hours," he said. "One never has an idea after five o'clock in the afternoon." He informed me he was going to tell my chief, General Handy, that he didn't want me working so late. At four o'clock that afternoon he called me to his office and gave me a job that kept me at work all night with my "pick and shovel" boys to have an important paper on his desk when he arrived at eight the next morning.

To do Marshall justice, this matter of overwork was on his mind a week later when he asked me if I would like to visit the Mediterranean Theater to observe the Sicily operation as a temporarily attached officer on Patton's staff. I told him I would be delighted.

Although I had felt great satisfaction in being assigned to the War Plans Division of the General Staff before our entry into the war, I had longed to command troops in battle and had frequently requested such an assignment. Since this was not to be, the next-best thing was to be enabled—if only for a few weeks—to accompany our forces in the invasion of Sicily. Strange as it may sound, being sent to a theater of war was in the nature of a vacation from my gruelling desk job. I knew I could easily leave my planning group now that we had so many supporting committees at work, and Marshall suggested that a break in routine might refresh my creativity.

Early in June I set off for North Africa, charged by the Chief of Staff with the duty of becoming acquainted with lower-echelon planning, particularly for landing operations, and with gaining first-hand experience in amphibious assault. Marshall told me to stay away until I had learned everything from HUSKY that would stand me in good stead as a War Department planner.

I arrived at Algiers on the 12th of June to join Patton's staff. I was at first billeted at Mostagenem, on the north coast of Africa about fifty miles east of Oran. Patton asked me to analyze the entire operational plan for HUSKY and to make any suggestions I deemed appropriate. This was very much to my liking. I suggested there were two respects in which the plan seemed inadequate: first, there was no provision for a diversion or a feint; second, I was not satisfied with the arrangements for direct air support. Moreover, I did not agree with the air leaders in the theater, Air Chief Marshal Sir Arthur Tedder and General Spaatz, that air power should be used in direct support of troops only when enemy air forces had been neutralized. I thought that this doctrine was not applicable in the situation confronting us in Sicily, where the defense forces were numerically stronger and had the advantage of fortified positions.

I learned later that General Sir Harold Alexander, General Eisenhower's British Deputy, and other British ground and sea officers had expressed views similar to mine. General Alexander directed the HUSKY air commanders to provide direct air support. Patton, however, did nothing to inject a diversionary effort or feint, although he told me he agreed in principle with the suggestion.

In addition to participating in some of the staff preparations for the HUSKY operation, I was active in other ways. As I reported to Handy, I was engaged in "strenuous observations" and "innocuous participation" in amphibious exercises from Tunis to Oran involving all the American units which were scheduled to take part in HUSKY.

At times I accompanied the landing-craft units; at others I walked along the beaches to observe the troops coming ashore and attacking inland; on one occasion I observed the landing operations from a small Cub plane. As I explained in my letter to Handy, I had at first been a little vague about what to do in the theater, but I tried to see everything that went on from top to bottom without getting in the way. General Patton wrote Handy:

> We are delighted to have him [General Wedemeyer] and have given him a complete run of our staff and have also sent him to see several of the divisions and to watch three landing operations. At the moment he is learning what he can (if anything) around AFHQ and will come aboard this ship the night we sail.

I frequently had dinner with Patton and his staff. Over a little wine or other stimulant he always became a most interesting and provocative talker who elicited information from others by encouraging them to give their real views and opinions. Emotional, and with a tremendous capacity for dynamic action, Patton was an unusual type of military man who was not only physically courageous but also possessed the rare quality which the Germans call "civil courage." He dared to speak his mind and act according to his convictions. The American people were given a picture of him only as a swashbuckling, intrepid combat leader; but he had a scholarly bent and a profound knowledge of strategy, tactics, and military and political techniques. He had studied the campaigns of von Schlieffen and Frederick the Great and was more interested in them than in Napoleon's campaigns, which were more familiar to most American staff officers.

On July 3, 1943, just a week before we were to land on Sicily, I'd been having dinner with Patton and his deputy Major General (later Lieutenant General) Geoffrey Keyes, and Patton asked me how I estimated the situation in Europe. Years before, he had read and discussed with me the report I submitted in 1938 on my return from the Kriegs Akademie concerning German strategy, tactics, and capabilities. Since then we had kept in touch through meetings and correspondence, exchanging views on the progress of the war and German capabilities. I told Patton and Keyes that I had read a World War I Allied intelligence estimate concerning Germany's power and will to resist and that this estimate was very wide of the mark. Prime Minister Lloyd George and General Jan Smuts of South Africa, attending a meeting of the Imperial War Cabinet in London on August 13, 1918, predicted that the Allies would never be able to win a victory over the Germans prior to 1919. On that very same day, August 13, 1918, the German military leader, von Ludendorff, advised his high command that it was absolutely impossible to defeat the enemy. He recommended that inasmuch as continued defensive action wouldn't win the war, a resort should be made to diplomatic means to bring about an armistice. Lloyd George and Smuts had a good intelligence service, but no appreciation of the psychological state of Germany in 1918.

Here, I said, was an example of a fine estimate of military capabilities but a poor estimate of the over-all capacity of Germany to win the war or to continue the fight. Keyes reminded us that the German Army was never defeated in the field, and when the armistice was effected on November 11, 1918, all the German units were fighting with excellent discipline and determination. Patton added that actually Allied forces hadn't reached German soil when the armistice was declared, which was a good point. Other information which was available to the British Cabinet at the time indicated the blockade was beginning to have a very serious effect upon the economy of Germany. The Germans at home had lost faith in their leadership and faith in victory, and there was increasing unrest due to mounting casualties and food shortages.

In reply to a question by Keyes concerning the situation now, I said that in my judgment the turning point of the war had occurred when the Russians had destroyed the bulk of the German military formations at Stalingrad. From there on out I felt that the Germans had lost the initiative and were on the downgrade. Patton then asked me if I felt military men would take control and compel the political leaders to ask for an armistice. I mentioned General Beck but commented that I didn't think he had the prestige of Ludendorff. Perhaps Rommel might do the job. "Unconditional surrender" was, of course, operating against this.

When the armada of ships dropped anchor off the southern coast of Sicily on July 9, all was quiet except for the swishing of water against the side of our flagship. Admiral Henry K. Hewitt, General Patton, and I, after eating a good-sized hunk of the birthday cake which the Admiral had provided for me, went topside on the Captain's bridge. The ships were silhouetted against the gray skyline, and the stars shone bright above.

I felt that the silence was ominous. The shoreline was plainly visible, yet there was no indication that our presence had been discovered. This was my first experience in an amphibious operation. Only a few hours later all hell was breaking loose. I went ashore with the assaulting troops and visited the beach west of Gela where Colonel (later Major General) William O. Darby's commandos were landing. Different-colored lights were visible on the beach as I went ashore, and I knew they were markers for different units as they proceeded to their assigned sectors. On the right was the 1st Division and on its right the 45th Division, and then the Canadians farther to the east.

Darby's commandos quickly penetrated the edge of the town, taking many prisoners, both Germans and Italians. The naval bombardment continued from our combat ships supporting the operation. The naval gunfire, interspersed with the staccato of machine guns and the occasional boom of artillery, created a din that caused one to shout in order to be heard.

After spending most of the morning with Darby I moved on down eastward to visit the 1st Division. There I ran into Brigadier General Teddy Roosevelt, Jr., who was second in command of that famous fighting outfit. The forward echelons had advanced well in reaching their phase line as scheduled. Succeeding waves were offloading and proceeding in, but occasionally a GI would stop and dig in because the beaches were being subjected to hostile artillery fire. Teddy Roosevelt, oblivious of his own safety, was walking around coolly with a swagger stick, calming the soldiers. He would kneel down beside a GI who was trying to get as close to the earth as he possibly could, throwing up a little sand revetment with his shovel. I overheard him talking to a few of these men. He would ask them where they were from. Invariably he knew someone in that town or would talk about a building or a landmark. This served to steady a nervous chap. Then he would admonish the boy in a friendly way to push forward, pointing out that it was dangerous to stop on the beaches where the enemy naturally would direct his shelling. I moved on along to the advance CP. The command post had not yet been established but there were several officers setting up communications and arranging for a field headquarters to be used by Major General "Terry" Allen, the indefatigable and gallant division commander.

I was much impressed with the Navy's efficiency in the HUSKY operation, particularly the wonderful liaison, co-operation, and integration of effort provided by that outstanding admiral, Richard Conolly, who commanded the fleet that put General Truscott's 3rd Division ashore in Sicily on the morning of July 10. Not only did the Navy land troops but it continued close support of the infantry as they advanced rapidly inland. I visited Truscott's division and watched it in combat. In my judgment it was the best-trained, the most aggressive, and the best-led outfit in Sicily. Truscott was one of the best combat leaders that I observed during the entire war. He was very high in his praise of Admiral Dick Conolly and most enthusiastic about his own division. His book, *Command Decisions*, is a modest account of the experiences of this brave and able commander.

I was particularly interested in the maintenance of troops over the beaches, for I had in mind at all times the problems that would arise in 1944 on the north coast of France. I had helped Colonel W. E. V. Abraham, a British officer I had known in Washington, prepare a long report on this subject. Our combined observations certainly strengthened my confidence in our contemplated large-scale amphibious operation against the north coast of France, and I so reported to the American Chiefs of Staffs.

After my six weeks' "vacation" in the Mediterranean Theater, I was recalled to my desk job. A radiogram came from General Handy instructing me to come home by way of London, where I was to spend two days ascertaining British views on preparations for another world conference scheduled to be held at Quebec in August.

I parted from George Patton with sincere regret for I had a great affection and admiration for him as a man. My high regard for the General, whom I considered the outstanding field commander of the U.S. Army in the Second World War, is recorded in a letter I wrote to General Handy in April, 1944, when I was again in London attending a conference arranged by Mountbatten with the British Chiefs of Staff and the Prime Minister. I had been contacted by a colonel of the U.S. Army's Inspector General's Department, concerning investigation of an incident which had occurred in North Africa involving General Patton. An American captain and sergeant were being court-martialed for having shot German prisoners during the Sicily operation and their defense had been that Patton had told them, during a critique prior to the operation, to shoot prisoners. Excerpts from my letter to Handy follow:

> While visiting with General Patton before the invasion of Sicily we arose in the morning of July 2nd and proceeded to a sector of the North African coastline to observe an amphibious landing by the 45th U.S. Division. We watched the men coming ashore and at the conclusion of the exercise each regimental combat team was assembled for a critique. Patton addressed the men, exhorting them to advance rapidly after getting ashore.
>
> He admonished them to be very careful when the Germans or Italians raised their arms as if they wanted to surrender. He stated that sometimes the enemy would do this, throwing our men off guard. The enemy soldiers had on several occasions shot our unsuspecting men or had thrown grenades at them. Patton warned the members of the 45th Division to watch out for this treachery and to "kill the s.o.b.'s" unless they were certain of their real intention to surrender.
>
> I am sure that the captain and sergeant who are now under investigation for shooting German prisoners misunderstood Patton's instructions as well as his intentions.

I took off from Sicily for Algiers in a transport plane accompanied by Major General William J. Donovan of the Office of Strategic Services (OSS), who, like myself, had been an observer at the Sicilian operation. At Algiers I visited with Eisenhower, talked to Bedell Smith and other friends, and saw General Mark W. Clark and Major General (later General) Alfred M. Gruenther at Fifth Army Headquarters. I spent four valuable days in London discussing not only the cross-Channel operation (soon to be called OVERLORD) but also ANAKIM, the Burma operation. I still found strong opposition to the cross-Channel plan. The Prime Minister seemed to be seeking every honorable avenue of escape.

I got back to Washington early in August, benefited by some exposure to combat and with a considerable amount of useful information for both my strategic planners and General Hull's group in Operations. In a long, informal report to General Handy, I observed that it was only with great difficulty that Patton's staff had been able to get in touch with the authorized representatives of air and naval commanders in making his own plans for HUSKY. I thought that such a failure of liaison should be remedied. I also recommended that military resources, the means for carrying out an operation, should be available early and then frozen in order to give a commander the feeling of stability. There is nothing like knowing that you have complete control of the movement, discipline, morale, and employment of all forces assigned to you if you are a commander in the field.

On the basis of my experience I became convinced of the value of observers overseas, watching the preparations and actually participating in combat operations. It would also have been a constructive move to send division commanders who were training in the United States overseas to see how divisions worked in the final phases of training and in combat.

CHAPTER XVII

THAT "SOFT UNDERBELLY"

Since some of my colleagues had acquiesced in the Mediterranean strategy, I tried to be objective and find affirmative reasons for continuing to climb the Mediterranean ladder. It would be perfectly logical, I conceded, to conduct operations through the Balkans if port facilities and air and naval bases permitted, and if the terrain would permit maneuver after we got ashore.

If we could get through the Balkans I foresaw the accomplishment of my ulterior but quietly guarded political objective of keeping the Russians from overrunning Central Europe. If we could get Anglo-American forces up into Poland by attacking from the south, the Mediterranean, I would gladly jump at the chance. But after careful scrutiny of all the possibilities, I couldn't see a chance of success. The terrain was against it.

Sir Alan Brooke regarded the Mediterranean Campaign as a great success because it had released "about a million tons of shipping." But his argument for pushing on and on in accordance with the "soft underbelly" concept was not supported by sound strategic principles.

At the TRIDENT conference Churchill had been disturbed by the evidence of increasingly articulate and resolute opposition by the Americans to this strategy. He was dissatisfied because the Combined Chiefs of Staff had not categorically stated that at the conclusion of the HUSKY operation, Italy would be invaded. This in spite of the fact that the United States representatives had agreed to submit the following resolution:

> That the Allied Commander-in-Chief, North Africa will be instructed as a matter of urgency, to plan such operations in exploitation of HUSKY as are best calculated to eliminate Italy from the war and to contain the maximum number of German forces. Which of the various specific operations should be adopted, and thereafter mounted, is a decision which will be reserved to the Combined Chiefs of Staff.

Churchill at this time seems to have been mainly concerned with giving all-out immediate aid to Communist Russia. As he himself wrote subsequently, "The Russians were fighting every day on their enormous front and their blood flowed in a torrent. We were then to keep over a million and a half fine troops, and all their air and naval power, idle for nearly a year!"

We Americans had tried by every possible argument to show the Prime Minister that Allied troops and supplies could and should be quickly removed from the Mediterranean to the United Kingdom for an operation that would definitely give us military and political advantages. Instead of listening to us, Churchill resorted to every known means of getting his own way. He successfully persuaded Roosevelt to have Marshall accompany him to Eisenhower's headquarters in Algiers immediately after TRIDENT and then assembled his senior commanders—Alexander, Montgomery, and others—at a conference to work on Eisenhower.

Whenever we Americans attempted to obtain agreements from our British friends on an operation outside the area of British interests we were always "lacking in landing craft." But whenever Churchill recommended an operation in the Mediterranean Theater, immediately all resources were readily available, even landing craft, which proves that where there's a will there's a way.

At one conference Mr. Eden was present, reinforced, of course, by Montgomery. (Concentration of British top-drawer leadership was obviously planned, but they tried to make it appear that they all had just dropped in.) General Alexander and Admiral Cunningham supported the Prime Minister, as did all the British, so the foregone conclusion was that after HUSKY we would go into Italy.

Eden, not schooled as to what he should say when he made his supporting talk, expressed the conviction that knocking Italy out of the war would go a long way toward bringing the Turks onto the Allied side. The Turks, he said, would be much more friendly "when our troops have reached the Balkan area." The Prime Minister knew, of course, that mentioning the Balkans was anathema to Marshall, as it was to all American military men. So when he recognized that Eden had let the truth slip out, the wily Winston jumped at once into the breach and made a clear-cut statement to allay Marshall's concern. As Churchill later wrote in *The Hinge of Fate*, he "intervened to observe" that he was not advocating sending an army into the Balkans now or in the near future.

In any event, the proposal to save the Balkans from communism could never have been made good by a "soft underbelly" invasion, for Churchill himself had already cleared the way for the success of Tito, the avowed Communist. Tito had been firmly ensconced in Yugoslavia with British aid long before Italy itself was conquered. True, if we had invaded the Balkans through the Ljubljana Gap, we might theoretically have beaten the Russians to Vienna and Budapest. But logistics would have been against us there: it would have been next to impossible to supply more than two divisions through Adriatic ports.

Roosevelt, it is apparent from Churchill's own memoirs, did not agree to the Italian campaign without a struggle. Churchill reports that the President . . .

. . . questioned the occupation of Italy which would release German troops to fight elsewhere. He thought the best way of forcing Germany to fight would be to launch an operation across the Channel.

But Churchill bore down on the reluctant Roosevelt. According to the British Prime Minister's own account:

> I now replied that as we were agreed that the cross-Channel operation could not take place until 1944, it seemed imperative to use our great armies to attack Italy. I do not think that an occupation of all Italy would be necessary. If Italy collapses, the United Nations would occupy the ports and airfields needed.

As things turned out, after the Anglo-American forces got into Italy, Churchill did everything in his power to prevent their movement back into England to participate in the cross-Channel operation of 1944. Later he did everything possible to sabotage the ANVIL plan for the invasion of Southern France after it had been accepted by Stalin, Roosevelt, and himself at the Teheran conference. Although committed to ANVIL, Churchill still hoped to scuttle it in favor of a push through the Balkans. He was steadfastly determined to have his strategy implemented, and fought so hard for his predilections that he managed to delay OVERLORD almost to the point where its value as a decisive operation was lost.

I have personal knowledge that Churchill vigorously opposed the ANVIL operation. He was in constant communication with Roosevelt, Hopkins, and Marshall, in fact with anyone in Washington who might have sufficient influence to persuade the Americans to give it up. I happened to be passing through London in July, 1944, when the great argument over ANVIL was at its height. Churchill showed me a sheaf of telegrams that he had sent to Roosevelt, Hopkins, and Marshall urging them to abandon the operation. He said the beaches of Southern France would be strewn with the bodies of American doughboys and British tommies. He was very dramatic in his description of the debacle that would surely occur if we ever launched such an attack. I expressed tactfully but firmly my disagreement with his views. I politely refused to radio my chief in Washington as he requested. After I left the Prime Minister I visited the joint intelligence offices and asked for an appreciation concerning the enemy's capabilities in Southern France and I was given an excellent résumé. Apparently Churchill did not trust his own intelligence agency's estimate of the enemy dispositions and strength, or he was interpreting military intelligence to support his own concept of strategy. When I had pointed out to him that the difficult terrain of the Balkans would result in far greater losses to our forces, he shook his head so violently his jowls trembled. When he eventually learned that the Americans were adamant in their determination to carry through the ANVIL plan, he went to the area himself aboard a destroyer, participating courageously in the very operations which he had violently opposed. Whatever his purpose, to me he recalled an admirable quality: "If you can't lick 'em, join 'em."

Anyone with an appreciation of the logistical factors in modern war should have realized that ANVIL was an important subsidiary operation that would support our campaign in Northern France. It was the only underbelly operation that had any justification in a war of decision for both tactical and logistic reasons. Tactical because it compelled the enemy to disperse his forces and posed a real threat to his southern flank. Logistical because it gave us the port of Marseilles in which to unload supplies for transport to our troops battling the Germans in the main theater of operations in Northern France.

In combat, a World War II division consumed daily about 700 tons of supplies. As the number of divisions in the cross-Channel operation was increased, obviously the tonnage which must flow through the lines of communications and into ports, thence to the fighting fronts, was mounting rapidly. By August, 1944, there were more than 30 divisions in France; therefore, approximately 21,000 tons of supplies had to be brought in every day. Initially the supplies came over the beaches; later, the fine port facilities of Cherbourg were rehabilitated and usable. The best port on the north coast of Europe was Antwerp, in Belgium. Therefore, our tactical scheme of maneuver correctly included that port as an important objective to be seized as soon as possible.

There was another important tactical reason for ANVIL. The danger of a right (south) flank attack on the Anglo-American invasion forces had to be provided for as our troops advanced eastward. Without ANVIL it would have been necessary to leave divisions along the lines of communications and at critical points. This would have so weakened the strength of the over-all attacking force that by the time it reached the Seine or points farther east it would have lacked sufficient strength to carry on and penetrate into Germany.

American and British war objectives were identical; namely, crush the enemy militarily. The only argument concerned two widely different concepts of the broad scheme of maneuver. Which was better, the British idea of invading through the "soft under-belly" or the American trans-Channel invasion? We Americans thought that we could and should launch an all-out invasion of France in 1943, assuming of course that a realistic BOLERO (assembling of forces in the U.K.) was accomplished. By no stretch of the imagination could the British have launched their "soft under-belly" invasion until after the force-consuming Mediterranean operations had been completed and then naval and air bases established to give support to the invading forces. After landing, our forces would still be terribly handicapped in trying to negotiate the rugged mountain mass.

Churchill all along magnified the value of Mediterranean victories. In Washington in 1943, before Congress, he made a typically dramatic speech which had a powerful emotional impact on the assembled legislators. In the course of his eloquent discourse he said:

> In North Africa we builded better than we knew. The unexpected came to the aid of the design and multiplied the results. For this we have to thank the military intuition of Corporal Hitler. We may notice as I predicted in the House of Commons three months ago the touch of the master hand. The same insensate obstinacy which condemned Field Marshal von Paulus and his army to destruction at Stalingrad has brought this new catastrophe upon our enemies in Tunisia.

Actually, there were only three German divisions operating in Africa. It is true that the German General Rommel, a master tactician and a bold, intrepid leader, had several Italian divisions under his command. But, though Italians are individually brave, they were not effective as organized units. Churchill grossly exaggerated the magnitude of the Allied victory in Africa. Montgomery had an over-whelming force—manpower, firepower, and air support—a marked advantage over Rommel. Nevertheless the German Desert Fox was able to outsmart the British for a considerable length of time. His generalship was so outstanding that the British troops who fought him carried pictures of Rommel in their knapsacks.

CHAPTER XVIII

FROM "TRIDENT" TO QUEBEC

FOLLOWING THE TRIDENT conference, Churchill had returned to London via Algiers, smarting over his failure to win a complete victory over the American Chiefs of Staff. He had some success, however, in the presence of Marshall and, assisted by his senior military leaders, in convincing Eisenhower that he should continue up the Italian boot after Sicily. Once again, the oratorical powers of Churchill, instead of sound strategic thinking, were to influence the operations of the Allies. While insisting that he did not want to interfere with the cross-Channel attack for 1944, Churchill said he wanted to take full and immediate advantage of all the opportunities opened up by the capture of Sicily. He declared that his "heart lay in an invasion of Southern Italy." General Eisenhower said that if the Allies were going to knock out Italy, they should go in immediately after HUSKY with all available means.

Our own air people submitted a plan at this time for a major operation against Italy designed to seize the boot up to the Pisa-Rimini line. They were interested in establishing bomber bases which could be used for strikes against South German industrial regions. This caused me no end of concern back in Washington and when he returned I pointed out to General Marshall the danger inherent in the plan. Marshall agreed that we should not commit real strength to any such goose chase. He insisted that seven divisions should be withdrawn from the Mediterranean area not later than November—four American and three British.

This set the stage for a continuing duel between Americans and British over the relative claims of Italy and the Normandy invasion. In London, during a summer visit in 1943, Mr. Stimson, still our most stalwart champion of concentration for OVERLORD, reported that Churchill . . .

. . . virtually took possession of my movements for the first week and I found myself launched in the discussion of subjects and with people which I had not expected. These unexpected subjects were so important that I devoted the bulk of my time to their consideration and altered my trip accordingly.

Although I have known the P.M. for many years and had talked freely with him I have never had such a series of important and confidential discussions as this time. . . . I told him the American people did not hate the Italians but took them rather as a joke as fighters; that only by an intellectual effort had they been convinced that Germany was their most dangerous enemy and should be disposed of before Japan; that the enemy whom the American people really hated, if they hated anyone, was Japan who had dealt them a foul blow. After setting out all the details upon which my conclusion was predicated, I asserted that it was my concerted opinion that if we allow ourselves to become so entangled with matters of the Balkans, Greece, and the Middle East that we could not fulfill our purpose of ROUNDHAMMER [the combination of the former code names ROUNDUP and SLEDGEHAMMER] in 1944, that situation would be a serious blow to the prestige of the President's war policy and therefore to the interests of the United States.

In the course of his discussions Mr. Stimson learned that the Prime Minister believed any blow to the prestige of the American President's war policy would be easily and quickly overcome by victories. The Prime Minister maintained his position of favoring a march on Rome with the idea of knocking Italy out of the war. Mr. Stimson reported that Eden, on the other hand, continued to argue for a thrust into the Balkans and Greece.

Stimson was gratified to note that Lieutenant General Freddie Morgan, who was British Chief of Staff for planning OVERLORD, the cross-Channel operation, was aware of all of the implications of Churchill's diversionary instincts. As "Lord Overlord," Morgan was prepared to combat them. Stimson was favorably impressed with our own general, Ray W. Barker, who was Morgan's deputy. Said Stimson of the Morgan-Barker team:

> He [Morgan] was very frank . . . in stating his fear of delays which might be caused by getting too deep into commitments in the Mediterranean. . . . Barker who explained the details of the plan showed the same fear. In other words they both felt that the plan was sound and safe but there might be subsequently yielding to temptation to undertake new activities which would interfere with the long stage of preparation with a false hope that such interference could be atoned for by subsequent speeding up.

To combat Churchill's table talk, Secretary Stimson submitted a memorandum to F.D.R. on August 10, 1943, designed to hold the President to a firm line against the temptation to "soft underbelly" extensions at the Quebec conference scheduled as QUADRANT. I did my best also to create a proper atmosphere for this conference. Just before boarding the flagship of Admiral Hewitt to accompany the task force in the operation against Sicily, I wrote a long letter to my Chief, General Handy, dated 4 July 1943, from Algiers:

> Even though HUSKY is successful after a bitter struggle [I said], we could never drive rampant up the boot as the P.M. so dramatically depicted in his concept of our continued effort over here. However, if we do decide to continue operations directly against Italy, greatly increased resources than those now invisaged or available in the area would be mandatory—to insure our position in the western Mediterranean and concurrently to provide sufficient punch in our blow against Italy proper. ROUNDHAMMER would be even more remote, in fact, may be crossed off the books for 1944. If we could only convince our cousins that this European theater struggle will never be won by dispersing our forces around the perimeter of the Axis citadel! I lay in bed the past several nights trying to evolve an overall concept of winning the war in Europe—one that would stir the imagination and win the support of the P.M., if not that of his recalcitrant planners and chiefs of staff.

Back home after Sicily I discovered that my co-partner in Operations Division, General Hull, had somewhat shifted his ground on strategy. His subordinate in the Operations Division, Colonel Vorys H. Connor, had prepared a memorandum for him recommending a reversal of our position on the Mediterranean. General Handy showed me the memorandum. Its conclusion read:

> Although from the very beginning of this war, I have felt that the logical plan for the defeat of Germany was to strike at her across the Channel by the most direct route, our commitments to the Mediterranean have led me to the belief that we should now reverse our decision and pour our resources into the exploitation of our Mediterranean operations.

I experienced my familiar sense of frustration concerning the firming up of strategy. Apparently the proponents of this reversal had abandoned all consideration of the basic ideas which caused the first Joint Staff Planning team back in early 1942 to discard any idea of a major invasion of Europe through the Mediterranean, namely, the mountainous terrain (which would preclude maneuver or at least restrict mobility to an unacceptable degree) and the dearth of air and naval bases.

Two of the keenest planners in the Joint War Plan Committees, General Bissell of the Army and Colonel Lindsey of the Army Air Force, submitted at this time an excellent memorandum on the subject of continued strategy. They discussed their views in my office. They maintained that the United States had been outmaneuvered at all of the world conferences because British political aims were clearly enunciated and their representatives in uniform or in civilian government positions acted as one team in support of the realization of those aims.

General Bissell provided me with considerable data concerning our failure to implement BOLERO. He pointed out to me that the original plans and agreements reached for the BOLERO build-up had contemplated a total of over one million men, or 17 army divisions, 60 air groups, and 4,000 airplanes in the United Kingdom by April 1943. Actually, as of the summer of 1943, we had only 110,000 troops and some 900 airplanes in England.

My informal meeting with Bissell and Lindsey occurred shortly after my return from Sicily during the first week of August. We were all busy preparing for the meeting in Quebec. Bissell emphasized that we had more than 500,000 troops and 4,000 airplanes in the Mediterranean. Dick Lindsey mentioned the fact that, so far, the only army that had really come to grips with the Germans had been the Russian. Unless we could persuade the British to go across the Channel, we never would make a contribution except by naval blockade and air power.

It was at this point that Lindsey broke with the BOLERO strategy to suggest we should continue to fight the Germans by a combination of air and sea forces. He thought this would eventually break the German war economy and, by weakening the effort on the Eastern Front, also perhaps destroy the will of the Germans to continue the fight.

By such counsel these two brilliant young planners urged me to support a strategy that envisaged continued operations in Italy until that country was knocked out of the war, meanwhile continuing to build up in the United Kingdom for the cross-Channel invasion insofar as was practicable. They urged me to recommend to General Marshall that if the British would not approve of this strategy we should turn our attention to the Pacific as soon as Italy had been defeated.

Even my old planning sidekick, Admiral Cooke, who was thoroughly honest at all times, finally deserted the cause. Cooke now took the position that there were so many contingencies involved that the cross-Channel move should be regarded as something to be undertaken only if favorable conditions arose. Meanwhile we should carry out scheduled operations in the Mediterranean and Pacific.

Naturally, I took exception to all of these views but I did recognize the merits of my colleagues' arguments. General Anderson had been relieved as air planner for the Joint Staff and replaced by General Lawrence S. Kuter. Quite independently, Kuter took the position that we should continue the strategy of concentrating in the United Kingdom and crossing the Channel for a decisive blow at the enemy. He did not agree with Cooke that conditions had changed sufficiently to justify a modification of our strategy.

On the eve of the QUADRANT conference at Quebec we were all at sixes and sevens in the planning agencies. But General Marshall continued to support the cross-Channel operation. With Marshall sticking to his guns we finally presented a united front. We also had the promise of Presidential support.

In the period intervening between TRIDENT and QUADRANT, plans for the Pacific were stepped up both as to time and scope. This can be attributed, I am sure, to the inability of the American Chiefs of Staff to obtain enthusiastic and loyal support for decisive action against Germany. The augmentation of the south and southwest Pacific theaters went on steadily, drawing in valuable resources that should properly have gone to the United Kingdom for the big blow. At this time we planners were asked to consider six major undertakings for the Far East. First, there was the extension of the MacArthur-Halsey advance along the New Guinea-Mindanao line. Second, there was the drive in the central Pacific, under Nimitz. Third, there were the operations against the Japanese in the Aleutians. Fourth, the augmenting of air resources in China via an increase in Hump tonnage. Fifth, the initiation of realistic offensive operations in Burma. Finally, there was the need to crystallize a plan for converging on Japan itself. My group had to consider these many proposals not only on their own merits but also with reference to commitments for OVERLORD and the idea of beating Germany first.

We had continuing jousts with the Navy over the Pacific. When MacArthur and Nimitz were fighting for Pacific priority as a whole, they presented a united front. But they had their own quarrel over the claims of the southwest and central Pacific strategies. A characteristic message from MacArthur read:

> From a broad strategic standpoint I am convinced that the best course of offensive action in the Pacific is a movement from Australia through New Guinea to Mindanao. This movement can be supported by land based aircraft which is utterly essential and will immediately cut the enemy lines from Japan to his conquered territory to the southward. By contrast a movement through the mandated islands will be a series of amphibious attacks with the support of carrier based aircraft against objectives defended by naval units and ground troops supported by land based aviation. Midway stands as an example of the hazards of such operations. Moreover, no vital strategic objective is reached until the

series of amphibious frontal attacks succeeds in reaching Mindanao. The factors upon which the old ORANGE plan was based have been greatly altered by the hostile conquests of Malaya and the Netherlands East Indies and by the availability of Australia as a base.

This not only reflected the rivalry between two theaters of operations, it also pointed up the eternal dispute between Naval and Army Air over spheres of responsibility involving carried- and land-based planes. But the message was noteworthy for a more important reason: it reflected MacArthur's strategic desire to go by the most direct route to critical areas which the enemy could not afford to lose for either psychological, economic, or military reasons. In other words, MacArthur adhered to the root principle of military strategy, namely, concentrating for a decisive blow against the most critical target.

Whenever one of MacArthur's reports came into the War Plans Division, I was impressed with the sound strategic concept behind his proposals. How often I wished that he could be in a position of authority in our Government to help the planners or the Joint Chiefs of Staff. He would surely have sought to compel the British to stop their indecisive operations. In relying upon the land forces of the Soviet Union to deliver the knockout blow, we were storing up infinite trouble for ourselves at the peace table. At the war's end the Communists would be in a favorable position to deliver mighty blows in political, economic, and psychological fields against their allies.

On August 10, just before leaving for the QUADRANT conference, the Joint Chiefs of Staff met with the President at the White House. Secretary of War Stimson was present. Roosevelt referred to the memorandum he had received from Stimson embodying the latter's observations and conversations in London. The President told the Joint Chiefs of Staff that Mr. Churchill was still looking toward operations in the Balkans. Mr. Stimson modified the President's remark to the effect that the Prime Minister wanted to give aid to the guerrillas in the Balkans in order to bring about uprisings. He told of Churchill's hopes of stirring up defections by parachuting agents and making air drops into those countries. It was Anthony Eden, said Stimson, who wished to conduct military operations through the Balkans.

Commenting on Mr. Eden's interest in invading the Balkans, Roosevelt said that the British were desirous of preventing Soviet influence from spreading into Yugoslavia and Bulgaria. The President added the curious statement that he did not understand the British viewpoint in this connection, for he, Roosevelt did not believe that the Soviets wanted to take over the Balkan states but wished only to establish "kinship with other slavic peoples." It is odd that the President, who was certainly aware of the fact that Churchill was already supporting an avowed Croat Communist, Tito, against the Serb patriot Mihailovich, should have thought that communism represented no menace in Yugoslavia. The President said it was "unwise to plan military strategy based on a gamble as to political results." Since the very purpose of military strategy is to gain a political end, the remark made very little sense. Nevertheless, it was reassuring to learn that Mr. Roosevelt was against trying to climb over the Balkan mountain passes in a vain attempt to reach Germany from below.

During my few days in London on the way home from Sicily I had mentioned to General Ray Barker that in my judgment certain leaders in Germany recognized that Stalingrad was the turning point of the war. I was sure that, of their enemies, the Germans would much prefer to let Anglo-Americans overrun their country than the hated Bolsheviks. Barker felt badly that we hadn't already made "Herculean" efforts to improvise an invasion of the Continent using a "Dunkirk fleet" of small craft in addition to more conventional landing craft. We might have thus been ready to exploit Stalingrad.

In London we had discussed the strength of the assault echelon needed for invasion. I felt that this echelon might be increased somewhat in the Morgan-Barker plan in order to give a broader front in the initial assault. I had learned at the German War College that it was advisable to attack in this manner, with mobile reserves available to exploit the point of air-isolated break-through. The exact location of the main effort should not be fixed until a break-through had occurred. No enemy can be strong everywhere, and after a penetration of his lines has been made, flexibility can exploit his weakness. That is why I felt that the initial cross-Channel assault should be on a broad front, with the mobile reserves standing ready to pour in anywhere.

2 CENTS PAY NO MORE!

Chicago Daily Tribune

THE WORLD'S GREATEST NEWSPAPER

FINAL

VOLUME C—NO 290 C | THURSDAY, DECEMBER 4, 1941.—46 PAGES | PRICE TWO CENTS

F.D.R.'S WAR PLANS!

REDS BEGIN NEW DRIVE TO BREAK VISE ON MOSCOW

Strike at Nazi Line South of Leningrad.

BULLETIN.

BERNE, Switzerland, Dec 4 (Thursday).—A special bulletin from Moscow early today announced soviet forces had launched a heavy attack along the entire northern line from Kalinin to Leningrad in a terrific effort to crush the German threat against Moscow. The main fighting was believed to be in the Lake Ilmen district 120 miles southeast of Leningrad where Russian forces were reported breaking thru the German lines on the Volkhov river.

(Maps on Page 17.)

LONDON, Dec. 4 (Thursday) (AP)—Russian troops were reported early today to have captured two Italian divisions which the Germans, falling back west of Rostov, had thrown into the path of the soviet steamroller.

The Italians, identified as members of the Union and Tuscan divisions, "hardly reached the battle lines before they began giving themselves up

LEIBER TRADED TO GIANTS; CUBS GET BOWMAN

The Chicago Cubs early this morning traded Outfielder Hank Leiber to the New York Giants for Pitcher Bob Bowman and an unannounced sum of cash. The deal was completed at the minor league baseball convention in Jacksonville, Fla. Leiber was one of three Giants sent to the Cubs after the 1938 season in exchange for Bill Jurges, Frank Demaree, and Ken O'Dea.

(Details on sports pages.)

NEWS SUMMARY of The Tribune

(And Historical Scrap Book)

Thursday, December 4, 1941

WAR SITUATION.

BERNE—Russians launch offensive to end Moscow threat. Page 1.

Germans unifying European industry, says Tribune man. Page 14.

CAIRO—RAF presses war during lull in Libya fighting. Page 15.

HELSINGFORS—Finns begin to occupy Hango as Reds pull out. Page 17.

WASHINGTON.

Roosevelt war plan calls for armed force of 10 million. Page 1.

House passes drastic anti-strike bill, 252 to 136. Page 1.

White House reveals Turkey put under lend-lease aid. Page 1.

President seeks to avoid shooting war over Finland. Page 12.

HOUSE ADOPTS DRASTIC BILL TO BLOCK STRIKES

Goes to Senate on 252-136 Vote.

BY WILLIAM STRAND.

(Chicago Tribune Press Service.)

Washington, D. C., Dec. 3.—The house of representatives, by a vote of 252 to 136, today passed sweeping anti-strike legislation designed to prevent work stoppages because of labor disputes in arms industries.

Rep. H. W. Smith.

The final vote was on a compromise measure introduced yesterday by Rep. Howard W. Smith [D., Va.]. It was regarded as the most drastic of four anti-strike measures before the house.

A coalition of 123 Republicans and 129 Democrats prevailed over 108 Democrats, 24 Republicans, 3 Progressives and 1 American Labor party member in adopting the bill.

Bill's Major Provisions.

As sent to the senate, the measure

THE STRONGHOLD OF PEACE

GOAL IS 10 MILLION ARMED MEN; HALF TO FIGHT IN AEF

Proposes Land Drive by July 1, 1943, to Smash Nazis; President Told of Equipment Shortage.

BY CHESLY MANLY.

(Copyright: 1941: By The Chicago Tribune.)

Washington, D. C., Dec. 3.—A confidential report prepared by the joint army and navy high command by direction of President Roosevelt calls for American expeditionary forces aggregating 5,000,000 men for a final land offensive against Germany and her satellites. It contemplates total armed forces of 10,045,658 men.

One of the few existing copies of this astounding document, which represents decisions and commitments affecting the destinies of peoples thruout the civilized world, became available to The Tribune today.

It is a blueprint for total war on a scale unprecedented in at least two oceans and three continents, Europe, Africa, and Asia.

The report expresses the considered opinion of the army and navy strategists that "Germany and her European satellites cannot be defeated by the European powers now fighting against her." Therefore, it concludes, "if our European enemies are to be defeated it will be necessary for the United States to enter the war, and to employ a part of its armed forces offensively in the eastern Atlantic and in Europe and Africa."

July 1, 1943, is fixed as the date for the beginning of the final supreme effort by American land

REVEAL TURKEY GETS LEND-LEASE

Roosevelt, Churchill, and "unconditional surrender" at Casablanca.

Giraud (left) and de Gaulle meet at Casablanca.

Conference at Quebec; seated at left, Marshall, Arnold, Deane; standing, 3rd from right, Wedemeyer.

Generalissimo and Madame Chiang Kai-shek with friends at Cairo, Thanksgiving Day, 1943.

The Big Three, seated at Teheran, December 2, 1943. Hopkins at far left, Eden between Roosevelt and Churchill.

Allied leaders in Burma: Wedemeyer (standing); left to right, seated, Sultan, Mountbatten, Donovan.

Wedemeyer and Chennault with
Governor Lung of Yunnan.

Wedemeyer and Hurley in the
Philippines, February, 1945.

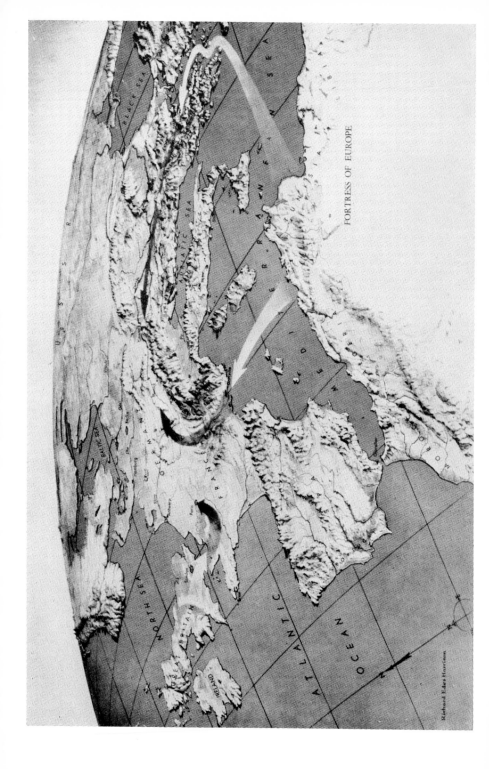

FORTRESS OF EUROPE

Richard Edes Harrison

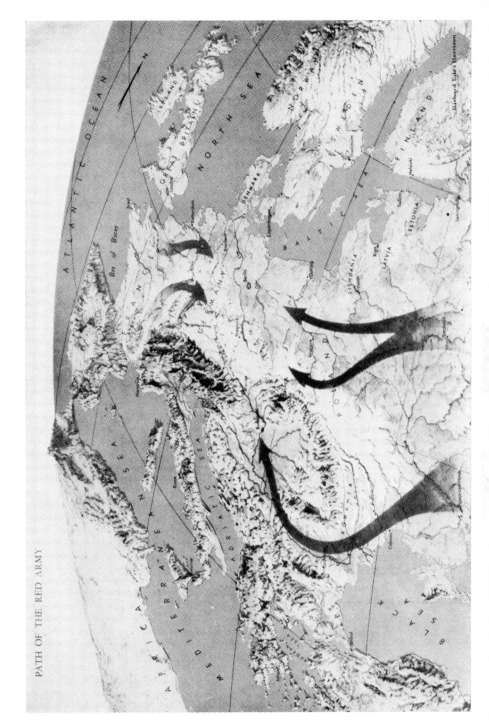

PATH OF THE RED ARMY

Wedemeyer greets a villager on an inspection trip in southeastern China, July, 1945.

Chungking, China, 1944. Left to right, Gen. Chu Shih-ming; Chiang Kai-shek; British General de Wiart; Wedemeyer; Ferris.

American-Sino staff meeting at China Theater Headquarters, Chungking, May, 1945.

At Kunming, China, July, 1945: left to right, Chennault, Aurand, Wedemeyer, Simpson, Davidson.

Victory Parade at Chungking.

Bishop Yu Lin presents a gift to General Marshall as General Wedemeyer and General Ho Yung-chin look on.

The Wedemeyer Mission, September, 1947: left to right, Watson, Walker, Wedemeyer, Lycurgus (hotel owner in Hawaii where photo was taken); Trexel, Jenkins, Sprouse.

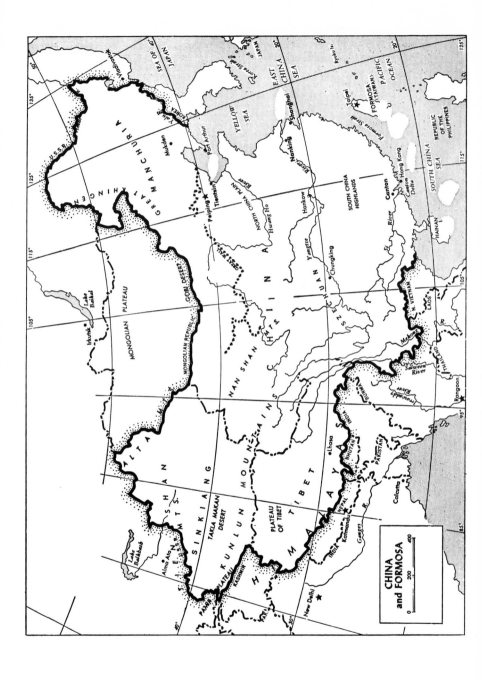

CHINA
and FORMOSA

0   200   400

The British planners who ostensibly supported the Prime Minister's Mediterranean strategy seemed to have no clear idea of where to commit themselves on the north shore of the Mediterranean. I sensed that they were taking instructions from higher up. The information I elicited in London was useful in making our plans for QUADRANT. General Marshall authorized a considerable group of U.S. planners to accompany him to Quebec, including my chief, General Handy. Later, Marshall said, "Handy was a tower of strength on this important occasion." It was my considered opinion that Handy was a tower of strength on all occasions. I never worked under any man for whom I had greater respect and admiration. In fact, almost without exception, I found the military men in all of our services and the officials in other government agencies to be dedicated men.

Our group in Quebec included the planners from the Operations Division and also the planners in the Joint Chiefs of Staff planning committees. Two outstanding officers, Lieutenant Colonel L. J. Lincoln and Lieutenant Colonel A. B. Starboard, were included in the party. Though they were from the Operations group under General Ed Hull, they were invaluable to those of us responsible for strategic planning, for they were charged with the implementation of our plans. One of the Army's most knowledgeable logistical planners, Colonel V. J. Esposito, accompanied the party. From the Joint War Planning Committees, there was a representative from each of our three teams: the Red team was represented by Colonel E. H. McDaniel; the Rainbow team, by Lieutenant Colonel H. H. Fisher; the Blue Team, by Colonel V. P. Armstrong; all carefully selected for the exacting job of war planning. Colonel W. W. Bissell represented a senior Joint War Planning team. There was also Colonel V. H. Connor from the Operations division and my ground and air deputies, Colonel F. M. Roberts of the ground force and Colonel W. E. Todd of the air force. Altogether we had a formidable planning group which was prepared to analyze British proposals and pass up important information and data upon which the Joint Chiefs could base the logic that would get us across the Rubicon. It was now either a final decision for OVERLORD or a choice after Italy of the Balkans or the Pacific.

Right from the beginning of the conference, General Marshall made it clear in the Combined Chiefs of Staff meetings that the

Americans were determined to give overriding priority to the OVERLORD operation. At a Joint Chiefs of Staff meeting on August 15, Generals Marshall and Handy pressed strongly for an unequivocal decision in consonance with the agreements reached at TRIDENT, that we would stage the cross-Channel operation in 1944, and that the forces in the United Kingdom would be increased by seven veteran divisions from the Mediterranean which were to be moved from that area not later than November, 1943.

On the morning of August 16, General Marshall told me personally that the Prime Minister had said the evening before that he would support the OVERLORD operation. A twinkle came to Marshall's eye when I asked, "What did you answer?" Marshall said, "I told the Prime Minister I could not agree to the past British position of supporting BOLERO-OVERLORD and at the same time taking major resources away from it to undertake operations in the Mediterranean. That has been our experience all the way through."

I had returned to Washington from London with information upon which we could base some of our anticipatory planning for QUADRANT, but the British had also learned something about our attitude in discussions with me. They knew for example that we had not changed our stand in connection with European strategy. Moreover, the British were now confronted with a well-conceived and meticulously prepared plan delivered by "Lord Overlord," Lieutenant General Freddie Morgan, one of their own officers. General Morgan believed in concentration for decisive blows as strongly as Marshall.

Immediately prior to the conference in Quebec, Mr. Churchill visited Roosevelt at Hyde Park. This scared us all. To forestall trouble, General Marshall sent Handy to explain to the President that a firm decision must finally be made on a cross-Channel date. The President confirmed his faith in the OVERLORD operation and announced his determination not to permit any American forces to enter the Balkans.

At Quebec the Joint Chiefs and their assistants lived at the Château Frontenac high above the St. Lawrence River. The senior political leaders and their immediate entourage were taken care of in the Citadel, the summer home of the Canadian Prime Minister located on the famous Plains of Abraham. Probably the most important meeting of the conference convened at the Citadel on August 19, with the President and Prime Minister and all their military advisers attending. Mr. Churchill again announced his belief in OVERLORD for 1944; his reasons for being against the operation in 1943 were, he said, no longer valid. However, the Prime Minister still managed to insinuate into his support of OVER-LORD certain debilitating conditions. For example, there must not be more than twelve German mobile divisions confronting us at the chosen time in France. There must, so Churchill continued, be alternative operations if the Germans had more than twelve mobile divisions. Once again the Prime Minister recommended the invasion of Norway.

Another strategic plan was introduced at Quebec. It bore the code name RANKIN. This plan had been outlined by General Barker in London, under Freddie Morgan. It envisaged an opportunistic entrance into Europe should a rapid deterioration of the German resistance occur. RANKIN was actually a streamlined version of the old SLEDGEHAMMER. Mr. Roosevelt seemed very much interested in it, and at the second meeting of the Combined Chiefs at the Citadel he wondered within Churchill's hearing if the West could use it to get to Berlin as quickly as the Russians.

Later on, in talking with General Marshall about the President's remark, I asked if Roosevelt was beginning to have some concern about Communist influence in Middle Europe. Marshall said he did not think so. He felt that it was just a question of prestige and ability to carry out the reorganization of Europe on an equal status with the Soviet Union. Marshall said Roosevelt recognized the importance of capturing Berlin as both a political and psychological factor.

In the discussion of RANKIN, General Morgan brought up the question of a division of territory between the occupying nations. Certain areas were tentatively sketched out. Americans were to occupy France and Belgium with a spillover into southwest Germany. The British were to be responsible for Norway, Denmark, and northwest Germany through the Ruhr. The Russians were not consulted; their day would come when the European Allied Commission (EAC) met in London to determine areas of territorial and occupational control in Germany. The EAC was composed of one representative each from the United States, the Soviet Union, and Great Britain.

QUADRANT ended with the acceptance of OVERLORD as the major effort for 1944. The Americans agreed that if OVERLORD could not be executed the Norway plan might be revived. General Marshall, however, was hardly serious about this; I felt he was just biding his time.

The question of command for OVERLORD was settled when Churchill agreed that it should be an American. By this time I was so suspicious of the Prime Minister that I wondered if he wanted no part of a possible debacle for an English officer.

Another matter that was brought up at Quebec involved Stilwell, who was serving at the time as Chief of Staff of Generalissimo Chiang Kai-shek and doubling in brass as commander of all Americans in the China, India, and Burma areas. Because of his peculiar personality Stilwell was having difficulties in resolving overlapping problems with Wavell. It was decided at Quebec that a new Allied Command would be created in Asia along the lines of Eisenhower's Mediterranean Command.

Admiral Louis Mountbatten, who was currently running the combined operations group in London, was designated to be the supreme head of a new Southeast Asia Command.

There were other changes made at Quebec. Averell Harriman told me confidentially that he was about to be sent to Moscow with ambassadorial rank. He invited me to have lunch with him the following day, at which time he asked me if I would be willing to accompany him to Moscow as a member of his staff. I admired Averell, although I felt at times that he was too subject to the whims of Harry Hopkins. I thought it would be interesting to go to Moscow but what I really wanted was to have command of troops, either an armored or airborne division. I explained to Harriman that the creation of the Southeast Asian Command had made my future uncertain. The day before, Admiral Mountbatten had told me that he had spoken to General Marshall, requesting my assignment to New Delhi. Marshall said it would be up to me. While I told Mountbatten of my hopes to command a division in combat, I said that I felt complimented by his asking for me and would abide by General Marshall's decision.

On a pleasant steamer trip down the St. Lawrence, General

Marshall told me that President Roosevelt felt I could make a real contribution toward bringing about better co-operation in a complex area by accepting the Mountbatten post. It would mean a promotion. Although I would naturally be glad to get my second star, I still felt better-qualified for my job as strategic planner in Washington. I told General Marshall I had enjoyed very much serving with him in that capacity. But no matter what Marshall intended for me, I had to give Averell Harriman a final turndown. When he asked me to recommend another officer, I suggested Johnny Deane or Ed Hull. Ultimately Johnny Deane was assigned to Harriman's staff and promoted to major general. He was later to write *The Strange Alliance,* perhaps the best book on the subject of Soviet intrigue and recalcitrance in existence.

I returned to Washington with my planners, stopping on the way at West Point to see my older son Albert, who was a cadet. When Marshall confirmed my shift to Asia, General Handy asked me to recommend my replacement. I suggested my ground force deputy, Colonel Frank Roberts.

Roberts had a pleasing personality and a fine analytical mind. He was fully aware of the difficulties inherent in the position, for he had practically grown up with it.

I left my fellow planners with a feeling of sadness and regret. In the field a military man must be firm, perhaps unpleasantly peremptory; commands must be obeyed unequivocally for human lives are at stake. Hesitation or vacillation in carrying out an order under combat conditions may cost many lives. But in strategic planning, there is no place for unquestioned conformity to the leader's will. Criticism and questions are absolutely essential. The planner's job demands a balance between decisiveness, tact, and a facile mind sufficiently open to entertain alternatives. At all times I encouraged the officers in my planning agencies regardless of rank to speak out their views, giving all of us the uninhibited benefit of their knowledge and experience. I stressed that it would be far better to expose the weakness of our proposal or plan than to have the enemy—or even our principal allies, the British and the Russians—do so. I had enjoyed the planning atmosphere and I really hated to leave the fine group of officers with whom I had been closely associated for approximately three years.

CHAPTER XIX

EASED OUT TO ASIA

MY TRIP to join Mountbatten in India in October, 1943, took me to
Brazil, thence over the Atlantic to Accra, and straight across the
heart of Africa to Khartoum, before turning north to Cairo, along
the valley of the Nile. I spent two days in Cairo conferring with
American officials, then proceeded on to Tel Aviv, Teheran, Bahrein,
Karachi, and finally New Delhi.

Crossing ocean, jungle, and desert, I had ample opportunity to
think about my new assignment. Were both Mountbatten and I
being kicked upstairs? The Southeast Asia Command obviously had
considerable importance so long as the Japanese were pressing in
Burma and the Chinese were cut off from the outside world. However, India was bound to become a strategic backwater as the
Allies closed the ring on the Nazis in Europe and MacArthur and
Nimitz pressed their advantages in the Pacific. I looked forward
to a vegetative period in comparison to my embattled career with
the planners, who had continually to fight for America's interests.

The War Department had assigned a nucleus of experienced
planning officers who would serve on my staff in New Delhi.
Gradually additional officers from both the Army and Navy would
be sent for integration in the Allied staff of the theater. Admiral
Mountbatten had asked General Marshall to assign a WAC detachment, stating that he planned to have WRENS and WAVES of the
British services detailed also for secretarial work. Initially I opposed

the assignment of women in advance battle areas, but when I arrived in New Delhi and became acquainted with conditions there, I realized that possibly it would work out all right. The women, both British and American, proved to be invaluable, and I felt very fortunate in having the detachment of approximately fifty members of the Women's Army Corps in the headquarters, for they released ablebodied men for more arduous duties on the front. The conduct of the American women was exemplary; later, when in command of the China Theater, I raised no objection whatsoever to Colonel Oveta Hobby's proposal to send a detachment there.

Knowing that Mountbatten had a reputation for getting in the hair of the British Chiefs of Staff, I couldn't stop thinking that possibly we were both the victims of a readiness to speak our minds. I abhorred sycophants, and I soon discovered that Mountbatten was of like mind. The British softened the blow for Mountbatten by giving him his fourth star, and they had taken it upon themselves ostensibly to compliment me by having Mountbatten ask for my assignment to his remote and relatively unimportant sphere. It was in the atmosphere of a promotion that was no promotion that I had taken leave of my official duties in Washington and left for the Southeast Asia Command.

My suspicions that I was being eased out to Asia were confirmed when my secretary informed me of a conversation she had overheard outside my office in the Pentagon. Several British officers who were waiting to see me regarding a strategic plan were wondering audibly who would replace me—would it be Colonel Roberts or Colonel Lincoln? They had remarked that either one of those officers would be much more acceptable. In other words, they would welcome a change.

I was not averse to serving with Admiral Lord Louis Mountbatten for I found him intelligent, amenable, and apparently willing and anxious to get on with the job. Some of his own British friends insinuated that he might prove devious, but only on one occasion did he assume that I would go along with him when he had no right to do so. Unlike many other Britishers, Mountbatten saw nothing singular when I held out for the American point of view.

My feeling that I would get along with him was reinforced by no less a person than General Eisenhower. In one of his letters to me he had chaffed me on my report that he, Eisenhower, "sometimes favored the British." General Ike wrote:

> If you could be present to hear some of the hard-boiled instructions they occasionally get, I think you would discount any such reports. I have the earnest conviction that an Allied Command can be made to work only if the Chief is truly self-effacing so far as glory grabbing is concerned and succeeds in establishing among all the senior subordinates the honest belief that he is working for one cause only—winning the war. . . .
>
> You will have a most interesting job in the Far East. Lord Louis is occasionally belittled by people who think they know more about war than he does, but in my honest opinion he has a lot on the ball and you will find that you are under a man you can respect in every way. Moreover, he is a man who will listen to advice and soak it up.

Eisenhower's opinion directly contravened the judgment of Sir Alan Brooke, the British Chief of Staff, who confided to his own diary that Lord Louis Mountbatten "had never commanded anything more than destroyers . . . What he lacked in experience he made up in self-confidence. He had boundless energy and drive, but would require a steadying influence in the nature of a very carefully selected Chief of Staff."

Admiral Mountbatten was already at New Delhi when I arrived. He had provided every facility for our comfort. Together with a few staff officers, we were ensconced in a beautiful palace belonging to the Rajah of Faridkot—a large building, square in shape, three stories high, of white stucco, very much in the Hollywood motif. There was a courtyard in the center with a fountain. One could hardly believe that we were to live in such luxurious surroundings while charged with the task of planning operations to kill and destroy. The whole atmosphere seemed utterly incongruous. When I attended the swearing-in ceremony for the new Viceroy, Sir Archibald Wavell gave it a Gilbert-and-Sullivan touch with his robe and wig, accentuating the atmosphere of luxurious incongruity.

Immediately after my arrival I had a conference with Mountbatten concerning his staff organization, which was to consist predominantly of British officers; however, an appropriate number of Americans was assigned to all echelons. I was to be in charge of planning operations, working directly under the British Chief of Staff, Sir Henry Pownall. Mountbatten had already discovered that Stilwell was having considerable difficulty in China with the Generalissimo. He expressed deep concern about this but felt he could win the full and loyal support of Vinegar Joe. Shortly after Lord Louis' first conference with Stilwell, T. V. Soong, Chiang Kai-shek's brother-in-law, arrived in New Delhi with the information that the Generalissimo was considering seriously the relief of the controversial American General. Admiral Mountbatten urged Soong to do everything possible to get Chiang to change his mind. I got the impression that Mountbatten was really in earnest about trying to make a go of it with Stilwell. After Soong's visit, Mountbatten immediately took off for Chungking to ensure that the Generalissimo understood the operations of the Southeast Asia Command, which included giving Stilwell the opportunity to drive the Japanese out of Upper Burma. Obviously, Mountbatten didn't want to give credence to a New Delhi rumor that he had come out to Asia to get rid of an American hero.

The SEAC Theater was directed by the Combined Chiefs of Staff to conduct operations that would facilitate the opening of a road to China. Personally I did not see much sense in making great efforts to recapture a jungle area merely to open a mountain road that would carry the veriest trickle to Chiang's beleaguered Chinese armies. But, given the command from Washington and London to proceed, the problem of sustaining a North Burma offensive was to be our challenging task. A British expert on parachute glider units, Major General "Boy" Browning, arrived in the theater to confer with Sir Henry Pownall and me with reference to the projected employment of airborne units in the jungle area. We reached general agreement that the Southeast Asia terrain rendered the employment of airborne divisions highly desirable. I suggested the U.S. might, after German surrender, provide at least two airborne divisions.

General Orde Wingate, one of the most interesting figures in the British Army, had come up with the idea of using long penetration groups in the jungle. His idea was to drop men by parachutes or gliders far behind the Japanese lines. The men would be charged with forming up to conduct sorties against communication lines, to destroy supply centers, and so on. Wingate was an imaginative man of great force and certainly a most interesting conversationalist. He put great emphasis upon keeping his men physically fit and spent much time teaching them jungle lore. His men were even trained to eat pythons, which abounded in the jungles of Burma, and which he claimed tasted like tender chicken.

Wingate often came to my room to talk about his experiences, and I was almost spellbound. He had quite a background of experience in the Near East, particularly among the Arabs. He had known Colonel T. E. Lawrence and described his unusual attributes of leadership and how much the Arabs admired him. Because Wingate had imagination and was willing to undertake bold operations, he struck a responsive chord in the Prime Minister, with whom he communicated directly. The British officers in India admired Wingate's initiative and bold spirit; but most of them never put much faith in his operations behind the Japanese lines and refused to give him much tangible help. Mountbatten was the exception; and he, along with the Americans, supported this strange individualist in every way possible. Wingate was elated at the achievements of two of our outstanding airmen, Colonels Philip Corcoran and Johnny Allison, who trained their air units to fly in men and equipment with gliders and drop them by parachute in isolated spots in the jungle. Wingate was tragically killed on one of his own parachuting exploits in Burma in 1944.

When I arrived in India I knew that I was going to be confronted with a battle of personalities. But I hardly realized that I would be right in the maelstrom from the start. There was, to begin with, a serious lack of co-ordination among the Americans, the Chinese, and the British due to personal animosities and cross-purposes. For example, shortly after my arrival, Mountbatten informed me that tonnage over the Hump into China during September had reached only 4,400 tons. Nobody had bothered to tell him that actually over 6,700 tons had gone to China by air. Someone had given the British incorrect data, and nobody had corrected it.

Also surprisingly, there were language difficulties to be surmounted. I had to confer with a British Major General concerning some supply matters. I reported to his office and after initial formalities, noted that he was very reserved. He was a fine looking chap with a bristly moustache, immaculate uniform, and rows of campaign ribbons. During the course of our conference, we had occasion to use the word "schedule" frequently. Each time, he would pronounce it "shed-u-al." I had never heard such pronunciation and decided he was pulling my leg. Therefore, whenever I had to use the word, I pronounced it "ske-doo-ley." The conference was concluded and I took my leave. Several weeks later, after I had an opportunity to be better acquainted with this officer, I discovered that he was a fine man and I liked him every much. At a small gathering for libations before dinner one evening, he approached me in a friendly manner and said, "Say Wedemeyer, you Americans really don't say 'ske-doo-ley' do you?"

The Southeast Asia Command had an immediate mission: to open at the earliest possible moment a supply route to China from Burma. The ultimate objective was to deliver 85,000 tons a month of munitions, and, in addition, 55,000 tons of gas and oil. It was planned to take care of this delivery of fuel for the planes by installing a four-inch pipeline by way of Fort Hertz into Kunming, capable of delivering about 20,000 tons of gasoline per month, and by laying a six-inch pipeline along the Burma Road capable of carrying 36,000 tons a month.

The delivery of 85,000 tons a month of equipment for the Chinese Army was to be accomplished as follows: 20,000 tons were to be taken in by air over the Hump, and the balance would be carried in over the Burma Road and the four-inch pipeline just as soon as the Japanese were driven south and the road rebuilt.

Since the American Chiefs of Staff had agreed to the equipment, the supplies, and the engineering units required to construct and operate the road from Ledo to Kunming, China, it was not up to me to dispute the idea. Pursuing my investigations of the amount of tonnage that might be taken over the road, however, I discovered that the whole business was completely unsound from an engineering standpoint. It was true the road could be built; but the maintenance made necessary by slides resulting from the torrential rains and remoteness from appropriate repair facilities, and the tremendous service equipment and number of stations that would have to be installed, rendered the project economically as well as militarily unsound. I confirmed all this in conversations with an able American engineer, General Wheeler. He felt that it was a mistake to undertake building the road. He agreed with me, however, that the rest of our Burma mission was sound. We should put our emphasis on driving the Japanese as far south as possible in order to deny them bases for fighter aircraft. This would insure the passage of our air transport unmolested into China.

The Commander-in-Chief in India, General Claude Auchinleck, had certain responsibilities independent of the Southeast Asia Command. For example, he was required to provide for the defense of India proper. This responsibility would certainly have higher priority than the operation against the Japanese. Assuming the safety of India, however, the Commander was to hold himself in readiness to co-operate in all missions of Mountbatten's over-all command. One of Auchinleck's principal missions was to develop an Indian base for the eventual launching of major overseas operations against Japan. He was directed to carry on consultation with the Southeast Asia Command to this end.

Mountbatten's chief role at the outset was diplomatic, one in which he excelled. He had to get along with the anti-British Stilwell, the anti-Stilwell Chiang Kai-shek, and the many veteran British officers in the theater who were dubious of Mountbatten's own ability to command a huge theater due to his youth and inexperienced background.

My own reputation for being anti-British didn't help him much at the start. This drawback was somewhat alleviated, however, when it became known that Stilwell thought I was extremely pro-British. Lord Louis' troubles with Stilwell remained; for Vinegar Joe was constantly making wisecracks to the effect that the British had no intention of fighting, that they would do everything possible to avoid getting involved themselves but would push the Americans and Chinese into doing the job against Japan.

Admiral Mountbatten was extremely lucky in getting Spec Wheeler to serve as his principal administrative officer (PAO). In our own service Wheeler would have been called Chief of Service of Supply. Spec Wheeler had character and outstanding professional ability; everyone respected him. Furthermore, he was tactful in resolving difficulties between Americans and British concerning the allotment of equipment, supplies, transportation facilities, etc. Spec was really a master at any job, as he was to prove later in the clearing of the Suez Canal in 1957.

In my own task of bringing British and Americans to an agreement on strategy there were some rather touchy moments. Seeking a solution, I would quietly consult with Spec Wheeler for sound and objective advice. Spec was senior to me both in years and rank. I always felt that I had a great and good friend in him as well as a wise confidant.

Since India, Burma, and Ceylon were all British spheres of interest, it would not have been possible to give Spec Wheeler the command in the Southeast Asia Theater. Even though he was the ablest officer around, he never gave his own preferment any thought. He was intensely loyal to Mountbatten, who was years younger and had much less knowledge and experience to equip him for his position of great responsibility.

Mountbatten's rapid promotion created both jealousy and envy among British officers, particularly among his senior commanders. The Naval officers made fun of him in a restrained way. By and large, however, he did as good a job as anyone could expect, given the limited means and the diverse, contradictory objectives of his command.

At all of the big conferences—Casablanca, Washington and Quebec—the Combined Chiefs of Staff, with the approval of Roosevelt and Prime Minister Churchill, had accepted plans to open a land route into China. So one of the most important tasks confronting the SEAC planning group was to submit a scheme of maneuver to Admiral Mountbatten as early as possible, utilizing all available forces, land and air as well as naval. We had studied carefully a plan prepared under the direction of General Auchinleck. This plan was a sound, simple maneuver which called for converging attacks from Ledo and Assam in the northwest and from Yunan Province in China from the northeast, to be followed by an attack on the Burma Coast from the Bay of Bengal. I talked to General Stilwell about this plan and he ridiculed it. The British, he said, would certainly not be sufficiently vigorous and aggressive. I promised Stilwell that we would do everything possible to insure coordination of British and American forces, and also that we would hope to step up the timing, taking into consideration the climate and the terrain in which our troops would be operating.

There were three general schemes of maneuver that might be used to attain our objective. My planners and I preferred one that provided for an airborne landing by two divisions in central Burma. The code name for this was TOREADOR. It was our conviction that if we could cut the main artery of the Japanese lines of communication leading out to their dispositions in northeast and western Burma, the enemy at the front would die on the limb. Certainly they couldn't afford to disregard a force of two divisions in their rear. Such a force would be of immeasurable help to Stilwell's force operating in the northwestern part of Burma and the Chinese operating out of Yunan. Assuming co-ordinated, aggressive action, we might hope to converge rapidly on the Mandalay plain.

Another plan called TARZAN envisaged an airborne landing at Indaw, which was located on the railroad leading to Myitkyina. This was to be co-ordinated with an advance by the Ledo forces on Myitkyina. There would also be a push eastward by the British IV Corps looking to a secure lodgment on the east side of the Chindwin River before the rainy season began. Finally, there would be an advance by British forces along the Arakan coast.

Over Stilwell's objections, Admiral Mountbatten favored the TARZAN operation. Stilwell felt that the British had limited their objectives too much. He wanted a two-pronged attack across the Chindwin and an aggressive drive along the Arakan coast in order to pin down or occupy the attention of the Japanese forces while the Chinese Ledo and Yunan forces were advancing in the north.

At a final meeting to consider our projected operations, the Admiral decided upon TARZAN. His judgment was confirmed by General Auchinleck and by his senior commanders, Admiral Sir James Somerville, Air Chief Sir Richard Peirse, and Army Commander General Gifford. When asked for my comments, I had expressed the view that TARZAN would not accomplish the objective as given to the Southeast Asia Command in its directive from the Combined Chiefs. I felt that the objectives were too limited and feared that by the time monsoon rains began we would have only a small lodgment on the other side of the Chindwin.

In December, 1943, Mountbatten and I flew to Cairo to attend the world conference called SEXTANT. This was the first of many peripatetic missions I was to experience while in the Southeast Asia Command. The SEXTANT conferences developed nothing new for our Command, but it gave short-lived encouragement to Generalissimo Chiang Kai-shek. He, his charming wife, and an entourage of Chinese generals were present when the Anglo-American leaders decided that additional forces and shipping could be made available to the Southeast Asia Command for amphibious operations in

Burma. Informed of this, the Generalissimo and his party returned to China highly pleased. After his departure the American and British conferees went to Teheran where they were joined by Generalissimo Stalin. At his insistence, definite plans and allocation of resources were adopted by the Allied leaders to insure a cross-Channel (OVERLORD) operation in the summer of 1944. The equipment previously earmarked for Burma would now be sent instead to England. This had been China's experience throughout the war—promises and high hopes to be followed by disappointments, with other areas draining off most of the equipment she so sorely needed to fight. Stilwell was, as usual, assigned the difficult task of breaking the bad news to the Generalissimo.

The SEAC joint planning staff, also deeply disappointed, worked feverishly on the preparation of operational plans that would make the most effective and prompt use of the means available. These plans envisaged offensive action in Burma with a view to driving the Japanese from the northern section and thus facilitating the completion of a secure land route from India, through Burma to beleaguered China. Personally I had never accepted the Stilwell premise that an all-weather road should be constructed and maintained through the jungles and rugged terrain of northern Burma. He accepted the estimates of his engineers that 100,000 tons of supplies would flow into China when the road was completed. However, General Wheeler had emphasized again that the road was impractical. Slides, washouts, and monsoons would necessitate prohibitive amounts of time, labor and matériel to keep the road in operation.

But Stilwell was adamant and had Marshall's backing. The Japanese had driven him out of Burma earlier in the war, and he was determined to return and fight it out in the jungles. In my opinion such operations were tactically unsound because our air and mechanized advantages would be of little use.

The British had been unco-operative, stuffy, and seemingly resentful of the American Commander who was striving to get on with the fighting. Stilwell told me that Festing (Major General F. W. Festing) and Lieutenant General Stopford were the only British officers who would get out and fight. I remarked that General Slim, commanding the Fourteenth Army, was an aggressive and outstanding combat commander. He replied with a wry smile, "So

Slick Slim continues to fool 'em." Stilwell's unfortunate experience in that complex area was not all of his own making. I think Mountbatten realized this and was sincere, although unsuccessful, in his effort to create mutual trust and friendly co-operation. However, he was by training, experience, and background the exact antithesis of Vinegar Joe, a typical old-fashioned Indian fighter, reveling in the rugged life of a field soldier.

On January 31, 1944, Mountbatten assembled the senior officers of his command at New Delhi Headquarters and asked me to give a brief résumé of our projected plan called CULVERIN involving an attack against Sumatra, to be followed by operations against Singapore and northward along the coast of Malay and China. Comments were favorable as to the soundness of our strategy from all sources except General Stilwell. He said that the way to defeat the Japanese in this area was to build a strong Chinese Army and drive to the sea. I agreed with him but added, "*if* it were logistically possible." "Clive wasn't worried about logistics," he said. "No," I answered, "but Clive did not have airplanes, either. We just can't do it unless we can install and maintain lines of communication to the interior of China. Our technical experts tell us that we cannot do that for at least two years. In the meantime Nimitz and MacArthur will have won the war in the Pacific."

Stilwell went back to China frustrated and furious.

In February a group, * headed by myself, flew first to London to present our plan (CULVERIN) to the British Chiefs of Staff and planners; and then to Washington where we tried to sell our strategy to their American opposites. Our mission was called AXIOM.

Enroute to London, we stopped at Marrakech and stayed at the Villa Taylor, where Churchill, his wife and entourage had been spending almost a month after the Cairo Conference. He let it be known he was suffering from a bad cold, but actually, I was told he did not want to return to London and face a hostile Commons after having his nose twisted by Stalin at Teheran.

Before our first meeting in London, all the members of our party

* *British members:* Gen. MacLeod, Gen. Harrison, Brig. Bourne, Capt. Goodenough, RN, Lt. Col. de Chassiron, Lt. Col. Chapman, Mr. Dening, 1st Off. Hayes, 2nd Offs. Trubody and Gwynne. *American members:* Gen. Wedemeyer, Lt. Col. Lincoln, Lt. Col. Cary, Col. Mason, Capt. Lutze, Lt. McAfee, M/Sgt. Duval.

were carefully briefed on our presentation. I learned that, as chief planner, I was going to have a very difficult time. "Pug" Ismay dropped over to see me soon after I arrived and warned me that the Chief of Staff and all the planners were opposed to the strategy we were proposing. Only the Prime Minister agreed with us; he had been asking Pug daily when I would arrive, and said he wanted to see me. I felt, however, that it would be unwise to see the PM before presenting my case to the planners, then the Chiefs of Staff, and finally to the War Cabinet. Sir Richard Pierse, British Air Commander in Chief, SEAC, whom I saw later, said that it was just as well that I was presenting the SEAC strategy, because they would not be rude to me—an American—but that I should not be surprised if they went after me with everything they had from the strategic viewpoint. I told him that I expected this, and hoped that when he returned to New Delhi he would pass all this information on to Admiral Mountbatten so that he would be prepared for the worst if they threw us out.

Later that day I saw General Eisenhower, who was as pleasant and unaffected as always. He discussed at some length the OVERLORD operation and showed a considerable interest in our plans in SEAC. I told him that I was scheduled to appear before the British War Cabinet that evening in order to present our plan CULVERIN. Ike admonished me to be very firm, particularly with the Prime Minister, and not to permit him, a politician, to tell me how to conduct world strategy. "Don't forget Gallipoli," he said. "The Prime Minister will run roughshod over anyone who appears subservient or meek."

I was glad to get this information, as it confirmed a British Parliament Member's views expressed to me on a previous visit in London. Ike asked me to drop by and see him before I left for Washington, saying he had an important message for General Marshall that he wanted me to deliver.

That evening all the members of the AXIOM party went to No. 10 Downing Street Annex where the Prime Minister held a conference in an underground bombproofed map room. We met with the British Chiefs of Staff, the Prime Minister, and members of the War Cabinet, including Anthony Eden. The PM acted as chairman and asked me to sit next to him. Without any formalities, he stated simply that they were assembled to hear General Wedemeyer present the views of SEAC with reference to continued operations, and then asked me to proceed.

My presentation was received courteously but coolly by the Chiefs of Staff and enthusiastically by the Prime Minister. He kept urging me to say more, even to the point of repetition. Upon breaking up the meeting the Prime Minister gave instructions to the British planners to prepare a report on CULVERIN as soon as practicable.

The next evening I was invited to dinner by the Prime Minister at No. 10 Downing Street. Among the other guests were the King, Ambassador Winant, Count Lascelles, Air Marshal Tedder, Air Marshal Leigh-Mallory, and Admiral Ramsey. We assembled in the living room and waited for the King. We had been asked to arrive punctually at 8:15 in order to be sure that we were all present before the arrival of the King, who appeared at 8:30, wearing the uniform of an admiral. After cocktails were served, we went into the dining room. I was seated between the King and Air Marshal Tedder. The King asked me at some length about the situation in India and his cousin, Lord Louis, to whom he referred as "Dickie." The Prime Minister sat opposite the King and recounted many interesting anecdotes. Champagne was poured from a jeroboam, a bottle almost three feet high like an enormous fire extinguisher full of "fire water." A French friend had presented the Prime Minister with twelve such bottles of this excellent champagne just prior to the outbreak of the war. After dinner we went into the living room again and the Prime Minister asked me to sit next to the King. Ambassador Winant sat nearby, and we three talked about the war and postwar collaboration between the British and Americans. Somewhat later the Prime Minister asked me to join him and a group of British officers. He emphasized how anxious he was for our plan CULVERIN to be implemented, adding, "But I am sure it can be accomplished with fewer resources. We must not permit the logistical tail to wag the tactical dog. After all, the Germans assume administrative as well as tactical risks."

"Don't forget Gallipoli!" I thought.

Everyone was by now in a jovial mood, with whisky and soda flowing freely, and it was 1:30 A.M. before the King arose to go home. After he left we all bade the Prime Minister good night.

On February 16 I wrote a letter to Mountbatten in order that he and the SEAC staff would be kept informed about AXIOM's experiences. Pertinent extracts follow:

DEAR ADMIRAL:
I want to review briefly events as they have transpired here since the arrival of AXIOM.

. . . .

The Prime Minister, in talking about the size of the forces involved in CULVERIN, used figures rather loosely. He tried to persuade me to agree to greatly reduced forces. I told him that it would not be honest on my part if I gave false impressions relative to the estimated forces required for the operation.

. . . .

The First Sea Lord was firmly opposed to the employment of the British fleet in the Indian Ocean. He is determined to participate in the Pacific with the U.S. Fleet. Admiral "Savvy" Cooke is in London with General Ed Hull and Colonel George Lincoln of OPD, and while their mission does not involve Pacific strategy (it is concerned with the allocation of Landing Craft for the European operation OVERLORD), Savvy gave me the straight dope about the American Navy's attitude toward the employment of British forces in the Pacific. He stated that Admiral King had never approved combining the two fleets. He questioned seriously the capacity of existing maintenance facilities in the Pacific to service and maintain combat effective the combined U.S. and British Fleets. He said that it would require a prohibitive amount of time to expand shipyards and similar facilities to take care of both fleets and that the American Navy was now self-sufficient and capable of accomplishing any foreseeable tasks in the Pacific.

. . . .

One bit of interesting news reached me from Washington, namely, that "Spec" Wheeler ran into a nest of hornets in the Pentagon when he informally discussed our strategy and advocated the discontinuance of the Ledo Road project. Perhaps Bill Somervell was the chief stumbling block. This portends hectic days ahead but it is a challenge to Yankee and Limey ingenuity, and the will to win.

Faithfully yours,

A. C. WEDEMEYER

After the London conversations, the AXIOM party moved on to Washington. I recorded my experiences and reactions in Washington in a letter to the Prime Minister. Extracts follow:

21 March, 1944

DEAR MR. PRIME MINISTER:

The members of the AXIOM party have been busily engaged in discussions and conferences since arrival in Washington. We have been received with every consideration on all levels although we have not as yet received encouraging signs of agreement.

. . . .

My talk with the President was most satisfactory. He was pleased when I reassured him that Admiral Mountbatten is determined to employ the maximum Allied resources that can be maintained effectively against the enemy. I emphasized that we recommend strongly against the construction of the Ledo Road through Upper Burma to China and explained very carefully our reasons. Instead of the unfavorable reaction which I had anticipated, he did not appear to attach importance to this matter—at least not as much as he had on previous occasions. I explained that we felt that the Allies could assist China more realistically and earlier by placing emphasis upon the expansion and security of the air ferry route to China; by providing maximum assistance to Chennault's air forces; and by conducting military operations in Burma that would assure the security of our lines of communication, including the air ferry route.

. . . .

The AXIOM party is tentatively scheduled to leave Washington on Sunday, 26 March, and should arrive in London about the 29th or 30th of March. Prior to my departure, I will see the President again and the U.S. Chiefs of Staff for final indication of their views and any messages which they desire me to convey.

Faithfully yours,

A. C. WEDEMEYER
Major General, G.S.C.
Deputy Chief of Staff
Southeast Asia Command

A few days later we returned to London.

Brigadier Bourne met us and reported the happenings in London during our absence. Most important of all, he said that he, as a member of an *ad hoc* team, had drafted a new CULVERIN, at the behest of the Prime Minister. The object, of course, was to reduce the forces we had estimated as the minimum required for the operation. I decided to wait a few days before seeing the Prime Minister or British Chiefs of Staff and in the interim to examine carefully the new plan.

But the Prime Minister had other ideas. Later the same day Pug Ismay called and said the PM wanted to see me at 10 o'clock that night for a conference. When I reported to the PM, he told me he expected Mr. Eden in a few minutes. The three of us discussed what had occurred at Washington. It was readily apparent that the Prime Minister was determined that Mountbatten should execute his new CULVERIN plan. He was almost rude in his cherubic way when referring to the British Chiefs of Staff and their "sticky notions" concerning a CULVERIN operation.

I told him that I was glad he agreed with Mountbatten's plan to undertake the operation but that a cursory examination revealed that approximately the same forces would be required for the new CULVERIN as were estimated for the original AXIOM CULVERIN. It was like serving the old boy quince juice to tell him anything that he did not like to hear.

Later that evening the PM asked me to spend the next week end at Chequers, his country home. Here we continued our interesting discussions, but he continued to pressurize for a reduced CULVERIN.

Before leaving London, I asked him if he would join the AXIOM party for cocktails. "You might come incognito as Air Commodore

Spencer," I wrote, "I know that the American and British members of my party would greatly enjoy a final contact with you, who have so ably and loyally championed our views concerning strategy in the Southeast Asia area."

"Air Commodore Spencer" came and had a thoroughly good time. Whenever I watched him relax, I thought of his characteristic wartime toast, offered in imported brandy: "We will forego our necessities but never our pleasure."

Back "home" in India at SEAC's new headquarters in Kandy, Ceylon, I made a trip to the front which I described in a letter to the Prime Minister on June 15. Extracts follow:

> MY DEAR MR. PRIME MINISTER:
>
> The return of the AXIOM party from London to Kandy, Ceylon, was uneventful. I intentionally postponed writing to you because I wanted to observe conditions within the Southeast Asia Command, particularly in the battle areas, and then transmit my impressions.
>
> The site of our new headquarters in Kandy is ideal, for we are centrally located with reference to the battle front in Burma vis-à-vis the projected areas for operations east southeast. Furthermore, communications have been just as efficient, if not more so, than they were in Delhi.
>
> . . . .
>
> My recent visit to the front included the Arakan-Imphal-Kohima areas. The spirit and condition of men [British-Indian troops] are excellent. I find it hard to understand how our [numerically] superior ground forces with overwhelming air support, both combat and logistical, can be denied liberty of action and immobilized by the enemy. Accepting the fact that the terrain is difficult, that the Japanese have trained for years in jungles preparing for "Der Tag," that our troops are unaccustomed to the hardships and deprivations imposed by jungles, swamps, and limited supply lines of communication, we can and must overcome these difficulties. We know that British-Indian troops do not lack courage. They fought well in the last war, and they have been fighting valiantly in the Mediterranean Theater. We are seeking the solution, you may be sure, and we are determined to evolve ways and means of seizing and maintaining the initiative.

I motored down the entire length of the Ledo Road in a jeep from Ledo to Stilwell's forward combat headquarters near Shaduzup. One could see many potential slides along the route, but the engineer officer-in-charge assured me that such slides could be quickly alleviated as the result of a very carefully organized road maintenance system, with equipment distributed along the road readily available for every contingency. The Chinese were fighting aggressively when I was in their area, and the sudden capture of Myitkyina seemed to stir their enthusiasm for the job and they were steadily advancing on Kamsing.

. . . .

Personally I feel that the most realistic justification for a land route across Upper Burma is the fact that such a route would clearly facilitate the installation, maintenance, and protection of vital pipelines to support our air effort from bases in China. The tonnage that we could actually move over the road itself would in all probability be absorbed by troops maintaining and defending the road, so that a mere trickle of supplies would reach combat areas in China for employment against the enemy. But pipelines could carry approximately 75,000 tons monthly of POL to nourish the remunerative efforts of Chennault's air force.

I also visited China and talked to leaders there, including the Generalissimo, General Chennault, General Carton de Wiart, Ho Ying Chin, and others. When I reported to SEAC several months ago, I was informed that the relations between the British and Chinese were far from friendly. It will please you to know that quite the converse is true now, and I attribute the change to the splendid work General de Wiart is doing. He was a most fortunate selection. His straightforward and friendly manner have won the confidence and admiration of the Chinese. I might add that the Americans I contacted in China also respect him.

My tour of China included a visit to the airfields radiating about Kweilin, located at or near Suichwan, Hengyang, Lingling, and Liuchow. I also visited some of the advance U.S. airfields north of Chungking and the fields in the vicinity of Chengtu. The spirit of the U.S. air men in these stations was most commendable. Their only grouse was the lack of gas, although they are living under rugged conditions. I must emphasize that I was impressed with the apathetic view of the Chinese military toward the provision of security forces for these valuable installations. There is practically no ground defense established at or near the fields, and I doubt seriously whether anyone has given careful consideration to plans and proper distribution of anti-aircraft and infantry for such purpose. When talking to the Generalissimo, I mentioned this, and also, upon my return to Kandy, in a letter thanking him for his hospitality, I reiterated my concern, hoping that this would stir him and his subordinates to appropriate action in the premises.

. . . .

Sincere good wishes for your health and happiness.
Faithfully yours,

A. C. WEDEMEYER
Major General, G.S.C.
Deputy Chief of Staff

Although far removed from the scene, I could not help following the progress of the Anglo-American forces in France. After working so hard with my colleagues in American planning agencies to convince our British friends that this decisive operation would bring an early victory, it was only natural that I should take some pardonable pride in its success. Admiral Mountbatten continued to urge the British Chiefs of Staff to release additional resources for SEAC so that we might launch a worthwhile offensive in the fall. Convinced that a personal presentation would be more efficacious, he asked me to accompany him to London where, again, I was to experience hours of discussion with British planners and the Chiefs of Staff.

One meeting held on August 8 was particularly notable, not only because of the prominent positions the conferees occupied in the British Government but because of an incident involving Deputy Prime Minister Attlee and me. Several times the Deputy Prime Minister raised the issue that the British were making a tremendous effort in the India-Burma area, in fact using all of their effort to provide a trickle of supplies to China. The Prime Minister commented that this was being done so that the Americans could construct and protect a supply line to China. At this point Attlee burst out angrily, "What do we care what the Americans want?" There was hushed silence. I was the only American present. I asked the Prime Minister for permission to answer Mr. Attlee. It was granted, and I told Mr. Attlee forcibly that I was surprised to hear him make such a remark and that it was just as much in the British interest to strengthen China as in my country's, and pointed out that Stilwell's forces, which had done most of the fighting in North Burma, consisted primarily of Chinese and Americans. Admiral Mountbatten was visibly embarrassed by Attlee's remarks, as were others present.

The discussion turned to other subjects, but my encounter with Attlee was to have its effect. When the meeting broke up, I was told that we would all assemble at 6:00 P.M. the following day. I proceeded to the War Cabinet office at that time, and while waiting in the room with the others for the Prime Minister to arrive, I received a message that he wanted to see me in his private office. He was most friendly when I reported and insisted that I sit down. He said, "I want to tell you, Wedemeyer, that you were perfectly right when you defended your country's position with reference to the supply line into China. I was glad that you did this and admire you for it." He went on, "As you know, I am partly American and my sympathies are very much with your country. This evening we are going to discuss some matters that pertain to the Southwest Pacific and we may say things that might embarrass you, so I feel that it would be better if you did not attend the meeting."

I told the Prime Minister I fully understood and asked him if he wanted me to attend any of the subsequent meetings. He stated that he definitely wanted me to do so. However, I was later informed that it would not be necessary to attend subsequent meetings. Shortly thereafter I returned to India.

On October 27, 1944, I was lying in my bunk back at Kandy, Ceylon. The silver rays of a full moon shone through the Venetian blinds. Outside a civet cat was scrambling. My thoughts turned to a report that I had read, predicting the early surrender of the Germans. Certainly they would not last the winter out. There was a rap at my bedroom door and I called, "Come in." A British orderly apologized courteously for disturbing me and said, "A signal for you, sir." I never had become accustomed to the use of the word "signal" for a message, and it was unusual for me to be disturbed at such a late hour. Messages coming in during the night were normally placed on my desk in the morning. I thanked the orderly and dismissed him. The message read "For the Eyes of General Wedemeyer Only" on the envelope. This excited my curiosity, although during the past years of war I had received many secret communications. The whole world was afflicted with this new malady of secrecy—leading of course to a plethora of gossip and conjectures, at times malicious, always dangerous.

The "signal" was from General Marshall. In substance it read: You will hold yourself in readiness to depart for China within 24 hours after you receive the next message, which will explain in detail that you are to assume command of the China Theater.

I at once awakened my aide, Captain William McAfee, who lived in another room of the tea plantation owner's home in which we were billeted. We returned quietly to my room so that we would not disturb the other occupants in the house and proceeded to discuss my assignment and its implications.

We began by reviewing the situation relating to General Stilwell. I told McAfee that I had always considered Stilwell our outstanding expert on China and understood that he could speak the language fluently and also read and write it. I knew that he was greatly respected by Secretary of War Stimson, and particularly by General Marshall, with whom he had been a fellow instructor at Fort Benning, Georgia, prior to the war. McAfee listened with absorbed interest when I told him about a meeting with Stilwell, which had occurred in General Marshall's office in the Pentagon immediately prior to the TRIDENT conference in May, 1943.

On that occasion we had discussed the capabilities of air power based in China. General Chennault, the volunteer commander of the Flying Tigers in China and later commanding general of the newly constituted 14th Air Force in that area, was naturally a strong exponent of the use of the airplane, both in combat and logistically, in operations against the Japanese. But the over-all commander, General Joseph Stilwell, an infantryman, had little confidence in the value of air power except as an adjunct to army operations. In his enthusiasm General Chennault had made extravagant claims and even suggested that, given the proper logistical support, the

14th Air Force would stop the ever-advancing Japanese in the China Theater.

Free China was then completely blockaded from the sea by the enemy; the only source of supply was the tenuous airline over the Himalayas, known as the Hump. General Stilwell had insisted upon utilizing most of the Hump tonnage pouring into China to equip his ground forces, whereas Chennault was constantly demanding additional tonnage for the operation of his air force. General Chennault's aide, Captain Joseph Alsop, in corresponding directly with the President or the White House circle, which was within his cousinly right, created a rather difficult situation for General Stilwell, who, after all, had the responsibility as the Supreme Commander in China. McAfee asked me if I felt this was the cause of Stilwell's being relieved. I said it may have contributed indirectly. But there were other factors beside the ability of Alsop and Chennault to get through to the highest level with their views. The Generalissimo, Dr. T. V. Soong, and other influential Chinese leaders had all along been carrying the torch for the 14th Air Force.

True, the airplane had brought a new dimension to the war in China where communications were limited. But in the final analysis this new weapon also had its limitations. Actually it had proved to be the more important member of an air-ground team. I conjectured to McAfee that the wrangle between Stilwell and Chennault, which had many ramifications, was only the immediate cause of the difficulties. The antagonism between Stilwell and Chiang Kai-shek was fundamental. I recalled the description of the Generalissimo ("coolie class," prone to "tantrums," "incompetent") as I had heard it from Stilwell in Marshall's office. I could see that McAfee, his black eyes shining, a quirk on his lips, wondered what the future held for him as well as for me.

I told him that a year or so back I would have welcomed the opportunity to try to solve the problems of the China Theater, but by now the difficulties seemed practically insurmountable. I had heard many times over that China was a graveyard for American officials, military and diplomatic; that you couldn't do anything with the Chinese, they just wouldn't co-operate, they led you into difficulties with your own government as well as with theirs, and so on. Many a good officer had had his career ruined in China.

McAfee, who was a student of history, tried to cheer me up by mentioning the British general, "Chinese" Gordon, and the German general, von Falkenhausen, both of whom had had remarkable success in China. Von Falkenhausen had trained the Chinese Army prior to 1938, and more than a decade earlier the Russian general, Blucher, known under the pseudonym Galen, had won renown by his accomplishments in training the new Kuomintang troops who swept victoriously up to Shanghai from Canton in the period of Communist-Nationalist co-operation.

We talked into the small hours and finally went to bed.

The following morning I went to my office with new horizons opening before me. I knew that I would not have command experience in the Southeast Asia Command. Drew Pearson had written in his column that I spent considerable time there reading Carl Sandburg's *Abraham Lincoln,* and that I had been foisted into a comic-opera Hollywood setting with liveried servants at my beck and call while the foot soldier was slogging it out in the steaming jungles of Burma. There was an element of bitter truth in Pearson's remarks.

Almost everyone had been courteous to me, the only exceptions being a few American officers at General Stilwell's headquarters, which led me to presume that Stilwell himself was hostile to me. On the surface, however, my relations with Vinegar Joe had been good. The British had been uniformly correct, and many of them, for example, Mountbatten and his Chief of Staff, Sir Henry Pownall, Admiral Langley, and Air Vice Marshal Whitworth-Jones in particular, were very compatible.

Since Mountbatten was away on a trip and would not be back until the following day, I informed Sir Henry Pownall that I had been alerted to leave my present assignment. I also told my good friend Spec Wheeler, who was very happy for me. I told Wheeler that I would be leaving within twenty-four hours.

That evening I received a radiogram explaining that the China-Burma-India Theater had been broken up into two theaters. I was to command the China Theater and also serve as Chief of Staff to the Generalissimo, effective immediately. Lieutenant General Daniel Sultan, who had been Deputy Commanding General of the China-Burma-India Theater under Stilwell, was to command the Americans in the Burma-India area. His primary mission was to insure an uninterrupted flow of supplies to the China Theater. He would also command the five Chinese divisions operating in concert with the British in the Burma area, with the objective of opening land lines of communications to China by driving the Japanese from the northern half of Burma and ultimately from the whole area.

The China War Theater included the mainland of China, Manchuria, and Indo-China, as well as the islands immediately offshore, Formosa excepted. I was charged with the following mission:

> Your primary mission with respect to the Chinese Forces is to advise and assist the Generalissimo in the conduct of military operations against the Japanese.
>
> Your primary mission as to U.S. combat forces under your command is to carry out air operations from China. In addition, you will continue to assist the Chinese air and ground forces in operations, training, and logistical support.
>
> You will not employ United States resources for suppression of civil strife except insofar as necessary to protect United States lives and property.
>
> You are authorized to accept the position of Chief of Staff to the Generalissimo.

I dispatched a message to Marshall to the effect that I would appreciate some latitude in selecting my key personnel. I asked that Major General Thomas Hearn and Brigadier General Benjamin G. Ferris then on General Stilwell's staff be relieved immediately and that General Robert B. McClure (then a division commander with MacArthur) and Brigadier General (later General) T. S. Timberman be ordered to report as replacements. These changes, which were granted, implied no reflection on the character or ability of Hearn or Ferris. I just wanted to insure that I had men at least in key positions who would be sympathetic to my plans and methods.

I was authorized to take my aide-de-camp, Captain McAfee, and my private secretary, Captain Elizabeth Lutze; as well as several outstanding officers from the SEAC staff, to help me get under way in my new command. Mountbatten also loaned me his personal plane, the *Hapgift* to fly to New Delhi where I had scheduled a conference with Dan Sultan.

My orders for assignment to China came as a bombshell. I had been so deeply immersed in matters pertaining to the Southeast Asia Command that I felt rather cold on the subject of Cathay. Immediately after receiving General Marshall's message, many ideas and a multitude of doubts and unanswered questions permeated my mind. I thought of Stephen Leacock's remark, "He mounted his horse and rode off in all directions." Although the information that I had concerning Stilwell's headquarters in Chungking was rather limited, I realized that I probably would be required to start from scratch and create an efficient, well-balanced theater staff. I shared General Marshall's dislike of empire builders, and I made up my mind to proceed slowly in building up the requisite team. Having visited China on two occasions, I knew that Stilwell had the bulk of his staff located in New Delhi, with a small coterie of representatives in Chungking. I had been told that the group in Chungking was not equipped to analyze and/or plan operations effectively. I decided to wait until I could survey the situation on the ground before submitting requests for personnel and suggesting a table of organization for the theater headquarters.

I pondered how fate had now decreed that I should be pitted against the Japanese instead of the Germans. Often when working in the War Plans Division back in Washington I had hoped that one day I would be given an assignment in Europe. Having studied German tactics, I hardly expected to fight the war in the Far East, at the end of the pipeline, where modern warfare had limited application.

When my impetuous chief, Admiral Mountbatten, was informed about my abrupt departure, he was upset. Without my knowledge he dispatched messages to London and Washington immediately, indicating that his Chief of Staff, Assistant Chief of Staff, and Assistant Deputy Chief of Staff had all been ordered away and that he would have no experienced senior officer available to insure continuity of advice and assistance in conducting projected operations in Burma. He now disclosed to me that he had written a letter several months earlier from Cairo to Washington and London recommending my assignment in the Southeast Asia Command as Deputy Supreme Allied Commander with the rank of lieutenant general. I was sure that my friends back in Washington would be amused when they noted British reverberations in my behalf. How paradoxical! This was the antithesis of British feeling toward me when I fought for the cross-Channel operation (the heart) instead of TORCH-HUSKY (the umbilicus). But Mountbatten—yes, many other Britishers even though I did disagree at times with their ideas

—recognized that I was trying always to bring about sound strategy. I had been treated with every consideration and shown every courtesy by all of the British in my year's association with them in this area. Even the Prime Minister had been friendly at Cairo a few months earlier, although he had mental and emotional fits every time we discussed European strategy.

Admiral Mountbatten asked me to recommend a replacement for my position. I submitted the name of Brigadier General Ray Maddocks, who had been on my SEAC staff as a most effective planner. However, the Admiral did not agree. I told him frankly that in my judgment he was making a mistake. He reacted in a friendly way, saying that he had consulted with senior members of the planning staff and they felt that while Maddocks was a fine man and very capable that he did not possess the all-around qualifications for the job. I still disagreed but in the final analysis I could urge Maddocks on the Admiral only to a certain point. The situation involving Maddocks developed favorably in any case. If Mountbatten had taken him as my replacement, the China Theater would never have had the benefit later of his high professional attainments, tact, loyalty, and all-around qualifications for one of the most important jobs in the China Theater, namely, Chief of Staff.

At Admiral Mountbatten's request I submitted a list of American officers for consideration as my replacement. The list was quite long and was not arranged in any proirity. I recognized Mountbatten's predicament and urged the War Department to send a replacement as early as practicable, for the Southeast Asia Command was facing an operational period when planning and supervisory duties would be required. Admiral Mountbatten had developed a great deal professionally, essentially in air operations; however, I found that he still had certain limitations and was somewhat handicapped when he got far away from salt air.

Prior to my departure from SEAC I urged the promotion of Major General George Stratemeyer, who was in command of all Allied Air operations under Mountbatten. Under this command the U.S. Air Force performed very effectively and, as weather conditions improved, the intensity of the air effort was accelerated. Stratemeyer was involved in a very intricate command setup and yet emerged at all times in good heart and with co-operative spirit. There were many officers of the British Air Force with higher rank and yet operating under Stratemeyer who exercised tact and continued patience under the most trying circumstances.

While reporting back information which I felt might be of assistance to the War Department concerning developments in SEAC, I mentioned the fact that there were only two heavy bomber groups in the entire theater. I pointed out that Chennault's were Long-Range Bomber airplanes and consequently could not operate as a group striking force. The 7th Bomber Group, which was a very fine heavy-bombardment outfit, had to be used to fly gas, oil, and lubricants (POL) to the Kweilin area in support of Chennault's attempt by air strikes to save the eastern bases. The land lines of communications from Kunming to Kweilin had been blocked due to land slides and masses of withdrawing Chinese refugees.

I reported also that the Eastern Air Command (British and American air units) was rendering superior support to the ground forces in Burma and had maintained air superiority over the area. It had destroyed enemy lines of communications, bridges, and supply dumps, and in fact the air operations, both combat and logistical, were vital in stemming the Japanese advance in the Imphal area. I recommended that reports should be submitted concerning the air effort of U.S. units separate from others because I felt that the integration of our Air Force with the British had militated against a true picture of the American contribution.

My departure from Ceylon was both a sad and happy event—sad because my associates there, both American and British, went out of their way to indicate a feeling of comradeship. They presented me with a beautiful silver cigarette case, appropriately inscribed. Senior staff members were all present at a farewell breakfast, and there was a guard of honor lining the highway down which my car proceeded to the airport.

CHAPTER XX

FIRST MONTHS IN CHINA

I ARRIVED IN NEW DELHI in the afternoon of October 29 and went at once to the office of General Dan Sultan, a West Point graduate with a fine military record, and a man of the highest integrity and sense of loyalty. He was somewhat familiar with Chinese complexities, for, as Stilwell's second-in-command, he had visited the Chinese theater a few times. However, he informed me that Stilwell had run the Chinese show himself and had been secretive about tactical plans. Sultan knew a lot about Stilwell's difficulties with Chennault and with the Generalissimo. Like myself, he had little positive information about the incidents which had precipitated Stilwell's relief, but he surmised that it was due mainly to Stilwell's insistence that he command all the Chinese troops not only in Burma but also in China.

Sultan conjectured that the British also had had something to do with Stilwell's relief. The whole thing, he said, was extraordinarily complex, and he likened my problem to untangling a can of worms. General Chennault, he said, had often taken supplies for his air force without authority. When Stilwell had forbidden Chennault to send supplies to the Chinese General Hsieh Yueh, the orders had been ignored. Sultan warned me that I would have my own difficulties with Chennault, who was greatly beloved and respected by the Chinese.

I shall never forget how, when I bade Danny Sultan good-by late that evening, he promised to do everything possible to help me in China. He told me that, as he interpreted his directive, his major job was to get supplies to China and to give me every support. Sultan was at least fifteen years my senior. His attitude made a deep impression, and I resolved that I would try to justify in every way his confidence, loyalty, and friendship.

Early the next morning McAfee and I boarded a plane to Assam, where I spent the night with my West Point classmate, Brigadier General Joseph Cranston. He was the commander of the Service of Supply establishment in the area; and he, too, assured me that henceforward, there would be an additional oomph to the flow of supplies to China.

On October 30 I crossed the Hump at a 21,000-foot altitude. Below there were jagged peaks protruding through heavy cloud layers. Off to the left one could see three very high peaks. The middle one, Mt. Everest, reached over 29,000 feet into the blue sky.

When we dropped through rain and overcast to Kunming there was no one to meet us. My aide, however, noticed a long line of troops drawn up approximately a quarter of a mile away, with a band and a large crowd. Arriving at the Operations Desk, we were informed that the troops and the band were an escort of honor. The Operations Officer at once gave me a car to motor down to the gathering. There was some embarrassment: the pilot of my plane had misunderstood his instructions. He was supposed to have taxied down to that part of the field but had not done so. I made amends for the error by inspecting the Guard of Honor. General Chennault and his Chief of Staff, Brigadier General Glenn, were on hand, along with a number of Chinese officials. I had very little opportunity to inspect the terminal, which, I was told, was even busier than LaGuardia Field at New York.

The evening in Kunming was spent in pleasant discussion with Claire Chennault. I found that the famous boss of the Flying Tigers was very hard of hearing, which made his heroic accomplishments all the more remarkable. His objectivity contrasted strongly with my memory of Stilwell's diatribes against him.

The following morning we flew 800 miles to Chungking, which had been the capital of China ever since the fall of Hankow in 1938, the second year of the Japanese war. T. V. Soong, Ambassador Hurley, the Generalissimo's Chief of Staff, General Ho Ying-chin, and several other Chinese dignitaries were at the airport to meet me. McAfee and I were whisked off to the city and were billeted in quarters formerly occupied by General Stilwell. During the drive in from the airport I expressed my surprise to Pat Hurley at the many command changes which had occurred since my last visit. Hurley said it was he who had reported to the President that Stilwell must go. The Chinese, he said, had endeavored vainly to cooperate with Stilwell. Although Pat Hurley spoke very highly of Stilwell as an individual and said he liked him personally, it was clear that his sympathies lay with Chiang Kai-shek. Hurley told me he had personally recommended me as Stilwell's replacement. It is interesting to note that I was told by General Handy that General Marshall suggested my name. Later I read a magazine article by former Vice President Wallace, who stated that he had recommended me for the job.

Next day Hurley and I made a formal call on Generalissimo Chiang. When I had met him on my last visit to China, he had been dressed in a plain black jacket over a dark blue Chinese robe with no decorations of any kind. On this morning of my first official visit as U.S. Commander in the China Theater, he was attired in a dark greenish-brown uniform with the insignia of a five-star general and the Kuomintang blue button with a white sun in the middle. The insignia indicated he was Commander in Chief of the Chinese forces as well as President of the Republic of China. Again I was impressed by this small, graceful, fine-boned man with black, piercing eyes and an engaging smile.

The spacious room in which Chiang received me was to become familiar to me in the months to come. At this first meeting I noted the beautiful Chinese paintings and etchings on the walls, the rugs on the polished floor, and the Chinese-style teakwood tables and chairs with marble-inlay backs. Exquisitely fashioned vases filled with flowers stood on stands and tables. Servants in long blue robes glided in and out, serving tea and refreshments. So many curtains and screens were drawn around the room that I wondered how many people might be listening in and noting what we said.

The Generalissimo stood up when we entered and shook hands courteously, saying "Please, please," his only English words as he motioned for me to sit down. He had a fan which he fluttered constantly. I felt that he was nervous. He seemed shy but also keenly alert. Obviously he was judging me even as I was evaluating him.

Beside Pat Hurley and myself, T. V. Soong was also present. Chiang asked me to be seated on a divan next to him, and started the conversation by recalling our last meeting when I had been sent to China by Admiral Mountbatten to discuss the disputed China-Burma boundary line.

I said that I was honored and happy to be directly associated with him in the war against Japan. Chiang replied that he knew I was no stranger to China, since I had served there as a junior officer. He added that he had enjoyed his meetings with me in Cairo and greatly appreciated the report I had sent him concerning my observations in China after my last visit there. I said I had always admired the Chinese people and felt we would have no difficulties in bringing about an efficient, carefully co-ordinated employment of American and Chinese forces against the Japanese. We did not on this occasion discuss the military situation in detail, although I told Chiang that I was already fairly familiar with it through my talks with Chennault and Sultan.

My second night in Chungking there was an air-raid alarm. As sirens blew, masses of people scurried into caves located along the steep cliffs on which the town is built. Sometimes a bomb would strike near the entrance to a shelter, sealing it and burying the people alive. The air raids which I experienced in Chungking helped me to realize that China was indeed at the end of the pipeline. There were no anti-aircraft guns or modern warning equipment. The Japs consequently could bomb with impunity, particularly just before nightfall. Something had to be done about this and many equally important steps taken in order to fight the Japanese on more equal terms.

Here in China's beleaguered temporary capital in Szechwan Province, I was confronted with problems undreamed of by staff officers in the Pentagon or by combat officers fighting in the European Theater. I now suddenly found myself responsible for the conduct of military operations in an area most remote from the sources of supply and with the lowest priority of all theaters of war. The United Kingdom and the Soviet Union had been receiving the lion's share of the tremendous production of American industry. China, which had been fighting Japan since 1937 almost singlehanded, had received only a trickle of aid. Yet she had managed to survive as a national entity in spite of Western indifference and neglect.

At the beginning of the Sino-Japanese War Chiang Kai-shek was convinced that if he could hold on by "trading space for time," the United States would eventually be involved in war with Japan, and China would thereby be saved. But following Pearl Harbor—in spite of the natural pressure by Americans to fight Japan—Roosevelt had gone along with Churchill in considering the defeat of Germany our paramount objective. Thus China's situation, far from being improved over the early days of the war (when the West had positively assisted Japanese aggression by selling war materials to Tokyo) had now been rendered even more desperate by Japan's attack on the United States and Britain. The Japanese conquest of Hong Kong, Malaya, and Burma had cut off the hard-pressed Chinese forces from the military aid which we had denied her prior to Pearl Harbor when it could easily have reached her.

As the weeks passed I began to understand that the Nationalist Government of China, far from being reluctant to fight as pictured by Stilwell and some of his friends among the American correspondents, had shown amazing tenacity and endurance in resisting Japan. France had gone down to defeat six weeks after Germany launched her offensive. In 1944 China was still resisting, seven years after Japan had launched her initial attack.

As I learned more about the situation, I realized that it was part of China's tragedy that we Americans, for the most part, had been indifferent to her self-sacrificial efforts to stop Japan before 1941. Pearl Harbor alerted the Americans to the real situation. But China by then was already exhausted and was no longer capable of any such military effort as she had made in 1937–38. Few Americans even knew that in the summer of 1937 the troops of the Chinese Nationalist Government had resolutely fought for three months at Shanghai against the Japanese invaders in the "bloodiest battle that the world had seen since Verdun."

China's resistance had taken the Japanese by surprise. They had launched their war to prevent China's unification under the Nationalist Government and had never imagined that they would meet such heroic resistance. It has been argued that Chiang made a military mistake in sacrificing the flower of his armies at Shanghai and subsequently in the defense of Nanking. Perhaps if China had followed France's example and let herself be occupied with little resistance, waiting to be rescued eventually by the United States, her postwar fate would not have been so tragic.

Chiang Kai-shek had endeavored to avoid war with Japan at least until his political, economic, and social reforms, and the increasing authority his government was acquiring even in remote provinces, should have so unified and strengthened China that she would be capable of standing on her own feet and blocking the Japanese plans for expansion at China's expense.

When Japan struck in 1937, Chiang Kai-shek realized that China's only hope in her desperate situation was to demonstrate the capacity to fight and thus eventually secure Western aid. Precisely because China was still weak, she had to demonstrate that she could and would resist. In Chiang Kai-shek's words, China had "reached the limits of endurance" and would "throw every ounce of energy into the struggle for national survival and independence." In his historic pronouncement to his people in July, 1937, Chiang Kai-shek had also said: "Neither time nor circumstances will permit our stopping midway to seek peace."

Since China had far less expectation than England or the Soviet Union of being rescued by America, Chiang Kai-shek's words expressed a spirit more gallant and resolute than Churchill's famous "blood, sweat and tears" speech after Dunkirk. Said Chiang: "Let our people realize the meaning of the limits of endurance, and the extent of sacrifice implied, for once that stage is reached, we can only sacrifice and fight to the bitter end. Only a determination to sacrifice to the utmost can bring us ultimate victory."

Following the loss of her best soldiers and quantities of equipment during the early stages of the war, China could hope for victory only by hanging on against superior forces in the expectation that Japan would sooner or later become embroiled in war with the Western powers. Having proved to the world that the Chinese Army could fight, the Generalissimo adopted the sound strategy of endeavoring to dissipate Japanese strength and forcing the enemy to overextend his lines.

Through the years Japan made tempting offers of peace which were always rejected. Yet, while holding out against Japan, the Chinese Nationalist Government also had to contend with the Chinese Communist armed forces, which, following the Stalin-Hitler

Pact and the subsequent entente between Russia and Japan, withdrew from the united front and directed their main effort against the Nationalist forces instead of against Japan.

Chiang was all along fighting on four fronts: against the Japanese; against Russia in the person of the Chinese Communists; against the centrifugal forces in China, represented by former war lords or semi-independent provincial governors and generals; *and* against the "Western imperialists," meaning in particular the British who, thanks to their strategy of self-interest and their attitude toward China, he had no reason to trust. Both Chiang's greatness and his weakness lay in the fact that he never lost sight of the original objective of the Kuomintang, namely, the unification and independence of China. He perceived that the defeat of Japan would be meaningless if it led to China's once again becoming split up into warring factions or divided, impotent, and at the mercy of both Western and Russian imperialists, as she had been throughout the nineteenth and twentieth centuries. Paradoxically, it was the Communists who were to benefit in the future by the fact that the political unity of China was conserved by Chiang Kai-shek.

Americans for the most part either refused to recognize Chiang's problems or could not have cared less about China's postwar fate. Our main aim was simply to see to it that, in spite of her exhaustion and the terrible sacrifices and privations of her people, she should "play an active role in this war." These were the words used in my own directive from the War Department on my being assigned to the China Theater.

Although he refused all Japanese peace offers, the Generalissimo naturally wanted to have the pressure taken off China; at the least, he hoped to refrain from provoking the Japanese to advance any further in Chinese territory. This led to the charge (often made by John Davies and others) that a sort of *modus vivendi* had been worked out between the Nationalists and Japan.

To the Chinese Nationalists, Western imperialists, Russians, and the Chinese Communists were all enemies. The U.S. was allied with the British, who Chiang knew had a long record of exploitation and domination over China. The United States and Britain had supplied war matériel to Japan in the first years of the Sino-Japanese War. Just as it can be argued that it would have been the best strategy for America to let Germany and Russia knock each other out, so Chiang might well have thought it best for China to let the Westerners and the Japanese fight it out.

In any case, since Chiang was receiving little direct military aid from the U.S., he had to husband his limited resources; to use all of the small amount of modern armament he possessed in offensive action against the Japanese would (as he saw it) be fatal to the cause of Chinese independence after the war.

If Chiang had had firm assurances of U.S. postwar backing against Communists and Western imperialists, he might have dared to throw all his best troops into battle to stop Japanese advances in China and Burma. Because he came to trust Roosevelt and Hurley, he went a long way with us in the closing months of the war in implementing American strategy, whereas previously knowing the sympathy toward the Communists of Stilwell and his advisers, he had become more and more suspicious of American intentions and therefore refused to budge.

I do not pretend that from the beginning I understood or fully appreciated Chiang's dilemma, or the very real problems which faced him in his battle on four fronts. But I approached my duties realizing that they required me to improve Sino-American relations if I possibly could. I knew that this task demanded a sympathetic and friendly approach to the Generalissimo and his government in place of the "do what you are told or be damned" attitude which had got us nowhere. I may be forgiven for quoting here from the U.S. Army's official history, *Time Runs Out*, by Romanus and Sunderland (volume I, page 3):

> An intangible but constructive influence in the relationship may be found in the impression shared by several members of Wedemeyer's staff, that Wedemeyer and Chiang Kai-shek quickly established an easy and pleasant personal relationship. Wedemeyer's tact, his disarming personality, and his regard for the amenities made his advice palatable; the Generalissimo, as will be seen, was able to consider Wedemeyer's proposals on their merits.

In 1937 and 1938 the soldiers of the Chinese Red Army fought fairly well against Japan in spite of, or because of, their secret aim, as expressed in October, 1937, when Mao Tse-tung gave the following instructions * to his followers:

> The Sino-Japanese war affords our party an excellent opportunity for expansion. Our fixed policy should be seventy per cent expansion, twenty per cent dealing with the Kuomintang, and ten per cent resisting Japan. There are three stages in carrying out this fixed policy: the first is a compromising stage, in which self-sacrifice should be made to show our outward obedience to the Central Government and adherence to the Three Principles of the People [nationality, democracy, and livelihood, as outlined by Dr. Sun Yat-sen], but in reality this will serve as camouflage for the existence and development of our party.
>
> The second is a contending stage, in which two or three years should be spent in laying the foundation of our party's political and military powers, and developing these until we can match and break the Kuomintang, and eliminate the influence of the latter north of the Yellow River. While waiting for an unusual turn of events, we should give the Japanese invader certain concessions.
>
> The third is an offensive stage, in which our forces should penetrate deeply into Central China, sever the communications of the Central Government troops in various sectors, isolate and disperse them until we are ready for the counter-offensive and wrest the leadership from the hands of the Kuomintang.

As the result of this Communist strategy, it was not the Japanese but the Chinese people who suffered wherever the Communist guerrillas operated. The Japanese retaliated against Chinese Communist depredations by burning inoffensive villages. The Communists, for their part, killed those who refused to work with them, labeling them "collaborators." The Communist forces could not, and did not even try to, defend the people against the Japanese; and the Japanese had no interest in defending the people against the Communists. Caught between two fires, vast numbers of Chinese had no choice but to choose their executioners.

* As quoted in Freda Utley's *Last Chance in China* (Indianapolis, Bobbs-Merrill, 1947): from *Documents on the Problem of the Chinese Communist Party;* presented to the People's Political Council, March, 1941, and published in Chungking, 1944, by the Supreme National Defense Council.

The great advantage of the Communists both before and after V-J Day consisted in their utter irresponsibility for the fate of the Chinese people. The Nationalist Government was trying, however ineffectually, to defend what was left of Free China. The Chinese Communists were simply engaged in raiding Japanese or Nationalist Government–controlled areas. They played the role of jackal or hyena against the wounded and suffering Chinese elephant who would not submit to his enemy.

No Communist Chinese forces fought in any of the major engagements of the Sino-Japanese War—neither at Shanghai in 1937 nor at Taierchwang in the North in 1938 when General Li Tsung-jen of Kwangsi inflicted a major defeat on the Japanese, nor in defense of the Wuhan cities in that same year, nor in the battles for Changsha, nor later on the Salween and Burma fronts. According to the testimony even of Americans who were sympathetic to the Chinese Communist cause, Chinese Communists never challenged any important Japanese garrison post or Japan's control of China's railway system. Thus, for instance, Theodore White admitted in his and Annalee Jacoby's best-selling book, *Thunder Out of China*, that the Chinese Communists fought only "when they had an opportunity to surprise a very small group of the enemy. . . . During the significant campaigns it was the weary soldiers of the Central Government who took the shock, gnawed at the enemy, and died."

I do not pretend that the realities of the situation in China were immediately apparent to me. Like my chief, General Marshall, I had been prejudiced by General Stilwell's reports. But unlike Stilwell and Marshall I had had the benefit of experiences which had alerted me to the Communist menace. Although it took me some time to acquire confirmation of the ruthless objectives of the Chinese Communists, I had no illusions concerning them from the outset. I never believed with Stilwell that the Communists were China's last best hope. Nor did I ever subscribe to Ambassador Hurley's belief (later relinquished) that Moscow had repudiated them.

During the first months of my command in China I was subjected to pressures from many sources. But I realized that we had an opportunity at last to evolve and implement a strategy which would secure a real and lasting victory for America. In China the primary question for me was: What kind of conditions did the United States want to create or encourage?

While serving in Washington in the War Plans Division of the Army, and subsequently in attending the conferences at Casablanca, Cairo, and Quebec, I had endeavored to promote a strategy which would deny to the Communists an opportunity to supplant Nazi tyranny in Europe. In China I no longer needed to be overly cautious or equivocal in recommending constructive measures in the political, economic, social, and psychological fields, since Chiang Kai-shek and his government were as well, or better, aware of the reality of the Communist menace. America was on the front line in the battle against communism in this remote but important area. It was of vital importance that the Communists, who were even greater enemies of liberty than the Nazis, should not win out in China.

I was fully aware of the activities of the Communists in North China. I had appointed Colonel Ivan Yeaton, who had formerly been the United States military attaché in Moscow, to the U.S. Observation Group in Yenan, which had been headed by Colonel David Barrett under my predecessor, General Stilwell. Ivan Yeaton was supplying me with excellent first-hand reports concerning Communist machinations and their subversive operations among the Chinese people in the areas they controlled. I knew that Mao Tse-tung, Chou En-lai, and the other Chinese Communist leaders were not interested in fighting the Japanese because their main concern was to occupy the territory which the Nationalist Government forces evacuated in their retreat.

In discussing communism with Mao Tse-tung and Chou En-lai in my home in Chungking I asked them why they and their followers could not on their own initiative and without adopting a foreign ideology accomplish the excellent objectives embodied in the *San Min Chu I* of Sun Yat-sen. Chou En-lai replied that the Chinese liberators could not be separated from the socialist state nor could they operate without the aid of the international proletariat. I then asked, "Does this mean that you must obtain aid from the Soviet Union?" and he replied categorically that the Chinese Communists must accept the assistance of the Soviet Union as well as of the proletariat in the United States, Great Britain, and other countries of the world. "Otherwise we cannot win a victory over bourgeois dictatorship," he said.

Mao Tse-tung, who had been listening carefully to our conversation, translated for him by a female interpreter who accompanied them, interrupted: "Chinese revolution is an integral part of world revolution against imperialism, feudalism, and capitalism." He added: "We are definitely committed to the struggle for political and economic revolution in China so that the people will have a new system of politics, economy, and culture. Not only must we eliminate political oppression and economic exploitation but also we want to help our people who are so ignorant and backward to become educated, civilized, and progressive; in other words, a new culture for all our people."

I then recalled the period 1927–37 in China when Chiang Kai-shek and his government were striving to accomplish similar objectives. Neither Chou En-lai nor Mao Tse-tung would agree that forward steps had been made; in fact they emphasized the poverty, squalor, corruption, and maladministration which they maintained were directly attributable to the Kuomintang. I then commented that many of the objectives of Marxism when read or even expressed by an ardent Communist would seem humanitarian and constructive, but uniformly after the Communists came into power these worthy objectives proved to be a delusion and a snare. The so-called proletariat were denied freedom of speech, the opportunity of determining how and by whom they would be governed, commensurate reward for their work, and even freedom to worship their God. Chou En-lai was very anxious to interrupt but I continued: "The methods employed by the Communists to obtain control—lying, intimidations, murder, and enslavement—have in every instance been the hallmarks of Communist acquisition and maintenance of power."

Chou En-lai was obviously aroused by my remarks, because he burst forth in Chinese. Then, realizing that I did not understand, he returned rather haltingly to English, trying to find the correct words to refute my statements. He emphasized that the power of the reactionary forces in the world was so great that the common people were compelled to resort to any means in order to accomplish the overthrow of their deadly enemies. He then quoted Lenin:

"The proletariat must continue the struggle against capitalism until it is destroyed."

This discussion, much of which was conducted through the interpreter, was slow and painful, the latter because I was trying to establish unmistakably the objectives of these two Communist leaders. I had heard many times that they were not true Marxists but were simply agrarian reformers interested in the welfare of the Chinese people. However, this historic meeting under informal circumstances gave the lie to such reports, which were being widely disseminated in the United States. I recorded this provocative discussion immediately after my Chinese Communist guests had departed.

Occasionally Communist troops would make limited sorties against a Japanese blockhouse in order to capture arms and equipment. In preparing plans for an all-out effort to reach the east coast, I asked Communist leaders to participate with their available troops and exert pressure against the Japanese in the northern part of the country. This request was agreed to in typical Communist fashion. They stipulated that I should first send American equipment, guns, and ammunition to Yenan.

At one time, curiously enough, I was offered the command of the Communist armies by Mao Tse-tung and Chou En-lai. I politely refused, referring to my directive as theater commander which required me to support the Chinese Nationalist Government. I should mention, however, that on the occasion of a severe epidemic in the Communist area, I sent eleven tons of medical supplies to alleviate the situation, with the approval of the American Ambassador and the Generalissimo.

But this is getting ahead of my story. Shortly after my arrival in Chungking I held a meeting with the members of my General and Special Staffs and explained that I would make no immediate changes. I expressed the hope that they would continue to give me the same loyal and effective support they had given to my predecessor. I told them I would be making rounds of inspection, not with a view to finding fault but in order to ascertain how we were organized to carry on our job and how best we could hasten the defeat of Japan.

At the outset I found there were many purely administrative matters that had not been processed by General Stilwell, who had no doubt been preoccupied with the matters pertaining to his relief and sudden departure from the area.

I found numerous recommendations for battle awards and decorations on my desk. A sergeant major told me that some of them had been there for months awaiting General Stilwell's decision. He said General Stilwell considered the award of combat medals had been greatly abused, especially by the 14th Air Force. I consulted Stilwell's Chief of Staff, General Hearn, who confirmed the sergeant major's statement. Thereupon I ordered the immediate approval of all the awards and decorations that had lain neglected at Stilwell's headquarters. I also instructed my Chief of Staff to appoint a permanent Awards and Decorations Board, with representatives from my own headquarters, the 14th Air Force, the Services of Supply, and the Ground Forces. I gave instructions that recommendations for awards and decorations would henceforth be acted upon by this board as soon as it could convene, and that I wanted no delay in action on such recommendations. General Chennault told me later the approval of the decorations recommended by the 14th Air Force had had a most salutary effect upon the morale of his young pilots, who were daily risking their lives and enduring hardships and dangers for their country.

Gradually I was compelled to make some changes in the personnel of my headquarters. Every commander has certain ideosyncrasies, and my changes were in no way critical of my predecessor. But in order to ensure that my ideas would be carried out, I needed officers who were familiar with staff procedures as I understood them. This, of necessity, meant that many loyal officers who had been with Stilwell, and who had served him as conscientiously and as effectively as their knowledge and experience would permit, were relieved of their duties in the China Theater.

I gave the generals and special staff officers under my command considerable latitude in performing the duties I assigned them. I demanded only that they act in consonance with my strategy and policy. I tried as far as possible to decentralize command responsibility. I assured my key men that, although they would inevitably make mistakes, I would support them so long as they tried to carry out the instructions I had given them. I also emphasized that we must set the best example we possibly could, not only in the efficient performance of our duties as American officers, but also in establishing friendlier co-operation with the Chinese at all levels.

In Chungking, as I gradually became adjusted to my new surroundings and the tasks confronting me, I agreed at the request of the Chinese Ministry of Information to hold a weekly press conference. The purpose, I was told, was to inform the Chinese as well as the outside world about the situation and of course, if possible, to give out information that would bolster morale and condition the minds of the people to the hardships and sacrifices still before them. At my first press conference, held in my headquarters about a week after my arrival, I indicated clearly that my name would be de-emphasized in all press reports emanating from China Theater Headquarters, and that communiqués would be referred to as China Theater communiqués and not General Wedemeyer's communiqués. Also, I asked that I not be quoted. Of course, the fifty or more correspondents who attended these meetings were always eager for a tidbit which could be blown up into an exciting article. They were permitted to ask questions, and my answers had to be carefully phrased so that I would not violate military security or give rise to malicious conjectures and speculations. I found that my press relations officer was inexperienced, and radioed to General Marshall requesting a replacement. I made up my mind to do everything possible to co-operate with the press and establish an atmosphere of friendliness and mutual trust. I knew that they could help me, or, conversely, make my task more difficult. As time went on, I felt amply rewarded for this attitude toward Chinese and foreign correspondents. On several occasions correspondents traveling about in the theater and noting something definitely in need of correction, instead of writing a dramatic or nasty article for home consumption, sent an informal note to me.

Facilities for health and comfort of our men were difficult to establish and maintain in the vast area over which they were deployed. Imagine an air unit in Billings, Montana, with terrible roads and no railroads connecting with Chicago, the location of the supply center. It was indeed a terrific problem to maintain contact with my far-flung units, and added to communications difficulties was the fact that the China Theater was not given much by the "powers that be" in Washington, London, and Moscow either for fighting purposes or for modicum of comfort. I had visited all of the theaters of war except the Russian, prior to assuming command in China so I was forced to make comparisons—millions of tons of supplies to the Russians and the British and only a trickle to China.

The few officers who had either accompanied me or joined my staff a week or so after my arrival were working day and night against the pressures from the enemy as well as those caused by lack of organization, lack of co-ordination, lack of co-operation, and lack of appropriate facilities in Chungking; daily conferences with the Generalissimo; urgent radios from the field asking for reinforcements, equipment, air support, and transportation. In addition to building up an effective headquarters we had to cope with a rapidly deteriorating military situation which we found among staff and troops in the Kweilin-Liuchow area.

The first week after my arrival in China, the Japanese pushed forward rapidly, attacking and capturing Kweilin and Liuchow. As these disturbing reports came in I conferred with the Generalissimo and his military leaders and arranged to move additional Nationalist armies to blunt the enemy attack. The Generalissimo would assure me that the units we were moving were highly effective and would not melt away as the units they were relieving had uniformly done. It was very discouraging when even the highly touted divisions which at great effort we had moved by air or motor transport to the Kweilin-Liuchow area also fell back, introducing the possibility of an enemy advance on Kunming or Chungking. Actually there had been practically no fighting worthy of the name on the part of the Chinese since the Changsha battle in May, at which they had made a most gallant stand. Now, however, the Chinese troops appeared to lack spirit and simply would not hold ground. The Japanese had approximately twelve divisions concentrated south of Changsha and extending down to Liuchow. I felt that that was double the number they required to conduct limited-objective attacks and protect the line of communications running from Hankow to Canton. So I concluded that the enemy had continued offensive intentions, and realized that drastic measures must be taken immediately to stop their advance. We simply could not lose our supply terminal at Kunming, and psychologically it would be a serious blow if we lost the wartime capital, Chungking.

In redisposing forces to block the advance of the Japanese, I recognized that practically everything I did would impinge upon military operations in other areas, particularly Burma. Having just left Mountbatten's command I was thoroughly familiar with his plans, and I did not want to do anything to militate against his success. On the other hand, I also knew that the major objective of the United States, as explicitly spelled out in directives from the Joint Chiefs of Staff, was to establish and maintain a line of communications to China and to maintain the Chinese in the war as an effective fighting force. I reasoned that if we lost China there would be no necessity for the operations in upper Burma to which the Americans seemed to have been irretrievably committed since the time that Stilwell had announced his intention to return to Burma. Further, if China were knocked out of the war, the approximately one million Japanese fighting there could be moved elsewhere—for example, to the Philippines, Malay, or even Burma, and thus make it tougher for Nimitz, MacArthur, and Mountbatten.

Thus I became a competitor for American resources against my former chief, Admiral Mountbatten. Naturally he was disturbed. Members of his staff were reported as highly critical, for they felt that I was taking advantage of the fact that I had complete knowledge of their plans and purposes, whereas they had to rely upon the intelligence that I provided concerning the situation in my theater. Actually, the intelligence experts on Mountbatten's staff underestimated the enemy capabilities in China while my own intelligence people had overestimated and depicted a critical situation. Carton de Wiart, however, the British Prime Minister's Special Representative to the Generalissimo, agreed with my own analysis of the situation and thought that I was fully justified in requesting that two of the American-trained and equipped divisions be returned from Burma to save the situation in China.

The British reaction in India was amusing to some of the members of my staff, who knew that shortly after my departure from the Southeast Asia Command His Brittanic Majesty King George VI had graciously decided to bestow upon me a valued decoration, the Order of Companion of the Bath. One wag said that before we got through competing for resources with the British, Mountbatten would surely pull the plug and let the water out of the tub so that I could not be his Companion of the Bath! This did not happen and

I was very happy and honored when my former chief, Mountbatten, presented me with this greatly coveted honor.

In conferring with the Generalissimo concerning Japanese capabilities, I discussed the defense of both Kunming and Chungking. I pointed out that if the Japanese captured Kweiyang, which I felt they definitely would do unless the Chinese forces opposing could be compelled to hold, they could in a short time turn north to capture Chungking. However, the other Japanese alternative, turning west to capture Kunming, would not only be a psychological and political blow but disastrous since this was our one terminal of supply in China. I pointed out that we could no longer conduct a military effort worthy of the name. The Generalissimo understood the implications of losing our one and only supply terminal. I told him that I would do everything possible to defend Chungking but I cautioned him that I could not possibly recommend that our efforts to defend Chungking be given priority over the determined defense of our supply terminal, Kunming.

Based on intelligence estimates of these dangerous Japanese capabilities, and on reconnaissance reports from the 14th Air Force to the effect that the Japanese were assembling large numbers of planes and gliders in the Hankow area, we were greatly concerned. We had little confidence in the ability of available ground forces to fight effectively. In order to preclude chaos in Chungking should the Japanese attempt to capture the capital either with ground or airborne units, I directed my staff secretly to make plans for the orderly evacuation of Americans as well as the seat of the Chinese Government to Chengtu, seventy miles to the west. I was not an alarmist but I could visualize the confusion if three battalions of Japanese were parachuted down on Chungking with millions of refugees already jamming roads and buildings. Also, I knew that Japanese plain-clothes agents could add to the tumult by broadcasting conflicting orders over loudspeakers. In fact it could develop into a situation with which I simply could not cope. Anticipating the worst, I quietly evacuated American women and some military personnel in the area to Kunming. Every move that I made and every statement that I uttered was being carefully evaluated by the Chinese. Rumors spread rapidly to the effect that we were going to pull out. I issued firm denials and outwardly exuded confidence in our ability to stop the enemy. I never confided my real apprehensions to anyone. At that time Tokyo Rose was broadcasting popular music interspersed with subtle propaganda—for example, in her lilting voice she announced that "General Wedemeyer will eat his Thanksgiving dinner in India if he eats any at all."

In this atmosphere the Generalissimo firmly announced his intention to remain in Chungking—even though the Japanese should invest the place—adding stoically "and die if necessary." This impressed me and I admired his stand, but I also had heard that on two other occasions he had expressed similar intentions, once at Nanking and the second time at Hankow. However, when the Japanese finally approached he yielded to the persuasion of his advisers to evacuate. I made it clear to the Generalissimo that it was not my intention to remain in Chungking and be captured or killed by the Japanese, but that I would go if I could to Kunming and there organize as strong a defense as the circumstances permitted.

In November, Pat Hurley, who had been appointed ambassador to relieve the departing American official Gauss, was ordered back to Washington for a conference with the President. I sent two of my ablest staff officers, Colonel (later Major General) Paul Caraway and Colonel John H. Caughey, with Pat to explain first-hand the over-all situation and the various problems confronting us, including the aggressive enemy in the theater. I told Caraway and Caughey to emphasize that if we could ride out the crisis that confronted us at the time, and if we could parry the blows of the Japanese until June, I hoped in the interim to create in the rear areas a well-equipped, trained, and led group of approximately thirty divisions with which we could make a concerted drive against Canton in the fall of 1945 in order to open up sea communications to the theater. These projected plans were predicated on a continued flow of increased tonnages of supplies and equipment over the Hump by air, pipeline, and road. Logistic experts, including Sommervell and the U.S. engineer, Brigadier General (later Lieutenant General) Lewis Pick, who was in charge of constructing the road, estimated that I could plan on 100,000 tons per month after the road was completed. But my good friend, General Wheeler, who was now Deputy Supreme Allied Commander in SEAC and who was recognized as a sound engineer, again informed me that we would never be able to transport payloads over the Ledo Road to China. He pointed out that maintenance would consume a prohibitive amount of labor and supplies, resulting in very little reaching China.

On my arrival in the China Theater I asked General Hearn to explain the plans which had been prepared for projected operations there and how General Stilwell had visualized bringing about a co-ordinated, decisive effort against the Japanese. Hearn said that he was not familiar with operational plans, because the "old man had carried such information in his hip pocket."

I thought at first that Hearn was joking. However, I soon learned that he was speaking the literal truth. However, there were some plans, and quite good ones, which Colonel "Tommy" Taylor, the Chief of Operations under Stilwell, outlined for me. These plans were admittedly not complete and required considerable additional effort, but were definitely sound in concept and were helpful later when my new planning staff evolved an over-all theater plan. I learned that two outstanding officers, Colonel William Creasy (later a Major General and Chief of Chemical Warfare, U.S. Army) and Colonel Dean Rusk had done considerable work on projected plans for China. I knew from contacts earlier in the war back in Washington and in New Delhi that Creasy's and Rusk's work was always of the highest quality. My new theater staff was gradually becoming integrated, and new officers were arriving to be assigned in key positions. In addition to Lieutenant Colonel (later Colonel) B. F. Taylor and Lieutenant Colonel (later Colonel) J. H. Caughey, Major General Robert B. McClure, whose assignment I had officially requested from the War Department, had arrived. Brigadier General (later Major General) Ray T. Maddocks was assigned to the theater and ultimately became my valued and trusted Chief of Staff.

My staff was beginning to work along lines that would ensure speedy and efficient processing of administrative matters as well as preparation of sound operational plans. Concurrently I was doing my utmost to learn all I could about the complex problems of the China Theater. I had to decide what we could do immediately with the limited means available. What obstacles would the Japanese put in our way? How could I bring about the maximum co-ordination of effort? I had to draw on the staff of General Sultan for information as to the availability of supplies. The Chinese must be induced to tell me their own industrial and transportation capabilities. Finally, I had to have the unqualified support of my principal arm in the theater, the 14th Air Force and composite wings. There was plenty of written data available, but I had also to survey for myself the terrain and get first-hand information concerning the Chinese and American units-in-training and in action. Leaving my then Chief of Staff, General McClure, to run Headquarters, I flew to Kunming and other key areas, accompanied by appropriate staff officers. We visited American and Chinese commanders in the field to learn their problems and to effect better co-ordination.

While endeavoring to promote good team spirit among the Americans, I was increasingly concerned with the problem of establishing co-operative and mutually advantageous relations with the Chinese military and government officials.

Shortly before General Hearn returned to the States, I discussed the over-all situation with him. He echoed the belief of his former chief, General Stilwell, when he warned me that it was impossible to learn anything, or to secure any co-operation, from Chiang Kai-shek's military headquarters or from any of the government bureaus. This feeling was widespread among the Americans at that time. When I went to the American Embassy to pay my respects to Ambassador Gauss, he shocked me by his attitude of complete despair. He said, "We should pull up the plug and let the whole Chinese Government go down the drain."

General Hearn told me that the Chinese were both noncommital and deceitful. He thought they were hopelessly embarrassed or ashamed at their poor war effort against the Japanese. I myself also soon came to the conclusion that the Chinese Nationalist Government was not fully informed about the location, operations, or capabilities of the Chinese armies.

General Hearn told me that every Thursday morning Stilwell, or a representative of his headquarters, had visited the Chinese headquarters ostensibly to discuss and evaluate the week's operations. Stilwell had rarely attended these conferences himself; he regarded them as nothing but a tea-drinking, time-consuming farce. Although General Hearn continued to warn me that I would learn nothing, and would be regarded with suspicion by the Chinese if I asked many questions, I told him I would attend the next Chinese staff meeting.

The following Thursday morning, accompanied by General Hearn and Sergeant (later Captain) Horace Eng (my interpreter), I went to the Chinese War Ministry. We were ushered into a conference room, and after introductions and courteous amenities had been dispensed with, we examined the maps which were spread out on a table. General Ho Ying-chin, the Chinese Chief of Staff, gave a brief résumé of the over-all situation. I couldn't follow the presentation very well and I made no effort to elicit more information.

After spending about half an hour hopefully waiting for concrete information, I knew that I had met defeat. But already I had thought of a way of breaking the impasse. I told General Hearn on our drive back to my office that I intended to organize a Joint American-Chinese Staff which would schedule meetings every week, or more often if the situation required, at my own headquarters.

There was no War Room or large conference room in my theater headquarters, but the Generalissimo assured me that I could make any changes or procure additional space to provide adequate facilities. General Hearn was sure that my honeymoon with the Chinese would soon be over. I was new and they would test me out, making lots of promises that would never be fulfilled. I felt depressed by his skepticism but I would not admit defeat and continued to exude enthusiasm, for which up to that time I had had little basis.

The Generalissimo approved the joint staff idea and as soon as a War Room was set up at my headquarters the meetings I had proposed started on a regularly weekly basis. General Chen Cheng, the newly appointed Minister of Defense, sat next to me at the head of the table. To our right the Chinese and American Chiefs of Personnel (G-1) sat side by side; on our left the Chinese and American Chiefs of Intelligence (G-2); and next to them the Chiefs of Operations (G-3); and so on, with complete Chinese and American integration in each major staff division.

Initially the Chinese did not contribute much. They were shy but not indifferent. They made notes of the questions we raised, and I was gratified to observe gradually increasing participation in the discussions by the Chinese representatives. It was not long before they were differing with suggestions made by the Americans; this was exactly the atmosphere I had hoped we would create. Our different views were resolved in a spirit of good fellowship and mutual respect, and we all recognized that it would be better for us to discover weaknesses in our proposed plans than to have the enemy expose them on the field of battle. The Generalissimo heard so much about the success of these meetings that he suggested he would attend one. I, of course, was overjoyed to have him. He had never seen a War Room so modern and complete. My wonderful staff had set up sliding easels on a large wall on which they could depict graphically the various areas and troop dispositions. Charts, graphs, tables, and pictures of weapons, silhouettes of enemy planes, and all types of information that would be helpful in the evolution of our plans were visible from any seat at the conference table. The Generalissimo was highly gratified and enthusiastic.

This spirit of friendly co-operation accomplished at the top level began gradually to permeate the entire theater down to the lowest echelon far from the wartime capital.

The reorganization of the combat forces was our next task. There were about 350 divisions in China when I assumed command of the theater. The tables of organization called for about 10,000 men to a division. The Joint American-Chinese Staff recognized the inability of the United States or China to provide even the barest essentials and equipment for so many divisions and so many men; accordingly, it was agreed that we would concentrate on training and equipping only 39 divisions. I told the Generalissimo that with a comparatively small number of well-trained divisions we could drive the Japanese from Chinese soil; assuming, of course, our continued overwhelming air superiority in the area.

We assigned American advisory groups equipped with radios to each Chinese division and army. The senior member of each advisory group served as the military adviser to the Chinese unit commander. If it developed that the Chinese commander did not agree with the advice, he was free to exercise his own judgment. However, in so doing he was required to notify the next higher commander in the Chinese chain of command that he was overriding his American adviser and give the reason. Similarly the American adviser was required to notify the next higher American commander that his advice had been overruled by his Chinese opposite number. Usually the differences in judgment were resolved at the lower echelons. If necessary, they could continue on up for consideration by the Generalissimo and me for final decision.

While these steps were being implemented to improve efficiency and to create a spirit of friendly co-operation in all echelons between the Americans and Chinese, a sufficient number of experienced highly qualified officers had arrived from the U.S. so that I could now organize a War Planning Division on my staff. I was proud of the work performed by this group of officers. The plans which they submitted for the Joint Staff's consideration were invariably approved almost without change. When V-J Day came, we were preparing to execute their excellent plan for the capture of the Canton–Hong Kong area.

Let us return now to the immediate situation confronting us in the fall of 1944. We had forces operating in the Salween area against a Japanese division based in Northeast Burma. Marshal Wei Li-huang, known as "Hundred Victories Wei," was in command of the Chinese in that area. His principal American adviser was Brigadier General Frank Dorn. I received a message from General Sultan, who commanded the five Chinese divisions in Burma, that the Allied forces in Burma, including the British and Chinese ground troops and U.S.-British air units, were planning to converge on the Mandalay plains, driving the Japanese southward. This campaign, if successful, would free North Burma of enemy troops and thus permit uninterrupted construction of the Ledo Road.

General Sultan asked me to insure that the Chinese Salween forces would advance, exerting maximum pressure against the Japanese there in order to pin them down while he was attacking out of the Myitkyina-Bhamo area. I discussed Sultan's request with the Generalissimo and he gave full approval to my plan to visit Marshal Wei at the front in the Salween area and authorized me to order him to launch an all-out attack against the Japanese.

Accordingly I flew to Kunming, where I was met by Brigadier General Dorn. From Kunming we took a smaller plane to a point nearby. We then proceeded by jeep to Wei's headquarters.

The Marshal was friendly and hospitable. I quickly got down to business by inquiring about Japanese strength and capabilities. The replies tallied more or less with information I had previously received. Then we reviewed the strength of the Chinese forces and the number of days of fire available to the troops, and, in general, made a comparison of capabilities, the Japanese and our own. I had done all of this in Chungking before recommending the attack plan to the Generalissimo, but I thought it would be helpful to review the entire situation with the responsible commander, Marshal Wei, and his staff.

At the conclusion of the evaluation, I informed Marshal Wei that I wanted him to attack the Japanese at a certain hour on a certain date and expected his forces to reach specified objectives which I pointed to on the map. I indicated that this order was given in the name of the Generalissimo, who was fully acquainted with the situation and understood the necessity of attacking at the agreed-upon time and place. I mentioned that General Sultan would be pushing hard against the Japanese opposing him in the Myitkyina (Burma) area, that the British would be advancing out of the Chindwin Valley eastward, and that it was important that this over-all effort be conducted vigorously.

I gave these instructions exactly as I would have given them to a group of American officers, courteously and with confidence. There was a moment or so of silence; then Marshal Wei informed me that the attack just simply couldn't be mounted at the time and under the conditions that prevailed. He said he would require considerable reinforcements, more troops, and also more ammunition. Here was my first test with the Chinese. I was wearing two hats: Commanding General of the theater and also the Generalissimo's Chief of Staff. The advisers attached to Marshal Wei's headquarters and to each major echelon, including divisions throughout his command, were Americans under my direct control. The equipment of his troops was preponderantly American. I had to be firm, for I knew if I vacillated that my position would become untenable in future contacts, not only with this particular Chinese commander but with the others.

So I said, "Marshal Wei, I have carefully considered all of the factors involved, and it is my considered judgment, with which the Generalissimo agrees, that we can and must attack on the date and hour specified. Therefore, I am ordering you in the name of the Generalissimo to launch the attack as I outlined."

Marshal Wei's eyes narrowed and I sensed that he was reserving his action. There was not much more to be said. In fact, I felt further discussion would weaken my position; so I took my leave, shaking hands all around and wishing the assembled group of Chinese officers with their American advisers good luck. I told them that I would be following closely the reports of their successes on the scheduled day of the attack. I shook hands again with Marshal Wei and bade him a friendly good-by, leaving the tent. I noted that Brigadier General Dorn had his hands cupped together and was backing out of the tent and bowing slightly—a recognized and very polite Chinese gesture on taking leave of a senior or important official.

Dorn and I jumped into the jeep and went back to the airport to board my plane for Kunming. En route Dorn said, "General Wedemeyer, I presume you always want me to be frank with you and make criticisms when I think they are appropriate." I assured Dorn that that was the case and that I would always appreciate criticisms and advice from any of my people. I emphasized that he would be doing me a disservice if he didn't give me the benefit of his knowledge and experience after his long duty in China. (Dorn was a Chinese-language student and had been assigned to the area many years before the war.)

He then launched forth. He said I had insulted the Chinese marshal, and offered to wager that the attack would not be made as I had ordered.

Covering the first point raised by Dorn, I replied that I had lived in China many years earlier and was fairly well acquainted with their customs and manners. I said that in my judgment I had been firm but courteous in the American tradition. I added that if the cupped-hands, bow-out-backwards method had been successful, perhaps I would not have been ordered to China to succeed Stilwell. I said I was going to try my own method, which I believed to be direct as well as courteous.

With reference to the second point, that Marshal Wei would not attack, I told Dorn that if he didn't I would relieve all of the Americans now on duty with Marshal Wei and take all of the American equipment from him. Both the men and equipment would go to Chinese units and leaders that would obey my orders. Then I added, "In the future, don't you ever let me see you kowtowing to any Chinese official. I expect all officers to be courteous, tactful, and completely honest in their contacts with Chinese, but I want them always to be so in the American tradition."

I flew back to Chungking and reported my experiences with Marshal Wei to my Chief of Staff, but to no one else. The day of the scheduled attack arrived, and I arose early because I wanted to receive the first reports coming in. There were none. I felt uneasy all that morning. All day long I made inquiries in the War

Room concerning enemy dispositions and the operations reports from our own troops in the Salween front. There was nothing but silence. I went home that evening with a heavy heart.

Perhaps (so I thought to myself) Dorn was right after all. If so, what should I do now? My Chief of Staff joined me for dinner, and afterward we had a long private conference. I finally decided to wait another day before taking action. The following morning before I left my quarters for the office a radiogram arrived. It said: "Attack jumped off at 5:00 A.M., first objective captured. Our troops advancing steadily but Japanese resistance seems to be building up."

I was overjoyed. When I went to the Generalissimo's office for my daily conference at 11:00 A.M., I told him that our troops in the Salween area had reported successful advances and suggested that he send a radiogram to Marshal Wei congratulating him. This was done. Later, when I talked about this matter to Dorn, he told me that while he agreed with my own estimate of the situation, namely that Marshal Wei had sufficient forces to make a successful attack, nevertheless he had not believed that Wei would comply until I gave him the additional resources. He thought I had made Wei lose face in front of his entire staff. He added that he was surprised that the attack had been pulled off. Perhaps Marshal Wei would now feel better and would in the future carry out my orders.

I wonder whether we Americans, impetuous, impressionable, and attuned to the automobile era, are possibly as wise as our Chinese allies who counseled us to go slow in rickshaw cadence: "To make haste by eating our tea with a fork."

Whether or not Americans could learn some lessons from the ancient civilization, philosophy, and precepts of the Chinese, I was soon convinced that Chiang Kai-shek was a sincere patriot, preeminently concerned with the interest of his country and his people. He knew very little about modern military strategy, for he had been trained in guerrilla war concepts; but he knew a great deal about the political art of holding his people to the job at hand. He was skillful in playing one person against others. Using honey for my part instead of vinegar—as suggested in the phrase of F. F. Liu, the Chinese military historian—I discovered Chiang was eminently willing to accede to planning in which he had primarily an onlooker's part.

CHAPTER XXI

STILWELL, HURLEY, AND
THE COMMUNISTS

WHEN I ARRIVED in the China Theater in the fall of 1944, Major General Patrick J. Hurley had already been in Chungking for several months serving as the Special Representative of the President. He had for long been an effective trouble shooter for Mr. Roosevelt. In the early days of the war he had been sent to Australia to organize a fleet of small ships to deliver supplies to the beleaguered Philippine Islands. Later he was sent to Moscow to discuss Far Eastern affairs with Generalissimo Stalin. He was one of the few American officers who had been permitted to visit the scene of the most important battle of the war, Stalingrad.

Hurley, an ebullient and colorful character, was not always long on tact, but he enjoyed the advantage of President Roosevelt's complete trust and confidence. He had found a deplorable situation existing in the relationship between General Chiang Kai-shek and the American military commander, General Stilwell. In the interest of using the maximum available Chinese manpower against the common Japanese enemy, he was striving to bring about a *modus operandi* for the employment of Chinese Communist troops alongside the armies of Nationalist China.

It was important that a clear-cut understanding be established between General Hurley and myself. Accordingly I made it crystal clear that I would endeavor not to become involved in political or diplomatic matters; and that if this inadvertently happened, I would keep him fully informed. When Hurley was appointed to succeed Ambassador Gauss, I told him that my headquarters would do everything possible to co-operate with him and the members of the Embassy.

To assist General Stilwell in his multifarious responsibilities in the complex area of China, Secretary of War Stimson had arranged with Secretary of State Hull to have four career men of the State Department assigned to the staff of China Theater Headquarters as political advisers to the Commanding General. Mr. Hull had reluctantly acceded to this unusual arrangement. However, the Secretary of State was often bypassed by the President of the United States, who actually assumed the responsibilities of the Secretary of State as well as those of the Chief Executive. When I relieved General Stilwell, these four political advisers were John Davies, John Service, Raymond Ludden, and John Emerson. The first three possessed extensive knowledge of conditions in China and were acquainted with the principal Chinese miltiary and civilian leaders. They were students of the language as well; and Mr. Davies, who had spent considerable time in China, spoke the language fluently. Mr. Emerson had made an extensive study of the Japanese language and the country at first hand.

All these State Department men were permitted to travel widely in the country and rendered reports to General Stilwell concerning their observations and analyses of the situation. Their reports uniformly expressed strong disapproval of the Nationalist Government and invariably embodied favorable views of the Communists. Their comments frequently covered military matters. When I assumed command, I directed that they submit thumbnail sketches of the principal Chinese officials with whom I would come in contact, so that I would know something about the background, abilities, and character of the individuals with whom I had to deal. Accepting the fact that my political advisers had definite animus against the Nationalists, these thumbnail sketches were helpful.

One might have expected that General Stilwell, whom I relieved, would have remained in the theater until I arrived, in order to give me information concerning both Americans and Chinese in the area—what positions they occupied, how effectively they co-operated, and what I might expect them to do. Also, it would have been helpful if Stilwell had stayed only one day longer to give me a briefing concerning his plans for projected operations. I do not know exactly what instructions Stilwell had received from the War Department. It is difficult to believe that General Marshall would not have permitted him to remain on, to give me even a single day's briefing concerning his projected plans and to supply me with other vital information.

When I arrived in Kunming, I was still confident that there would be a memorandum from Stilwell pointing out to me what I must look out for, telling me in which men he had placed special confidence, their capabilities and their key jobs, and advising me concerning the Chinese and Americans of whom I should be careful, indicating their weaknesses and what difficulty he may have had with them. But there was nothing whatsoever, no message wishing me good luck, or go to hell, or anything else. I then thought that perhaps he had left some memorandum for me with his Chief of Staff, General Hearn, or some other senior American officer in Chungking. But there was no word; none of them was particularly well informed about the main problems in the area, and some were woefully uninformed. Later I learned that General Stilwell had found sufficient time in New Delhi to hold a press conference of several hours' duration; so it seemed to me that he might have waited to give me a hand.

I soon learned that both Stilwell and Chennault were sensitive and apparently rubbed each other the wrong way. But this was not the principal reason why they were unable to co-operate in a friendly and effective manner. I had often heard from Stilwell and members of his staff that General Chennault was an intriguer; but after studying the records at headquarters and talking to both Americans and Chinese, I came to the conclusion that Stilwell was no mean intriguer himself. Both he and Chennault had jockeyed for power and position and, to ensure that their ideas were put into effect, had sought support among both Chinese and Americans. Each had tried to ingratiate himself with powerful Chinese, Chennault more successfully and deservedly so for he was a superb commander, capable of deep loyalties to friend or principle. He was in the good graces of the Generalissimo, Madame Chiang, and T. V. Soong, and was a hero to most Chinese and the members of his command. Stilwell had some very devoted friends among the Chinese military leaders, and his American staff members were fanatically loyal to "Uncle Joe" as many affectionately called him.

Many of our military men who were in China during the war did not recognize the evolutionary processes of history and were not cognizant of the implications of the struggles between old order and the new in the Middle East and Far East and their direct effect upon the situation in China during World War II. General Stilwell was regarded as the leading expert on China in the War Department. Yet I found much evidence indicating that he, too, had failed to understand the complex political and psychological problems which were the result of China's past experiences at the hands of Westerners.

My military problems in the Chinese Theater were perplexing and absorbing. The last thing I desired was to get mixed up in politics, like my predecessor. I had locked up the papers relating to the relief of Stilwell in a file called "Oklahoma" (after Pat Hurley's native state) and decided not to read them until after the war. At the outset I made a solemn agreement with Ambassador Hurley that I would never send any information back to Washington pertaining to political, economic, or diplomatic matters without affording him an opportunity to make comments or suggestions.

Reciprocally, he had agreed that he would not send any military information back to the President (with whom he was in direct communication) without giving me an opportunity to comment. This mutual agreement resulted in appropriate instructions to the members of my staff, including the political advisers, that all material of a political and diplomatic nature would be sent to the Embassy for the Ambassador's attention.

On a visit to the Salween front early in December, 1944, far from any spot which could provide security in communication, I received a message to the effect that an urgent EYES ALONE, TOP SECRET message was awaiting me at Kunming. This caused me to cut short my visit with the troops and return to Kunming, several hundred miles away. The top-secret message was from General Marshall. It informed me that Ambassador Hurley had reported to the President that members of my staff had undermined the delicate negotiations Hurley was conducting with the Communists in his attempt to secure Communist troops for use against Japan along with the

Nationalist armies. I was ordered to investigate and make prompt report.

I immediately flew to Chungking and got in touch with the Ambassador, to whom I expressed my disappointment at not having been shown his report to the President before it was dispatched. Wasn't this, after all, a breach of our agreement? Hurley maintained that the matter was so serious and urgent he had not been able to wait for my return. I agreed that if his information were correct, drastic measures should be taken, and assured him that I would investigate immediately.

Pat Hurley's allegations concerned John Davies and John Service in particular. But he had also cast aspersions on the loyalty of General McClure and Colonel David Barrett. I had implicit confidence in the loyalty and sound judgment of my Chief of Staff, Bob McClure; and Colonel Barrett was an old China hand whom I had no reason to distrust. Barrett had been functioning with the Yenan liaison group created by General Stilwell; and while he was friendly with his Communist contacts in Yenan and often expressed agreement with the critics of the Nationalist Government, I found it hard to believe that he could be disloyally scheming against Hurley or myself.

The perilous military situation in China had naturally caused me to investigate every possibility that might bring about effective co-ordination of all China's armed forces as well as our own against the Japanese. In the studies submitted by my staff there was a plan involving the employment of the Chinese Communist troops which envisaged their advance out of Yenan eastward to bring pressure against the Japanese operating in North China. In my absence on the Salween front this plan had been elaborated upon; and General McClure had discussed it with the Minister of War, General Chen Cheng, and other Chinese officials. In doing so he had assured me that his presentation and discussion were all of an exploratory nature, and that by my approval as responsible theater commander and finally the Generalissimo's as overall commander would naturally be required.

I had known General McClure for twenty years. In World War I he was wounded and decorated for gallantry in action; in the interim peacetime service he was recognized as a superior officer. Serving in General MacArthur's command in the southwest Pacific, he had again distinguished himself as an outstanding combat leader. I could not and would not believe that he had had any part in the conspiracy which Hurley thought he had uncovered.

After a thoroughgoing investigation I concluded that Ambassador Hurley had been incorrectly informed. But having got to know Pat well, I thought I understood the reasons for his hasty action.

In order that the reader may also understand, I must explain what our Ambassador was endeavoring to accomplish in China and also try to give a character sketch of my dear and valued friend, Pat Hurley.

Like President Roosevelt, General Hurley was a great believer in personal diplomacy. Both of them imagined that charm, or a trusting, comradely approach could disarm Communists and convert them into friends—or at least induce them to co-operate in what was assumed to be a common aim. Although after his disillusioning experience in China, Hurley became an irreconcilable opponent of communism in Russia, China, or anywhere else, he would seem originally to have had no better understanding of the real nature of communism or its aims and methods than President Roosevelt. He had arrived in China during the first week of September, 1944, fresh from an interview with Molotov in Moscow, apparently believing in the assurances given him that the Soviet Government was not "associated with" or "responsible for" the Chinese Communists. According to Hurley's own account of this interview, Molotov told him that some of those who called themselves Communists were related to communism in no way at all, but were simply expressing dissatisfaction with their economic conditions, and would forget their political inclination when their economic conditions improved.

Thus Hurley, in 1944–45, like Marshall after him, in 1945–46, approached the problem of unifying China on the false supposition that the Chinese Communists were not real Communists under Moscow's command but simply a Chinese faction that could be induced by diplomatic negotiations to come to terms with the Nationalist Government. Unlike Marshall, however, Hurley never wanted or tried to compel Chiang to share power with the Communists. Before he left for China as President Roosevelt's personal representative, Hurley and the President agreed upon the following formula (as reported in Don Lohbeck's authorized biography, *Patrick J. Hurley,* page 280):

> The purpose of the armed Communists being the overthrow of the Government of the Republic of China, it would be futile for the United States to attempt to uphold the Republic while arming a force bent upon its destruction. The President therefore decided that lend-lease material could not be used to arm the Communists unless and until they acknowledged the National Government of the Republic of China, and the leadership of Generalissimo Chiang Kai-shek.

The original purpose of his mission as stated in Hurley's directive was "to promote efficient or harmonious relations between the Generalissimo and General Stilwell to facilitate General Stilwell's exercise of command over the Chinese armies placed under his direction."

On arrival in China in September, 1944, Hurley found Chiang increasingly alarmed at the efforts being made by the State Department and by Stilwell to force him into an agreement with the Communists. Stilwell had gone so far as to tell his cronies (in *The Stilwell Papers,* page 321) that "the cure for China's trouble is the elimination of Chiang Kai-shek." Chiang told Hurley that instead of trying to force him into an agreement with the Communists, the United States ought to be telling the rebellious Communists to submit to the authority of the Nationalist Government; that if the Communist armies were armed and equipped by America, China's whole war effort would prove futile, since China would end up by being turned over to the Communists.

Hurley sympathized with and understood Chiang's position and valid arguments and quickly established friendly relations with him. Nevertheless, he advised the Generalissimo that the United States would be better disposed to give increased aid to the Chinese armies if the threats of civil war were brought to an end by an agreement with the Communists.

Chiang was, of course, in a desperate situation. Chennault had told him that Stilwell had deliberately refused to give him help in the defense of Kweilin in order to compel Chiang to yield command of the Chinese armies to Stilwell. And on September 16, ten days after Hurley's arrival in China, Stilwell had sent a note to T. V. Soong, who was then Foreign Minister, saying that "if the Generalissimo did not meet the demands concerning his appointment to command all of the Chinese forces, he [Stilwell] would recommend that the United States withdraw from China and set up its Asiatic base in the territory of the Soviet Union." (This is reported in *Patrick J. Hurley*, page 290.)

Confronted with the demand that the Civil Government as well as all Chinese armed forces and resources should be placed under Stilwell's orders, and the threat that if he refused the United States would withdraw its forces and cease all aid to China, the Generalissimo courteously and firmly stated, in substance as follows: Inform President Roosevelt that I cannot surrender my responsibilities as President of China. If he withdraws American forces and lend-lease, we will do the best we can with what we have. We will continue to fight even though we receive no aid from outside sources. Tell the President that I desire General Stilwell to be relieved from all duties and responsibilities in China. Hurley told me that he had dispatched the above information to Washington.

It should be emphasized that Hurley supported Chiang at this critical juncture and subsequently summed up his own conclusions about Stilwell as follows (see Lohbeck, *op. cit.*, page 305):

> The record of General Stilwell in China is irrevocably coupled in history with the conspiracy to overthrow the Nationalist Government of China, and to set up in its place a Communist regime—and all of this movement was a part of, and cannot be separated from, the Communist cell or apparatus that existed at that time in the Government in Washington.

Hurley, nevertheless, still considered it his duty to bring about some sort of compromise agreement with the Chinese Communists which would bring their armies into the war against Japan. Following his appointment as Ambassador to China, he drew up a five-point proposal for a possible accord, which he himself described as "rather innocuous," and on November 7 he flew to Yenan to confer with the Chinese Communist leaders. As they were hurrying to meet him at the airfield, he performed his favorite stunt, yelling the loud and piercing Comanche Indian war cry which had, according to his own account, "delighted the Russian soldiers at Stalin-

grad." This was in accordance with his idea that "contagious friendliness could be made a fundamentally effective part of diplomacy."

That evening he was the guest of honor at a banquet celebrating
the Bolshevik revolution and felt he was getting along famously
with his hosts.

During the following two days, as Hurley informed President
Roosevelt, he argued with the Communists in "most friendly
fashion," and they "pulled and hauled his five points" until they
were finally revised. They were, in fact, so "revised" that they
became little more than a restatement of the same irreconcilable
position the Communists had for so long maintained toward
Chiang.

Once again the Chinese Communists refused to acknowledge the
authority of the Nationalist Government. As "revised," Point 1 re-
stated the Communist refusal to acknowledge the Nationalist Government as the supreme authority in China. Hurley's Point 2 was
twisted out of all recognition to include a demand that "the present
Nationalist Government is to be reorganized into a coalition Nationalist Government embracing representatives of all anti-Japanese parties and non-parties and political bodies." Point 4 as rewritten by the
Communists in Yenan now stated that American Lend-Lease supplies should be "equitably distributed" to the Communist armies
and the Nationalist Government forces. And Point 5 proposed the
legalization of the Chinese Communist Party.

This reformulation of his five points, which the Communists in
Yenan gave to Hurley, should have forewarned him that there was
in actual fact no possibility of unity except on terms which would
have destroyed the authority of the Nationalist Government.

Nevertheless, either because he was misled by his warm reception in Yenan, or because he thought he was attempting a task no
more impossible to achieve than arbitration between a trade union
and management in a labor dispute, Hurley told his hosts that he
could not speak for Chiang's reception of the Communist proposals
but that he would like Chou En-lai to return with him to Chungking to negotiate.

In Don Lohbeck's biography of General Hurley, we are told
(page 314, footnote) that "notwithstanding these concessions to
the Communist organization, Hurley felt that this proposal con-

stituted a basis for negotiations between the Nationalist Government and the Chinese Communist Armed Party."

No wonder that T. V. Soong told Hurley when he presented the Communist five-point proposal to Chiang that "The Communists have sold you a bill of goods." The Generalissimo's brother-in-law on this occasion also warned Ambassador Hurley that the result of accepting the Communist agreement would be the eventual control of the Government by the Communists. Still attempting to carry out an impossible task as set for him by his Washington directive, Hurley resisted the truth told him by Chiang Kai-shek and T. V. Soong that the admission of Communists to a coalition government in China, as in Poland and Yugoslavia, would result in the destruction of all democratic, anti-Communist groups.

Try as he might, Hurley naturally failed to square the circle. For all his charm, his engagingly informal approach to diplomacy, and his eloquence, Pat Hurley couldn't produce unity on the basis of a compromise settlement of internal differences among political factions which had absolutely opposed theories of society and government. Instead of realizing that Molotov had deceived him about the Chinese Communists, Hurley grew angry. Instead of revising his estimate of the political situation in China and Soviet Russia's role, he blamed John Davies and John Stewart Service and their backers in the State Department. This was odd, for Davies and Service had always agreed with Hurley (or at least they professed to agree) on the one point that the Chinese Communists were not Moscow's stooges but an independent force composed essentially of agrarian reformers. The dilemma into which Pat Hurley had worked himself was clearly posed when he was called upon to testify before the Senate Foreign Relations Committee in 1945. He then accused his enemies in the State Department of sabotaging United States policy by privately advising the Communists that "his efforts to prevent the collapse of the Nationalist Government did not represent the policy of the United States." But he still spoke as if he believed that the Soviet Government had no control over the Chinese Communists. In his letter of resignation, he said that there was no question but that the Soviet as well as the British Government supported the United States policy of unifying China.

Whereas many Americans were deluded by clever propaganda into believing that the Chinese Communists were not real Communists but agrarian reformers, Pat Hurley would seem to have fallen for a contrary but equally pernicious myth. To him it seemed that Stalin, Molotov, & Co. could be relied upon, or their words believed, and that the villains of the piece were the Chinese Communists and the State Department in the person of the political advisers on my staff whom I had inherited from Stilwell.

Looking backward and examining the evidence, I realize today that I was too preoccupied with my military duties in attempting to stem Japan's last offensive in China to have time to evaluate fully the reports of my political officers—Davies, Service, Ludden, and Emerson. Their sympathy for the Chinese Communists is obvious in their reports and in their recommendations that we back the Communists instead of the Nationalist Government. Whatever their motives, which may have been dictated by a number of reasons ranging from misplaced idealism to naked careerism or worse, their activities were not actually out of line with the policy that both Hurley and Marshall vainly endeavored to implement: namely, collaboration between the Nationalist Government and the Communists. At the time I had no reason to doubt the loyalty of my State Department advisers, even though I did not agree with their estimate of the situation in China and their proposals that we should eventually ditch Chiang Kai-shek.

In a radiogram I sent to General Marshall at this time I pointed out that Hurley had been striving to accomplish a coalition between the Nationalist Government and the Communists; and that, having been unsuccessful in his negotiations at the political level, he had turned to seek a solution through the military amalgamation of Chinese armed forces. He had known all along that the Communists, while refusing to place their troops under the Nationalist Government's command, had asked me to take command of their forces.

When Hurley saw my radiogram to General Marshall he was very angry. He was at this time living in my house, and for several days he refused to speak to me. It was most embarrassing, since we had to sit together at meals. I had conceived a feeling of genuine affection and warm respect for Pat Hurley, who bore a strong physical resemblance to my father, although his temperament was the reverse of my father's calm and reflective way of viewing the world. I was deeply grieved by Pat's hostility. I had already begun to understand his mercurial temperament. I also realized that he considered me as simply a military officer, incapable of analyzing the political situation in China in its true light. I never attempted to make him realize that my interests and studies had rendered me perhaps no less capable than he of understanding the political situation, particularly the implications of Communism, in China.

After many days during which we had not spoken to one another, Pat Hurley came into my room one evening while I was propped up in bed reading. He sat on the edge of my bed, clasped my right hand in both of his, and said that he was sorry for his behavior toward me. I assured him of my continued friendship and loyalty and suggested that he send a telegram to the President indicating that possibly his information had not been correct, or at least that the actions of my staff members had been misinterpreted.

Looking back, I must now frankly admit that I was somewhat naïve or uninformed in my estimate of John Davies and John Service. One evening, when we were having a discussion about a certain individual and his loyalty to our effort in the area, Hurley said, "When you have lived as long as I have, Al, you will learn not to trust anyone until he has proved worthy of your trust." I thought that over for a minute. Then I said, "But, Pat, I have always worked on the exact opposite theory. I believe in trusting people until they prove unworthy of my trust." I developed the thought a little further, pointing out that it had been my experience that if you expect people to measure up to a certain standard and to give loyal and effective service, they will as a rule not disappoint you. I said to Pat: "It seems to bring out the best in them."

Perhaps if Hurley had not unjustly impugned the loyalty of my Chief of Staff, General McClure, I would have paid more attention to his entirely justified suspicion of John Davies, John Stewart Service, and the other State Department political advisers on my staff. Today, reading through the reports sent to me and to the State Department by Davies, Service, Emerson, and Ludden, it seems obvious not only that their sympathies lay with the Chinese Communists, but also that they were either consciously or unwittingly disseminating exaggerated or false, Communist-inspired, reports concerning the Nationalist Government designed to stir up all manner of Sino-American distrust—as, for instance, when John Davies sent me long accounts of rumors or unsubstantiated reports that the Generalissimo was collaborating with the Japanese or had reached a tacit nonaggression pact with them.

John Davies might be held correct in his assumption that the United States intended to assist the Communists, in view of the attitude of the State Department at this time and the views of his former chief, General Stilwell. But I should have realized that it was strange, if not positive proof of John Davies' Communist sympathies, that in his report of his visit to Yenan, December 15–17, 1944, he should have been so concerned that a leading Chinese Communist general, Peng Teh-huai, had "little faith in what the United States will do to help the Communists."

John Davies had not been content to press for aid to the Communists. In one of his secret reports, dated December 12, 1944, he went so far as to recommend that the United States cut off supplies to the Nationalist armies unless they ceased fighting to contain Communist forces. He obviously wanted us to make a Mikhailovitch out of Chiang Kai-shek. His advice in this document, from which I quote below, is reminiscent of Churchill when the British Prime Minister told Brigadier McLean that his job in Yugoslavia was simply to help those killing the most Germans, without regard to the political consequences. Davies wrote:

> It is time that we unequivocally told Chiang Kai-shek that we will work with and, within our discretion, supply whatever Chinese forces we believe can contribute most to the war against Japan. We should tell him that we will not work with or supply any Chinese unit, whether Central Government, Provincial or Communist, which shows any inclination toward precipitating civil conflict. We should tell him that we proposed to keep him, as head of the recognized government, informed of what supplies we give the various Chinese forces.
>
> It is time that we make it clear to Chiang Kai-shek that we expect the Chinese to settle their own political differences; that we refuse to become further involved in and party to Chinese domestic political disputes. We greatly hope and desire that China will emerge from this war unified, democratic, independent, and strong. We feel that this goal is to be achieved most expeditiously and with the least possible expenditure of Chinese and American blood and treasure if the United States bends its efforts in China primarily toward

working with and assisting whatever elements can contribute most to the speedy defeat of Japan.

In another report of his, extracts from which were included in the 1949 State Department White Paper, John Davies wrote that although "We should not now abandon Chiang Kai-shek," because for the moment we would thereby "lose more than we could gain," we should "have no qualms in ultimately abandoning him in favor of the progressive—Communist—forces in China."

As Davies expressed it in one of his many dispatches:

> . . . If we openly declare ourselves for the Communists, the Chiang Government will promptly be reduced to the position of a local regime. . . . There will be some chaos (but not as much as anticipated in some quarters). There will be large-scale transfer of military, technical and administrative allegiance from Kuomintang to Communist China, and we *shall have aligned ourselves behind the most coherent, progressive and powerful force in China.*

The fact that the Davies reports of a truce between Chiang and the Japanese had no substance is proved by the postwar interrogation of senior Japanese staff officers of the China Expeditionary Army. Questioned in 1951 concerning Sino-Japanese relations in 1944, they denied that there had been any understanding between the Japanese and the Chinese Nationalist Government. According to Romanus and Sunderland, in *Time Runs Out*, the Japanese officers, however, agreed that there had been "extensive contact with dissident Nationalist Commanders in S.E. China," and that "through many channels they had sought to inform the Chinese that the East China drive offered no threat to them, but only to the U.S. airfields."

If this were the case, there was justification for Chiang's refusal to send arms from his own meager supplies to Chinese commanders whose loyalty to him was suspect. As Romanus and Sunderland comment:

> To sum up, when Wedemeyer took command of the U.S. forces in China Theater, there was extensive evidence of serious dissension among the Nationalist commanders, in addition to the highly publicized and generally known state of latent civil war between Nationalists and Communists, while the economic situation was an adverse factor that would

weigh heavily against any American effort exerted in China. Under these circumstances, preventing the dissolution of China into a group of warring factions—some supported by the Japanese, some by the Soviet Union, some by the United States and the British Commonwealth—in order for the nation to reach the end of the war as a state rather than a geographic expression would be a major achievement. Gradually, the appreciation of these circumstances molded Wedemeyer's interpretation of his mission.

My own experience with Chiang was considerably different from Davies' theory of Chiang's behavior vis-à-vis Japan. I had heard that the best Nationalist divisions were opposing the Communists north of Hsian, and I asked Chiang to release some of those divisions for use against the Japanese in the Kweilin-Liuchow area. Chiang Kai-shek did not hesitate to permit my flying two divisions from the Hsian area, where they were supposed to be indispensably engaged in encircling the Communists. One of my colleagues told me that when Stilwell had made the same request, he had been refused. The Generalissimo knew that I was just as opposed to communism as he was, but that calculated risks had to be accepted in order to stop the Japanese at this critical period.

Some of the difficulties Pat Hurley experienced in Chungking were made known in the United States when Drew Pearson in his column of June 15, 1945, wrote an article based partly on fact and partly on fiction. This is quoted here at length because it exemplifies the misinformation or misinterpretation of some American press and radio commentators at that time (and subsequently) concerning the Chinese Communists—if not their positive sympathy for them.

Referring to the *Amerasia* case involving the arrest of State Department and other U.S. Government agency personnel on the charge of having given secret government reports to the Communists, Drew Pearson said:

There is a lot more than meets the eye behind the arrest of two State Department officials and one Naval officer on a charge of passing out secret documents to magazine writers. Chief factor behind it is the intense cut-throat rivalry between two Chinese factions—Chiang Kai-shek's War Lords in the south of China, and the so-called Chinese Communists, actually an agrarian party, in the north. Mixed up in all this is the action of the Chinese Secret Service operating under cover in the USA against anyone opposed to Chiang Kai-shek. Also involved is the prima donna temparament of a very temperamental US Ambassador, and finally the issue of whether the United States will get itself caught between Chiang's political factions the same way it has between Polish factions.

It so happens that all three of the young Far Eastern experts arrested by the Navy and State Department feel ardently that the USA is backing the wrong horse in China. They feel that the northern Chinese Government [sic] is much more representative of the Chinese people, has done more fighting against Japan and that Chiang Kai-shek is chiefly an important prisoner of his own southern War Lords. Moreover, these three are not alone in this belief. General Stilwell emphatically believed it and was ousted from China as a result. John R. Davies, Secretary of the American Embassy, also believed it and was ousted by Ambassador Patrick J. Hurley after a bitter verbal battle. Also John Service, another Secretary of the Embassy, believed it, was fired out of China by Hurley and has now been arrested by the State Department. Finally, US military men solely concerned with winning the war quickly feel that the Northern Chinese can be a vitally important factor in defeating Japan on the vast mainland in China.

It was all too typical of the general attitude in America, as influenced either by unwitting misinterpretations or by treasonable manipulators, that Drew Pearson should have referred to the Chinese Communists as "the Northern Chinese."

My Chief of Staff, General McClure, was less discreet or restrained than I tried to be. Drew Pearson's account of what occurred when McClure met Hurley at a cocktail party at this time was exaggerated but substantially true:

At about the same time General McClure, Wedemeyer's Chief of Staff, encountered Hurley at a cocktail party and chided him for sending his telegram of protest without prior consultation.

"You pup," roared the former cowpuncher from Oklahoma, "I've hit men for less than that." Fists went up. McClure is no small man, neither is Hurley; but before anything happened, friends intervened. However, Chinese were present, and saw these two high-ranking Americans in a near fist fight. It didn't help American prestige. It was at about this time also that Embassy advisers, John Davies and John Service, the latter now arrested, were ordered out of Chungking by Hurley. He said that he did not want anyone around who sided with the Northern Chinese. Since then the rift between North and South China has become wider and wider with the result that Russia probably will officially recognize the North Chinese, leaving the USA with another Lublin-London Polish dispute on its hands. This has been one of the hottest debates among junior officers inside the State Department. Top officials, however, are dead set against discussion.

In view of Drew Pearson's column and other reports which distorted or exaggerated the situation in Chungking, Hurley and I gave the following statement to the press on June 19, 1945:

> The following statement is issued jointly by His Excellency, The American Ambassador to China, Patrick J. Hurley, and the Commanding General, United States Forces, China Theater, Lieutenant General A. C. Wedemeyer:
> "Reports of dissension between ourselves or members of our staffs, either personally or officially, are untrue. There have been differences of opinion; however, they have always been resolved promptly and amicably. The diplomatic and military representatives of the United States in China are working together harmoniously and will continue to do so."

At Hurley's insistence, John Davies was recalled by the State Department. Subsequently he was transferred to Moscow, where (as Pat said to me) he hoped John "would experience at first hand the chicanery as well as the tyranny of communism."

Before leaving Chungking, Davies came to bid me good-by. Hurley and I were seated together at the breakfast table. My relations with my senior political adviser had always been cordial and friendly, and I wished him good luck and asked him to keep in touch with me by correspondence. It was inevitable that he and Mr. Hurley should exchange some remarks, which became rather acrimonious. Other members of my staff were present, so I suggested that we three go to another room. The Ambassador and Mr. Davies then launched into a very heated argument during which Hurley accused Davies of being a Communist and of failing to support the directive of his country in support of the Chinese Nationalists. Tears came to the eyes of Mr. Davies as he heatedly denied Hurley's accusations. Hurley said that he was going to have him kicked out of the State Department. Davies begged the Ambassador not to ruin his reputation and his career. I endeavored to calm them down, and finally brought the conversation to a close, reminding Mr. Davies that he would have to hurry to the airport in order to catch his plane. As he was leaving, Hurley relented somewhat and said he would not immediately take action against Davies. Later I received a letter from Mr. Davies in Moscow, insisting that he had never accepted communism as a philosophy of life, and thanking me for having helped to soften Hurley's attitude toward him.

John Davies had given me valuable information concerning Chinese officials and had also helped me in making a survey of available river transportation. Some of his reports included suggestions pertaining to the employment of Communist troops, and uniformly included critical statements regarding the corruption, maladministration, and inefficiency in the Chinese Nationalist Army and often extolled the Chinese Communist Administration and Army. In evaluating these reports, I felt better qualified to pass judgments on the employment of military means, for I had spent my lifetime in the study of military tactics and techniques. Thus, when my political advisers made recommendations of a military nature, I was not influenced particularly by them. It never occurred to me that my four professional Foreign Service officers could be disloyal to me or to their country.

If I had been suspicious of their motives, I might have concluded that they were sympathetic to the Communist movement. Later, when I heard that these men were suspect, I was astounded. For example, it was difficult to believe that Jack Service would release secret documents to Mr. Jaffe, a Communist agent in Washington, as subsequently was charged according to articles in the press. On many occasions I was questioned by FBI agents and Congressional committees concerning my views about the loyalty of the four political advisers on my staff. I could understand more fully the feelings of those individuals toward whom the finger of suspicion was pointed as the result of their associations, actions, and philosophy of life, for I had been suspected of being pro-Nazi in 1941. Later on, some of the Americans in India thought I was completely in the British camp. At the same time I had a reputation among the British of being an Anglophobe, because I had so consistently opposed Churchill on the Mediterranean strategy. Because of my own experiences I was on all occasions meticulous about Davies, Service, and others in China. But it was no exaggeration to say that they were hypercritical of the Nationalists and commendatory with reference to the Communists.

This I felt was true about some of the correspondents in the China Theater. They may not have approved of communism, but they were drawn into comparing an inflation-ridden Kuomintang China with the promised agrarian reforms of the Communists, who posed as honest people interested in the welfare of the common man. Such pretense is in the pattern of communism everywhere. But after the party seizes power, usually by foul means, then the true picture is revealed. Communist leaders show themselves to be ruthless and barbaric, not at all interested in the welfare of the people.

CHAPTER XXII

TOWARD VICTORY

WHEN THE NEW YEAR DAWNED in 1945 I had been in China for about three months and had gradually oriented myself both toward the difficulties confronting and the great opportunities afforded by my command in this turbulent theater of war. My headquarters had been moved to a more suitable location for the efficient performance of the many duties involved in co-ordinating all of the activities within this vast area.

The China Theater was greater in expanse than the United States. The Japanese enemy occupied the eastern third of the country and controlled all the seaports and main railroads and highways. Our war effort against the Japanese was maintained by a tenuous airline of communications, which was gradually bringing in greatly increased tonnages of aviation gasoline and munitions of war. The Japanese two-pronged advance in South Central China had been blunted. Preparations had been made for a concerted drive to capture Canton and contiguous areas in order to open sea communications and thus greatly accelerate the flow of supplies into the China Theater. An improved relationship of mutual confidence and trust had been created between Americans and Chinese. A fine spirit of co-operation and comradeship was developing from the highest to the lowest echelons.

When I first arrived I noted many objectives that I wanted to accomplish. After carefully weighing the advantages and disadvantages I would submit proposals to the Generalissimo at my daily meetings with him. Although he apparently was in complete accord and expressed approval, action was not always taken.

By this time I had become convinced of the Generalissimo's sincerity of purpose, and my admiration and respect were unequivocal. However, in the interest of following through on proposed action, I discontinued making oral recommendations. Instead, I substituted carefully prepared memoranda embodying each problem requiring action. I submitted two copies: one in English which I signed and the other in Chinese which was sealed with my chop (Chinese seal). I retained copies of these memoranda in my headquarters and from time to time, if the contemplated action had not been taken, I invited the Generalissimo's attention to them.

I had gradually succeeded in effecting changes which, although not very far-reaching, had contributed toward creating confidence and mutual respect. I had put a stop to the all too frequent expression of derogatory remarks about the Chinese by American officers who had taken their tone from Vinegar Joe. And as soon as I felt sure that Chiang Kai-shek recognized I was a friend who was sincerely striving to help China defeat Japan, I began to make suggestions for reforms, which he received and acted on without offense. For instance, it had worried me that on many occasions I was invited to banquets given by Chinese officials at which some twenty courses were served. Having seen so many half-starved or emaciated Chinese, I felt this was fundamentally wrong, and I recommended to Chiang that such banquets should be discontinued for the duration of the war. I suggested that he could set an example by restricting the number of courses at his dinners to four. He enthusiastically agreed and the word got around in a tactful manner.

I expressed my concern for the health and feeding of Chinese soldiers. The conditions were terrible and I said, "Generalissimo, if I were a Chinese officer, I believe I would be tempted to "squeeze" or take money in order that my family could live properly and I could provide food and shelter for them." Chiang responded by doubling the pay of every member of the armed forces. I asked General Marshall to send a food expert to China to study the situation on the ground and make recommendations to alleviate the inadequate and improper diet the Chinese troops were receiving.

Of course, I realized such success as I had in gradually overcoming Chinese distrust and inducing the Generalissimo and his associates to accept recommendations was also, I think, due to never promising them anything without actually doing it. They came to realize that I expected them likewise not to break their pledges. The trouble was that all too frequently Chiang was unable even though willing to carry out my recommendations. ·

The history of China reveals that it had never been a political entity in the sense that we understand a nation. The Generalissimo's position was not secure. There were ambitious, self-seeking Chinese generals who continued to oppose his regime. The Communists represented a group of revolutionaries with a private army and with an ideology wholly untraditional in the Chinese sense, both inspired and supported by the Soviet Union. There were many intellectuals who opposed the one-party system as represented by the Kuomintang and yet were strongly opposed to communism. The common enemy, Japan, had served to unite many recalcitrants, at least for a time, but it was evident that the Generalissimo did not exercise full control. And one always had to remember that a large number of Chinese people were ruled by a puppet Government located at Nanking. Americans imagined that Chiang Kai-shek could simply give an order and it would be carried out. I realized that the Generalissimo, far from being a dictator, was in fact only the head of a loose coalition, and at times experienced great difficulty in securing obedience to his commands.

The German officers who had helped Chiang Kai-shek build the nucleus of a modern army in the early thirties had perceived the basic weakness of the Nationalist military establishment and had sought to remedy it. General von Seeckt, invited to China by Chiang Kai-shek in 1933 to pattern the Chinese Army on German models, had said that circumstances in China rendered this an impossible task. He had, however, presented a memorandum on China's military situation in which he clearly outlined China's problems, and gave Chiang Kai-shek advice and plans concerning the reorganization of the Nationalist Government's military establishment. The Generalissimo endeavored to carry out the plans, but the war with Japan intervened. Like Stilwell and myself, von Seeckt had found that "lack of centralized authority, ill-defined powers and responsibilities, and the absence of unity of command were weaknesses prevalent in the Chinese Army." Ill-defined powers and responsibility were almost as grave a weakness as the lack of arms and food. As von Seeckt reported to Chiang in 1933:

> A side-by-side arrangement of higher positions, as was the case in North China during the late war and which still seems to be in existence, can never lead to victory.
> When the Commander in Chief does not personally take charge of the command at the front, he must appoint a special person to serve in his place with unrestricted authority. Here at Peiping it is not clear whether the War Minister, the Minister of the Interior, or the representative of the Chief of the General Staff is in command of troops. In any case, there is no unity of command.

As F. F. Liu, the Chinese military historian, has said:

> The Chinese traditions of balances of power and the characteristic reluctance to delegate authority were seen by Von Seeckt as weaknesses which the army could no longer afford to permit. The first desideratum was a clearly organized, unified command; then, quality:
> "It appears to me that it is better to have ten good divisions than to establish twenty mediocre divisions within the same period."

Von Seeckt's task, like my own, was rendered easier by the fact that he "had a real admiration for the Chinese and especially for Chiang," whom he described to the Swedish explorer Sven Hedin as "a judicious, wise and prudent statesman, a skillful but careful strategist, and a splendid and noble personality."

China's gallant three months' stand against Japan in 1937 at Shanghai and then at Nanking owed much to General von Falkenhausen, who followed von Seeckt and who had accomplished far more by tact and patience in his dealings with the Chinese than Stilwell by his dictatorial attitude toward Chiang Kai-shek. Again, as recorded by Liu:

> Had the war been delayed for two more years, China might have had 60 German-trained army divisions to throw against the Japanese invaders. In the air Messerschmitt and Stuka planes would have carried her markings and, under the sea, Chinese-manned U-boats would have harassed Jap-

anese shipping in submarine wolf-packs. As it turned out, much of her equipment was German-made, many of her officers German-trained, and her whole military organization and industrial development German-inspired. Had German influence been given more time to work and spread in China, the Japanese might have met a far different foe. Continued German influence might well have drastically changed the world picture by eventually enlisting China as a partner of Germany and turning China's formidable manpower in an entirely different direction.

In my contacts with Chinese senior officers, I found very few whom I deemed efficient or professionally well trained. I did not question their loyalty to the Generalissimo, but as his Chief of Staff I had to estimate their military capacities and knowledge, their leadership qualifications, and their willingness to carry out orders in consonance with over-all war plans. Many excellent schools were established for the junior officers—an infantry school, artillery school, motor mechanic school, tank school—which helped to produce a stronger officer corps. General McClure, replaced by General Maddocks as Chief of Staff, and now the senior American combat commander, reported that the junior officers had greatly improved, particularly in the company officer rank, to such a degree that he was most optimistic about the success of our planned operations. As he put it, good company commanders will carry a mediocre division commander forward in combat.

Perhaps the most outstanding Chinese military leader with whom I came in contact was General Sun Li-jen. He had received his early military training at the Virginia Military Institute in the United States. He had the attributes of leadership, he knew something about modern military tactics and techniques, and he was flexible in adjusting to the guerrilla-type warfare which predominated in the fighting in China as well as in the jungles of Burma.

There were other Chinese generals who enjoyed good reputations as military strategists or military leaders. Chen Cheng, Fu Tzo-yi, Pai Chung-shi, Li Sun-jen, Chang Fa-kwei, Wei Li-huang, and Tang En-Po. It was unfair to compare these Chinese officers with our own, and in retrospect I realize that my early evaluations of them were premature. Naturally, when the Chinese armies, with their particular methods of fighting, were confronted by modern disciplined forces such as the Japanese, they would easily be routed or defeated in spite of the courage, stoicism, and guts which by and large one found in Chinese soldiers. General Okamura, the over-all Japanese Commander opposite me in the area, said after the war that usually one Japanese division could defeat four or five Chinese. Later on, in Korea, Chinese divisions, several of which had been American-trained and equipped or had nuclei of former Nationalist troops, fought like dervishes. I have often been asked why these Chinese troops fought so effectively against the Americans in Korea and yet, when fighting against the Japanese, seemed to lack the same spirit, *élan,* and military effectiveness. There are three possible reasons for this: First, at the time the Chinese Communists took over, these Chinese Nationalist units had reached a peak in equipment and preparation for combat. (They had been intended for use in the CARBONADO offensive against Japanese-held Canton-Hong Kong.) Second, the Chinese Nationalists had failed to explain adequately to their troops why they were called upon to fight. Third, under Communist leadership, the Chinese soldiers were driven by fear when not by conviction. If a soldier disobeyed or retreated in the face of the enemy he was summarily shot. He also knew that his family would be punished if he failed to fight. We Americans had striven to indoctrinate Chinese officers to lead, not to drive. Our idea was to enforce discipline by winning the respect and understanding of the soldiers, thus insuring willing obedience and high morale.

The basic attitude toward China, not only of the British but of our own American planners, is clearly revealed in the U.S. Army's official history of the war in the China-Burma-India theater. On the first page of Part I of this detailed and valuable book, Romanus and Sunderland write that in the period of December, 1941, and January, 1942, after Japan had "over-run American and British possessions in the Far East," such "gloom and despondency" had been spread in China "that it was feared she might make a separate peace with Japan;" and that the War Department, in starting a program of aid to China, hoped that a "revitalized Chinese Army" might "ease pressure on the United States and the British Commonwealth in the Pacific."

No word of recognition of the gallant fight which China had waged against Japan all alone during four and a half years, during the greater part of which period England and the United States had continued to sell the sinews of war to Japan. No word to China that henceforth, having been attacked ourselves, we would come to her aid and help her to drive the Japanese out of her territory. Instead we, fresh in the fight and with our enormous industrial resources, wanted China "to take the pressure off" us and the British Empire!

Similarly, as regards the later stages of the war, we read in the official U.S. history of the China-Burma-India theater that when the last Japanese offensive in China began in April, 1944, the JCS were worried only lest Japan capture the eastern Chinese airfields, centered around Kunming, from which support was expected for American operations in the western Pacific. Again no word concerning the vital interests of our Chinese allies, who were expected simply to go along with us, Britain, and Russia, at any cost to themselves. To complete the picture, it is recorded that following the U.S. Navy's decisive defeat of the Japanese at Leyte Gulf, and because of Stalin's promise in October, 1944, that sixty divisions for operations against Japan would be available three months after Germany's defeat, the JCS lost interest in China's war effort.

"The Joint Chiefs of Staff were aware," it is written, "that whatever might happen in China, sixty Russian divisions were promised against Japan, and these operations would sweep south and east below the Great Wall." Thus, "Chinese bases were no longer considered essential in the war against Japan." There remained only "the problems which would be created if the Generalissimo signed a separate peace. . . ." There was no thought at all of the fatal consequences to China and ourselves of bringing the Soviet Union into the Far Eastern War. Instead of trying to keep the Red Army out of China, we were happy to have her come in, and practically discarded a traditional friend, China.

It was inevitable that, having set our sights on "total victory" as our one and only war aim, regardless of the consequences in both Europe and Asia, we perforce hitched our wagon to the Soviet Red star.

In earlier chapters I have surveyed the disastrous consequences of our lack of a Grand Strategy in the war against Germany and recounted my own abortive attempts to call attention to the Communist menace. As regards China, although I tried to help her as well as my own country to avoid the consequences of a misplaced trust in Communist good intentions, I regret that I was not all along sufficiently aware of the devious methods by which the Kremlin and its stooges accomplish their nefarious purposes. It took me some months to get oriented to the realities of the power struggle between the Chinese Nationalist Government and the Communists, and even longer to realize that the political advisers provided by the State Department had been seduced for one reason or another into an undiscriminating, almost emotional, revulsion against the Nationalist Government.

The first few months in China were dismal, both as to climate and as to the military situation. We had many setbacks, heartaches, and disappointments. The Japanese continued to advance, taking important objectives without much difficulty in the area east of Kunming, particularly in the Kweilin-Liuchow area. One after another, key points would fall. I received radiograms at night requesting authority to blow up the facilities remaining on some of our advance airfields. The situation was deteriorating rapidly and in conference with the Generalissimo I emphasized that the Japanese capabilities to move on Kunming and/or Chungking were confirmed by the rapidity with which they advanced. None of the Chinese divisions which I interposed seemed able to remain steadfast. At great cost logistically, on account of the limited transportation means in the China Theater, we moved several divisions from the northwest in the vicinity of Hsian to block the Japanese columns south of Kweilin. The Generalissimo assured me that these divisions were all well-trained and equipped and would fight. However, after the Japanese came along they, too, melted away.

I had not been in the theater long enough to determine all of the angles, but it was apparent that I had to take drastic steps at once. My staff drew up a plan that envisaged bringing back two of the American-trained and -equipped divisions fighting in Burma with General Sultan. This would entail air movement across the Hump of personnel and equipment on a scale not hitherto imagined.

The Generalissimo arranged an evening conference of his senior cabinet and military officials to consider the plan. I presented the scheme of maneuver in the large sitting room of his home where I usually conferred with him and his representatives. The Generalissimo said that in his judgment all five of the Chinese divisions should be brought back from Burma, adding that if the situation were so desperate that the Japanese were on the verge of knocking China out of the war, the five Chinese divisions fighting in Burma should be used to protect their homeland. I conceded his point but explained that I had in mind interposing the two returned divisions on an escarpment which would increase our defensive strength just west of Kweilin, and I would mix the combat effectives brought over from Burma with some of our best divisions already present in the theater. I had talked this over with my most experienced combat officer, General McClure, and he fully agreed. Also, General Chennault had loyally suggested that the Air Force was prepared to go all-out in order to strengthen our defense and blunt the enemy advance.

The Generalissimo called for an expression of views from everyone present at the historic meeting. Only one officer supported my plan. The first official, sitting on Chiang's right, Dr. T. V. Soong, felt strongly that all five divisions should be brought back. Chiang Kai-ming, the Chinese Chief of Intelligence, agreed with Soong. General Lin Wei, whom I saw on almost every visit to the Generalissimo's home and for whom I had high regard, also voted to bring back the entire Chinese force from Burma. There were about a dozen officers present that evening. I was the only American present except for my interpreter, the Chinese-American Captain Horace Eng. He kept me posted as to the reactions that were being expressed in Chinese, and I could see that sentiment was overwhelmingly against my recommendation. All of them recognized the seriousness of the situation and agreed with the basic idea of appealing to the Joint Chiefs of Staff for permission to move forces from Burma back to China, but so far no one of them agreed with my compromise solution of bringing only two divisions. I acknowledged that they had good cause both to be alarmed and to insist upon stringent measures to alleviate the situation. But they were not acquainted with the serious problems confronting the Southeast Asia Command, which I had left only a few months earlier. I knew that the removal of the five Chinese divisions from Burma would practically negate the operations planned by Admiral Mountbatten. If we brought the five Chinese divisions back to China, it would require all of the transport planes available in the general area. A considerable amount of logistic support of the British divisions operating against the Japanese in Burma was taken care of by transport planes organized into combat carrier groups. It was my considered judgment that we could delay the enemy advance in China with two Chinese divisions from Burma reinforced by several less effective ones already available, while the three Chinese divisions remaining in Burma could at least carry on a limited offensive there and maintain pressure against the Japanese, thus giving indirect help to the British advancing out of Imphal Valley. If the situation were to deteriorate further after we had disposed the troops as envisaged in the plan, I intended to request authority from the Combined Chiefs of Staff to fly in the remaining three Chinese divisions from Burma. When the opportunity came to the Minister of War, General Chen Cheng, to express his views, he stated succinctly and boldly that he agreed with General Wedemeyer. This was the first ray of light and the only one, for the others agreed with the Generalissimo and T. V. Soong—bring them all back! Then I had an idea. Knowing the Chinese love of intrigue, I quietly instructed Captain Eng as follows: "Explain to the Generalissimo and those present that I have not as yet described the deception plan which may be the keynote to the success of the over-all maneuver." With great solemnity I told the Chinese present that we would sell the Japanese information to the effect that we were bringing all five divisions from Burma and it would be difficult for them to check on the accuracy of this statement. This struck a most responsive chord, first in the mind of General Chiang Kai-ming, the Chief of Intelligence. Others quickly fell in line and there was considerable talking, most of which I didn't understand, but I could sense a growing approval. As it turned out, the plan was adopted as I recommended, but the Generalissimo insisted that I should notify the Joint Chiefs of Staff that conditions might deteriorate to such a degree that it would be necessary to bring all of the divisions back. This I agreed gladly to do, and the meeting broke up at about midnight.

The transfer of two American-trained and -equipped Chinese divisions was conducted successfully, and after the war I learned from Japanese officers that they had intelligence reports to the effect that we had interposed the five divisions that had fought so effectively against their forces in Burma. Ironically enough, although I had succeeded in my struggle to persuade the Generalissimo and his staff to allow some Chinese divisions to remain in support of British operations in Burma, the British Prime Minister is reported to have said: "Wedemeyer doesn't care. He would remove the sidearms off the British tommies."

The unconditional surrender of the Germans in June would release personnel and matériel sorely needed for the all-out effort against Japan, and I was informed by General Marshall that Generals Patton, Simpson, and Truscott would be made available to the China Theater if I felt I could use them effectively. I immediately accepted this offer of outstanding combat-experienced officers. There were important roles in the China Theater for men of their caliber. The Generalissimo heartily agreed. Inasmuch as Patton was senior to me, I assured General Marshall that I would be glad to step down and have him assume command of the theater and that I would continue to serve in any capacity under him. Marshall informed me that I would remain in command. This introduced the question of my own promotion to four-star rank. The Generalissimo expressed his intention, and Ambassador Hurley confirmed his own intention, to ask the President to promote me, stating that I had relieved a four-star general and had greater responsibilities than some of the European generals who had been given that rank. Actually I always felt that Pat Hurley was responsible for the idea and made the suggestion to the Generalissimo. I told both of them that I had been promoted rapidly, being much junior in years and experience to other theater commanders, and that I had been able in my present rank to manage all right in dealing with four-star generals and even marshals in the Chinese Army.

I planned tentatively to assign Patton to the northern sector of China with the mission of advancing eastward on the important objectives Peking, Tientsin, and Ching Wan Tao. Truscott would be assigned the central group operating eastward along the Yangtze Valley on Shanghai; and McClure, who was already thoroughly familiar with the southern sector and had performed in a superior manner the past several months as a competent and aggressive combat leader, would command the operations in the south directed against the important objectives Canton-Kowloon-Fort Bayard. I had previously recommended McClure's promotion to Lieutenant General, a rank commensurate with his capabilities and great responsibilities. Lieutenant General Simpson would serve as Deputy Commanding General of the theater and supervise all operations of ground units, American and Chinese. Lieutenant General Stratemeyer, an outstanding airman, who had been brought into the theater from India, was now Deputy Theater Commander and also Commanding General of Allied Air Forces in the area.

When mid-summer, 1945, arrived, the CARBONADO plan for seizing Canton was in its initial phases, and we actually were ahead of schedule in our preparations for the drive on Canton-Kowloon. I would have pushed eastward more aggressively in August; however, I wanted to assure myself that arrangements were made for the establishment of close-up logistical support including facilities for the care and evacuation of wounded with a steady flow of replacements. In other words, once the final drive was launched against Canton, I wanted to insure that the attacking forces would be appropriately supported and would not bog down due to the lack of strong air support and ammunition or replacements.

Tragically, General Patton was fatally injured in an auto accident in Europe. However, both Simpson and Truscott visited the area shortly after V-E Day to make an estimate of their staff requirements and to acquaint themselves with the over-all situation in this complex theater. Simpson made a most favorable impression on the Generalissimo and other Chinese officials during his visit. He returned to the States to assemble an appropriate staff with a view to coming back and giving us the benefit of his acknowledged leadership. Truscott returned to the States when V-J Day was announced and consequently did not have the opportunity of visiting the Generalissimo and the capital, Chungking.

The Generalissimo was very sensitive and almost as intuitive as a woman. There were many intricate problems confronting him, and frequently he discussed the internal affairs of his country, asking my advice. Uniformly I emphasized under such circumstances that my suggestions had no official cognizance, but I did try to advise as a friend. It was my feeling that he was not too well equipped, either in training or experience, to cope with the multitude of problems confronting him. Unfortunately there did not seem to be many men of character and ability available and in whom he could impose complete confidence or responsibility.

But the vagaries of the Chinese mind were at times disconcerting—for example, the Generalissimo suggested that I extend to General Marshall an invitation to visit China, either before or after the Potsdam conference. When General Marshall indicated that he could not at that time make such a visit, the Generalissimo expressed keen disappointment. He probably harbored in his mind the thought that General Marshall's attitude toward him and the Chinese in general was one of anger, particularly since the relief of General Stilwell the preceding fall. Certainly he evolved an obtuse approach to this subject. He stated that he would have extended the invitation directly to General Marshall, but was reluctant to do so because on the occasion of President Roosevelt's death he had sent condolences to the Chief of Staff and received no reply. Here was a veiled hint that Marshall might be vexed because of Stilwell's removal. I immediately assured the Generalissimo that General Marshall would never under any circumstances be discourteous, and that I was certain there was some mistake. Later, when in my office, I checked and discovered that a courier letter was delivered to the Generalissimo's headquarters on April 26 and that I had a receipt for the same from a Chinese colonel. I told the Generalissimo about this and confirmed that it was General Marshall's reply to the Generalissimo. He was most apologetic. Both he and I were disappointed that General Marshall's plans precluded a visit to China immediately after V-E Day, but I understood that there would be many demands on his time before and subsequent to the important Potsdam conference. The Communist activities to the north continued to disturb me. I received reports daily concerning an increase in the scale and tempo of clashes between Nationalist and Communist troops. If an all-out fratricidal war had taken place at this critical time, the diversion of the limited number of combat-effective Chinese divisions might have been catastrophic. I made a tour of the theater and found a number of divisions fairly well equipped and trained that General McClure assured me would be able to exert maximum pressure when employed in operation CARBONADO. So my real concern was to prevent considerable military strength from becoming absorbed in fratricidal war. I suggested to General Marshall in a radiogram sent immediately prior to the Potsdam conference that the only sure method of avoiding a blow-up between the Communist and Nationalist forces would be to apply strong outside pressure through the United States and the Soviet Union. I knew that a civil war in China would destroy the economic and political equilibrium in the Far East and would eliminate the opportunity for millions of Chinese to live in peace and prosperity under a government of their own choosing. It was my hope in expressing these views to General Marshall that President Truman and Generalissimo Stalin would jointly agree to avoid interference in the internal affairs of China. I had my grave doubts but at that time I could see no alternative. Stalin at Teheran, Yalta, and Potsdam had confirmed his recognition of the sovereignty of Nationalist China. I knew that the Nationalist Government was militarily strong enough to cope with the Chinese Communists provided the latter received no outside help from the Soviet Union or other sources. But after eight years of war with its killing and widespread dislocations the Chinese would have to have a continued moral and material support from the West.

I was on the opposite side of the globe when the Allied leaders assembled in Potsdam to determine the fate of Germany, and I was convinced that unless the dire consequences of neglecting China in its strategic and political considerations were considered by them, the situation would get out of hand very quickly.

In the meantime, in order to prevent a violent eruption between the Chinese Communists and the Nationalists, I proposed to the Generalissimo and Mao Tse-tung that I be permitted to attach a small cadre of Americans with radio equipment to each of the Communist and Nationalist divisions located in close proximity to each other. The reports coming in had been so conflicting, each blaming or denouncing the other, that I felt in this manner I could obtain correct information. There had been recriminations and misrepresentations perhaps on both sides but I felt that the presence of American representatives with both Nationalists and Communists in the field might act as a deterrent to surreptitious maneuver. My major purpose of course was to obtain a factual picture of the situation for authorities in Washington.

Earlier I mentioned that as a member of the staff of the Southeast Asia Command I was opposed to the construction of the road from Ledo to Kunming. Events proved that the road which, upon the generous suggestion of the Generalissimo, was now called the Stilwell Road, would be closed to traffic most of the time by slides and inundations. The maintenance of the road consumed time, effort, and matériel to a prohibitive degree and precluded the movement of sufficient tonnage to justify the tremendous expenditure of money and equipment, not to mention the lives lost in the military operations in North Burma. Even the six-inch pipeline leading from India to Myitkyina was damaged by slides, and the four-inch pipeline continuing on to Kunming was sabotaged by native Burmese. Of course remedial action was taken promptly, but the tonnages predicted by the proponents of this tenuous line of communications could never be attained. These developments, of course, had a dilatory effect upon our intensified activity at the front, both air and ground, as envisaged under the CARBONADO plan.

Also I experienced considerable difficulty in obtaining sufficient Chinese truck drivers and maintenance personnel for the motor transport in the theater. We had anticipated the requirements of such personnel and had taken appropriate steps in organizing training schools; but the dearth of American instructors, the fact that maintenance parts which had been requisitioned failed to arrive from the States, and the difficulties of language all militated strongly against the effectiveness of our program. Other transportation problems were injected by unfortunate attributes of the Chinese themselves.

The five Chinese divisions in Burma which, at war's end, had been returned to the China Theater (the 14th, 22nd, 38th, 50th, and 30th) formed a wonderful nucleus of combat effectives. They were definitely cocky and proud of their achievements. U.S. equipment, full stomachs, and thorough training as well as successful combat experience contributed to their confidence and *élan*. These units were provided a supplemented ration by the British while fighting in Burma, and Admiral Mountbatten generously agreed to send such rations into China for a period of six months after their return. I pointed out to the Generalissimo that this situation would create a serious morale problem among the other divisions within China. My staff had recently evolved a new ration plan which had been approved by the Generalissimo and which would provide appropriate and adequate food for all divisions. He agreed that the five elite divisions should be given exactly the same ration as all other divisions in the theater.

In connection with the new ration plan adopted in the China Theater, my early investigations indicated that no one in China had ever heard that an army marches on its stomach. The system had been that a stipulated sum of money, presumably adequate to provide food for the men, would be given to the unit commanders. These latter were inadequately compensated and were constantly seeking opportunities to insure that their own families had sufficient food and shelter. The temptation was very great, and "squeeze" (graft) among some of the unit commanders was rampant —I might add, understandably. Although the Generalissimo had already increased the pay of the Chinese Army, in an inflationary situation such as prevailed in China this was not permanent in its effect. The ration plan referred to visualized giving sufficient money to a central supply organization in Kunming. It was the responsibility of this supply center to purchase the food and distribute it to the units, and thus the handling of money by unit commanders in the field was eliminated. This had a very salutary effect throughout the country. In the past the men had gone scavenging in order to obtain adequate food, with the result that people living in the countryside hated them. Also, the Chinese soldier, feeling that he was fighting for his country and was entitled at least to food, was hostile toward his own countrymen who resented his efforts to obtain food in that manner. This new ration-distribution plan greatly alleviated that situation and promoted a wholesome relationship between soldier and civilian. Also we succeeded in obtaining vitamins from the States to supplement the men's diet.

Another constructive step that was undertaken pertained to the arrangements for the evacuation of wounded. In the past in most instances soldiers who were wounded were left on the battlefields to rot and die. But under the supervision of Brigadier General George Armstrong, theater surgeon and ably assisted by Chinese Surgeon General Lim, an excellent plan was evolved. Modern equipment—for example, ambulances, litters, etc.—was not available; however, improvisations were resorted to and a highly effective evacuation of wounded and proper treatment in crude but sanitary field hospitals was put into effect.

I made many trips to various air bases and to training areas. What we considered a short jaunt in the China Theater would have encompassed all of Europe because of the great distances. The most difficult job in the China Theater was that of the Service of Supply. Major General Henry Aurand worked diligently and effectively in surmounting what at times seemed to be impossible obstacles.

In August, 1945, the Japanese strategy continued to be defensive. There were indications in the situation reports confirming estimates made by my staff that sacrificial forces would be left by the enemy in Singapore, Saigon, Bangkok, Hanoi, Haiphong, Canton, Shanghai, and Hankow. If the Chinese-American forces were able to exert strong pressure against the Yangtze River bastion, we felt that the enemy would probably fall back to a rear defensive position generally along the Yellow River. Viewing the entire area and considering reports that some Japanese troops were being moved south from Indo-China into Malaya, I decided that the enemy was attempting to strengthen defenses against projected Southeast Asia Command operations. They realized that it would be very costly to move their forces back to Manchuria or to the homeland because of stepped-up Allied air and submarine operations against their shipping operating along the coast.

In the China Theater we adhered to an active defense, continuing pressure wherever and whenever feasible, but scrupulously avoiding piecemeal commitment of our forces. It was our determination that nothing should interfere with the successful execution of CARBONADO. I issued instructions from theater headquarters that our troops should follow up and press enemy withdrawals but avoid large-scale commitments. In the meantime troops and supplies were moved eastward in preparation for the big push. The fact that we had already attained in August, 1945, the initial CARBONADO objectives, of Nanning-Fuchow-Kweilin greatly heartened everyone. The entire theater was imbued with the idea of recovering sea communications. In my headquarters, however, with the complete understanding and approval of our over-all combat commander, Major General McClure, it was agreed that we should not accept a prohibitive loss in lives and resources in the attempt to capture the Canton-Hong Kong area should the Japanese elect to make a suicide "Manila" defense there. If this development occurred, we were prepared to seal off the area and take steps to establish sea communications elsewhere, for example at Swatow, Fuchow, Wenchow, Fort Bayard, and/or Amoy. We envisaged the employment of twenty thoroughly equipped and trained Chinese divisions to conduct the major offensive in September. The soldiers were fed and there were provisions for an uninterrupted flow of ammunition and equipment as well as for the proper evacuation of wounded. We knew that these factors would strongly influence the fighting spirit of the Chinese soldiers who, all of us agreed, were the equal of any fighting men in the world when properly fed, equipped, trained, and led.

I should like to go back to an important trip in February, 1945, when Ambassador Hurley and I were ordered to Washington for conferences with the President and officials of the Government. We were directed to visit MacArthur's newly established headquarters in the Philippines en route. We traveled in the same plane, flying first to Calcutta. I was not permitted to fly over Japanese-held territory, for with my knowledge of secret war plans it would be dangerous if I were to become a Japanese prisoner of war. Torture might await me if I fell in Japanese-held territory.

At Calcutta we were met by Richard G. Casey, the Australian statesman who was the Governor of Bengal Province; General Stratemeyer, the U.S. Commander of Allied Air Forces; and other officials. A short stopover and then we proceeded to Colombo, Ceylon, where Admiral Mountbatten and former associates of the Southeast Asia Command met us. Thence we flew to Darwin, Australia, a 3,400-mile overwater journey that I had made in a much slower airplane earlier in the war. In Darwin we were most hospitably received by the British military officials there. Pat Hurley, a fine figure of a man in the uniform of a major general with several rows of ribbons, rose to thank our genial hosts. Extemporaneously, I am sure, he made one of the finest talks I have ever heard concerning American ideas and ideals. He referred to the dangers of imperialism and colonialism and assured his listeners that we all should recognize the importance of permitting people to determine how and by whom they will be governed. In closing, he added that the great sacrifice in lives and treasure made by the Americans and the British during the war would otherwise be for naught. His choice of words and charming manner precluded offense, and his talk was well received.

Our next hop was to Leyte where we spent the night with the American Commander, then Lieutenant General (later General) Robert L. Eichelberger, and his able Chief of Staff, Major General (later Lieutenant General) Clovis E. Byers. The Surgeon General of the Army,

Major General Norman Kirk, was also present at Leyte and asked if he could travel in our plane on to Luzon. A radiogram was dispatched to MacArthur's headquarters concerning our imminent arrival and requesting authority for Kirk to visit the Supreme Commander's headquarters; this was refused. General Kirk was very much put out for he wanted to determine requirements for the medical services in the general area. I personally did not understand the matter but assumed that under duress of combat an effort was being made to curtail the number of visitors in the battle zone. Bitter fighting was still in progress for Manila. The Santa Tomas prison had just been captured by the gallant 1st Cavalry Division and the emaciated Allied prisoners released. In flying to Clark Field, north of Fort Stotzenberg, we passed over my former home, on Corregidor. The entire top area of the island was pockmarked with shell holes, and all of the buildings had been leveled. It was a shambles.

We landed at Clark Field north of Manila and were taken to MacArthur's office where we were briefed concerning his operations. I explained the projected plans for my own area. He was very much interested, and I marveled at his knowledge concerning the problems that confronted me. Apparently he had sources of information concerning developments in all parts of the world. His brilliant mind was incessantly evaluating and analyzing the implications of our Grand Strategy everywhere. He asked me to convey his warm good wishes to the President and to General Marshall, and added dramatically as I bade him good-by, "Al, we are on our way to Tokyo. Godspeed." His dramatic attitude confirmed a statement made many years earlier by my father-in-law, General Embick, to the effect that a successful commander must have color and a certain degree of histrionic ability.

From the Philippines we flew to Hawaii, stopping en route only to refuel. An incident involving protocol occurred at each stopping place. I was a Lieutenant General in the Army, and the Ambassador was in the uniform of a major general; so when we deplaned at various stopping places there was always an "Alphonse and Gaston" scene with my urging the Ambassador, who was really senior to me—not in the military hierarchy but as an American ambassador— to leave the plane first. On each occasion he graciously insisted on my stepping out ahead of him. Members of my staff accompanying me urged me to do so, but we all wondered about the Ambassador's reaction if I had flaunted protocol.

Arriving in Washington in March, 1945, I found that appointments had been made with the President, the Joint Chiefs of Staff, and other officials. I had luncheon alone with Mr. Roosevelt in his office and endeavored to discuss the many problems of the China area with him. I had not seen the President for several months and was shocked at his physical appearance. His color was ashen, his face drawn, and his jaw drooping. I had difficulty in conveying information to him because he seemed in a daze. Several times I repeated the same idea because his mind did not seem to retain or register. He evinced considerable interest in French Indo-China and stated that he was going to do everything possible to give the people in that area their independence. He believed that colonialism must be abandoned by our allies. He admonished me not to give any supplies to the French forces operating in the area. I explained that there were not many there; that requests had been made by the French General Sabattier for arms and equipment and that I had in each instance refused on the grounds that my directive required me to give the equipment to the Chinese Nationalist forces and that my supply was wholly inadequate even for that purpose. I did tell the President that I had made available medical supplies and facilities to French units which had straggled up into the Yunnan Province from Indo-China. It was difficult to handle this situation in China, because I greatly admired the French and also knew that General Sabattier was a courageous leader who was sincere in his endeavors to continue to fight against the Japanese. Of course, he could not expect to receive help from his own country, which was occupied by the enemy; so he naturally turned to me, an ally, for help.

The President told me that he had received communications from the Generalissimo to the effect that I had made revolutionary changes in China which would bring victory. He asked me many questions concerning the Generalissimo as a person and also asked about my relations with Ambassador Hurley. I assured him of my admiration and respect for both men and told him that they had been most co-operative in supporting my efforts to insure that the Chinese forces would make a realistic contribution to the war effort. I told the President that the Communists were not of immediate concern but I felt certain that they would cause trouble as soon as the war ended. He did not seem to understand what I was talking about. I was in the process of explaining when we were interrupted by a secretary who announced another appointment. I bade the President good-by after conveying General MacArthur's message and assuring him that we Americans in the China Theater would do everything possible to help bring the war to a successful conclusion.

The Joint Chiefs of Staff invited me to give a résumé of the situation in China. After describing our projected plans to seize a port on the east coast (CARBONADO) I mentioned the problems inherent in the limited communications. They were most sympathetic and confirmed arrangements to increase the Hump tonnage and to proceed with the construction of the pipeline as well as the road leading into China.

I had a rather embarrassing problem which was caused by the presence of a U.S. Navy group within my theater under the command of Commodore Miles. I explained that this organization was undertaking operations of a clandestine nature which were not co-ordinated by my headquarters. Also I pointed out that they required logistical support from my limited supplies. It was therefore difficult to allocate the tonnages arriving in the area unless I, as the responsible commander in the area, knew what contribution their operations were making against the Japanese. Finally I concluded my remarks about the Navy Group China by pointing out that it was militarily unsound to have an organization working within my area of responsibility and yet not under my command. Admiral King, who was very interested in this organization, assured me that Navy Group China would immediately be put under my control.

I had lunch with Secretary of War Stimson, who was much interested in the China Theater. He asked me questions concerning the Generalissimo. It was evident that he felt bitter toward the Chinese leader because of the Stilwell episode. Mr. Stimson and General Marshall had always been very loyal champions of Vinegar Joe. They had resisted for a long time the British and Chinese efforts to have him relieved of his command in the Far East. Stimson said that the President had shown him letters from the Generalissimo and also reports from the Ambassador indicating that I had no difficulty whatsoever in my relations with the Generalissimo and his officials. I replied that my experience had been very satisfactory and I had come to respect and admire the Generalissimo as a person.

Mr. Stimson asked me what I thought of the Generalissimo's military ability. I told him that he was not, in my judgment, a highly trained or skillful military strategist in the modern sense of the word. He had been very successful in leading Chinese troops against war lords and the Communists in the area. But he evidenced little knowledge of modern military tactics and techniques. I added that the pressure of many problems—political, economic, and psychological—would tax any man's capacity and strength. Certainly it was important that he have a few military advisers around him in whom he could place implicit confidence. I told Mr. Stimson that the Generalissimo was supporting the American effort to bring order out of chaos and to insure the sound employment of his troops against the enemy. I explained that I found him sincerely appreciative of our assistance and related this story: On one occasion when I was visiting with the Chinese leader, as I did daily, he thanked me most heartily for a local but rather encouraging success that our troops had experienced in combat. He seemed to want to convey his gratitude to me, as an individual, for helping him, as an individual, and I tried to make it clear that I as well as the other Americans were there not to help him personally but to help the Chinese people whom he so ably represented.

I had never accepted the idea that the bottomless poverty of the masses in China precluded improvement, but I knew enough about this poverty to know it couldn't be blamed on Chiang. There was a considerable gap between the rich and more fortunate Chinese families and the millions of hungry, ill-clad, illiterate people whose daily concern was simply to get food for empty stomachs and provide meager shelter against the elements.

Stimson again brought up the fact that the Chinese seemed to be co-operating so well and I told him about the reaction of Mr. John Hersey of *Time* magazine, who had remarked, "It seems that you are getting very good co-operation from the Chinese." I had replied to Hersey, "I feel that I am," and he commented, "Unquestionably they feel that if they do not co-operate with you that there will not be any more American assistance, that you are their last hope." I admitted that that might be true.

The Secretary then told me that Hurley had described the situation with reference to the Foreign Service officers on my staff. Mr. Stimson asked me if I would be willing to have them relieved and returned to the Embassy. I sensed that their assignment to the theater staff having been his idea originally, he was hoping I would not desire a change. However, I replied that I would have no objection to their being relieved from my staff. I also assured the Secretary that my relations with the Ambassador personally and with the Embassy staff were excellent. I told him about my reciprocal arrangement with Hurley concerning the exchange of information.

Mr. Stimson asked me about my conference with the President and I recounted the instructions I had received concerning the French. He expressed surprise and suggested that I mention this to General Marshall, which I did at the earliest opportunity. Stimson now pressed me for information about how I felt the President looked. He was obviously concerned about F.D.R.'s health. I told him that I was shocked to find that the President seemed to be in a Never-Never Land most of the time that I spent with him, picking nervously at his food and going off on tangents during our discussion. The Secretary admonished me quietly but firmly not to mention the President's physical condition to anyone. This admonishment was reminiscent of the situation that prevailed when President Wilson was so ill and his condition was not revealed to the American people.

CHAPTER XXIII

AFTER VICTORY

As INDICATIONS INCREASED concerning war's end, my staff was busily engaged in planning for the many new problems that would arise. In China Theater headquarters we recognized that there would be grave difficulties involving the Communists. There had been a stepped-up program of propaganda emanating from Vladivostok, Yenan, and Moscow. The central theme of these messages from Communist key points was that Americans were in the Far East to exploit and conquer; in other words, that we were imperialists. The Nationalist Government and its leaders were depicted as a group of collaborators with imperialists and exploiters of the common people. Therefore, Chiang Kai-shek was an enemy of the people. Exaggerated and unsubstantiated reports of dishonesty and maladministration in Chiang's government were constantly beamed throughout the Far East and were repeated in the American press. Thus we had ample forewarning about the situation that might develop as a result of the machinations of the Soviet-sponsored Chinese Communist Party. This party was obviously not a political party in the Western sense of the word for it had a private army and was composed of conspirators operating under the aegis of the Kremlin with the objective of gaining complete control over the whole of China.

It was essential to insure that the Chinese Nationalist forces would be in a position to accept the surrender of the Japanese forces ahead of the Communists. U.S. policy in the Far East was vague, but I was directed to assist the Chinese Nationalist Government in arranging for the surrender and repatriation of the 3,900,000 Japanese in China, Korea, Manchuria, Indo-China, and Formosa. In the decisive weeks immediately after V-J Day, I used U.S. planes and ships to rush Nationalist forces north and east. This, of course, infuriated the Communists, and they began to make vitriolic attacks on me personally in their press and radio.

On November 2, 1945, Vice Admiral Barbey, while in command of the U.S. ships transporting Nationalist troops to Manchuria, was compelled to withdraw from the port of Yingkow after a conference ashore with the Soviet representatives, and after seeing thousands of Chinese Communists digging trenches there. A few days before, he had perforce put back to sea from another Manchurian port, Hulatao, after Communist riflemen had fired on his launch. Together with Dairen and Port Arthur these were Manchuria's only southern ports. The American Navy, compelled to withdraw before the Russians and the Chinese Communists, had no recourse but to land its convoy of Nationalist troops at Chingwantao in North China.

A struggle for positions of strength was already in progress between America and the Soviet Union in Manchuria and North China; but unfortunately Americans were for the most part unaware of this fact. We were still in the sunset period of the "Trust Uncle Joe" war era—still imagining that we could and should get along amicably with our Russian ally. It was taboo for any American in an official position to expose, denounce, or openly oppose Stalin's aggressive action and sinister aims. I could not admit that I was endeavoring to stymie the Chinese Communists and their masters in the Kremlin by giving as much help to the Nationalist Government in its endeavor to establish its sovereignty over the liberated territories as my directive permitted.

The fact that I was both the U.S. Commander in the area and Chiang Kai-shek's Chief of Staff further complicated my problem. I was frequently placed in an awkward and embarrassing situation when, week after week, I was needled by Communist-sympathizing American and other correspondents concerning the help I was giving to the Nationalists, under cover of my directive to arrange for the repatriation of the Japanese. I tried to remain calm and keep my wits about me so that I would not be betrayed into any indiscreet remark. I answered those who baited me by telling them that I did not formulate policy but simply carried out operations in consonance with directives from Washington.

Realizing that my government would not give Chiang the logistical and arms aid he must have to take over Manchuria, and also that the Chinese Nationalist Government unaided would not have the strength to re-establish its authority over North China if it also attempted to occupy Manchuria, I suggested to the Generalissimo that the Chinese Government propose a temporary five-power guardianship over Manchuria by the United States, Great Britain, France, China, and the Soviet Union. At the same time I recommended to Chiang that he would be wise to send his best administrators as well as military leaders to North China, south of the Great Wall, to insure that his control there would be firmly established.

My fundamental purpose in making the guardianship suggestion was to preclude unilateral action on the part of the Soviet Union in Manchuria. I knew that Communist power, once established in any place, would not voluntarily be withdrawn. The Soviet Union, unfortunately at our own urgent request, had entered the war against Japan only after her defeat was a *fait accompli*. Manchuria was a rich area which, agriculturally and industrially integrated with the economy of China proper, was essential to the establishment of a stable and viable Chinese economy.

Chinese sovereignty over Manchuria had been solemnly recognized at Cairo and subsequently reconfirmed at other world conferences. But at Yalta, Roosevelt and Churchill had secretly promised Stalin such far-reaching concessions in Manchuria that Russia would be enabled to step into Japan's shoes and dominate the area. It was agreed that Port Arthur should once again become a Russian naval base as in the days before the Russo-Japanese war of 1904–5; Dairen was to be a free port to and from which Russia could move goods without inspection or the payment of customs, and in which she would own half the harbor installations and equipment. Soviet Russia was also to be given joint ownership of the Manchurian railways. Stalin had been assured that pressure would be exerted on Chiang Kai-shek to compel him "unquestionably" to agree to all these concessions, which would give Russia *de facto* control of Manchuria. In sum, Roosevelt and Churchill at Yalta promised Stalin that Chiang would be induced to give Russia the imperialist privileges in Manchuria that China had struggled for fifteen years to deny to Japan.

Chiang was not told of this until months later. And I shall never forget his reaction when Ambassador Hurley in my presence performed the highly distasteful task of informing the Generalissimo of the Yalta betrayal of China's national interest.

However, rather than make a public protest, Chiang and his government went along with the U.S., by sending T. V. Soong and Wang Shi-Chieh to sign the Sino-Soviet Treaty of August, 1945, which sanctioned the concessions to Russia that we had made at China's expense. No doubt he expected that we would at least give him the necessary backing to insure that Moscow would honor its pledge in this treaty "to render to China moral support and aid in military supplies and other material resources, *such support and aid to be given entirely to the Nationalist Government as the recognized Government of China.*"

Operating through the Chinese Communist Party, which had been its obedient servant during all the twists and turns of Soviet policy, the Kremlin sought from the outset to wreck the Nationalist Government.

Having rushed into the war for the kill only eight days before Japan's surrender, the Red Army naturally met practically no enemy resistance and was soon in complete control of Manchuria. Establishing themselves in key positions and dominating all communications in the area, the Russians received the surrender of Japanese arms and equipment, which they overtly and covertly made available to the Chinese Communists. Furthermore, they immediately in high-handed arrogant manner exploited the country, dismantling all removable industrial equipment and destroying most of the rest.

It seemed strange that they should destroy installations that their own sponsored Chinese Communist forces might use or which they themselves could operate if they remained in occupation of Manchuria. I came to the conclusion that the reason for their seemingly illogical behavior was that the Kremlin leaders never dreamed that the U.S. would be so supine as to permit them to remain in Manchuria or enable the Chinese Communists to take it over. Clearly, Stalin was not yet convinced at this date that America would refuse to give adequate political and military support to the Nationalist Government of China.

Stalin and his henchmen were trying us out; but their calculated risk was small since they were all along well informed of American attitudes and intentions by Communist stooges in Washington. As described in J. Edgar Hoover's excellent book *Masters of Deceit,* some U.S. government bureaus were infiltrated both by Communist sympathizers and Soviet agents and that U.S. policies, plans, and official attitudes were not only influenced by these infiltrators but also promptly reported to Moscow. Moreover, the U.S. was an adolescent in the field of international intrigue and had no conception of the cross-currents of interest that were muddying the waters.

To me it seemed that we had a moral obligation to give China the necessary political, military, and economic support to insure that Soviet Russia would not be able with impunity to ignore her pledges in the treaty we had practically compelled China to sign. But more than that, it was also obviously in our own national interest to prevent China from becoming a Soviet satellite.

Hence my efforts to contain the Communists by interpreting my vague and contradictory instructions from Washington in the most elastic fashion possible. It was by now all too clear that the Soviet Government had no more intention of honoring the Sino-Russian Treaty of August, 1945, than its pledges and agreements in Europe. The Kremlin was not only denying the Chinese Nationalist forces access to Manchuria, but it had also supplied the Chinese Communist Party with surrendered Japanese arms and equipment, and was backing them with its powerful propaganda apparatus in America and elsewhere in the world. Realizing that the Chinese Nationalist Government could not possibly cope with the situation unaided, I asked the War Department to send seven American divisions to China in order to create a barrier through North China and Manchuria against Soviet Russia.

The Joint Chiefs of Staff replied that the divisions I called for were not available. However, two Marine Corps divisions under the command of Lieutenant General Keller E. Rockey, were sent out, and established headquarters in Tientsin. I disposed these inadequate but extremely valuable reinforcements in North China, from Peking to the sea, including the Shantung Peninsula.

In submitting the recommendation to both the Generalissimo and

Washington that a UN-sponsored guardianship be established over Manchuria, I had carefully avoided using the word "trusteeship" because this term had a connotation of permanence or at least, long duration. I thought my careful choice of words would assuage the sensitivities of the Chinese and yet provide for a sharing of responsibilities on the part of all five major powers in insuring a stable administration of Manchuria until such time as China had recovered from the devastation of the long war against Japan.

The Generalissimo did not accept my recommendation concerning a guardianship over Manchuria and it may have been politically impossible for him to do so. The conflict with Japan had begun over Manchuria in 1931. Now after her long ordeal China was flushed with victory, joyful and hopeful. Perhaps the Generalissimo felt that if he did not attempt to re-establish Chinese sovereignty over Manchuria he would lose face throughout the Orient, and might lose authority among his own people, who would find it hard to understand any such arrangement. Whatever his reasons at the time, my suggestion was not accepted; and he immediately attempted to establish effective administrative control over the area by designating a governor and also by sending some Nationalist troops into Manchuria at the conclusion of the war.

Since winter was approaching and sub-zero temperatures would be experienced in Manchuria and the northern provinces, I insisted that the Chinese troops sent there be provided with appropriate clothing. The U.S. Army co-operated and shipped warm winter clothing by air from Alaska. Also, I insisted that all of the troops be given smallpox vaccinations and inoculations against typhoid and cholera. This was a tremendous undertaking and delayed the movement of the troops, much to the concern of the Generalissimo, who wanted his armies to reoccupy Manchuria, and particularly the northern provinces, immediately. I was adamant, and the Generalissimo acceded to my plans for proper immunization of the troops as well as adequate protection against the elements.

The American Vice Admiral, Dan Barbey, who was in command of the Seventh Fleet, operating under my direction, told the Generalissimo that he had the shipping available and could move his troops immediately. I felt compelled to flash a radiogram to the Generalissimo stating that as long as I was his Chief of Staff my plans, which had been carefully prepared with due consideration for the combat effectiveness of the troops on their arrival in the North, must be carried out. If the Generalissimo wanted Admiral Barbey to be his Chief of Staff and take charge of these troop movements, I would immediately step down.

I should here recall that being myself cognizant of the importance of "face," I had urged that the Generalissimo personally accept the surrender of the senior Japanese commander, General Okamura. In his typical self-effacing manner he wanted me to represent him. I countered with the suggestion that either General Chen Cheng, the Chinese Minister of Defense, or General Ho Ying-chin, the Field Commander of the Chinese forces, should accept the surrender. "After all," I had said, "China has lost several million lives and has been ravaged by the enemy for eight years. No representative of a foreign power should receive the surrender of the enemy within the confines of the China Theater."

The Generalissimo, realizing the symbolic significance of the surrender ceremonies, agreed, and General Ho Ying-chin was sent to Nanking.

I appointed Major General Robert B. McClure, the senior American field commander, to represent the United States.

In the several other areas where large Japanese contingents would be laying down their arms, I arranged to have Chinese generals present for the formal acceptance of their surrender. Besides Manchuria—where the Red Army under Marshal Malenovsky accepted the surrender of the enemy troops—there was one other exception, namely, Hong Kong. The Generalissimo informed me that he had received notification from Admiral Mountbatten that British representatives were en route to Hong Kong to receive the surrender of the Japanese there. This presented a delicate situation, for Hong Kong and Kowloon were recognized as sovereign territory of the British and yet both of those areas were included in the China Theater; and the Supreme Allied Commander, General MacArthur, had directed that the Generalissimo arrange for the surrender of all enemy forces within his area of responsibility. Chiang discussed this matter with me and was determined that a Chinese representative should receive the surrender in Hong Kong, and I communicated this information at once to Washington. Belatedly I received information back that this was a question that should be settled between the Chinese and the British. The Generalissimo was disappointed that his position was not supported in Washington, particularly in the light of General MacArthur's instructions. In the final outcome, the British permitted Chinese representation but they themselves took first place at the ceremonies.

While of necessity engaged in political as well as military maneuvers, I also had to attend to my supposedly major postwar task, namely, the repatriation of almost four million Japanese soldiers and civilians. As it proved, this was among the least difficult of my problems, although it required skillful logistic planning and close collaboration with General MacArthur and his staff. About two and a half million of the 3,900,000 Japanese were civilians who had lived in China all their lives. The remainder were members of Japan's military forces and were scattered all over the huge area of North China, Manchuria, East and Southeast China, as well as Korea and Indo-China. Gathering together all these Japanese for repatriation was indeed a major operation requiring careful co-ordination. They had to be assembled in increments at suitable ports along the east coast of China. Some measures had to be taken to protect their health and prevent epidemics. Transport to Japan had to be provided; and MacArthur's headquarters had to arrange for their reception at the designated port in Japan and their assimilation in their homeland.

Plans were prepared in the G-3 General Staff Division of China Theater Headquarters, in charge of Colonel Roland W. McNamee. This officer had arrived rather late in the theater but quickly distinguished himself; and the plans from his division were outstanding, showing sound military judgment and thorough knowledge in troop-training, tactics and techniques. This General Staff Division was very close to the G-2 division of my General Staff, whose chief was Colonel Joseph Dickey. The latter was the only key officer of the former Stilwell staff whom I had retained, and he had fully merited my confidence. Having been a Japanese-language student earlier in his career he was well acquainted with Japanese military organization and methods.

Shortly after V-J Day and prior to executing the Japanese repatriation program, I had visited MacArthur's headquarters accompanied by my Chief of Staff, General Maddocks, and the G-3, Colonel McNamee. We had explained our plans to assemble and transport the Japanese to the Chinese coast, and the Navy's preparations for their transportation to Japanese ports. Maddocks and McNamee conferred with MacArthur's staff, and Dick Sutherland, MacArthur's Chief of Staff, informed me that they thought the China Theater would not be able to carry out this huge task.

General Sutherland reported these misgivings to General MacArthur in my presence. General MacArthur turned to me and asked, "Al, are you familiar with this plan?" I replied, "Completely, sir." "Can you do it?" was his rejoinder. "Yes, sir," I replied. MacArthur thereupon turned to his Chief of Staff and directed that the plan be executed insofar as it related to his command.

I am happy here to pay tribute to Colonel McNamee who, along with his principal assistants, was primarily responsible for the preparation and implementation of the plan, which was carried out with superb efficiency.

This would not, of course, have been possible had the enormous number of Japanese prisoners and civilian internees resisted or attempted to sabotage the operation. However, following the Emperor's surrender statement, the Japanese in China were so amenable that we felt confident of their disciplined co-operation.

On the occasions when I visited the areas where the Japanese were being assembled, and deloused before moving to the ports, I was struck by the attitude of most of them, which verged on servility. In one concentration area where there were some ten thousand Japanese men, women, and children, I was acutely embarrassed and dismayed when they all went down on their knees and bowed to the ground in my direction. Was abject servility the goal we sought? Or did we fight to enable all men, regardless of race, color, or class, to hold up their heads and look other men fearlessly, challengingly, in the eye? I thought we had fought the war to deprive power-drunk, arrogant megalomaniacs from enforcing servility and fear. Our leaders often alluded to preserving the dignity of man. Yet, due to our "unconditional surrender" demand and Japan's consequent complete dependence upon our mercy, I wondered whether we too might one day be forced to our knees, should the Communists acquire superior power thanks to our own blunders and follies.

Now that the war was over, there would be many appointments to important government positions, governors, mayors, and district magistrates in areas recovered from the enemy. I urged the Generalissimo to name qualified civilians, not military men. There was a dearth of executives and administrators in the country, but it seemed important at the time that the Generalissimo should avoid establishing a military hierarchy. However, I had failed to take into consideration Chiang's need to be certain of the loyalty of the men he appointed if China was not to fall apart again. As always he had to contend with the centrifugal forces in China. It was natural that he had more confidence in some of his generals than in anyone else. In any case, he did not follow my recommendations.

The condition of millions of Chinese was even worse than that of the now destitute Japanese civilians we were repatriating to their homeland. During the eight-year war, millions of Chinese had been driven from their homes by the Japanese, or had voluntarily taken refuge in the western provinces rather than remain in enemy-controlled areas. Arrangements now had to be made to enable them to return to their former homes and somehow or other earn a living in this war-ravaged country. Japan had long occupied the eastern provinces and seaboard, which were the industrial, commercial and cultural heart of the country. She had also been in control of the North except for some rural areas where the Communists had established centers of power. The Nationalist Government was confronted with a well-nigh insuperable problem of reconstruction and rehabilitation. This task, which the industrially advanced countries of Western Europe—who had suffered less than China—were unable to accomplish without billions of dollars of American aid, was rendered practically insoluble in China, because immediately following the end of the war with Japan she had to meet the onslaught of the Moscow-directed Communists.

Nor was this all. England was apparently as desirous as the Soviet Union, although for different reasons, of keeping China weak and disunited. Intent mainly on their commercial interests, the British opposed America's fumbling efforts to help China become strong and independent. This fact, which could be supported by more weighty evidence, was brought home to me by an incident in the course of my endeavor to help China institute minor as well as major reforms in order to become more self-sufficient.

The Generalissimo had made it clear before the war's end that he wanted to continue utilizing American equipment for his military forces. He wanted to purchase machinery and communications and transportation equipment from the United States sources. He also mentioned China's need of truck transportation and buses; of employing technicians, engineers, agronomists, fiscal experts, and professional military advisers.

It was only natural that China with its memories of past foreign domination and economic exploitation, and also because America alone had given her aid during the war, should have looked to us as her source of supply for postwar reconstruction. But here, as today in the Near East, the British were naturally suspicious of American action that could be interpreted as paving the way for American products to supplant theirs in markets which they had formerly supplied.

This was brought home to me even before the war ended when I endeavored to reduce the disproportionately large number of traffic accidents in China. For thousands of years, Chinese traffic—sedan chairs, camel caravans, rickshas, horses, and carriages—had moved on the left side of the road as in England. One reason for the large number of accidents was the fact that the vast majority of vehicles in China, both automobiles and trucks, were of American manufacture, with steering mechanism and lights designed for driving on the right side of the road. Although we established driving and maintenance schools for the Chinese, the number of vehicles immobilized by traffic accidents continued to increase. Several months before the end of the war, I decided that drastic measures must be enforced to prevent our truck convoys moving supplies to the front for the CARBONARO offensive from meeting with accidents. I thereupon suggested to the Generalissimo that all traffic in China be transferred to the right side of the road. He promptly approved and said that new traffic regulations would be put into effect throughout the area under Nationalist China's control immediately. I, however, cautioned him that we should not make the change for several months until we had thoroughly indoctrinated drivers and pedestrians to it. Otherwise it would result in an even greater number of accidents. Chiang therefore set the date for September 1, 1945 —by which time Japan had surrendered.

Posters were placed on telephone poles and shop windows, showing diagrammatically how traffic would move and giving instructions to pedestrians in order to minimize accidents. Articles were published in newspapers throughout the country. When the first notices concerning the change-over appeared in May and June of

1945, I was informed that articles were appearing in the vernacular press strongly criticizing the idea of breaking an old Chinese tradition and urging the Generalissimo to reconsider and uphold the old and the tried method of moving traffic.

Wondering who was responsible for these critical articles, I asked one of my secret service officers to investigate. A month or so later he reported that the opposition to the change-over had its genesis in the British Embassy, possibly with the full cognizance or at the instigation of the British ambassador, Sir Horace Seymour. I now for the first time realized the *economic* implications of my recommendations; but in all honesty, I had not given this factor any thought when I made them originally. Since British traffic moved on the left side of the road and all of their motor vehicles were manufactured to provide safety in driving in that manner, they might well oppose the new order, which would destroy their market in China for British cars.

I frequently met Sir Horace Seymour, the British ambassador, at cocktail parties and dinners; and at one of these gatherings I mentioned that the Generalissimo was enthusiastic about changing traffic over to the right side of the road. I had hoped to draw him out, but he was somewhat evasive. He asked me if I had ever ridden in a British car. I replied that I had rented one in London in 1937 and had driven it on a most enjoyable tour of England, Scotland, and Wales. He inquired whether I had had any difficulty in driving on the left side of the road; and I admitted that I learned very easily to adjust myself to the left-hand steering mechanism. But I added in carefully phrased words that the American motor industry would probably not be interested in changing its tooling to produce cars for left-hand driving.

Following Japan's surrender, the Generalissimo issued an order postponing from September, 1945, to January, 1946, the date on which the right-hand rule of the road would become effective. Realizing that the British had won out for a while, I was somewhat miffed that the Generalissimo had not told me of this decision.

But on December 31, 1945, I had the thrilling experience of standing on the balcony of my tower apartment in the Cathay Hotel in Shanghai to watch the traffic at midnight change over to move along the right side of the road. I was informed that this drastic change occurred all over China without any mishap and was still in effect when the Communists took control in 1949.

America had fought the war like a football game, after which the winner pulls up stakes and goes off on a celebration; consequently there was no realization that it would be disastrous to demobilize our armies until we had insured that the aims for which we fought would be implemented in spite of the very different objectives of our "allies."

So after V-J Day, like every other U.S. commander in the theaters of war, I received instructions for the demobilization of our armed forces. My G-1 (personnel staff) set up plans to comply with the order to send home, as rapidly as military transport permitted, every soldier and officer entitled to be demobilized under the point system, regardless of whether he was performing essential duties and would be hard to replace.

This arbitrary ruling was most harmful, since a military organization like any other is built around key men qualified for specific duties. At this time I was receiving hundreds and hundreds of letters from wives, parents, and sweethearts, urging me to release their loved ones. It was impossible to reply in each instance; but some of the letters were so vitriolic I felt impelled to take time out to answer them. I recall one woman living in Long Island who wrote that I wanted to keep her son in China so that I could enjoy the exalted rank I had reached during the war. I made inquiries concerning this woman's son and learned that he was a sergeant performing his duties in an exemplary manner, but that under the point system he was not yet due for release. So I wrote to his mother, explaining that her son was a credit to her and to his country, and assured her that he would be sent home just as soon as he had acquired the points stipulated in the War Department program, an explanation of which could be obtained by direct application to the Adjutant General of the Army in Washington. I added that my rank had not and would not influence my attitude, but that I was proud of the thousands of American men and women who were serving in my command, including her son. I also said that I too wanted to return to the States but that we had a job to do in the Far East to protect the military victory we had won against a new threat to the free world—the Communist menace. After I had shown the sergeant the letter and my reply, he assured me that he had no desire to go back until the job was done, and he apologized for his mother's action. A month or so later I received a wonderful letter from this woman, the gist of which was: "I agree. We still must protect our victory; and my son is proud to be a member of your command in your efforts to do it. My husband and I are proud of him and of you, too."

The trouble was that the American people did not realize the conditions existing in distant areas after the war. It did not occur to them that a vacuum had been created in Europe and Asia by the unconditional surrenders of Germany and Japan. All they knew was that the enemy had surrendered and that tumultuous celebrations had taken place in every city, town, and village square in America. Since victory had been won, they naturally thought that their boys should at once come home. And our leaders were either too naive or too impotent to speak out frankly and acknowledge the fact that strong American military forces must be kept in being to win the peace.

Many Congressmen were urging that the boys be sent home in order to please their constituents and assure their return to office in the next election. They were for the most part unmindful of the fact that the Communist international conspiracy constituted an even greater danger than the Nazis and the Japanese we had soundly defeated. It was a time when strong intelligent leadership was needed. Instead, Congress almost without exception yielded to the demand, "Bring our boys back," and in turn exerted pressures on the military establishments to denude and emasculate our forces abroad. All of this was part of the postwar hysteria which the Communists so cleverly and widely exploited.

In September, 1945, Pat Hurley and I were again ordered back to the States. We both flew direct from Chungking to Manila and thence across the Pacific to San Francisco and on to Washington; but the Ambassador arrived first. I stopped off in Manila and picked up Colonel Jack Vance, a West Point classmate who had been a Japanese prisoner for three and a half years. He was in Manila awaiting transportation back to the States and I made arrangements for him to accompany my party to Washington. I had admired Vance when we were cadets; and later we had been happily associated on various assignments. He was one of the most highly respected men in my West Point class; and if he had not been captured by the Japanese he would unquestionably have attained to much higher rank.

When our plane arrived at the National Airport in Washington, we were all peering out of the windows. I saw that there was a large crowd, a guard of honor, and a band. Jack Vance had not seen his wife for three and a half years. I gave instructions to everyone on the plane that we would all wait to deplane until he had gone down the ramp and greeted her. The plane stopped, the ramp was pushed up to the door, and Jack rushed out. The band started playing ruffles and flourishes, followed by the *General's March;* but Jack was wholly oblivious when the guard of honor commander assumed that he was General Wedemeyer. Many of our West Point classmates had come to the airport to greet Vance, and it was a touching scene when he ran into the arms of his happy wife.

As on our visit several months earlier, appointments were made for Pat Hurley and me to visit the President. We also talked separately to members of the Cabinet and the Joint Chiefs of Staff and other key officials in the Government. Hurley mentioned to Mr. Truman that his health might not permit him to return to China as Ambassador. Living conditions had been rather rugged in Chungking; but when we reached the east coast and opened sea communications, provisions for the supply of Stateside food had been made. Hurley suggested to Truman that I be designated to replace him; and later when I saw the President alone, he asked if I would like to be appointed Ambassador to China. I replied that I would want first to talk to General Marshall before deciding. General Marshall's advice was unequivocal: "Do not get mixed up with the State Department unless you are interested in that kind of work. I think you should remain in the Army."

General Marshall was at that time preparing to leave his post as Chief of Staff to enjoy a richly deserved rest at his beautiful home in Leesburg, Virginia. He said that he was receiving offers from various organizations in industry and other activities, but that he had so far not accepted any of them. Some of these offers, he stated, were accompanied by fabulous salaries; and he added, "But those of us in the military know we get something from life that money cannot buy."

Ambassador Hurley, after a check-up at Walter Reed Hospital, was told that he was in excellent physical condition; so he decided to return and serve as ambassador for a longer period. This pleased me because it would not be necessary to re-establish relations with a new diplomatic leader at present; and further, I felt very close to Pat Hurley, both officially and personally.

My report (see Appendix IV) concerning the progress being made under the point system seemed to be of great interest to the Chiefs of Staff. They were subjected to terrific pressure from Congress and from thousands of relatives throughout the States urging that the boys be brought home. Apparently it never occurred to them or to the people making the requests that the Communists were working to build up this hysteria. During my brief visit to Washington both President Truman and the Joint Chiefs of Staff directed me to write a report on China, covering both United States interests there and future prospects for the Chinese people. On my return I visited Mukden and Peiping, and then Shanghai, to study conditions before reporting. The President and General Marshall felt that I should refrain from coming to any definite conclusions, and had asked me to suggest several alternative lines of action rather than make definite recommendations, lest the State Department accuse the military of attempting to formulate policy.

Accordingly in my long, coded message of November 20, 1945, to the Joint Chiefs of Staff (a paraphrase of which is included in the Appendix) I could do no more than make my views of the situation clear, while refraining from stating definitely that only one course in China could preserve American interests and those of the free world: namely, unequivocal assistance to our ally, the Chinese Nationalist Government.

Neither then, nor before, or subsequently, did I receive a clear-cut directive from Washington, in spite of my efforts to explain the ominous situation in China and to stimulate the formulation of a clear and resolute American China policy.

The contradictory or inconsistent nature of my directives is illustrated by the report I made to Chiang Kai-shek on November 10, 1945, on returning to China from my conferences in Washington with President Truman and the Secretary of State and Joint Chiefs of Staff. I was happy to report that President Truman had "pledged his continued support of Generalissimo Chiang Kai-shek and the Nationalist Government of China." But this assurance was rendered well nigh meaningless by the JCS which, while expressing full agreement with the President's policy, and approval of "military assistance to China," had also . . .

> . . . emphasized that U.S. Forces must not be involved in fratricadal [sic] warfare; that Americans in areas must remain non-partisan in relations between the Chinese Government and the British, French, Soviet and other foreign powers. Stipulated clearly that U.S. assistance in the development of Chinese Armed Forces would be discontinued if it is established to the satisfaction of the U.S. Government that such Chinese Armed Forces are being used in support of an administration not acceptable to the United States, to engage in fratricidal warfare or to afford a threat of aggression. The extent to which political stability is being achieved in China under a unified, fully representative government is regarded by the United States as a basic consideration which will at all times govern the furnishing of economic, military or other assistance to China. The question of continuing such assistance will be reconsidered periodically by the U.S. Government in relation to this basic consideration.

This directive not only put the economic cart before the political and military horse, in that stability could be assured only with American aid and support, while we were making our help dependent on stability. It also meant in effect that American aid to China depended on the Nationalist Government's coming to terms with the Communist-armed party. And since the Chinese Communists were under Moscow's orders, the United States was in fact, even if unwittingly, demanding submission to Moscow as the price of American aid.

When the plan for the redistribution of Chinese Nationalist Government forces had been made by the combined Chinese and American Theater Chiefs of Staff in September, 1945, I further reported to Chiang Kai-shek, it had not been "visualized that obstacles would be placed in the way, or conditions would be created by either the Chinese Communists or the Soviet." Consequently the redistribution was originally considered as sound and the troops "adequate to cope with the envisaged situation." Later it was recognized all too clearly that the situation "manifestly requires deployment of increased numbers of Nationalist Government forces in the areas [formerly] occupied by the Japanese."

In sum, I had perforce to tell the Generalissimo that the United States, if not precisely throwing China to the wolves, was not going to save her from the embrace of the bear. In my report to him I said further that I had been instructed that:

> As American commander I cannot become involved or permit my forces to become involved in the difficulties between the Nationalist Government Forces and the Chinese Communists, Soviet Communists, and other dissident elements in China and Manchuria. The instructions, received in Washington, visualized settlement of problems by the Chinese Nationalist Government with the Chinese Communists as strictly Chinese Nationalist Government function. However, as the Generalissimo's Chief of Staff, I will be glad to study all of the implications and give my considered opinion to assist in the solution of the problems presented.

I also had to tell the Generalissimo that we were not going to give him the backing he required to deal on equal terms with the Soviet Union in Manchuria. "I am authorized," I reported, "to assist the Chinese in the planning [for the occupation of Manchuria] but cannot send Americans to that area. The United States feels that the arrangements should be accomplished between the Chinese and Soviet Governments."

I also had to indicate to Chiang Kai-shek that he could not afford to alienate Western opinion. "In the press of America," I said, "there have been suggestions of an anti-foreign wave in China." I recommended that "everything be done to foster good will with all the other powers." And, recognizing the strength of British influence in America, I suggested that since "China is not prepared to stand alone militarily or economically," she should abrogate extraterritorial rights and other foreign-power privileges only "in a firm and courteous manner."

Years later, on September 26, 1949, it was revealed by Senator Knowland in the Senate that my confidential report to Chiang Kaishek at this time had been made available to the Communists by one of their agents, a Chinese named Ching Nu-chi, who had occupied the position of Chief Secretary of the Chinese Documents Secretariat—first at my own headquarters and subsequently at General Marshall's. In this position Ching Nu-chi had handled all types of American documents and made the necessary translations. In April, 1949, after going over openly to the Communists he published a book called *Secret Report on the United States-Chiang Kai-shek Conspiracy,* in which he told all.*

In December, 1945, I received word from General Marshall that he had been requested by the President to serve as Special Envoy to China and would shortly arrive. He asked for recommendations concerning personnel and equipment. I suggested that he appoint a keen young officer to serve as Executive in his office in China and recommended Colonel Henry Byroade. I also suggested that he appoint a rear-echelon representative to process messages back to the President, the State Department, and the War Department, and recommended Colonel (later Major General) Marshall S. Carter for this post. I thought he should also have a confidential secretary and recommended that he bring Miss Mona Nason, an attractive and intelligent young lady who was then serving as his personal secretary in Washington.

The announcement that General Marshall would arrive in China with ambassadorial rank as the President's representative roused great interest among the Chinese as well as at the American Embassy. Hurley had resigned and an ambassador had not yet been appointed to replace him. Walter S. Robertson was the senior diplomatic official representing our country. He had never met General Marshall, however, welcomed the news of his imminent arrival. Mr. Robertson was not a professional Foreign Service officer, but had made an outstanding contribution in various important government posts during the war.

The Generalissimo was particularly inquisitive and asked me many questions as to the real purpose of General Marshall's visit. I always felt that Chiang was not certain about General Marshall's attitude toward him as the result of Stilwell's removal from China. I expressed the opinion that China and the United States were fortunate in having a man of his caliber visit the area and help in bringing about political stability and economic recovery.

The Generalissimo made elaborate plans for the reception and accommodations of General Marshall and his party. An American and Chinese Guard of Honor was drawn up at the Shanghai airport when his plane arrived. I met the General and accompanied him

* *The Enemy Within,* by Raymond de Jaegher and Irene Kuhn (New York, Doubleday, 1952), p. 277.

to the Cathay Hotel, where I had reserved a suite of rooms in the tower. After seeing that the General and his entourage were comfortably installed, I went back to my office in the Development Building. A short time later General Marshall phoned to ask me to come to his suite at the hotel. He was unpacking his effects while we discussed plans for his first call on the Generalissimo. He showed me a copy of his directive from the President, which required him to bring the Nationalists and the Communists together in a coalition government. I told General Marshall that he would never be able to effect a working arrangement between the Communists and Nationalists, since the Nationalists, who still had most of the power, were determined not to relinquish one iota of it, while the Communists for their part were equally determined to seize all power, with the aid of the Soviet Union.

General Marshall reacted angrily and said: "I am going to accomplish my mission and you are going to help me."

I replied by saying that there was no question of my desire to give him every possible help; that all the resources of the China Theater would be placed at his disposal, and that I had already assigned to him two of the ablest officers on my staff, General Paul Caraway and Colonel J. H. Caughey.

George Marshall was not in good spirits. Even during dinner he continued to show his displeasure. That night I was in a quandary. Certainly he must know that I was devoted to him personally and respected him greatly. I recalled that at the Casablanca conference he had said: "You will be doing me a disservice if you do not always give me the benefit of your thinking." I wondered what had happened to cause him to assume his present attitude of aloofness, almost of hostility, because I had spoken my mind frankly and freely. Finally I decided that the gruelling work and tremendous strain of the war had exacted a heavy toll both on his physical condition and his nerves, and that he was also fatigued by his long air trip from the United States.

The following day General Marshall flew to Nanking and called upon the Generalissimo. I accompanied him and the meeting was very cordial. I began to feel confident that these two men would co-operate in the task that lay before them.

George Marshall next had a long conference with Minister Walter Robertson, who gave him a report on the operations at the Embassy and placed his personnel at the disposal of General Marshall. I should state that Walter Robertson and I had worked closely together during the preceding months, and he had been particularly helpful in the negotiations pertaining to the disposition of surplus U.S. property in China. In these negotiations Robertson's realistic and firm attitude and sound judgment saved the United States millions of dollars (see Appendix I).

General Marshall had decided to make his headquarters, at least temporarily, in Chungking, where he and his staff were installed in quarters provided by the Generalissimo. I visited him each week, flying from my headquarters in Shanghai to Chungking, and keeping him informed of the progress made in demobilizing the theater and repatriating the Japanese to their homeland.

During the latter part of December, Secretary of War Robert Patterson arrived in China on a world tour. My staff briefed him concerning the activities in the theater and he expressed his desire to pay his respects to the Generalissimo, feeling that as a Cabinet officer he should not omit this courtesy. General Marshall, however, asked me to discourage the Secretary of War from visiting Chungking because he was then in the throes of delicate negotiations between the Communists and the Nationalists. I knew that the Secretary was already behind schedule in his world tour and was due in Manila, so I suggested to him that I would frame a radiogram to the Generalissimo expressing his regrets at his inability to pay his respects. I also mentioned to the Secretary of War that we had limited navigational aids in China and that bad weather frequently precluded flying so that he might reach Chungking but be unable to leave for several days. Patterson sent the radiogram to the Generalissimo, who graciously replied that he fully understood and wished him Godspeed on his trip.

Before departing, Secretary Patterson told me that he had been asked to find out if I would be willing to serve as ambassador to replace Ambassador Hurley, who had finally decided to resign. I replied that the President had previously mentioned the possibility of my accepting that position, but that I had discussed the matter with General Marshall who had strongly advised me to remain in the Army. I asked the Secretary of War to thank the President and to explain that much remained to be done in my military command

in China, particularly with reference to dismantling the theater
and repatriating the Japanese.

After Patterson's departure, I flew to Chungking to visit General
Marshall. In reply to his questions I told him that the Secretary
of War's principal interest seemed to be in the demobilization of our
army. I also casually mentioned that the Secretary had said he had
been instructed to ask me if I would be willing to serve as Ambassador to China to replace Hurley. Marshall replied that he thought I
should accept, adding that he had learned in the few weeks he had
been in China that both the Nationalists and the Communists respected me, so that he thought I could help his very difficult mission.
I replied that I wanted to help, and if he wanted me to, I would accept the post, but that I would first have to return to the States because I needed an operation to alleviate a sinus condition which had
troubled me for a long time. Marshall radioed to the President, telling him to disregard my negative reply to Secretary of War Patterson and asking that I be appointed as Ambassador to China.

In April, 1946, I again left for the States. The China Theater had
been demobilized and Lieutenant General Alvan C. Gillem was designated as the Commander of American Forces remaining in China.

Although General Marshall had recommended my appointment
as Ambassador to China, I felt certain that his concept of what
American policy should be was not mine. As with Pat Hurley the
year before, I knew that there was no possibility of an accommoda-
tion between the Nationalists and the Chinese Communists controlled by the Kremlin. I acceded to General Marshall's desire that
I should become Ambassador to China only because I still hoped
that I might help him to realize the danger to America of the Communist menace in China.

CHAPTER XXIV

DIVERSE VIEWS ON POLICIES

UPON MY ARRIVAL in the States in May, 1946, I reported to an Army Hospital for surgery and then was assigned to temporary duty in the War Department while awaiting my appointment as Ambassador to China. Early in July I was asked by Under Secretary of State, Dean Acheson to come to his office in the State Department. He showed me a radiogram from General Marshall to the President stating that the news concerning Wedemeyer's appointment as Ambassador to China had leaked and was causing him considerable embarrassment in his delicate negotiations with the Communists. They had protested my appointment on the ground that I would not be impartial as between them and the Nationalists, since I had been closely associated with the Generalissimo during the war years, and because I had taken prompt steps to insure that the Nationalist armies were moved to key positions in North China immediately after the war.

Dean Acheson said that he was sorry, but my appointment as Ambassador must be cancelled. I replied that I had not wanted to be Ambassador in the first place and had agreed to accept the appointment only at the urgent request of General Marshall. But, I told Acheson, I did not like the idea that the Communists had the power to determine who might be appointed to positions of responsibility within the United States Government. I also drew his attention as a minor consideration to the fact that I had already spent about $800 on the civilian clothes required to perform ambassadorial duties. Acheson paid no attention to the main point—namely, the outrageous appeasement of the Chinese Communists signified by the cancellation of my appointment as ambassador—but hastened to assure me that I would be reimbursed for my expenditures!

Following the information that I was *persona non grata* to the Chinese communists, the War Department was notified of my availability for reassignment. General Eisenhower had suggested that I might replace General Thomas Handy because the latter was being assigned to Germany. Handy offered to place a desk at my disposal in his office and suggested that I could start work immediately. I told him that the Chief of Staff had not personally spoken to me about a particular assignment but had indicated his intention to give me a very important job. I added that I was confused and tired and would like to get away from Washington for a while to think things through. Handy replied that senior commanders had been given a month or two of vacation upon their return from overseas and suggested that I go to Florida for a good rest. I told him that I was not physically tired and would rather be busily employed somewhere, but not in Washington. Actually I suppose I was seeking the opium of hard work in order to dull my apprehension and worry concerning the policy the United States was pursuing in China and elsewhere, which I feared would be disastrous. Handy said there were two armies which I might have, the Second or the Sixth. I could take command of the Second Army immediately if I wished, since General Simpson was being retired. Or I could wait until spring and take command of the Sixth Army when General Stilwell would be retired. I elected to go immediately to the Second Army and was assigned to that command, with headquarters in Baltimore. Later on I realized that Handy was right in urging me to take a vacation, and I spent six weeks in Florida at the beautiful island of Sanibel.

Although I longed to get away from it all by commanding troops and leaving policy to the politicians, my concern for my country and my mounting fears concerning U.S. policy in China compelled me to make another effort to point out the danger of the course being followed by General Marshall, first as Special Envoy to China and subsequently as Secretary of State.

On leaving Washington to command the Second Army at Fort

Meade in Maryland, I wrote a memorandum for Secretary of Defense Forrestal (at his request) which widened the rift with my esteemed chief, General George Catlett Marshall, who I fear has never forgiven me for opposing his China policy.

General Marshall, I wrote, had "tried to get a quick solution to the China problem." Now he was pessimistic. Some people, perhaps in responsible positions, I wrote, might feel that China would be regenerated by first permitting the destruction of the old order, after which a new and better order would arise. This, I pointed out, was the Marxian doctrine which had been applied in Russia. A better solution in consonance with American interests and those of the whole free world was to recognize that China would be in trouble for a long time to come; that Soviet communism would be "the force moving into the vacuum created by the fall of the Nationalist Government," and that the United States therefore had "no other resource but to support Chiang Kai-shek and his government."

Openly challenging General Marshall and the powerful political forces he represented at that time, I wrote in my memorandum:

> There is a question as to whether Marshall realizes the delicate situation revolving around the peace conference in Paris and the necessity for keeping our political policies and relationships on a very even keel at the present time.
> There is a question that Secretary of State Marshall is fully aware of all the implications of the present world situation as it concerns the Soviet Union and the vital place China (good or bad) plays in maintaining some sort of world equilibrium. It is unfortunate that General Marshall does not have available the clear and forceful studies on the Russian situation which have been prepared at the request of President Truman.

I knew that the President had asked for a complete analysis of our relations with Russia and asked also for recommendations. All our military studies had led to the conclusion that it was vital to U.S. interest to have a China friendly to the United States—a strong and unified China if at all possible. The only alternative was by now recognized in the Pentagon—a Russian-dominated China. The Army Intelligence Division of the General Staff (G-2) had irrefutable evidence proving that the Chinese Communists were directly linked with Moscow. "There exist," I wrote, "in the Secretary of War's files official documents indicating that a few days ago the President was convinced the U.S. had to continue to support the Chinese Nationalist Government as a basic element of U.S. policy." General Marshall's statements concerning China were being taken as equivalent to Bible texts by the U.S. people and most of the remainder of the world, so that, when he said, "There is and will continue to be civil war in China," there was grave danger that the United States would decide to wash its hands of China. I concluded my written statements of my views by saying:

> For the time being, the only useful action which can be taken is an indication to General Marshall that the suggestion by implication or otherwise of possible change in our Chinese policy (civil war or no civil war) is so serious that he should withhold comment on the U.S. position in any way at present. Further, he should not imply recognition of the Communists (which he has not done as yet in so many words). Finally, if General Marshall has not been briefed on the world and Russian situation, he should receive a message from the President, outlining the seriousness of the problem.

I had been shocked by General Marshall's recommendation that my appointment as Ambassador to China be cancelled on account of Communist objections. Nevertheless, I believed, or wanted to believe, that once he was properly informed, he would come to understand the realities of the situation in China and its implications for the world-wide struggle between the U.S. and Soviet Russia which was later to be called "the cold war."

Neither at this time (1947) nor later did I ever impugn General Marshall's motives. I emphatically disagreed with Senator McCarthy's attempt to represent him as having willingly associated himself with traitors, or as having been the tool of subversive, Communist-sympathizing elements in our Government. Today, as during the war years when I served under him and helped to formulate his plans for victory, I believe in General Marshall's devotion to his country. But I also realize that by the time he assumed responsibility for United States policy in China, he was getting on in years and that he had been exhausted by his superlative efforts as Chief of Staff to secure victory.

He had been subjected to such constant pounding by many and diverse people intent only on their own self-interest or that of the nations or ideologies they represented, that he had been deafened to the long-range interests of the United States. He had been continually harassed by the British, who sabotaged the U.S. strategy by their "periphery pecking." He had had neither time, inclination, nor opportunity to study the methods of communism; and he had implicitly believed the reports of his old friend, General Stilwell, who ascribed all the ills of China to the government of Chiang Kai-shek. Marshall had also to contend with the vagaries of President Roosevelt who, even before his faculties failed during his fourth term, had been surrounded by intriguers and the soft-on-communism eggheads who enjoyed his wife's patronage and were given formidable power by Harry Hopkins and others in the President's confidence.

General Marshall was primarily a military man who had little knowledge of the complexities of the world conflict and no conception of the skill with which the Communists pervert great and noble aspirations for social justice into support of their own diabolic purposes. Moreover, by the time he arrived in China on his fatal mission, George Marshall was physically and mentally too worn out to appraise the situation correctly. Finally, as I hate to admit because I never revered anyone more than General Marshall, he was not immune from the besetting sin of most human beings who rise to the heights of power or influence.

According to Lord Acton's famous dictum: All power corrupts, and absolute power corrupts absolutely. General Marshall never had absolute power; but his reputation at the war's end was so great, and his political influence consequently so overpowering, that he thought he could accomplish the impossible. Thus he became an easy prey to crypto-Communists, or Communist-sympathizing sycophants, who played on his vanity to accomplish their own ends. Otherwise he would never have believed that he could mix oil and water by reconciling the basically antagonistic aims of the Chinese Nationalists and the Moscow-supported Chinese Communists.

On November 18, 1946, I gave a lecture at the National War College in which, after carefully outlining my experiences in the China Theater, I said:

These experiences taught me that the Chinese situation was capable of rapid improvement. The great gains made, and the lessons learned in 1945, were too late to contribute much to the timing of final victory; however, one cannot dismiss the fact that a million and a half Japanese were held in China that might have been employed against our men in the Pacific. We learned that the Generalissimo and his associates can and will co-operate. They can and did improve the condition of their armies and people. They made rapid strides when they had the benefit of friendly and concrete American advice.

Taking issue with General Marshall and State Department policy, I went on to say that, in my opinion, the Generalissimo could make progress toward the unification of China and the constitutionalization of his government, "if he had realistic American aid—not measured by its bulk but by the wisdom with which it is applied and offered."

Chinese complexities, I said, were compounded by a full-scale, name-calling—and sporadic-shooting—civil war. "We are told," I continued, "that the Generalissimo and his Kuomintang Government are totalitarian, corrupt, and oppressive, and that the Chinese Communists are democratic in their agrarian economy and political organization." I admitted that there were elements of truth in these reports, but that they did not give a true picture of the situation in Asia.

It had been obvious to us who were there that, at the time when Japan surrendered, China would be confronted with many grave and pressing problems, not only because of the terrible devastation and dislocation of her economy during eight years of war and occupation by the Japanese, but also because of the "deeply rooted internal problems and bitter hatreds and political calumnies that had their inception twenty-five years ago."

Taking issue with General Marshall's analysis of the situation in China, I continued as follows:

> The question is often asked: Are the Chinese Communists real followers of the doctrines of Karl Marx? The basic tenets of Karl Marx have undergone many changes in their interpretations and applications, even by Lenin and Stalin. Outside of Soviet Russia one finds marked differences in the

tactical implementation of communism by individuals, groups, and political parties that definitely claim allegiance to the ideologies of the Kremlin. One must watch the basic doctrine and not be misled by local or transitory applications. The Chinese Red leaders themselves state plainly that they find their lives to have meaning only in the context of contemporary communism. I am certain that the Chinese Communist movement follows the Moscow line from week to week, insofar as conditions permit. One has only to read the regulations of the Chinese Communist Party to confirm the fact that the fundamental philosophy and aims of the Chinese Communists differ very little if at all from their Communist brethren the world over. There are striking diversities in application, but definitely no real differences in ultimate objectives. I have talked often with the Chinese Communist leaders, Mao Tse-tung and Chou En-lai, particularly with the latter, who speaks English. Their loyalties are first in the interest of Stalin and his program and then in the welfare of their own countrymen.

As proof of my thesis I pointed to the fact that before June 22, 1941, when the Nazis attacked Soviet Russia, the Chinese Communists had bitterly denounced the British war effort. Subsequently they had made a complete about-face, like our own American Communists and fellow travelers. And it was common knowledge that the Soviet Russians had collaborated all along with the Chinese Reds in spite of the Soong-Molotov agreement of August 1, 1945, in which Moscow had promised support exclusively to the Nationalist Government of China. The Russians had even denied China use of this port of Dairen (stipulated to be an open port) when the Generalissimo was redisposing his forces after the war's end. For all these and many other reasons, I said: "I reject altogether the idea that the Chinese Communists are not true Communists aligned with Moscow."

I told my National War College audience that although I was a soldier and had devoted my principal efforts to the military operations against the Japanese in my theater, it had been impossible to divorce myself entirely from political and economic events. As the Generalissimo's Chief of Staff I had had access to all sources of information, and my duties had required me to travel the length and breadth of the land.

I had contacted all classes of Chinese and discussed political and economic, as well as military, problems with Communists, Kuomintang members, Social Democratic League adherents, Chinese youth-movement leaders, peasants, businessmen, and scholars. I had strived to be objective and unemotional in my analysis of the momentous events transpiring in the China Theater. And on the basis of my experience I had come to the honest conviction that "the Chinese Communists are revolutionary Marxist zealots, whose efforts are dedicated to the realization of communism in China by whatever means may offer the best prospect of success."

I added that the Chinese Communists were "not presently emphasizing the application of the Soviet economic system," because their immediate objective was "to obtain political control"; and that therefore they did not for the moment "hesitate to use certain democratic methods to further attainment of their ultimate goal."

In this same lecture I said that, although the Nationalist Government of China was frequently and derisively described as authoritarian or totalitarian, there was a basic difference between it and its Communist enemies, since the Kuomintang's ultimate aim was the establishment of a constitutional republic, whereas the Communists wanted to establish a totalitarian dictatorship on the Soviet pattern. In my two years of close contact wih Chiang Kai-shek I had become convinced that he personally was a straightforward, selfless leader, keenly interested in the welfare of his people, and desirous of establishing a constitutional government according to the precepts of Sun Yat-sen. This was obviously impossible so long as China was fighting first the Japanese and then the Communists backed by Soviet Russia. "One man alone cannot solve the complexities of China," I subsequently stated, in answer to a question. "I can only assure you that the Generalissimo is sincere; that he is a real Christian gentleman, and I have never found him guilty of artifice or subterfuge. He was always straightforward with me."

Chiang Kai-shek's gravest weakness, it seemed to me, was his loyalty to friends and old supporters. Among his coterie of advisers there were both unscrupulous and incompetent men. If he could not be persuaded to remove them, it was difficult to conjecture how the situation in China might develop. I had myself pointed out to him that many of his officials were so incompetent or dishonest that the fine program which he visualized for his people could never be accomplished so long as he retained them. For his coterie of officials prevented him from contacting and winning the support of many of the most patriotic and capable men in China. I recognized the fact that Chiang was politically astute, had a logical mind and force of character. However, it also seemed to me that he was weighted down by the Confucian philosophy which required loyalty to family and friends. He had alienated some of the best and most able men in China by his refusal to jettison the cliques around him.

The Generalissimo, in my view, was further handicapped by "the appalling deficiency of trained administrators and technicians." Eighty per cent of the Chinese people were peasants, and it would be difficult even to estimate the degree of illiteracy. There was a thin crust of extremely wealthy Chinese, a very small white-collar class, a small middle class, and a great mass of people living in abject poverty and ignorance. All the difficulties which confronted a Chinese government endeavoring to lift China out of age-old poverty, unite her, and enable her to progress had been immensely aggravated by the cruel and devastating eight-year war against Japan, and subsequently by Communist depredation and destruction. Asking China to reform and democratize her government in these circumstances was like telling a man in the midst of a hurricane that he ought to repair and paint his roof.

In the question period that followed my lecture, I remarked that the process of reform in China would of necessity be slow, and said:

> We Americans are impetuous. We are efficient. The British
> are, too. We see the goal and we want to attain it. We are in-
> tolerant of delays and circumventions. Often I would estab-
> lish objectives that I wanted to accomplish. I recommended
> them to the Generalissimo, but there would be discourag-
> ing delays. I had to continually check myself. The cadence
> and methods of life in China are not going to be changed
> radically or quickly. You gentlemen are familiar with Euro-
> pean history. You know that hundreds of years were re-
> quired there to formulate and then implement the Bill of
> Rights and to create constitutional government. They are
> passing through a period of transition in China, passing
> from a feudal or medieval condition, gradually, toward
> modernism. The degree of accomplishment and the rate at
> which they move forward will be influenced by many im-

ponderables, intangibles, and unpredictable influences from within and from outside China's borders.

Asked by one student whether anything could be done to give the American people a true picture of the situation in China, I replied that, whereas the Communists had a marvelous propaganda system and a disciplined, vociferous minority all over the world to propagate their cause, the Generalissimo was very poorly organized for the dissemination of information or propaganda. I had been impressed (I told my audience) when I returned to the United States, to read editorials and periodicals giving what I considered to be distorted information about China as well as about Communism. I felt that the information the American people were getting was not correct and was often distorted.

Our stake in China, I said, is just as important and has similar basic justification as our European stake. "The same basic philosophy behind our interests and behind our participation in Europe pertains to the Far East."

I also reminded my National War College audience some twelve years ago that, in determining policy and attitude toward the Generalissimo and his government, we should not forget or lightly dismiss the fact that during the war Chiang Kai-shek had on numerous occasions rejected very favorable terms of peace offered by Japan. If these terms had been accepted, approximately one and a half million Japanese troops would have been released for employment against Americans in the Philippines, the Bonins, the Marianas, and the Ryukyus. The Generalissimo's adamant refusals and firm loyalty to his pledge to fight on with his Allies had "saved countless American lives and naturally contributed to our final victory."

I concluded by saying that, since the U.S. objective in China was to assist the Chinese people in establishing a unified democratic country, thus insuring our own interests in China and in other parts of the world, we should take appropriate steps, including . . .

. . . the deployment of military forces to insure that no other nation or group of nations will attempt to interfere with the realization of our aims. . . .

A realistic approach to the current situation in the Far East requires our immediate and continued support of the Generalissimo and his government. We should continue economic assistance in the form of loans and supplies, accompanied by appropriate safeguards to insure that our aid is employed for the purpose we intend.

All of us make mistakes. Great or humble men admit their errors and seek to rectify them, knowing that, as Confucius said: "He who makes a mistake and refuses to admit it commits an even greater mistake."

I should still esteem General Marshall as one of the great men of our generation if he had ever acknowledged his fundamental mistake in China: namely, that of believing that the Nationalist Government and the Communists were simply two Chinese factions striving for power, and that he was therefore justified in embargoing all arms and ammunition supplies to China in 1946–47 in order to force Chiang Kai-shek to come to terms with the Communists. But he has never repudiated his mistaken China policy of endeavoring to force the Nationalist Government to make concessions to the Communists. On his departure from China in January, 1947, to become Secretary of State, he castigated "the dominant group of reactionaries" in the Nationalist Government who had been opposed "to almost every effort I have made to influence the formation of a genuine coalition government." In his public statement on January 7, 1947, General Marshall further unmistakably revealed his lack of understanding of the Communist menace when he described as reactionaries those Chinese who "were quite frank in publicly stating their belief that co-operation by the Chinese Communist Party in the government was inconceivable, and that only a policy of force could settle the issue."

General Marshall would seem to have failed to understand the nature and aims of communism in general and of the Chinese Communists in particular. He admitted in his January 7, 1947, statement that there were some "dyed-in-the-wool Communists" who were wrecking the Chinese economy in order to facilitate the overthrow of the Nationalist Government. But he continued to insist, in spite of all evidence to the contrary, that there was "a liberal group among the Communists who put the interests of the Chinese people above ruthless measures to establish a Communist ideology in the immediate future."

The revenues of the Nationalist Government shrank instead of increasing when "peace" came after V-J Day. More and more appropriations had to be made for the repair of railways, mines, and industries, and military expenditures were swollen to ever greater proportions. Hence the demoralizing inflation, resulting corruption, and a general decline of morale greater than during the long years of holding out against Japan. Then there had always been hope. But now America seemed to have become the friend of the enemy, namely communism, or at least to be refusing support to the anti-Communist forces in China.

We were insisting that Chiang both institute democratic reforms *and* collaborate with the Communists. We said we wanted a strong and independent China but refused the Nationalist Government the material and political aid and support without which it could not crush the Communists.

The reforms we kept urging the Nationalists to institute would have been hard enough to carry out in peacetime even with U.S. aid, and were totally impossible in the midst of the civil war, which was in fact a Sino-Russian War.

China's real need was for a government with the power to govern. As I saw it the worst ills of China—corruption, maladministration, inefficiency, and the like—were the result not of the dictatorial nature of its government but of its lack of power and authority to get its orders carried out. And Chiang Kai-shek could to some extent, although not entirely, be excused for his failure to clean up his administration by having all along had his hands tied both by the endless war and his need to retain loyal cadres if China was not to fall apart. To call Chiang Kai-shek a fascist dictator, as was the fashion in America, was a ridiculous reversal of the truth, but was tragic in its consequences since it led to U.S. policy being based on a false premise. The powers of the Chinese Nationalist Government, far from being totalitarian, were much too limited. It interfered with the individual too little, not too much. Its sins of omission, not of commission, were the cause of its eventual downfall. Its gravest defect was the ineffectiveness of its administration and its consequent failure to enforce reforms which were all beautifully worked out on paper and decreed.

Since most Americans have little knowledge of history prior to 1776 and also had never traveled abroad and gained a conception of the condition of the greater part of mankind—particularly in Asia

—it is only natural that when they came to China, they should have attributed the appalling poverty and squalor and mismanagement to the Nationalist Government.

As Colonel Linton, an able and perceptive officer in the Education Department of my headquarters, had written, back in 1945, in *Stars and Stripes:*

> It is almost tragic that American soldiers have eyes and do not see, ears and do not hear, minds and do not understand. They see the poverty, the filth, and humanity serving as beasts of burden, but they do not see how all these things are inherent in the history of a great nation struggling to emerge from the days of handicraft to the day of modern technology. They hear a strange language, but they do not hear the voice of a people singing faith and hope for its future. Their minds tell them that China is different, very different from the life they know, but they do not understand that, like ourselves and like all peoples, China must begin today from where she is.

I was appalled when General Marshall, on his departure from China in January, 1947, to become Secretary of State, washed his hands of the conflict between the Western-oriented Nationalists and the Soviet-backed Communists, as if it were no concern of ours. Subsequently as Secretary of State he seems to have failed to appreciate the ambiguity of his policy when he recommended that $400,000,000 be given to Greece to keep the Communists out of power, while continuing to deny military or economic aid to our Chinese ally unless and until Chiang Kai-shek should agree to take the Communists in.

As late as March 10, 1948, Secretary of State Marshall "replied in the affirmative" to a question whether President Truman's December 15, 1945, statement demanding that the Communists should be included in the Chinese government was still our policy. And on March 11, 1948, President Truman at his press conference replied to questions concerning the inclusion of the Chinese Communists in the Chinese Government by saying that his December 15, 1945, statement of policy regarding this as the *sine qua non* of American aid and support, "still stood."

It should here be noted, however, that President Truman, wanting to have it both ways, made confusion worse confounded by his contradictory statement that "we did not want any Communists in the government of China or anywhere else if we could help it."

In spite of my endeavor to return to military life and eschew politics, I could not refrain from expressing my profound dismay and sympathy for the Chinese when, in April, 1948, President Truman replied to Chiang Kai-shek's desperate appeal for a firm statement of support against the onrush of communism by a formal repetition of his March 11 statement which had reiterated the demand for a coalition government.

I realized all too well that both Chiang Kai-shek and every anti-Communist (whether for or against the Generalissimo) must have thrown up their hands in despair when President Truman said that his statements had made the position of the United States Government clear.

Clarity was about the last thing that could have been claimed for these ambiguous and contradictory statements. From the Chinese point of view, all they added up to was the conclusion either that the United States Government did not know what its policy was, or that it still favored China's submission to Moscow, but was endeavoring to hide this fact from the American public.

Nor was the promised aid, voted by Congress in April, 1948, and referred to in President Truman's letter to Chiang Kai-shek, forthcoming. The Administration succeeded in thwarting the intent of the China Aid Act by delaying the shipment of munitions to China until the end of that critical year.

I have made as many mistakes as other men, and in the year following my November 18, 1946, lecture to the National War College I was to make what may have been the greatest mistake of my life. I accepted an assignment which I had every reason to believe (I was permitted to write my own directive) would afford an opportunity to help formulate a realistic U.S. policy in China and throughout the Far East. My disillusioning experience is related in the next chapter. But without vanity or false pride I may perhaps be permitted to take satisfaction in having seen the shape of things to come somewhat more clearly than many contemporaries who lacked the advantage I had had in Europe and Asia to learn the truth about communism.

At the time of my National War College lecture I was asked whether I believed that either China or Korea would be capable of resisting Russian encroachment following the withdrawal of American power from the continental limits of Asia. I replied:

> I definitely do not. I do not think that any power or any area or political structure contiguous to Soviet Russia is capable of resisting Russian aggression, Russian penetration, or infiltration without the assistance of outside powers comparable to Russia.

In answer to another question, I said:

> The Nationalist Government has the capacity to defeat, to crush militarily, the Communist forces right now. Most of the equipment of the Nationalist Government forces is American. If we do not continue to sell them ammunition to maintain or implement that equipment, they will be very greatly crippled in their military campaigns. Again, it is contingent upon the assistance that the Chinese Communist troops receive from outside sources, and that is very, very nebulous.

My audience, of course, knew that it was General Marshall who, four months before, had embargoed all arms and ammunition shipments to China unless and until the Nationalist Government came to terms with the Communists.

Knowing that my views as expressed in this lecture were contrary to General Marshall's, I realized that I had crossed, if not the Rubicon, at least one of its tributaries. I settled down to perform my duties at Fort Meade believing that the bolt I had shot would preclude any future diplomatic assignments. However, the end was not yet.

CHAPTER XXV

MY LAST MISSION TO CHINA

In THE SPRING of 1947 General Eisenhower, then Chief of Staff, sent me to England to deliver lectures at the Imperial Defense College in London, the Staff College at Camberly and The Royal Military College at Sandhurst. In his will, the late Kermit Roosevelt had generously provided a fund to pay for exchange lectures between the American and British armies. While I was lecturing in England, the British Major General Hull was lecturing at the National War College in Washington, the General Staff College at Fort Leavenworth, and the Military Academy at West Point.

In London I paid my respects to the American Ambassador, Lewis Douglas, and visited many of my British associates of World War II. As I was preparing to return to the United States, I received a message through Ambassador Douglas from Secretary of State Marshall saying that he had tried to reach me at Fort Meade and only then learned that I was in Europe. He suggested that I visit several European countries and make a report to him upon my return. I traveled to a number of countries but spent most of my time in Germany. I saw many widows of my former classmates of the German War College, including Frau Nina von Stauffenberg and Frau Mady Freitag von Loringhoven, both of whom had spent several months in Nazi prisons after the execution of their husbands for their complicity in the abortive attempt to kill Hitler. Also I saw former German General Gunther Lohmann and his wife Maria, who had endured a precarious life in hiding during most of the war. I arranged to have their daughter visit us in America.

During the first week of July (1947) I reported to the State Department and gave General Marshall a brief résumé of what I had learned on my European trip. He thereupon asked me if I would be willing to go to China to serve as Ambassador, adding that Dr. Leighton Stuart's health had not been good and for that reason he was not sufficiently forceful.

I reminded General Marshall of his request a year earlier that I accept this post and how subsequently my appointment had been cancelled because I was *persona non grata* to the Communists. Far from showing any embarrassment or expressing regret at having permitted the Communists to veto my appointment, General Marshall laughed and said that he, too, was probably *persona non grata* to them.

Without hesitation I replied that I would prefer to remain in the Army.

Marshall then told me that he had been discussing the Far Eastern situation with the President and other members of the Cabinet, and it had been decided that an objective survey should be made of conditions in China and Korea as a basis for future policy. He wanted me to undertake this mission and assured me that this would be only a temporary assignment requiring no more than two or three months.

I asked Marshall exactly what he expected me to uncover that was not already available in many State and War Department reports, or which the Embassy staff could not obtain. Marshall then admitted that pressures in Congress (from Congressman Walter Judd, Senator Styles Bridges, and others) and from other sources accusing the Administration of pursuing a negative policy in China were compelling a reappraisal of U.S. policy.

In all my contacts with him in the War Department—on trips to world conferences, in hiking down from Fort Myer quarters to our offices in the Pentagon, and in China when he was sent there as President Truman's special envoy—Marshall always seemed preoccupied. There was a reserve or hint of some mysterious, unseen but always present, force which had first call on his deeper thoughts.

I now tried to understand his purpose in suggesting that I go to China. My confidence in his integrity, his loyalty to principles and friends had been shaken but not destroyed by the testimony he gave before the Army Board investigating Pearl Harbor, and by his angry reaction in Shanghai in December, 1945, to my warning that a coalition government in China was neither possible nor desirable. But my respect and regard for my former chief were still so great that I was all too ready to believe that he had at last realized that the Administration's assumptions concerning U.S. policy in the Far East were unsound and was now seeking to rectify the situation. Why also, I asked myself, would he have chosen me for this mission unless a radical change of policy was envisaged, in line with my formerly rejected recommendations? Perhaps we would now deal realistically and firmly with the Commies!

When Marshall told me I could write my own directive for my mission to China, I was convinced of this. I agreed to go, under the impression that I had been appointed not simply to give a superficially "new look" to our China policy but to provide the basis for a fundamental change. Only much later, after the suppression of my report to the President, did I come to realize that I may have been chosen to allay doubts in Congress and in the country and to provide justification for continuance of the old disastrous China policy.

As I sat down to draft my directive at General Marshall's desk in the State Department, he left to attend a Congressional Committee hearing. At the door he turned and said he would speak to the President about giving me ambassadorial rank. I told him that this was not necessary. He insisted it would be important for prestige reasons. I replied that I felt the Chinese respected me and that my entrée would not be difficult in any circles in the Far East regardless of the title I bore.

Inasmuch as General Marshall had said my mission was urgent, I returned to my headquarters at the Second Army in Baltimore and prepared for an early departure for China. Next day I conferred with Marshall again and he told me my drafted directive appeared all right to him but he had turned it over to Mr. John Carter Vincent, the Chief of the State Department's Far Eastern Division, for his comment. He suggested that I should see Mr. Vincent to discuss the directive, which I did.

In my draft I had carefully eliminated any suggestion of amalgamating the Chinese Communists and the Nationalists, and in discussing my proposed instructions with Vincent and other State Department representatives I was determined not to accept substantive changes. However, I had no difficulty with the State Department China experts, who recommended only a few changes in phraseology which did not alter the basic concept of my directive. As the paper was finally phrased and signed by President Truman, I was directed to appraise the political, economic, psychological, and military situations—current and projected—in both China and Korea.

The full text of my directive is given in Appendix V. However, it should be noted here that I was instructed that in reporting on my "fact-finding mission," I should endeavor to state as concisely as possible my "estimate of the character, extent and probable consequences of assistance which you may recommend, and the probable consequences in the event that assistance is not given."

Remembering my past ordeals with the press in Shanghai in 1944–46, I had asked General Marshall for permission to select someone to help me in public relations, in particular to enable me to cope with newspaper correspondents. Accordingly an outstanding member of the *Baltimore Sun* staff, Mark Watson, a Pulitzer prize winner, was invited to accompany me. He proved to be an invaluable and loyal member of my mission. I was also accompanied by political, fiscal, economic, and engineering experts assigned to act in an advisory capacity.

When we arrived in Nanking in July, 1947, we were met by many Chinese and American officials, including Ambassador Leighton Stuart. After I had inspected the Guard of Honor and greeted many old friends, the Ambassador insisted that I accompany him to his quarters. A Chinese official had already informed me that the Generalissimo had assigned a beautiful house and servants for my use. I would have preferred staying with the members of my mission so that we could be together to discuss our plans. In the end, Ambassador Stuart, with kind intentions, prevailed upon me to stay with him. He also provided accommodations for the executive officer of the mission, Colonel C. E. Hutchin; Captain J. J. Boyle, my aide-de-camp; and my still-trusted, former interpreter, Captain Horace Eng.

As we were driving to the Embassy, the Ambassador explained

that he had every facility, clerical help, and so forth, available for my convenience at his residence. He also outlined the preparations he had made to facilitate my fact-finding mission, including reports by members of his staff covering the situation in China.

The other members of the mission stayed in the house provided by the Generalissimo. The Ambassador's home was very comfortable and commodious; but nothing could be done to alleviate the oppressive humidity and heat that settled like a canopy from Hades over central China at that time.

I inquired of American officials what the reaction was of the Communists, both Chinese and Soviet, to my arrival. They told me that Moscow considered my mission to China and Korea as the turning point in the United States policy in the Far East. This attitude of the Soviet confirmed my belief in 1945 that the Kremlin never expected the United States to let them get away with their plots, first, to take over Manchuria and, finally, to communize China. Otherwise they would not have removed or destroyed Manchuria's industrial equipment immediately after V-J Day.

I was told that the Communists thought my arrival was the result of a major United States decision to prepare plans for a new war. They had come to the conclusion that my mission was designed to prepare the ground for this purpose with the full co-operation of General MacArthur. Second, they conjectured that I was there to ascertain what form American aid to China should take. Moscow was now convinced that, in the current situation, Kuomintang China could not possibly survive without substantial help from the United States. All Soviet representatives throughout China had been instructed to follow my movements and actions as well as the contacts that I made. Many Soviet officials in Shanghai had expressed the opinion that events in China in the next six months would develop into a struggle between the United States and the U.S.S.R. for the control of China and might possibly lead to an open conflict. The Chinese Communists disseminated information to support these views and privately indicated that they expected very grave developments throughout the Far East because of (a) the Wedemeyer mission, (b) the scheduled visit of the British Field Marshal Bernard Montgomery to Japan, and (c) repeated accusations in the press of the Western powers that the U.S.S.R. was developing an aggressive policy in China.

My informants then pin-pointed some of the information obtained from individual Soviet representatives. For example, Yak Shamin, the official correspondent of *Tass* in Shanghai, had stated that General Wedemeyer had been known for a long time as a man of strong anti-Soviet tendencies and was considered by Soviet officials to be a reactionary. When he was under consideration the year earlier for appointment as Ambassador to China, the Soviet press and Soviet officials had informed Washington that his appointment would be considered as an expression of anti-Soviet policy in China. Yak Shamin also said that the U.S.S.R. had been greatly relieved when the appointment of Ambassador Stuart was announced. Now that Washington had approved of General Wedemeyer's assignment to his current mission to China and Korea, Soviet officials naturally felt that this marked a turn toward a strongly anti-Soviet American policy in China and in the whole Far East. They expected that the United States would start giving unofficial military support to Generalissimo Chiang Kai-shek. Yak Shamin added that the Wedemeyer mission was the main topic of discussion in the Shanghai Soviet community.

The Chinese Communist reaction to my mission is further reflected in the following quotation from a Chinese Communist broadcast:

From North Shensi Province,
July 16, 1947

By sending the infamous General Wedemeyer back to China, American imperialists hope to carry out aggression in China with a free hand and to prop up Chiang Kai-shek's moribund rule. The Chinese people are all too familiar with Wedemeyer, American imperialist educated in Prussian militarism. His record in China reads as follows:

After the Jap surrender he hastily sent American troops to occupy Tsingtao, Tientsin, Peiping, and Chingwantao, all of which had been surrounded by Peoples Liberated Armies [Chinese Communist armies], while directing Jap and puppet troops to hold those cities and refuse surrender to peoples armies. At the same time he organized his biggest air transport feat, flying six of Chiang Kai-shek's armies to Shanghai, Nanking, Peiping, Tientsin, Tsingtao and Tsinan. Later on he shipped five of Chiang's armies through American-occupied Chingwantao to fight the civil war in Manchuria, where the Manchurian Peoples Volunteer Army had been active for fourteen long years and which territory had long ago been renounced by Chiang Kai-shek.

After all these nefarious activities—helping Dictator Chiang and opposing the Chinese people—the name of Alfred [sic] Wedemeyer became as odious as that of Patrick Hurley. When Marshall wanted to appear as "Neutral Mediator" therefore he had no choice but to send Wedemeyer back to the United States.

Now American imperialists, Truman and Marshall, see that Chiang is tottering on the brink of collapse and that American imperialism's position in China is imperiled. They have tossed their "Neutral" masks into the rubbish heap long ago and now they send this infamous Wedemeyer back to China with a free hand and to prop up Chiang Kai-shek's moribund rule. All of which goes to show that American imperialism is now quite panicky and required the adoption of barbarous, open, and direct methods of intervention in China, just as in Greece.

The people of China are just as courageous and resolute as the people of Greece, but their strength is many times greater. The Chinese people drove out Jap imperialism and they will certainly drive out American imperialism as well.

I did not, of course, confine my observations, interviews, and discussions to Nanking; but traveled extensively north, east, and south, visiting Mukden in Manchuria, Peiping, Tientsin, Formosa, Shanghai, and Canton. Everywhere I discussed the situation and ascertained the views of a multitude of Chinese and foreigners, including Americans. I consulted Chinese of various political persuasions as well as government officials and military leaders. After several weeks of travel I went to Nanking to prepare for my return to the States and to start writing my report.

The Generalissimo asked me to make an address to his officials, both civilian and military, giving them my observations, impressions, and advice. He urged me to speak frankly and to have no compunction in saying exactly what I thought in an informal and off-the-record talk. I had grave misgivings as to the wisdom of acceding to Chiang's request, which were subsequently to prove more than justified. However, Ambassador Stuart insisted that I accept, saying, "Your address might do a world of good and no one else—

no Chinese and no foreigner—could make such a valuable contribution." He said that I enjoyed a unique position in the hearts and minds of the Chinese people and that they would accept criticism from me in the spirit in which it was given, as a friend.

When I finally agreed to make this talk, I was influenced by the following considerations: I had already decided to recommend to President Truman that immediate aid be given to China, including military as well as material and moral support. I had high hopes of persuading my government to take the steps necessary to block the spread of communism by assisting the Nationalist Government to establish political tranquillity and economic stability. But I was well aware that this would be possible only if America were given some assurance that our aid would be constructively and effectively used.

I had found evidence of maladministration, corruption, and lethargy. I knew all too well that there were strong forces in our Government and press which were violently opposed to the Chinese Nationalists and to the Generalissimo in particular. I also realized that the influence of the American friends of the Chinese Communists could not be discounted. If my recommendations were to be accepted I must convince American Government circles and the public that I saw the Chinese situation whole and clear and was not influenced either by my personal regard for the Generalissimo or my affection for the Chinese people.

On the one hand I must demonstrate that my primary concern was the security and interests of my country; on the other hand I must endeavor to use such influence as I had in China to convince the Nationalist Government that, unless it instituted some essential reforms, it would not be able to secure American aid to save China from the Communists. In a word I had a double task: to convince the Chinese that they must produce proof that American aid would not be wasted; and to convince Washington that such aid must be given. Had I known that "The Wedemeyer Report" would be suppressed by the Secretary of State, I would never have made my speech in Nanking, since my two aims were interdependent.

In addressing the assemblage of China's most important officials, I prefaced my remarks with the statement that I was appearing before them at the urgent request of the Generalissimo and that I was *not* speaking as an envoy of the President of the United

States but simply as a friend. I also said that I was speaking to them with reluctance and would tell them the truth as I saw it. I hoped that my remarks would not offend but would be accepted in the constructive spirit in which they were intended. I then proceeded to describe conditions as I had found them, and to enumerate the instances of maladministration and corruption that had come to my notice.

There was a hushed silence as I earnestly recounted the defects in organization, the shortcomings of officials, and the inefficiency and ineptitude I had discovered.

At the conclusion of my talk the Generalissimo, with Madame Chiang, and a few other officials shook my hand warmly and thanked me.

On the ride back to my quarters with Ambassador Stuart, he complimented me and assured me that what I had said could not possibly offend, and that no one else that he knew could have presented the information so convincingly and with such beneficial effects. I still had misgivings, but I hoped that my frank disclosures would strengthen the Generalissimo's hand in taking drastic steps to eliminate corruption and correct maladministration.

Later I was informed that an old, highly respected member of the Executive Yuan who was present at the meeting wept. When asked why he was weeping and whether General Wedemeyer had given offense, he replied: "I am convinced that General Wedemeyer is a friend of China and what he has told us is the truth; and that is why I am weeping."

Back in Washington a month later, when I reviewed the dispatches concerning my visit sent in by the American Ambassador, I was astounded. They gave the impression that I had wounded Chinese sensibilities, including those of the Generalissimo. Leighton Stuart made no mention of the fact that it was at his insistence that I had spoken.

I should here recall a most disturbing incident which occurred prior to my fateful address in Nanking. The night before, I had made some notes outlining the salient points of the speech I was going to make and had placed them on my bedside table. In the morning they were missing. I questioned my staff members—Colonel Hutchin, Captain Boyle, and Captain Eng—who reported they knew only that they had seen me place them on the table beside my bed just before retiring. Tactfully I questioned the servants, but they all disclaimed any knowledge. I did not mention the matter immediately to Ambassador Stuart but I discussed the situation with a member of the American Embassy staff. It soon became evident that my notes were appropriated by some individual within the household of the Ambassador. As mysteriously as they disappeared, several hours later the notes reappeared, but still no evidence concerning the person who appropriated them. I relate this incident hoping to alert Americans serving abroad in a diplomatic, military, or other official position. Obviously every precaution must be taken to safeguard classified documents. It must be assumed at all times in American embassies, consulates, and in the private homes of our officials abroad that there could be agents of foreign governments striving to obtain intelligence information, either written or oral.

On August 24, 1947, immediately prior to my departure from China, I had released a statement to the press embodying some of the more important conclusions I had reached during my fact-finding mission there. I was frank in my criticisms concerning the corruption and maladministration in China. As in my speech to the assembled civilian and military leaders of Nationalist China, my purpose in publicizing these defects was to insure that drastic action would be taken and a climate created for the realistic and effective use of the military and economic aid I intended to recommend to President Truman.

My wise press relations assistant, Mark Watson, strongly advised me not to issue this critical statement. Unfortunately, I didn't take his advice. There is no doubt that I conspicuously failed on this occasion as on others to be a clever diplomat. Instead of furthering the cause I had at heart, I merely added fuel to the fire of the Communists' vicious propaganda against the Nationalists. Instead of accomplishing a constructive purpose, I helped to weaken the Generalissimo's position and unintentionally cast aspersion on his ability to provide inspirational leadership. I soon thereafter realized that I should have followed Mr. Watson's advice, which was to issue only a statement of appreciation of the co-operation and kindnesses extended to the members of my mission during our stay in China.

Not as an alibi, but simply in order to explain my grave error, I would again remind my readers that I was strongly influenced by my knowledge that responsible officials in our government had practically written off China; and that they regarded her difficulties as internal problems because they failed to realize that the Soviet Communists were inciting, inspiring, and supporting the subversion of the Nationalist Government and rendering impossible the accomplishment of reform or any other democratic objectives. I hoped to jolt the Nationalist leaders into taking action which would convince America that they were worth supporting. And again I repeat, I had no means of knowing at this time that my report to President Truman and Secretary of State Marshall, recommending increased aid to China, would be suppressed and ignored. Instead, I was confident that when I returned to the United States and pointed out that if we did not immediately help our loyal wartime ally, the Chinese Nationalist Government, the Communists would take over. I had no doubt that my recommendations would be accepted and implemented. My fundamental mistake was due to my anxiety that the American people should realize I had not been namby-pamby in my examination of the situation in China. In other words, that I had not been biased or influenced by friendships or close relationships of wartime in the area—had not been taken in, so to speak. My eyes were fixed on America, upon whom the fate of China depended. I hoped that by honestly stating all that I found wrong in China, my *bona fides* in nevertheless advocating aid to her would be established.

In the preamble to my "Report on China" (see Appendix VI) I emphasized the fact that the goals and principles and aims of the United Nations were being jeopardized by "forces as sinister as those that operated in Europe and Asia during the ten years leading to World War II." There was the same familiar pattern of the employment of subversive agents, infiltration, incitement of disorder and chaos to disrupt normal economy and thereby to undermine popular confidence in government and leaders; seizure of authority without reference to the will of the people—all the techniques skillfully designed and ruthlessly implemented in order to create favorable conditions for the imposition of totalitarian ideology.

In a word, long before the phrase "indirect aggression" was coined by John Foster Dulles in 1958, it was clear to anyone who knew the score that China was menaced by direct aggression as well as insurrection.

"Soviet practices in the countries already occupied or dominated," I continued, "completes the mosaic of aggressive expansion through ruthless secret police methods and through an increasing political and economic enslavement of peoples." In sum, Soviet Russia had already revealed in word and act "a definite plan for expansion, far exceding that of Naziism in its ambitious scope and dangerous implications." Therefore, I wrote: "Events of the past two years demonstrate the futility of appeasement based on the hope that the strongly consolidated forces of the Soviet Union will adopt either a conciliatory or a co-operative attitude, except as tactical expedients."

It was therefore essential, I concluded, that America "should seize every possible opportunity to create bulwarks of freedom."

I observed: "Notwithstanding all the corruption and incompetence that one notes in China, it is a certainty that the bulk of the people were not disposed to accept the Communist political and economic structure," although some had become affiliated with Communism "in indignant protest against oppressive police measures, corrupt practices, and maladministration." It was all too clear why some Chinese had "lost all hope under existing leadership" and turned to the Communists in despair. But, I pointed out, Americans must realize that we ourselves bore a large share of responsibility for this outcome, thanks both to the Yalta Agreement—which facilitated Russia's entry into Manchuria—and our subsequent withholding of arms aid and political support to our loyal ally, the Chinese Nationalist Government. The United States had "facilitated the Soviet program in the Far East."

"If the recommendations of this report are approved," I concluded, the United States should suggest to China that "she inform the United Nations officially of her request to the United States for material assistance and advisory aid in order to facilitate China's postwar rehabilitation and economic recovery."

As in the case of Greece and Turkey, such action would demonstrate that the UN was not being circumvented and that the U.S. was "not infringing upon China's sovereignty," but on the contrary "co-operating constructively in the interest of world peace and stability in the Far East, concomitantly in the world."

I also repeated the arguments I had made a year and a half before in favor of a guardianship over Manchuria, to obviate the danger that Manchuria "may be drawn into the Soviet orbit, despite U.S. aid, and lost, perhaps permanently, to China." The situation in Manchuria had by now deteriorated to such a degree that prompt action was necessary to prevent that area from becoming a Soviet satellite. I therefore suggested that the United Nations might take immediate action to bring about cessation of hostilities as a prelude to the establishment of a guardianship or trusteeship, to be initiated by China.

I placed major emphasis in my report on the fact that the economic deterioration, incompetence, and corruption in the political and military organizations in China should be considered against an all-inclusive background, "lest there be disproportionate emphasis on defects."

It seemed to me that in the West we were all too prone to pride ourselves on the material prosperity, freedom from fear, and all the other liberties and opportunities which our forefathers had won. We often failed to understand the problems of less fortunate peoples and nations who were being subjected to trials and tribulations of which we ourselves in our generation had no conception at all. This was particularly true of our view of China. So I wrote:

> Unlike other powers since V-J Day, China has never been free to devote full attention to internal problems that were greatly confounded by eight years of war. The current civil war has imposed an overwhelming financial and economic burden at a time when resources and energies have been dissipated and when, in any event, they would have been strained to the utmost to meet the problems of recovery.

The Generalissimo had categorically stated that, "regardless of moral encouragements or material aid received from the United States" he was determined "to oppose Communism and to create a democratic form of government in consonance with Dr. Sun Yat-sen's principles." He had assured me, and I believed him, that he planned to make sweeping reforms in the Government, including the removal of incompetent and corrupt officials. But I understood as well as he did that "with spiraling inflation, economic distress and civil war," it had been impossible to accomplish these objectives. It was all too obvious that the Generalissimo could not drastically reduce the size of the Army and concentrate upon political and economic reforms, unless and until the Communists backed by Soviet Russia could be suppressed, or at least halted in their tracks.

Although I believed that Chiang Kai-shek was sincere in his desire to establish a democratic form of government, I was not certain that he had sufficient determination to do so if this required "overruling of the political and military cliques surrounding him." The receipt of realistic U.S. aid required that he show evidence of such determination. As I wrote: "Adoption by the United States of a policy motivated solely toward the expansion of Communism without regard to the continued existence of an unpopular, repressive government would render any aid ineffective."

I was in a dilemma. I recognized the weaknesses and the oppressive character of the Nationalist Government and its decreasing popular support, but I was equally well aware that Communist totalitarian tyranny would be infinitely worse. Finally I realized that only American military, economic, and political support of the Chinese Nationalist Government against the Communists would establish a climate in which the best, most progressive, and liberal forces in China could win influence and power and an opportunity to reform their country. The real liberals in China had so far been given a choice only between adherence to the Kuomintang, in spite of its degeneration and corruption, and Communism. We ourselves were largely responsible for this tragic fact. We had rendered confusion worse confounded by making our aid and support conditional on the establishment of a Chinese Government deemed to be democratic by both ourselves and the Communists. Since the Communist view of what constitutes democracy is diametrically opposed to that of the free world, we had impaled the Chinese on the horns of an insoluble dilemma. By equating democracy with willingness to collaborate with Communists, and by castigating as reactionaries those who believed that "co-operation by the Chinese Communist party in the government was inconceivable and that only force could settle the issue" General Marshall had positively encouraged the liberals to go over to the Communist side, or at least support it against the Nationalist Government. The tragedy was that, had it not been for the false equation on which U.S.-China policy was based in the Truman-Acheson-Marshall era, we could have strengthened the influence of the real liberals and reformers instead of either driving them to retire from the struggle in despair or go over to the Communists in the hope that the Americans' favorable view of them would be justified.

In 1947 on my mission I believed it was not yet too late to remedy the unfortunate consequences of our former China policy, which had been formulated on the basis of illusions and myths about communism which had already been discarded in our policy toward Greece and Europe in general. I thought that if we gave Chiang Kai-shek military aid and moral support against the Communist menace, but also compelled, or galvanized him into instituting vitally necessary reforms in administration, the best elements in China would once again rally to the Nationalist Government. In my report I wrote:

> Although the Chinese people are unanimous in their desire for peace at almost any cost, there seems to be no possibility of its realization under existing circumstances. On one side is the Kuomintang, whose reactionary leadership, repression and corruption have caused a loss of popular faith in the government. On the other side, bound ideologically to the Soviet Union, are the Chinese Communists, whose eventual aim is admittedly a Communist state in China. Some reports indicate that Communist measures of land reform have gained for them the support of the majority of peasants in areas under their control, while others indicate that their ruthless tactics of land distribution and terrorism have alienated the majority of such peasants. They have, however, successfully organized many rural areas against the Nationalist Government. Moderate groups are caught between Kuomintang misrule and repression, and ruthless Communist totalitarianism. Minority parties lack dynamic leadership and sizeable following. Neither the moderates, many of whom are in the Kuomintang, nor the minority parties, are able to make their influence felt because of Nationalist Government repression.

I shall here pass over my visit to Korea and my recommendations concerning that unhappy country which had been divided at the 38th parallel by another of the disastrous Yalta agreements. Briefly, I recommended the formation of a trusteeship over Korea comprising Great Britain, the Soviet Union, France, China, and the United States operating under the aegis of the United Nations. My purpose was to preclude subversive action in Korea by the Soviet Union.

While under the leadership of the great patriot Syngman Rhee, the Koreans established conditions for their complete control of the entire area.

After I had submitted my report to the President, I temporarily occupied an office in the State Department, holding myself in readiness to amplify the premises established and the background of my conclusions and recommendations. General Marshall, who was at the United Nations at Lake Success, suggested that I visit New York to see him there. He complimented me orally upon the report but said he had not as yet had time to study it thoroughly and that we would discuss it on his return to Washington.

While in New York I had luncheon with my friend, Mr. Henry Luce, publisher of *Time, Life,* and *Fortune.* We had an interesting chat in his Waldorf Towers suite; but since Marshall had admonished me scrupulously to avoid discussing the contents of my report with anyone, I had to parry Luce's searching questions and explain the reason why I could not give him any details concerning my report and recommendations.

Other members of the press, as well as radio commentators, members of Congress, and officials in the Pentagon, constantly importuned me, trying to elicit some information or obtain hints of the contents of my report. I couldn't understand the decision to handle the report so secretly. I felt that at least top officials in the Pentagon, and certainly members of the Senate and House Foreign Relations Committees, should have full access to it and to members of the mission if explanation or amplification were required. Pressures were brought to bear on other members of my mission, who had been similarly warned not to divulge the contents. Soon it became known in all circles that a rigid clamp had been put down by the President and Secretary of State. In subsequent testimony, before Congressional committees, Secretary Marshall accepted full responsibility for this decision. (See Appendix III.)

While I continued to sit in the State Department expecting that eventually my report and recommendations would be discussed, the then Chief of the Far Eastern Division, Mr. Walton Butterworth, visited me several times. But on only one occasion did we consider the findings on which my report was based, and Mr. Butterworth then told me that the Secretary of State wanted me to delete certain specific portions. I told him that I could not agree to do this. He then suggested that the Secretary might be angry if I did not accede to his wishes, because he wanted to publish my report but could not do so unless certain statements were removed. I told Mr. Butterworth that I would see the Secretary right away; and I telephoned his office but was informed that Marshall was again attending the United Nations sessions in New York. So I put in a long-distance call and told Marshall that I could not in clear conscience delete the parts of my report that he requested. Secretary Marshall, far from showing anger, understood and accepted my position.

I then explained to Butterworth that considerable research, analysis, and thought had gone into the preparation of the report. If the sections he indicated were deleted, the continuity of thought and, in fact, the very heart of the report would be removed. He himself did not at any time comment on the merits or demerits of my recommendations, nor did anyone else in the State Department ever do so to me. No one asked me to explain or amplify. I was just left to twiddle my thumbs in a spacious office at the State Department until at last it dawned on me that all my work had been to no purpose, and the recommendations I had made with such high hopes were being quietly ignored.

No doubt I had been naïve. I had had many warnings concerning the negative attitude of the State Department toward giving any military aid to the Nationalist Government or taking any concrete steps to dam the advancing Communist tide in China. It had refused all along to give even the political and moral support to the Chinese Government which might have sustained the morale of its armed forces. I felt more and more frustrated and alarmed. I knew that the delay in implementing my recommendations for immediate moral and material support to the Chinese Nationalist Government was serving the purpose of the Communists. The State Department knew as well as I that the situation was deteriorating rapidly, yet the hands-off attitude prevailed. I asked myself with increasing anxiety why I had been sent to China. Had General Marshall simply wanted me to reinforce his own views by submitting a report completely confirming his existing do-nothing policy? Had he wanted me to join the host of sycophants whom he had despised in the earlier years when he told me that he valued most those who frankly expressed their honest convictions?

When questioned by Congressional committees and the press as to why my report to the President had been suppressed, Secretary of State Marshall indicated that it contained confidential material the publication of which might cause embarrassment to the nations concerned. Of course it was not my function to determine the effect of the information embodied in my report and certainly I did not feel qualified to make such determination. But the conclusions and recommendations were carefully phrased to insure that no offense would be given, and practically all of the ideas had been previously discussed in a most friendly atmosphere with Generalissimo Chiang Kai-shek. I feel positive today that the publication of my report would not have caused embarrassment to my Government or to the Chinese and Koreans. If I am wrong, then it would appear that the subsequent publication of my report in the White Paper in 1949 was a serious mistake in diplomacy.

I visited General Eisenhower and told him I wished to be returned to duty with the Second Army, since I was doing nothing in the State Department. He agreed to ask that I be reassigned, pointing out that I would be readily available for conferences, inasmuch as my headquarters were located in Baltimore, Maryland.

Not that I was ever again consulted, nor my report discussed. It was simply buried until in the course of time it was exhumed by Senate Committee investigators alarmed at the imminent loss of China to the Communists. Long before this, Ambassador Leighton Stuart's dispatches from China (which are to be found buried in the 600 pages of annexes to the unindexed State Department White Paper of 1949, in which my own suppressed Report was eventually published) had begun to echo the recommendations I had made in the spring of 1947, and which he himself had failed to support.

On July 1, 1947, Stuart reported:

> Persons in direct contact with the Nationalist troops in rural areas state there are insufficient small arms and ammunition to arm all combatant troops in the field.

By September 20, 1947, he reported:

Political, military, and economic position of Central [Nationalist] Government has continued to deteriorate within recent months in accordance with previous expectations. Currently, the cumulative effect of the absence of substantial financial and military assistance expected from the Wedemeyer Mission and renewed Communist military activity are intensifying the Chinese tendency to panic in times of crisis.

And on March 17, 1948, realizing that the Nationalist forces were at the limit of endurance, our Ambassador reported:

In their despair all groups blame America for urging structural changes . . . or reforms which they feel they themselves would carry out if their immediate internal problems were not so acute, while America still delays the long-promised aid upon which the survival of democratic institutions depends.

A few days later, on March 31, 1948, Leighton Stuart wrote:

The Chinese people do not want to become Communists, yet they see the tide of communism running irresistibly onward. In the midst of this chaos and inaction the Generalissimo stands out as the only moral force capable of action.

Finally on August 10, 1948, in a panic at the imminent success of the Marshall-Acheson policy designed to establish a coalition government in China, Mr. Stuart reported:

Even though at present some form of coalition seems most likely, we believe that from the standpoint of the United States it would be undesirable. We say this because the history of coalitions including Communists demonstrates all too clearly Communist ability by political means to take over complete control of the government and in the process to acquire some kind of international recognition. . . . We would recommend therefore that American efforts be designed to prevent the formation of a coalition government, and our best means to that end is continued and, if possible, increased support of the present government.

In November, 1948, the Chinese delegate to the United Nations, Dr. T. F. Tsiang, appealed to Secretary of State Marshall in Paris, asking if anything would induce the United States to help China. He offered to put United States officers in actual command of

Chinese troops "under the pretense of acting as advisers as in Greece." He begged for munitions. And, finally, he asked General Marshall "as to the advisability of Chinese appeal to the United Nations because of Soviet training and equipping of Japanese military and also the Koreans."

General Marshall thereupon said he would refer Tsiang's requests and suggestions to Washington, but "did not offer encouragement." And he rejected the Chinese proposal to appeal to the United Nations, saying: "I thought it an inadvisable procedure and discussed possible Soviet moves to take advantage rather than to counter such a move."

The U. S. Administration's refusal to give Chiang Kai-shek the military advice he had long requested was perhaps even more helpful to the Communists than General Marshall's 1946 embargo on arms and ammunition to China, and the failure of the Administration to implement the China Aid Act of April, 1948, which provided $128,000,000 worth of arms aid to China that was not delivered until the end of that year when it was too late to stop the Communists.

The Chinese Nationalist armies had few generals capable of commanding large forces, and Chiang Kai-shek had therefore asked America to allow United States officers to give him the same help that the Russians were giving the Communist forces and that we were giving to the Greeks. But his request was refused.

Back in the summer of 1945 when Japan surrendered, the program for the modernization of the Chinese armed forces had only begun. Because the project had been started under the guidance of American Army personnel, and because of the success which even our limited effort had achieved during the war, the Generalissimo had asked that this assistance to China be continued. With the approval of the United States War Department, immediately after V-J Day a tentative plan for the establishment of a Military Advisory Group had been drawn up under my direction.

The proposed Military Advisory Group was to be subdivided into two sections, one conducted by personnel of the U.S. Army and the other by the U.S. Navy. The Army section would have been further divided into Ground Force, Air Force, and Service Force contingents. The American personnel required from both the Army and Navy was estimated at 1,000 officers and 2,600 enlisted men, for the first year or so, with subsequent reductions. The plan called for a five-year period of training, with an extension to depend on agreement between the Chinese and United States governments.

An effective Military Advisory Group could have conferred numerous benefits on the United States as well as China. The close connection between two governments established during the war would have continued, and friendly contacts could have contributed a great deal to world peace. American Army and Navy personnel would have gained valuable experience in the language, customs, and civilization of the Far East. The personnel of the advisory group was to have consisted of veteran members of the U.S. Army serving on a volunteer basis.

Chief beneficiary, of course, would have been China. The Chinese Government, if assisted in establishing the internal peace that only military strength can guarantee, would eventually have been able to progress toward the modern, democratic state which had seemed to be in sight in 1937 before the Japanese aggression. A reform in China's military organization would also undoubtedly have led to reforms in her civil administration.

This plan never materialized. A very small American Military Advisory group was established, but it was ordered not to enter combat areas to assist the Chinese Nationalist armies in the use of the limited amount of equipment we had given them. (American personnel serving in similar capacity with the Greeks were permitted to accompany Greek units into combat areas.)

Dean Acheson was either misinformed or was deliberately misleading Congress when he cited "our military observers on the spot" as the authority for his statement that the Chinese Nationalist forces had lost no battles against the Communists for lack of arms or ammunition. Thanks to the State Department, American military observers had not been permitted to enter combat areas and therefore could not render first-hand reports of that nature. A civilian engineer representing the J. C. White Company of New York was present in the Soochow area during the fighting and told me personally that the Nationalists fought tenaciously against the Communists. He saw thousands of wounded and dead, both Communists and Nationalists. The latter withdrew only as the ammunition supply was exhausted.

Perhaps I made a grave mistake and was derelict in duty to my country when I returned to military duties following the suppression of my report on China and Korea. Maybe if I had resigned and spoken my mind I might have brought the truth home to the American people and thus saved China from the Communist conquest which led inevitably to the bloody, futile Korean war. But I was a soldier trained and taught to eschew politics, and conceiving it as my primary duty to perform my military tasks even though I might personally disagree with the policy of my Government. Also my respect and affection for General Marshall made it all the more difficult to abandon my military career in order to challenge him (*actually his advisers*) in the field of policy. At the same time *I was well aware of the implications of my stand.* One hesitates to question the judgment of others—particularly those in high positions of responsibility with access to classified information and expert consultants. However, I sensed that our top leaders were virtually captive to those around them—their advisers, now often alluded to as the palace guard. Information presented to a busy President, Secretary of State, or any high official must of necessity be brief, succinct—almost in capsule form. The ingredients put into that capsule become very potent—influencing the decisions in highest quarters. With due modesty, I felt qualified to contribute ideas, based on knowledge and experience in international developments. At least I knew in my heart that my motives were the best—namely, to protect America's interests. I did not question the motives of others unless and until I had irrefutable evidence, but at times I was compelled to question judgments, policies, and decisions. No one is omniscient, and I tried to keep an open mind in weighing the advantages or disadvantages to our country of courses of action proposed by the State Department experts, in relations with the British, the Chinese, the Russians, the Hindus—in fact, with any nation.

When a situation develops wherein a member of a team feels he cannot in clear conscience subscribe to and support the leader, it is mandatory that he resign from the team. This does not mean that he should stop fighting, if his knowledge and experience still support his convictions. Accordingly, I finally left Government service in the hope that I could present my views and support those in the Government who were of like mind. In leaving the Army I did so with regret for I loved the service. I owed much to West Point and the Army, and valued the years of happy association with the dedicated men and women in the government services.

I never believed that the Chinese Communists were a totally different species from all others. Therefore, I couldn't imagine that they either could or would establish a democratic government in China. It seemed obvious that the kind of government they would set up would be the same type of totalitarian dictatorship as the ones which had already been imposed by the Red Army in Poland, East Germany, Roumania, and other countries within the Soviet orbit. However reactionary and corrupt the Chinese Nationalist Government might be, I thought that we could help to cleanse it by supporting the truly liberal and progressive, as distinct from the Communist, elements. On the other hand I knew that no regime constitutes so great a threat to liberty and progress as a Communist group backed by Soviet Russia.

Nor was it understood in America that the amount of aid we had given to China was infinitesimal as compared to that which we had given to the U.K. and the Soviet Union.

In a later book I hope to provide detailed evidence of the "China thesis," which I have only briefly outlined in this and preceding chapters. In concluding my sad story of American bungling in China I am now attempting only to summarize a few salient facts.

First and foremost, we should realize that had not the time-honored U.S. policy of United States-China friendly co-operation been reversed by the State Department in the Acheson era, China would not now equal or surpass her master and ally, the Union of Soviet Socialist Republics, as a menace to American security. The State Department's "wait and see," or "let the dust settle," China policy rendered inevitable the Communist conquest of China. The Chinese people are realists. They became so disheartened and demoralized by our attitude that they finally ceased to resist the Communists. What reason could there be for continuing to oppose them if even America wanted China to come to terms with them? What other alternative was there for the great majority of the Chinese people than to submit to Communist conquest, since even the United States demanded they do so as the *sine qua non* of American aid?

Thinking back through the years, I now freely acknowledge that I myself was not sufficiently cognizant of the almost insuperable problems faced by the Chinese Nationalist Government.

CHAPTER XXVI

THE WAR NOBODY WON: 1

It is always tempting to be a Monday morning quarterback, or to exercise 20-20 hindsight. The spectacle of two old soldiers, Eisenhower and Montgomery, rambling around the battlefield of Gettysburg and deciding that *both* Lee and Meade should have been sacked for their errors is always good for a laugh. Across the river Styx the vilified Civil War heroes must have been amused and compassionate as they in their own turn reviewed the bloopers of a later generation of strategists and tacticians. People who live in glass houses have to be careful of the sunlight as well as of stones. Nevertheless, Monday morning quarterbacking is particularly valuable to the military man. It affords an opportunity to evaluate policies and decisions, to conjure up alternate courses of action, and to bring into focus valuable lessons in strategy or in tactics for application in the future.

World War II offers the richest possible field for the Monday morning analyst. To begin with, as Charles Lindbergh warned in 1939, the war itself was a supreme mistake from both the German and the Allied points of view. Nobody could, nobody did, win it.

The double mistake of Germany and Britain was to repeat the lamentable history of the Peloponnesian War of ancient Greece. As Edith Hamilton has explained in her chapter on Thucydides in *The Greek Way*, Athens, the democratic sea power of the ancient world, and Sparta, the totalitarian land power, fought each other

405

for reasons of greed and power-seeking passion. Meanwhile, Macedon, the Asiatic power, waited in the wings for the two strong Greek city-states to mangle each other. The parallel of 1939–45 is obvious. While Germany (Sparta) and Britain (Athens) were chewing each other to pieces, Russia (Macedon) became the sole beneficiary of the suicidal internecine quarrel of the West.

This, of course, is seeing things *sub specie aeternitatis*—or, as it might be put more colloquially, simply crying over spilt milk. Perhaps I, as a former professional military man, should narrow the focus to consider what might have been done by the leaders on both sides after the war began.

In commenting on World War II decisions, I do so with some temerity, for I know that I made many mistakes—errors of judgment and wrong decisions. Sometimes I discovered and corrected them. In other instances I did not learn about them until the war was over. My analyses and reactions were based on the limited information available at the time.

It is a military axiom, far older than Bedford Forrest's "git there fustest with the mostest," that the major objective of war should be to smash the enemy where he is strong. In modern war, this "principle of the objective" must be to reach the heart of the enemy's homeland—to destroy or capture his war-making industrial complex and to break the will of the people to fight.

In examining Western Europe, the Allies should never have been diverted from the obvious fact that the Ruhr was the key industrial area of the German war effort. From the German viewpoint the heart of the Allied war effort, at least prior to U.S. entry, was the compact, highly industrialized British Isles. But, strangely, both sides seemed to compete in ignoring the major or decisive objectives; and the Western Allies and Russia won the war precisely because Hitler dawdled longer and interfered to a greater degree with his professional soldiers in their attempts to apply sound military doctrine.

Hitler even began the war in 1939 with a thundering mistake when he elected to attack Poland before completing his defenses in the west. The Siegfried line (Westwall) was weak and vulnerable. There remained much work to be done to give greater flexibility in defending against an enemy employing modern air power and armor. Consequently, the Nazis were compelled to deploy more highly effective combat units along the Westwall than would have been necessary had the fortifications been completed. Not only this, but provision for anti-aircraft defense of vital communications and industrial centers in Western Germany was neglected to the point of stupidity.

The British and the French saved Hitler from the consequences of his folly when they failed to launch an all-out attack against him while he was irretrievably tied up in Poland. True, it was a mistake on England's part to guarantee Poland's territorial integrity once the Czech bastion and the small, though formidable, Czechoslovak Army had fallen to Hitler without an effort to stop him. But the Allies might have done much to compensate for their earlier errors in statecraft if they had seized the initiative in the West at the very outset of the war. If they had attacked then, I am confident that the Allies would easily have reached the Rhine; possibly they might even have smashed into the Ruhr.

The French, it must be remembered, had the largest standing army in Europe in 1939. In the judgment of some German military experts, the French Army was the best trained and equipped on the Continent. General Ludwig Beck, the Chief of Staff of the German Army, who knew the French Chief of Staff General Gamelin both personally and professionally, told me that Gamelin was one of the ablest field generals among the Allies. Together, the French and British had available over 100 divisions supported by an effective British Air Force.

When the Germans, on September 1, began their advance against the Poles, they employed 44 divisions, including all of their mechanized and motorized formations. The bulk of the *Luftwaffe* (Air Force) was also concentrated in the east for close support of Army operations. Remaining behind in the homeland were only a few divisions in process of mobilization. Some 35 additional German divisions of reserve or home defense units were scattered along the Western Front. If approximately 70 divisions of French and British, supported by the British air units, had launched a vigorous attack on the Westwall along a broad front in the first week of September, they would have compelled the Germans to divert strong forces from their operations against Poland. Even then the Allies might have reached into the Ruhr to weaken or destroy the dynamo of the Nazi war effort. But the Allies did not exploit this opportunity at the outset of the war, and the phony war, or sitzkrieg, prevailed in the West while the Nazi blitzkrieg was pushed to a successful conclusion in Poland.

The most critical bungling of the war should be attributed to Hitler. Despite the evidence available to him in history books, he had no concept of British pugnacity and determination once these people set their stout hearts and stubborn souls to a task. Just a smattering of English history would have set him straight. His professional military advisers—Keitel, Jodl, and Halder—warned him not to turn his back on England.

When he finally realized that he could not flatter, cajole, or intimidate the islanders across the channel, he initiated steps to strengthen the Westwall. With bitterness in his heart and in defiant spirit Hitler adopted an arrogant "I'll bring them to their knees" attitude. Hadn't Goering assured him that the *Luftwaffe* could blast them to oblivion? Hitler's preliminary steps to tighten his hold on Western Europe and to improve his military position vis-à-vis the British included a blitz advance into Norway, where he beat the British to the punch. Then, in May of 1940, his columns dashed rapidly through Holland, Belgium, and France. At that time there seemed to be no way of stopping the Nazi legions. Their armored columns, combining a tremendous fire power and mobility, had no difficulty in quickly overcoming resistance. The Germans used close-support aviation in conjunction with armored columns most successfully, a new technique thoroughly tested in Poland.

Even in the vanguard of their miraculous success in the west the Nazis lost golden opportunities to weaken their most indomitable foe, the British. The Germans were advancing rapidly westward and could easily have captured the 300,000 men of the British Expeditionary Force. However, General Heinz Guderian, who commanded the armored corps near Dunkirk, was ordered to stop his advance. The order explained that Dunkirk was to be left to the *Luftwaffe*. In reporting this, Guderian says, "We were utterly speechless but since we were not informed of the reasons for this order it was difficult to argue against it. . . . Later we attempted once again to attack toward Dunkirk and to close the ring about that sea fortress, but renewed orders to halt arrived. We were stopped within sight of Dunkirk! We watched the *Luftwaffe* attack.

We also saw the armada of great and little ships by means of which the British were evacuating their forces. . . ."

What could have been Hitler's reason for giving Guderian the order to hold back his armored divisions at Dunkirk? Hitler disregarded the British who were rapidly evacuating by boat at Dunkirk and drove on to capture Paris, the French capital. While it was an important political and psychological objective, it could not be moved by boats to safety. Apparently the thought still lurked in Hitler's mind that if he were lenient he might persuade the British to come to some form of agreement in the west, thus permitting Germany to concentrate her strength in carrying out the policy of *Drang nach Osten*.

Churchill himself has suggested that by holding back Guderian at Dunkirk, Hitler was hoping to induce Britain to ask for a settlement. But, says Guderian, "Only the capture of the British Expeditionary Force could have influenced the English toward making peace with Hitler or could have created the conditions necessary for a successful German invasion of Great Britain."

In any event, always uppermost in the Fuehrer's mind was the defeat of the dreaded Bolsheviki to the east, with concomitant acquisition of Caucasian oil, the rich wheat fields of the Ukraine, and *Lebensraum* (living space) for colonization by Germans.

Maybe Hitler was confident that he could charm, bluff, or flatter Churchill into an amalgamation of "enlightened" democracy and ruthless dictatorship. The German Fuehrer finally was fully convinced that the British bulldog, although practically toothless, retained his old ferocity of spirit. Shortly thereafter orders were issued for all-out preparations for SEA LION, an ambitious cross-Channel operation in reverse. Landing craft were rapidly built or improvised and troops were quickly trained for amphibious operations. Preparations along the coast from Holland to Normandy were made for the launching of an invasion of the British Isles.

As I have said, the heart of the Allied effort in 1940 was the British Isles. If sound strategy instead of numerology or the impetuous hunches of a megalomaniac were to govern, every resource at Hitler's command should have been concentrated on the conquest of the British in their homeland. No diversions should have been permitted unless they contributed directly or indirectly to the success of SEA LION.

Fortunately for the Allies, however, Goering, the vainglorious mastermind of the *Luftwaffe*, had convinced the Fuehrer that his Air Force could compel the British to choose between German terms and outright annihilation. He proudly predicted that any British resistance would be shattered and the Nazi invasion forces could go in practically behind the band.

Thus the Battle of Britain, the greatest air battle of history, was on. The RAF wrote an epic in defending their island, and the British people, with a stark and resourceful courage never before excelled, took everything that was thrown at them. The Nazis were surprised to see Hurricanes and Spitfires rising to meet them day after day when all their calculations, as German Air Force General Werner Kreipe put it, showed the "British Fighter Command should have already ceased to exist." The Germans did not succeed in gaining undisputed control of the air, a prerequisite for a successful land invasion. As later revealed, German production hadn't concentrated on building sufficient air strength, either in type or numbers. Moreover, Goering continually interfered with operations during the critical period of the Battle of Britain, ordering costly daylight bombing attacks that resulted in a tremendous attrition of Nazi planes. There seemed to be a total lack of firm objectives—"too many targets," as General Kreipe has said. Although Goering was a disciple of the doctrines of General Douhet, he was often guilty of dissipation of means.

The original directives issued by Hitler required the elimination of the Royal Air Force as a preliminary to landing operations on the British shore. But this proper objective was soon changed, and a higher priority was given to bombing English industrial areas and shipping facilities. The pattern was unrelated to the requirements of wiping out British air power and getting an invasion army ashore in Britain.

Professional *Luftwaffe* officers, realizing that German bombers were not armored or otherwise equipped for defense against enemy fighters, were opposed to the Battle of Britain. But Hitler, supported of course by Hermann Goering, overruled his professional airmen and insisted upon carrying through.

The heavy losses sustained by the Nazis in the Battle of Britain cannot be attributed entirely to lack of armor or armament on German planes. British pilots, ground crews, anti-aircraft personnel, warning-service operators, and fire fighters all worked together to form an invincible team, to the lasting credit of a great people.

If excessive losses had promised ultimate success, Hitler would have been well advised to risk them. But even if air superiority had been achieved, there was still the problem of landing craft to effect a Channel crossing. With both air forces practically depleted, England's Navy would have become an important factor against a cross-Channel operation mounted with an insufficient number of landing barges and escorting naval vessels.

The fact is that the Germans had never realized the requirements for a large-scale amphibious operation. Nazi air power had failed in its mission, landing craft and naval escort vessels were not available, and lack of unanimity among the three services concerning possible success of the invasion contributed to the utter collapse of SEA LION. This complete reversal—his wings clipped, his so-called omniscience placed in true perspective—should have made the impetuous German Fuehrer a wiser, more prudent man.

The knowledge and experience gained in the Battle of Britain, if properly analyzed from both strategic and technical angles, should have led Hitler to renewed preparations for a successful cross-Channel operation, including an allocation of a proportionate amount of the German production for landing craft, convoy ships, and armored bombers equipped with appropriate weapons. But Hitler had new horizons eastward—new pulls, new urges irresistibly tugging at his cruel heart. The most basic strategic blunder of the war on either side came when the German leader changed his main objective to the east, leaving a wounded and infuriated British lion to the west.

Hitler, of course, feared the Russians at his back. But the history of Russia had always been one of defensive posture. I question seriously that Stalin would have attacked Germany if the Nazis had concentrated against the British. Military history proves that the Russian soldier normally fights well on his own soil but is deficient if sent abroad. Even though the Ukrainians and the Russians in Byelorussia initially welcomed the advancing columns of German soldiers as deliverers because of the tyranny they had experienced under Stalin, it was not long before the Todt organization of civilian oppressors—the hardfisted Nazi civilian commissars moving in behind the armies—had undone the fraternal work of the German soldiers. The civilian commissars were harsh, unremitting, cruel. It was not difficult for Stalin to prove to his people that the Nazis were enemies of *all* Russians and were determined to destroy any kind of Russian state.

I am confident that Stalin would have liked to see the British and the Germans fight to the end on the theory that this would have weakened or rendered each power practically impotent. Well did Stalin know the stick-to-itiveness and the great capacity of both Hitler and Churchill to strive unremittingly to win. Stalin would have had England and Germany clawing, killing, and destroying until both were almost prostrate. Then communism might take over.

But Hitler was still confident. He was more ground-minded than sea-minded and had great confidence in his Army which looked backward for its traditions to the Kaiser's time. Then, too, Hitler had not yet been convinced of the great importance of air power. He could be called a land strategist primarily. Trusting in the Army, he overcame objections of his generals and decided to attack the Russians.

This was the inglorious end of the "thousand-year Reich," for now Hitler had an aroused Britain at his back and a two-front war (Bismarck's nightmare) on his hands. The British bulldog's dentures were being refurbished by American industry. Also, the U.S. was becoming more and more impressed by the stouthearted stand of the British on their island—"fighting the battle for America," as it was coming more and more to be said. Finally, the Russians had had almost two years in which to prepare for any contingency during the period from the Stalin-Hitler Pact of August, 1939, to the Nazi attack on June 22, 1941.

As Hitler's legions advanced farther and farther into Russia, the lengthening lines of communication became more tenuous and vulnerable. The point was eventually reached when Hitler was "out in the blue," unable to supply his armies. His strategic position had become precarious, if not impossible.

I do not know how much study Hitler ever gave to Napoleon's campaign against Russia, but certainly both space and weather conditions, plus Kutuzov's strategy of retreat, were important factors which broke Napoleon's attack. These same factors were now to prove the nemesis of the highly mobile flying columns of the Germans. As someone has said, there were no gas stations in Russia.

It is my understanding that Hitler did consider two ways of attacking England in case of continued opposition by Churchill to a "deal." One plan was to move on the Middle East, thus gaining access to the rich oil resources in that area. Success in this undertaking would destroy British influence; it would also cut the line of communications to Egypt, India, and Australia. For economic reasons, this course promised many advantages. In addition to denying oil to the West, it would permanently tie up Allied shipping by forcing it to go around the Cape of Good Hope. And, aside from its strong psychological effect on the Arab world, it might have persuaded the Turks to throw in their lot with Fascism. It would also have facilitated the advance of the Japanese against Ceylon, India, and Australia. The end might even have been the juncture of the two principal Axis powers, the Germans and the Japanese.

This particular plan for disrupting the British Empire had the defect of leaving the productive dynamo intact in the British Isles. Once the heartbeat of the Empire had been stilled by success in the alternative plan of invading Britain, Hitler could have driven to the Middle East at his leisure. Concentration on an attack against the British Isles was in conformity with the traditional German theory of going for victory at the decisive point.

Hitler's blunders were all incipient in the attitudes expressed in *Mein Kampf*. Hitler felt he could do no wrong; his intuition he considered to be infallible. But the intuition went astray from the Battle of Britain on. Hitler respected England; he feared her, too. I think he never contemplated her complete destruction and wanted always to make some kind of arrangement whereby the Germans would exercise a sphere of influence in Eastern Europe ranging down into the Middle East, whereas British influence in Western Europe would remain predominant. Some kind of mutual interest in exploiting the rich oil resources of the Middle East would have suited Hitler. Of course, if the Nazis had gained access to the Caucasus, Middle East oil would not have seemed so crucial to Germany. Ironically, while Hitler wished to preserve some semblance of the British Empire, President Roosevelt seemed to think one objective of the war was to create a state of affairs that would result in the Empire's voluntary dissolution.

Emotional hatred of the Bolsheviks, which is the leitmotif of *Mein Kampf*, kept Hitler from making judgments based on military reality. Always he reverted to the Grand Design. The *Drang nach Osten*, the drive to the East, was drilled into Germans in all walks of life. I listened to such propaganda on the radio and read columns daily in the press during my years in Berlin. Hitler, of course, was convinced that Germany had been mistreated after World War I when her colonies were taken away from her. Overseas *Lebensraum* was no longer available to the energetic German people. So why not look to the East? The influence of Alfred Rosenberg and the propaganda of Goebbels had convinced Hitler of the soundness of his policy of attempting to crush the Russians and reach the oil of the Caucasus, the resources of Byelorussia, and the vast areas that could be opened for colonization in the Ukraine. Then there was the traditional pull of the Baltic areas, where many thousands of German families had been settled for years. These were the lands of the old Teutonic knights who had protected the eastern marches of Germany from time out of mind.

After the decision to attack the Soviet Union was made in June, 1941, Hitler interfered increasingly with military operations, and as events proved, to a catastrophic degree. The Nazi columns advanced rapidly, gobbling up huge numbers of Russian prisoners with big pincer or enveloping movements. They were very soon knocking at the door of Moscow, and swift armored columns were piercing deep into the Ukraine.

Scorning the advise of his generals, Hitler wanted to push on everywhere with redoubled ferocity. There was considerable discussion about the main effort, whether it should be to capture Moscow or advance in the south. The Germans, as their generals told Hitler, should have chosen to do one or the other, but not both. Hitler, however, decided to try both; he was so flushed with success, and so impressed with the thousands of Russian prisoners in German camps, that he thought everything was his for the taking. Indeed, he might have been right if he had not originally permitted himself to be diverted in Yugoslavia and Greece. If Hitler had ignored the Balkans for concentration on Russia, which would have been strategically sound, it is possible that he might have captured Moscow before winter set in. As it was, the Balkan campaigns delayed the attack on Russia so long that the Nazis could not reach assigned objectives before snow and cold immobilized their heavily armored columns.

At one point General von Leeb, commanding the north group of German armies, was convinced that, after encircling Leningrad, he could practically have walked into the city. He said as much after the war to a fellow officer, General von Boetticher. However, he was stopped by Hitler's personal order. Years later in Washington von Boetticher told me that Hitler wanted von Leeb to continue his siege of the city so that its two million inhabitants would slowly starve. This tied down important elements of von Leeb's forces. Eventually von Leeb's reserves were taken away and moved to hard-pressed southern areas, with the result that he no longer had sufficient forces to capture Leningrad. Thus Hitler's demographic sadism kept von Leeb from delivering a decisive blow to Russian resistance. Today the Communists celebrate justifiably the heroic defense of Leningrad, but it was probably the intercession of Hitler that prevented professional German military leaders from taking the city.

Once committed in three massive spearheads, north, central, and south, Hitler would not permit commanders on the Eastern Front to shorten their lines and assume an active defense. Thus, by degrees, the stage was set for Stalingrad. Eventually the long line of communications to the Volga was broken, and vast numbers of German troops under General von Paulus were caught in a trap. There was to be no retreat from Stalingrad, for Hitler had ordered, "Stand or die."

Hitler had increasingly ignored his generals. He questioned even their loyalty, not only to him but to the Fatherland. From the beginning, as we have seen when Chief of Staff Ludwig Beck failed to dissuade him from invading Czechoslovakia, he had flouted their advice. At the end of the war he was making all of the major decisions.

Naturally, Hitler's suspicions concerning the military were confirmed by the July 20, 1944, plot to kill him. This plot had its roots in the genuine patriotism of the old German officer corps, which couldn't bear to see the Fatherland led into an irretrievable morass of disaster. The conspirators of July, 1944, headed by Ludwig Beck, were in almost continuous contact with American OSS representatives in Switzerland working under Allen Dulles, now the head of the Central Intelligence Agency. For four years of warfare, dissident German generals had been quiescent about their fears. The Fuehrer had enjoyed many lucky successes, and understandably many Germans were convinced of his wizard powers. A patient man, General Beck waited for the inevitable day when Hitler's ignorance of military science and paranoiac schemes would stand clearly revealed. Beck and his fellow conspirators wanted to gain their end by one bold stroke. It was agreed not to make Hitler a prisoner but to kill him outright, then establish a government responsive to the will of the people and bring about an honorable peace with the Allies.

In the spring of 1944, as head of the secret resistance movement, Beck arranged several contacts between his representatives and those of the Allies in Switzerland. He had hopes of arranging terms under which the Allies would be prepared to make peace with Germany. He was prepared to pledge his country to constructive efforts as a peaceful member of the family of nations. A thinking man, he realized that this could only be accomplished by renouncing every vestige of Nazi philosophy. It had been hard for Beck to win the allegiance of high-placed military and civilian leaders to conspiratorial plans, for no one was able to vouch for what might happen to Germany once Hitler was removed. Several of the senior military leaders, although in complete sympathy with the conspiracy's objectives, would not join the resistance movement because they felt that any effort on their part to remove Hitler would simply bring about an immediate military collapse, thus putting the German people at the mercy of the hated Kremlin.

It is understandable to any soldier that these men, dedicated to the protection of their homeland, could never in clear conscience make themselves party to the complete collapse of their country without first getting assurances of honorable conditions of armistice or peace. Accordingly, General Beck made overtures to the American OSS representative, Allen Dulles, in Switzerland. How unfortunate, in retrospect, that the sincerity of purpose, the sense of honor, the wisdom, and the humanitarian spirit of General Beck were not realized by responsible officials in our government.

The fate of any Allied official who wished for something better than unconditional surrender is illustrated by the story of what happened to George H. Earle of Pennsylvania, who was at one time associated with President Roosevelt. Earle served as Minister to Austria in 1933 and then resigned in 1934 to run for Governor of Pennsylvania. He became that state's first Democratic Governor in forty-four years. In reward for his services to Roosevelt, Earle was made Minister to Bulgaria, where he remained through 1940 and 1941, resigning to become commander of a submarine chaser when America entered the war. After winning a decoration for gallantry in action, Earle became U.S. naval attaché at Istanbul in 1943.

Turkey, of course, was neutral. In its capital of Istanbul, Earle was approached by Admiral Wilhelm Canaris, famous intelligence expert and Chief of the Nazi Secret Service, Herr Franz von Papen, who was German Ambassador to Turkey at the time, and Baron Kurt von Lersner, who had known Earle before the war.

What Canaris, von Lersner, and von Papen suggested was nothing less than a defection of the German Army from Hitler and a subsequent surrender to the Allies. Hitler was to be captured or killed. Canaris and von Papen had only one stipulation: That Germany's surrender was to be predicated upon the prevention, by a joint German, British, and American force, of a Soviet advance into Central Europe.

Earle conveyed the Canaris-von Papen proposal at once to the President. He waited expectantly for word from Washington. There were more conversations with von Lersner, who had some Jewish blood in his veins and could be accepted as a genuine anti-Nazi. Von Lersner assured Earle that many prominent Germans beside Canaris and von Papen were in the plot to get rid of Hitler. They all wanted a quick end to the war, to Nazism, and to the spread of communism, all wrapped up in one effective package.

After a long silence, Roosevelt's answer came. It was a definite brush-off: "All such applications for negotiated peace should be referred to the Supreme Allied Commander, General Eisenhower." Later, after a lapse of months, Earle flew to Washington to see the President. This was in May of 1944. While waiting at the White House he ran into his old friend, Secretary of the Navy James Forrestal, who said, "My God, George, you and I and Bill Bullitt are the only ones around the President who know the Russian leaders for what they are." But in spite of Forrestal's and Bullitt's support, all that Earle could get out of Roosevelt was, "Stop worrying, George, we are getting ready for this Normandy landing, it cannot fail, Germany will surrender in a few months." When Earle replied that the real menace was not German but Russian, F.D.R. smiled. "George, Russia is a nation of one hundred eighty million people, speaking one hundred and twenty dialects. When the war's over, she will fly to pieces like a cracked centrifugal machine at high speed."

Governor Earle's account of the Canaris-von Papen-von Lersner offer appeared in the August, 1958, issue of *Confidential* magazine. The story cannot be dismissed as flamboyant or unimportant, for it rings all too true against the plot to kill Hitler. The plot was under the direction of dedicated men. Besides Beck there were Count Rol Heinrich von Heldorf, Chief of Police of Berlin; Prince Gottfried Bismarck, grandson of the Grand Chancellor; Colonel Claus von Stauffenberg, Baron Freitag von Loringhoven of the Baltic nobility, and many others. The code name of their operation was VALKYRIE.

George Earle is right when he says that if the President and Prime Minister had accepted and followed through on the Canaris-von Papen offer, the war might have ended in 1943. Countless lives would in all probability have been saved and, of greatest importance, the Allies would not have supplanted one dangerous ideology with another. The Soviet hordes would have been stopped at the Polish border. The entire map of Europe would have been different if the territorial integrity of the principal countries could have been maintained on a basis of sound economics as well as traditional historical conditions.

CHAPTER XXVII

THE WAR NOBODY WON: 2

BECK'S OWN REPRESENTATIONS made to the OSS in Switzerland were duly forwarded to Washington and London. Among the Germans who acted as go-betweens was Hans Gisevius, who had been connected with anti-Nazi activities for a long time. I became acquainted with Gisevius after the war and through him and other German friends I learned many of the details of the anti-Hitler bomb plot. Admiral Canaris had developed an effective organization as chief of German secret intelligence. He had secretly turned anti-Nazi, for he recognized that Hitler would bring his country to no good end. His principal assistant, General Oster, agreed with him. The attitude of these key intelligence men was not known to many, either in or outside of Germany. It was Admiral Canaris who arranged for Gisevius to be placed in an innocuous spot with the German Consulate in Zurich, Switzerland, where he served as representative of the resistance movement. Gisevius slipped back and forth between Switzerland and Germany, acting as a messenger between Beck and Canaris and certain individuals in Switzerland. When the Gestapo began to watch him, he turned his job over to another conspirator. He lived to tell the story of the bomb plot.

There had been many attempts to kill Hitler and other key Nazis. All of them had failed. By July, 1944, the leaders of the resistance movement felt they must succeed in their gruesome task soon, for the Russians were advancing westward with great rapidity and might soon be overrunning the country. Therefore, on the 11th of July, Colonel von Stauffenberg volunteered to plant the bomb. He had already received orders to attend a military conference at Obersalzburg. He decided that this would be a good chance to kill Hitler. He carried a delayed-action bomb in his brief case, one of a type scavenged from the enemy. The English had dropped delayed-action bombs on Germany and France, many of which had been recovered by the German military.

When Himmler, the other Nazi leader whom the conservatives most wanted to kill along with Hitler, failed to put in an appearance at the Obersalzburg meeting, von Stauffenberg decided to postpone his dangerous mission. The next time he was summoned to a military conference, scheduled for July 15 in East Prussia, he once again stowed the bomb in his brief case. Unfortunately, though Hitler and Himmler were both on hand for the conference, they were seldom together. When Hitler left early, von Stauffenberg had to give up a second time.

The next opportunity for killing Hitler was at a conference scheduled for the 20th of July, again in East Prussia. This time it was decided to kill Hitler in any event without necessarily waiting for Himmler.

The room in which Hitler and the others gathered on the 20th was above ground and was constructed of concrete and wood. This meant the bomb would not have as strong a concussion effect as it would have had in an underground, completely concrete bunker. But von Stauffenberg had decided to take his chances. He sat next to Hitler and he made his official report concerning troop replacements, as prepared in the Headquarters of Home Forces in Berlin. The status of replacements had become increasingly important as both the Eastern and Western Front situations progressively deteriorated. Von Stauffenberg was invariably required to inform Hitler and his senior staff officers concerning Home Forces dispositions, strengths, and combat training status. Not only was he present in a perfectly legitimate capacity, but his reports were eagerly awaited by the conferees.

When he had completed his report, von Stauffenberg got permission to leave. It was a few minutes after one o'clock in the afternoon. Just before departing he triggered the bomb, which was well concealed in the brief case. He then casually placed the brief case against the leg of the table close to Hitler. Saluting smartly, he took his leave, confident and relieved. He could not know that Hitler would leave his chair and cross the room to examine a war map. A few minutes elapsed which to von Stauffenberg seemed an eternity and then the bomb went off with a terrific explosive effect. The pressure of the explosion pushed through the more vulnerable wooden sections of the room. Several of the conferees were tossed through gaps in the walls. Four were killed outright, including the Fuehrer's aide, General Schmundt; Colonel Brandt; Colonel General Korten of the Air Force General Staff; and Herr Berger, a secretary. The rest of the conferees suffered varying degrees of injury.

Hitler himself was only superficially hurt. Von Stauffenberg, who lurked about to make sure of the explosion, went quickly to his waiting plane at the nearby airstrip. He was certain that nobody could have survived the concussion. Satisfied that Hitler had been killed, von Stauffenberg immediately put in a call for Beck in Berlin. Once back in the capital, he repeated confidently that Hitler was dead.

The plan called VALKYRIE for taking over the government was immediately set in motion. General Beck, who was the acknowledged leader, phoned the chief commanders in the field. He ordered German forces to fall back from the Baltic territories into East Prussia. Then he called the principal conspiracy representative in Paris, General Stuelpnagel, to say that Hitler's death was still not fully confirmed. He added, "Whatever happens the die is cast, we can do nothing else but go ahead." Stuelpnagel reassured him by saying, "We'll go ahead, I'll see to that."

This was the last time Beck and Stuelpnagel were to talk together. An unskilled conspirator, Beck tried by long distance to persuade Field Marshal von Kluge in France to throw in with the rebels. Another conspirator, General Olbricht, went to the headquarters of General Fromm, Commander of the Home Forces, to tell Fromm that Hitler was dead. Fromm's answer was to pick up the phone and ask for Field Marshal Keitel at Field Headquarters in East Prussia. When Keitel came to the phone, Fromm said that he understood Hitler had been killed. Keitel replied that Hitler was very much alive. He had been hurt, but the injury wasn't serious.

At this point, Fromm hung up. Turning to General Olbricht, he refused to signal VALKYRIE, the password that was to have set the anti-Nazi rebellion in full swing.

While all this was going on, Count von Stauffenberg was on his way to the War Ministry Building. He joined General Olbricht in Fromm's office to "confirm" Hitler's death. Fromm's response was to shout, "This is treason!" He was tremendously angered when he discovered that the code word VALKYRIE had been broadcast without his authorization. When von Stauffenberg said that he himself had placed the bomb and that nobody in the room could still be alive, Fromm promptly placed von Stauffenberg under close arrest.

When Hitler's narrow escape was unmistakably confirmed, the whole plot collapsed. To prove his miraculous survival, Hitler broadcast to the people, ranting in high-pitched, crackling staccato about a "mad clique of generals, contemptible rats who sought to betray the Fatherland, [who] will be mercilessly exterminated. My life has been spared—proof given by Providence that I must carry on as your *Fuehrer*." This news spread through the War Ministry, nerve center of the conspiracy. Many of the rebels wavered, then deserted.

When Fromm, as Commanding General of the Home Forces, realized that Hitler was definitely alive, he instituted official court-martial proceedings against the generals involved in the plot. A court-martial was quickly convened and the evidence reviewed. Death sentences were pronounced summarily. Fromm ordered them to turn over their pistols. Beck refused. He pulled out his gun and tried twice to shoot himself. The second shot made him unconscious, but it failed to kill him.

Fromm ordered Olbricht, von Stauffenberg, and several others to be executed in the courtyard. When Beck lingered on, Fromm had him mercifully killed. Fromm had been half in the conspiracy and half out, and his flop-over in the moment of crisis was a devastating blow to Beck and von Stauffenberg. He did not save himself by his double-dealing, however, for Hitler had him killed in March, 1945, for his failure to warn the Nazis sooner about the plot.

With his growing conviction that practically everyone was conspiring to misinform or even kill him, Hitler naturally could not believe the reports that the Allies had concentrated sufficient strength to invade France. On the date of the Channel crossing, June 6, 1944, Field Marshal Erwin Rommel had secretly left his command post to be with his wife on her birthday. General Hans Speidel, another very able officer and Chief of Staff to Rommel, tried unsuccessfully to reach his chief and inform him of the invasion. He also sent a report through to Hitler's headquarters. Hitler had given instructions that his sleep should not be disturbed, so nobody dared wake him up. As for General Alfred Jodl, Hitler's chief strategist, he too was left undisturbed at that early hour; hence the news of the Allied landing did not reach Jodl until about 9 o'clock. Jodl waited for still another hour before he passed the news on to General Keitel. Both men were hesitant even then about waking the Fuehrer. So it was not until the usual meeting of the staff around noon that Hitler received the news of our landing in Normandy. By that time the Allied lodgment was beginning to take shape, with several American and British divisions fighting savagely as they advanced inland followed by tons of equipment, moving ashore close behind the troops.

It so happened that the failure to inform Hitler automatically immobilized an armored corps which might have been effective in swift counterattack against the first landings on the Normandy beaches. Hitler had stipulated that this armored corps was to be employed only on his specific authority. Since this could not be obtained while he slept during the night and early morning of the Allies' D Day, the armored corps might just as well not have existed.

By the time Hitler had been alerted to what was going on, the Allies had enough heavy close-support weapons ashore to cope with any Nazi counterattacks by infantry or armor. When Hitler's special corps was thrown in against the Allied bridgehead, it was much too late. The support of OVERLORD by the Allied Air Force was devastating and in my judgment decisive. Hitler was completely deceived about the location of the main effort of the invasion. He was certain that the main Allied landings would come far to the east, but this time his strategic intuition had been fatally debunked. An Allied diversion in the Calais area had fooled him and even some of his top military advisers. Many hours had passed before the German generals were able to convince Hitler that the major invasion effort was along the coast of Normandy.

Hitler's mistakes, both strategic and tactical, were compounded by the misadventures of his fellow dictator, Mussolini. Flushed with his "great" victory over France, the Duce had launched an attack against Albania and Greece without asking any by-your-leave from Berlin. He also pushed forward in Africa at a time when the British Navy controlled the Mediterranean. In both Greece and North Africa, Mussolini was confronted with an imminent fiasco. To bail his Italian partner out, Hitler had to send help. This frittered away several German divisions which were sorely needed for employment against the Allied invasion in the west and against the Russians along the Eastern Front.

In the Far East, Hitler's other partner, Japan, blundered badly by stirring up a caldron in the Pacific involving the United States instead of launching an attack against the Maritime Provinces of the Soviet Union. Instead of choosing to bring America into the war as she did, Japan should have attacked Vladivostok, the key to eastern Siberia. This would have accomplished many purposes. The Japanese Navy would have prevented the Russians from receiving Lend-Lease supplies from the U.S. via Vladivostok. The attack would have pinned down large numbers of Russian troops. Most important of all, it would have caused the Soviet Union to fight a two-front war and thus would have brought relief to Japan's ally, Germany, at a critical time. Stalin would not have been able to transfer his legion of Siberians to the Moscow front. Without the reinforcements from Siberia, Moscow would in all probability have fallen. I feel confident that the Russians would never have defeated the Germans at Stalingrad if the Japanese had moved again.ɔt the Russian Maritime Provinces. If the Germans had been successful in taking Stalingrad and capturing the Caucasus they would have been able to carry on the war for a long time. The tempo of U.S. involvement in the war might have been slowed to a point where the Axis could have achieved at least a stalemate.

Because of the many Axis mistakes, Hitler should and would have gone to his doom much earlier had it not been for the compensating Allied errors. In avoiding a showdown with the United States through 1940 and 1941, Hitler did show some wisdom but no diplomatic skill. However, the Japanese negated all this in a single hour at Pearl Harbor.

I have already indicated my belief that the whole Mediterranean strategy of the Allies was unfortunate and unnecessary, in that time, effort, and resources were consumed to such a degree as to render timely decisive blows infeasible if not impossible. The mistake grew progressively worse as TORCH and HUSKY were succeeded by the campaign against Italy. We took great risks in delaying our decisive attack against Fortress Europe, for if the Germans had perfected their ultra-destructive V-2 rocket a little sooner they might have reduced Southern England to smoldering ruins and made our invasion preparations a shambles.

After the invasion of the European Continent in June of 1944, all went reasonably well from a military standpoint. Eisenhower exercised tact and great judgment in creating a team which had strongly conflicting national interests but which was united around the one idea of defeating the Germans. Aside from the objective of "victory at all costs," the nations understandably had different ideas about postwar Europe, each inspired by selfish interests, each determined to get something at the expense of the vanquished. The Communists, more than anyone else, were well prepared for postwar looting and exploiting and subjugating of the conquered peoples. The United States had the most naïve concept of its postwar objectives and responsibilities.

I am not suggesting that we should have sought territorial reward or demanded crippling reparations. However, we had made tremendous sacrifices in lives and treasure and certainly should have had some constructive war aims other than crushing our enemies militarily. As I interpreted the hopes and prayers of millions of Americans, it was my own hope that our leaders would insist upon the following postwar conditions or stipulations: All peoples will be afforded the opportunity of worshiping God in an atmosphere of peace with honor; of exchanging their goods and receiving commensurate reward for their energy, talents, and ingenuity; of determining how and by whom they would be governed. Such goals are not nebulous. They are based on commonly accepted human values, responsibilities, and rights which were recognized in the Atlantic Charter. It was simply a question of simultaneously excluding Fascism, communism, and any other form of tyranny throughout Europe.

In the Far East the Americans and the Japanese engaged in a competition of blunders. Our major blunders were political. If we thoroughly believed in the policy of balancing the power in Asia, or in the time-honored policy which went by the name of the Open Door, we should never have permitted Nationalist China to be weakened to the point of falling like a ripe peach into the Soviet gullet. To keep Japan out of Manchuria, we simply traded off that part of the world to Stalin.

The original emergence of Japan into the role of an industrial, predatory nation was due to our own megalomania in trying to make the world over. In the mid-nineteenth century the Japanese were reluctantly pushed by Commodore Perry into admitting Westerners into their closed feudal preserves. Unable to isolate themselves any longer, the Japanese imitated a pattern of trade familiar to the Occidental world. However, they retained rigidly the trappings, the feudalistic notions, and customs of their fathers. They were fanatic in their patriotism, and the shoguns headed by the Emperor were not only temporal rulers but also spiritual leaders.

Very quickly the Japanese learned the more mercurial aspects of international trade. Much like the British, they expanded their industries and sought remote sources of raw materials and markets for their processed goods. As success met their aggressive and energetic efforts, they offered increased competition to the Western powers, particularly in the trade with Oriental countries. They proved to be the most efficient and dynamic peoples in the Far East, an area where half the world's population is to be found. There were abundant undeveloped resources in the area, particularly in Manchuria, China, and the Indies. The most important prize was Manchuria, which contained rich supplies of coal and some iron ore as well as vast expanses fit for Temperate Zone agriculture. The exploitation of Manchuria became Japan's Number One objective, for with coal and iron the Japanese felt they could develop into the strongest military and political power in the Far East.

In the 1930's, the Japanese succeeded in establishing undisputed control over Manchuria. This fact signalized the failure of the balance-of-power strategy of the British, French, and Americans; it was also a defeat for Russia, which from the time of the Czars had looked upon Manchuria as its own natural prey.

Roosevelt's strategy was to restore the balance in the Far East by accepting Kuomintang China as a potential democracy and a future Great Power. But he never faced the problems of providing Chiang Kai-shek with the stability and strength needed to realize the potentials: some officials in the lower echelons of the State Department saw to that. Furthermore, in concentrating too long on the

defeat of Germany, we let a friendly China become drastically en-
feebled. And after the war, as we have seen, we did nothing to help
the Chinese Nationalists recoup their strength and retain their control of the vital resources of Manchuria. So the Czars' historic strategy for Asia ultimately won, after all. The Communists simply
moved in.

The Japanese, I am sure, did not feel that they could defeat
America militarily. The military operations that they conducted during the course of the war would indicate that they hoped to create
a stand-off or stalemate situation by controlling mutually supporting
island bases extending from Sakhalin south to New Guinea, and
through the Marshall and Caroline Islands, meanwhile holding the
Malay, French Indo-China, and China seaboard. The control of this
vast area would insure access to raw materials and markets for a
rapidly increasing population and its concomitant, an expanded
economy. They unquestionably felt that the United States would
be at a marked disadvantage in attempting to wrest that area from
them except at prohibitive costs, because of the great distances involved. Eventually, so they must have thought, a negotiated peace
would leave them in possession of their strongly consolidated positions on the mainland of Asia and the interlocking island bases offshore.

The Japanese misjudged the American naval potential and our
logistical ingenuity, which rapidly surmounted the difficulties usually inherent in long lines of communication. They also misjudged
our industrial capacity to build ships and to replace the obsolescent
battlewagons lost at Pearl Harbor. As the war progressed and the
Americans became more convinced that the British had no intention
of launching the decisive effort against the Axis powers in Europe,
our operations in the Pacific were stepped up. The Japanese suffered tremendous losses in shipping, a vital necessity of an island
empire. Wisely the American strategy in the Pacific was designed
to strike at the heartland of Japan, particularly the island of Honshu
where great industries were concentrated. By turning our submarines loose and giving MacArthur and Nimitz their heads, Japan's
links with the oil regions of the Indies were snapped. The homeland
was thus bereft of its industrial sinews, and the Japanese war machine ground to a halt. The atomic bomb produced the *coup de
grâce* after the war had been won by the U.S.

It was a mistake ever to visualize a landing in force against the Japanese main islands. Such an attack would have cost us a tremendous number of lives and was not necessary. The Japanese lived by the sea, and once their Navy, shipping, and Air Force were destroyed it was certain that they could be starved into surrender. MacArthur and Nimitz could have maintained a tight blockade around the islands *ad infinitum*. Fortunately the war ended before OLYMPIC, the actual invasion of Japan, was ever mounted.

Our most costly strategic mistake in the Far East was our insistence that the Soviet Union enter the war against the Japanese. Early in 1945 intelligence reports and evaluation of the photographs made of aerial attacks on Japanese cities proved that the end in East Asia was a matter of weeks. The Mikado's war-making potential was rapidly deteriorating, and our air sweeps across the Japanese islands were wiping out the industrial and communications centers. It was just a matter of letting the ripe fruit fall, yet we connived and finagled to induce the Soviet Union to join us for the final victory. Eventually Stalin got it cheap; for four days only, Russia fought the Japanese, who were then already contemplating the atomized ruins of Hiroshima. Victory over Japan had actually been achieved much earlier when MacArthur and Nimitz converged in the Philippines to cut Japanese sea contact with the south. By the spring of 1945 most of Japan's shipping had been sunk, her Navy had been all but totally destroyed, and her Air Force had been driven from the skies. The Russians moved into Manchuria against merely token resistance by retreating Japanese forces.

In connection with the decisions at Yalta, I felt that it was right at the time to ask the Russians to fight the Japanese. Earlier in the year, on a visit to the States, I had said as much. Events proved me entirely wrong. I was, however, wholly unaware of the destruction of Japanese industries and shipping by our Air Force and Navy. Our intelligence reports should have told us not to use the atom bomb and not to give Russia an opportunity to enter the struggle. We learned by intercepts of code messages that the Japanese Emperor was instructing his Ambassador in Moscow to ask the Soviet to act as a mediator with the Americans in order to obtain an armistice. This was a month or more before the actual surrender in August. All through the war, our ability to break any Japanese code enabled us to listen in on what the Japanese were saying to their diplomats.

Actually, we knew early in 1945 that they were ready to quit provided we didn't insist on unconditional surrender.

Although not too much has been made of our code-breaking activities, we knew enough about Japanese intentions in November of 1941 to have forestalled any attack upon us, anywhere. It is not too fantastic to suppose that we might even have stopped the war before it started. Every individual who worked successfully on the codes of our enemies should be recognized as having made just as important a contribution to our victory as any front-line soldier. The Code Room was a test of perseverance demanding a high order of intelligence and dedication to duty.

When, on December 6, our intercepts told us that the Japanese were going to strike somewhere the very next day, whether in the Central Pacific or to the south in the Philippines and Dutch East Indies, the President of the United States, as Commander in Chief of our military forces and as the responsible leader of 135,000,000 people, could have gone on the radio and broadcast to the wide world that he had irrefutable evidence of an immediate Japanese intention to strike. This would have alerted everybody from Singapore to Pearl Harbor. Even though inadequate in some cases to defend effectively, nevertheless our forces would have been able to take a toll which would have blunted the Japanese attack. In Hawaii, the capital ships might have been moved out of the congested harbor to sea, where Admiral Kimmel had at least had the foresight to keep the far more vital aircraft carriers. Furthermore, our carrier task force in the mid-Pacific might have attacked the Japanese task force when its planes were aloft. There are many possibilities which would have given our men at least a fighting chance.

Captain L. F. Safford, U.S. Navy, in charge of the Communications Security Section of Naval Communications in Washington just prior to Pearl Harbor, testified before the Admiral Hart Board that "On December 4, 1941, we received definite information from two independent sources that Japan would attack the United States and Britain but would maintain peace with Russia." At 9:00 P.M. Washington time, December 6, 1941, we received positive information that Japan would declare war against the United States at a time to be specified thereafter. This information, so Safford testified, was positive and unmistakable and was made available to Military

Intelligence virtually at the moment of its decoding. Finally, at 10:15 A.M. Washington time, December 7, 1941, we received positive information from the Signal Intelligence Service, War Department, that the Japanese declaration of war would be presented to the Secretary of State at 1:00 P.M. Washington time that date; when it was 1:00 P.M. in Washington it would be daybreak in Hawaii and approximately midnight in the Philippines, which indicated a surprise air raid on Pearl Harbor in about three hours. According to Safford, Lieutenant Kramer of the Navy appended a note to this effect to the paper sent over from Secret Intelligence Service before presenting it to the Secretary of the Navy.

President Roosevelt had ample time to broadcast a warning. Conjecturally, such a warning might even have caused the Japanese to call off their surprise attack. In any event, we would not have permitted 3,500 Americans to die at Hawaii without an opportunity to fight back.

The argument has been made that we could not afford to let the Japanese know we had broken their code. But this argument against a Presidential warning does not hold water. It was not a mere matter of having broken a specific code; what we had done was to devise a machine which could break *any* code provided it was fed the right combinations by our extremely able and gifted cryptographers. The Japanese kept changing their codes throughout the war anyway. And we kept breaking them almost as a matter of routine.

In warning the world against a Pearl Harbor, President Roosevelt need never have given away the *methodological* procedure of our code-breaking. That was the vital secret. Without even a bare risk of the secret's disclosure, the war might have been called off by a bewildered Tokyo before it had ever begun.

The final and most egregious error of all was our failure to judge the postwar intentions of our ally, the Soviet Union. Franklin Roosevelt declared, on March 8, 1944, "I think the Russians are perfectly friendly. They aren't trying to gobble up all the rest of Europe. They haven't got any ideas of conquest. These fears that have been expressed by a lot of people here that the Russians are going to try and dominate Europe, I personally don't think there is anything in it." Before his death, approximately a year later, Roosevelt had presumably become completely aware of Stalin's diabolical aims. But his successors failed to see the handwriting on the wall in time. There were men, government officials, and private citizens, who likewise understood the full implications of communism—men like James Forrestal, Bill Bullitt, and Loy Henderson. Forrestal was actually hounded into suicide as a reward for his prescience and honesty. Throughout the war he had been an inspiring leader, a fine administrator who imbued his subordinates with enthusiasm for the job. When he became Secretary of Defense, he consciously made an effort to be objective in adjudicating differences among the three armed services.

Forrestal was fearless in assuming positions that were unpopular with the press and with certain elements in government. He was an indefatigable worker who spent long hours on the job, never sparing himself. He had the courage of his convictions and would not hesitate to speak up if he felt that American interests or principles were being violated. One such example was the partitioning of Palestine. He felt that it would be a mistake to alienate the Arab world, and for saying this he was most unfairly accused of being anti-Semitic. He was roundly criticized by correspondents of leading newspapers, some of the criticism amounting to reflections upon his personal honor and courage. One canard circulated in Washington was that he hid in a closet while Mrs. Forrestal was routing an intruder from their Georgetown home. Forrestal was sacrificed by Truman in order to enable the Democratic Party to pay a political debt to Louis Johnson, who became Secretary of Defense. Those of us associated with Forrestal in the Pentagon felt that this was a great injustice to a loyal and efficient public servant, and we were disappointed that the change was made at such a critical time when the Air Force had just recently been given its autonomy.

Inasmuch as we set things up for the Communists after the war, it is extremely lucky that Stalin made continuing mistakes on his own. The biggest mistake the Russians made after World War II was in not exploiting the good will they enjoyed in our country. In pursuance of their revolutionary ends they should have continued to deceive us by a show of false friendliness. If they had taken Marshall Plan money for themselves they might have rehabilitated their country far more quickly. Meanwhile we would have permitted them to infiltrate everywhere. Fortunately, they chose deliberately to alienate us. If we have emerged in the slightest bit from our former incredible state of naïveté, the Soviets have only themselves to blame.

CHAPTER XXVIII

"Statesman" Politician:
I fled him down the nights and down the days;
I fled him, down the arches of the years;
I fled him, down the labyrinthine ways
Of my own mind — -Francis Thompson

CONCLUSION

MANY MOTIVES inspire the writing of books, of which, as stated in
Ecclesiastes, there is no end. I was impelled both by the desire to
make some slight contribution to historical knowledge and by the
hope that my experience and reflections may contribute to a better
understanding of the present and the formulation of a viable strategy for the future. As Bismarck, the Iron Chancellor, wisely remarked: "Fools learn by experience; the wise man learns by the
experience of others."

I have endeavored to be objective, although I realize that, for
good or ill, one's views are influenced by environment, prejudices,

predilections, and hopes. As an American, my opinions are naturally colored by my desire to preserve and promote the interests of my own country and people. I have tried to understand, and to refrain from condemning, the motives and actions of the leaders and people of other nations, who have as much right as we to pursue national objectives. I get angry only when either our allies or our enemies deny America the same rights of self-preservation and self-interest.

Some readers may think that I am unduly critical of President Roosevelt; Prime Minister Churchill or the British in general; General George Marshall; or my predecessor in China, General Stilwell. I have never been and am not now moved by any personal animus or prejudices toward any of the individuals who happened to be in key positions of responsibility in America, England, China or anywhere else when the future of the world was being decided during and after the Second World War. I recognize that the individuals whom I have criticized, or with whom I have differed, were not always individually responsible for the policies and plans which led us to "snatch defeat out of the jaws of victory." Circumstances had enshrouded them in a mantle of authority which was beyond their capabilities, or they lacked sufficient knowledge and wisdom to meet their responsibilities. Some may have been compelled out of a sense of duty to take actions which they did not approve or concerning which they had grave doubts. Others again may have been intoxicated by their own propaganda or influenced by a fancied need to win approval by any and every means in order to continue in power. Whatever their motives, they cannot be absolved from responsibility for the decisions they made in the fateful war and postwar years.

Nowhere in this book have I imputed sinister motives to either the British or Americans with whom I disagreed. But it was difficult at times to understand the actions of some of the individuals whose attitudes seemed incomprehensible, since they were intelligent and experienced and had access to as much or more information as those of us who realized that communism constituted at least as great a menace to the free world as Nazism, Fascism, or Japanese militarism.

I have seen men march forward in battle. I have watched them die—their lifeless forms, sometimes terribly mangled, lying grotesquely about the battlefield. The bodies of enemy soldiers were intermingled with those of our own in areas that were strongly disputed as the tide of battle surged back and forth. These men had not hated each other. By accident of birth they lived in countries at war, all protesting their righteous cause, whose leaders had aroused hate and inspired others to kill and destroy. In each country men had put their faith in leaders who had refused or been unable to settle international affairs by peaceful and civilized means. The men on both sides who fought and bled and died on countless battlefields in both World Wars believed that their endurance and sacrifice would protect those near and dear to them and insure enduring and just conditions of peace. Yet even the victors found that their efforts had availed little or nothing, either in enhancing their security or establishing a better world order.

Man's nature being a compound of good and evil, even his best aspirations too often serve, against his will, to increase the power and advance the selfish designs of unscrupulous leaders. It may, therefore, be too much to hope that complete harmony and peace will ever be established in this world. The crusades and humanitarian endeavors in which Americans can justly claim to have taken the lead in good faith have twice in our generation been perverted. After setting out once more to destroy tyrants and increase the area of freedom and opportunity everywhere in the world, we found that we had succeeded only in extending the area controlled by totalitarian tyranny and had ourselves enhanced the power of the Communists, who now constitute a greater menace to our freedom and security than the enemy we vanquished.

During World War II, Allied leaders too often whipped up hatred and fear, causing us to forget that the people of enemy nations were as much the victims of circumstances as ourselves. The truly liberal American philosopher, John Dewey, believed that views and opinions are shaped by experience, associations, and knowledge. Today, however, we live in an age of propaganda. It would seem that our views and opinions are determined mainly by headlines, radio, and TV. The pace of modern living has almost eliminated dispassionate, reasoned deliberation or quiet contemplation of the issues involved. Articulate orators and sensational reporting too often shape our thinking and determine our course of action.

One often hears individuals state that they want good government; but many seem primarily concerned with security, material rewards, power, prestige, recreation, and entertainment rather than with their responsibilities as citizens. They are indifferent to the fact that the measure of success in a country, wherein people can determine how and by whom they will be governed, will be in proportion to their own active participation. A government will not be responsive to the will of the people if those in positions of responsibility have no indication of such will. We in America may be gradually losing by default our wonderful heritage. History may record that we reached our peak at the turn of the century and are now experiencing a decline in the pattern so poignantly recorded by Gibbon in *The History of the Decline and Fall of the Roman Empire*.

The foregoing remarks concern essentially individuals, and intentionally so, because nations are, after all, made up of individuals. Government policies and actions in a free society find their genesis in the hearts and minds of the governed. Perhaps the outstanding lesson I learned in my wartime experience was that Americans must discipline their emotions when dealing with foreign affairs. In Washington's "Farewell Address" he admonished our people to avoid *entangling* alliances. This sage counsel is even more pertinent today. It should be noted, however, that he did not warn against all alliances but only against *entangling* alliances.

Our most conspicuous lack in our war and postwar policies and actions was the absence of realistic and worthy national aims. Therefore, as I have again and again pointed out in this book, our war effort, involving over a million casualties and billions in treasure, achieved results wholly incommensurate with our sacrifices. In peacetime, or in the present era of cold war, it is equally important that we should know what we are *for* as well as what we are *against*. We should have a viable strategy for attaining our objectives instead of simply reacting opportunistically to Communist pressures and other challenges in the foreign field.

I am not sure that our nation's organization for the formulation of foreign policies and Grand Strategy is adequate in this complex world. The present set-up might have been satisfactory before international relations became so important a factor in our national life. But today the determination and enunciation of sound international policies and actions are as important to the survival of our American heritage as the interpretation and adjudication of laws by the United States Supreme Court. The members of the

Supreme Court are appointed for life. They are carefully selected, ostensibly for character, knowledge, and practice of jurisprudence. Would it not be wise to create a foreign policy group, presided over by the Vice President, with the continuing responsibility of formulating national aims and foreign policies for the consideration of the Chief Executive and the members of Congress? Such a foreign policy group, or Grand Strategy Board, would be comprised of carefully selected members representing collective knowledge and experience in the political, economic, psychological, and military fields. In order that they could recommend appropriate aims and sound courses of action in each country—friendly, neutral, or hostile—they would have access to all information available to the government as provided by the Central Intelligence Agency and other intelligence sources so that their determinations would not be made in a vacuum but would be attuned to developments in all parts of the world. To give continuity and to insure non-partisan evaluations, members of the foreign policy group, or Grand Strategy Board, should be appointed for life. The important tasks visualized for this group are today nominally performed by the National Security Council (the President, Secretary of State, Secretary of Defense, and Director of CIA). However, these individuals are weighed down with day-by-day administrative and perfunctory distractions which preclude careful study, analysis, deliberation, and evaluation.

We Americans, who are citizens of the most fortunate and powerful country on the globe, must search our hearts and minds to decide what we want and compel our government to pursue a consistent foreign policy. What kind of conditions do we want to create or maintain in the world? We know that we want an honorable peace, liberty, justice, and dignity for all peoples. We want to help people—all people—to enjoy opportunities to improve their lot, to receive commensurate reward for their talents, energy, and work. We want everyone to know the challenge and joys of an "open society" with its concomitants: freedom of worship, freedom of expression, and freedom to choose leaders and form of government. We do not wish to meddle in the affairs of other peoples or nations nor do we covet their lands and resources. We stand ready at all times to aid others in distress. We should be prepared to co-operate economically, militarily, scientifically, and culturally with others having compatible aims, but only on a reciprocal basis.

We have the responsibility of insuring that all other peoples and nations clearly understand America's motives and aims, but this is impossible unless we ourselves know what they are and approve them. Our sincerity of purpose can best be demonstrated by policies and actions in social, political, diplomatic, and commercial contacts which refute the vicious propaganda of those who would destroy freedom and opportunity everywhere in the world. Today the greatest threat to the realization of our aims is communism. We must check and destroy this world-wide conspiracy which is designed to destroy us, and we shall never succeed in doing so if we dare not take risks. We must have the courage to fight when there is no other way out.

We took a stand at the time of the Berlin airlift when the Communists imposed a blockade on that city. Again, in Korea, President Truman courageously adopted a firm policy of resistance to Communist aggression, but only after Secretary of State Dean Acheson had publicly washed his hands of American concern over the fate of both Korea and China. And once in the war against the Communists in Korea, the United States, under both Democratic and Republican administrations, was too fearful of Soviet intervention to go all-out to win. In 1956 we refused to support the Freedom Fighters of Hungary, although a year and a half later we intervened in the Middle East following a popular revolution in Iraq. We were told that that revolution was Communist-inspired and supported; a week or so later we extended diplomatic recognition.

Foreign aid in the form of money, materials, and technical assistance can help implement policy but it must be applied judiciously. In other words, we should not give aid directly to governments and thus create bureaucracies in competition with local private enterprise. It would be far better to give selective aid with a view to encouraging voluntary economic development.

Like my admired and dear friend, the late Robert A. Taft, I have been incorrectly described as an isolationist. In fact, like the great Senator from Ohio, I believe in friendly co-operation with other nations but am opposed to meddling in their affairs or becoming involved in internecine struggles. Taft's program, as I interpreted it while I was National Chairman of the Citizens for Taft Committee in 1952, would have provided aid to other nations having objectives compatible with our own. It was based on realistic reciprocal arrangements. We recognized that outright charity undermines the moral fiber of individuals as well as nations.

Taft is now dead, but the high esteem of his colleagues in the Senate on both sides of the aisle was revealed when he was chosen *by them* as a symbol of the finest traditions of American public life and was paid the richly deserved tribute of being one of the outstanding senators in our history.

There always have been and will continue to be struggles between individuals and nations for the attainment of security or power; for territory, wealth, raw materials, and markets. National aims must be flexible to facilitate adjustments to inescapable or desirable changes in the world. Compromises are necessary, but we should be inflexible in so far as integrity and sincerity of purpose are concerned.

I have repeatedly decried the fact that the Western Allies made great sacrifice and supreme effort in two world wars to win a crushing military victory and in the process tragically lost the peace. The most important lesson that I have learned in the field of Grand Strategy is clearly etched in my mind, namely, that greater responsibilities and challenges for the victors are always present after the military victory than prior to or during the actual period of combat. The end of a war is not, never has been, and never will be the end of the power struggle.

The Western Allies destroyed the time-honored "balance of power" in Europe and in Asia in World War II. We Americans certainly should have recognized the implications, for in formulating the Constitution, our wise founding fathers established "checks and balances" to preclude usurpation of power by any individual or by any echelon of government. The great British Prime Ministers Pitt, Palmerston, and Disraeli in peace or in war understood the dire necessity of policies designed to maintain neutralizing power alignments. Actually, in 1939 I thought that the British and French decided to fight Hitler primarily to preserve the "balance of power" in Europe.

After World War I, the League of Nations and after World War II, the United Nations Organization were formed, each to insure concerted international effort to preserve peace. The world is not yet ready psychologically for a world state, or federation. People everywhere cling tenaciously to their sovereignty as epitomized by language, customs, traditions, and territory. The alternative then would appear to be regional (geographical) organizations comprising nations having compatible objectives in the political, economic, and cultural fields. Participating nations in such regional organizations would understandably retain their separate identities but would make realistic and proportionate contribution toward the attainment of common objectives. Gradually, as the spirit of solidarity, which has its genesis in common interests, spreads, mankind may one day attain that goal of a world state dedicated to and realistically capable of promoting equity and opportunity for all, regardless of race, color, creed, or social status. The cohesive element under such conditions would unquestionably be the recognition and application of spiritual forces devoid of hypocrisy and bigotry.

Different peoples or nations have different aims and objectives and are swayed by differing compulsions. Yet in my travels to various parts of the world I have observed that the paramount desire of most people is to be let alone and to live in peace. They seek only opportunities to improve their lot and to enjoy freedom in developing their talents and realizing their interests. In all the great religions of the world one can find various expressions of the golden rule: "Do unto others as you would have them do unto you."

> New occasions teach new duties,
> Time makes ancient good uncouth;
> They must upward still and onward
> Who would keep abreast of truth.
>
> —JAMES RUSSELL LOWELL

APPENDIX I

SALE OF WAR SURPLUSES IN CHINA

1. On 29 November 1945, American Minister Walter S. Robertson and the Commanding General, China Theater, entered into an agreement with the Chinese Government whereby the Chinese purchased certain fixed installations and items of supply, material and equipment. This property was located generally west of the 110° meridian.

2. Estimated depreciated value of United States property was U. S. $67,371,000 and C. N. $5,160,000,000. The Chinese Government agreed to pay the U. S. $25,000,000 and C. N. $5,160,000,000, increased or decreased slightly to conform to the actual depreciated value of the material actually transferred.

3. The actual depreciated value was reported to the U. S. $62,773,442 and C. N. $9,278,114,670 so that the Chinese Government should pay U. S. $23,293,906 and C. N. $9,278,114,670.

4. The material sold included approximately:

    a. 37,000 tons of ground type supplies and equipment

    b. 22,000 tons of air type supplies and equipment

    c. 55 aircraft

    d. Fixed installations worth U. S. $4,000 and C. N. $980,000,000

5. A down payment of U. S. $5,000,000 and cancellation of the Yuan debt was covered in the Chinese Bulk Sale of 30 August 1946. The balance was to be collected by the Treasury Department.

APPENDIX II

MEMORANDUM FOR COLONEL HANDY:

Subject: Comments Pertaining to the British Chiefs of Staff Review General Strategy.

The Strategic estimate submitted by the Chiefs of the British Air, Ground and Sea forces definitely implies a realization on their part that defeat by Germany is inevitable and the disintegration of the British Empire is highly probable, *unless the United States becomes an active belligerent within a very short period of time.* Assuming full collaboration (military and economic) by the United States, the British chieftains reveal their basic strategic plan as follows:

1. Concentration of their own war effort, to ensure the continuity of the United Kingdom.

2. Dependence upon the United States, not only to assist them in that task, but also to undertake the security and preservation of the far-flung British Empire.

Prior to the war, there were evidences that the British Commonwealth of nations had begun to disintegrate. In India, the natives were clamoring for independence and in South Africa, similar defections were present. Promises by the Home government for increased autonomy were made, but the advent of war postponed the strong representations and increasing demands for independence.

Plans made to implement national policies must be based on a careful review of available potential forces, including manpower, industry, morale, transportation and raw materials. Comparisons with the corresponding potentials of nations which may oppose them will provide sound deductions upon which to base military operations. Have the British approached their study in such manner? Many definitely relevant matters are presented but in a disconnected manner, indicating perhaps a groping for a panacea which will bring relief from their unfortunate and not entirely avoidable predicament. Now they turn to any ally out of necessity. They have even risked the consequences of an alliance with Russia, a step which every European knows has dire implications.

There are 390,000,000 people in India. Why not import some to England to perform labor thus releasing able-bodied Britishers to carry on their job of fighting. The British have always fought bravely in defense of their homes, but in the past they have employed their own navy and the fighting forces of other countries most adroitly in the fighting to create and maintain their mighty empire.

Is it not logical that if the members of the British Commonwealth are not interested in its preservation, certainly the United States should not contribute blood, bombs, and bullets for such purpose? If on the other hand, the British had the full military and economic cooperation of India, Egypt, South Africa, Canada and Australia, supported by their uniform determination to present a united front to the enemy, then the United States might well be expected, as an associate in the present war, to participate in the plans suggested.

The British indicate that the security of the United Kingdom remains the overriding consideration in their strategy. Let us too be guided by hard-headed realism as they have always been, and immediately adopt and adhere to the policy, that our own overriding consideration in all planning, remains the absolute security of the United States and its possessions. Any assistance that we may give Great Britain, *after our own security has been provided for,* should be coordinated with the war effort of the British and associates, in order to accomplish our mutual objectives.

The British indicate that they expect to win the war by creating conditions in Germany which will permit them to invade the continent with ground forces. They expect to bring about these conditions by bombing German industrial areas, military centers, lines of communication and transportation facilities. The British do not really believe this is possible of accomplishment. Their courageous and dogged defense against a numerically stronger enemy last year, is cogent proof, that a nation cannot be brought to her knees through bombardment of essential installations. The Germans employed mass air concentrations under much more favorable conditions (concentrated targets, short operation radii, ample air bases which permit converging on objective) than would be possible operating bombardment planes against Germany from British Isles Bases, (long operation radii necessary to reach critical installations; dearth of operational bases, resulting in a saturation point which will never permit an over-all air superiority, widely separated targets resulting in dispersion of means). If our own strategic concept of the world situation, particularly with reference to the European theater is sound, we too visualize the necessity for the creation in Germany of the conditions indicated, but also we are confident that additional bases must be obtained, in order to facilitate the operations involved in softening up of the foe before combined air and ground efforts can possibly be launched against him.

Meanwhile what ideas and plans do the members of the German High Command have relative to possible developments in the situation? No other nation knew the Russia war potential better than the Germans. The 100 German economists sent into Russia in 1939 to facilitate the acceleration of Russian industry were primarily military observers and secondarily economists. Events are proving that Russia was well prepared for a major military effort. This spring (1941) Germany was confronted by two important decisions:

1. Extend her control over the Mediterranean and Middle East Area and thus insure oil, and limited industrial facilities and food stuffs. The campaign, militarily, was certain of success.

2. Assume the strategic defensive in all theaters except the Russian, where an all-out effort would be made to render Russia militarily impotent in as short a time as possible.

This was the toughest assignment of the many lines of action open to Germany (with the exception of possible attempted invasion of England or South America) and Hitler was no doubt so informed. However, he has been throughout his meteoric career a heavy gambler both politically and militarily. The industry twins (coal and iron) in the Donet Basin and the Ukrainian wheat fields complement his own highly industrialized nation. The pact with Stalin had already served its real purpose, permitting Germany to conduct a one-theater operation against France. Now a strong potential foe (Russia) might be liquidated. Hitler and Stalin trust few men and definitely not each other. Finally Germany could establish many of her industries deep in central Europe, thus facilitating their protection and continuous operation. If control of the Russian area as far east as the line: White Sea—Caspian Sea could be obtained, the economic possibilities of that vast region could be quickly exploited to Germany's advantage. If Russia could be rendered militarily impotent, the powerful military forces of the Axis could be safely employed in western theaters with their flanks and rear secure. If Bolshevism could be crushed, the Nazi-dominated hegemony of Europe would be practically assured. The stakes were high. The situation (August 1941) is not sufficiently developed to determine the wisdom of the Nazi choice, but it is now apparent that Hitler is involved in the decisive campaign of his career.

When considering the British paper in its entirety, I was impressed by its defeatism. The United States Military Forces stand today in a position similar to that of the British High Command in August of 1939. Our Government like the British is making commitments which may involve us in a war for which we are definitely unprepared militarily and apparently psychologically. No one questions the motives of our leaders in their quest for international idealism. However, history and particularly the events of the past thirty years that we have personally experienced, have proven conclusively that international morality is clearly impractical at this point in the development of mankind and that each nation must look out for its own interests, regardless of international laws, moral considerations or ethical implications. As soldiers we must make certain that the country's executives and law-makers are fully and continuously informed of our limitations, to preclude active involvement in any struggle until we are militarily prepared. The army will be judged by what it accomplishes on the battlefield. Daladier and Gamelin were aware of the serious situation which confronted their country in 1938 and 1939. They took steps to alleviate the very conditions which later resulted in their repudiation and condemnation.

It is my conviction that this British Staff paper should be answered in a spirit which unmistakably conveys to them as well as to our own governmental officials the following:

1. Our admiration for the gallant stand which the British are making against the Axis Powers.

2. Our determination to assist them in every possible way (short of war) and to continue our collaboration through the agencies and in the manner mutually agreed upon by authorized and qualified representatives in Joint Conference (ABC-1).

3. Our realization that we must not become an active belligerent until we have created the means by which we can accomplish our national objectives.

A.C.W.

APPENDIX III

DEPARTMENT OF STATE
WASHINGTON
September 25, 1947

MEMORANDUM FOR MR. CONNELLY

The following letter from Secretary Marshall to the President was dictated to me this morning over the secret telephone:

"Dear Mr. President:

"I understand General Wedemeyer is presenting his report to you at noon today. It seems to me mandatory that we treat Wedemeyer's report strictly top secret and that no indication of its contents be divulged to the public. This will allow us time to review our policy in the light of the report, giving due consideration to it in balance with our policies in other parts of the world.

"If you agree, I suggest Wedemeyer be informed by you accordingly.

"If questioned by the press, you might state that a summary of the report cannot be issued until careful consideration has been given it by the various Departments of the Government concerned.

Faithfully yours,

G. C. MARSHALL."

C. H. Humelsine
Executive Secretary

APPENDIX IV

THE PARAPHRASE OF THE AUTHOR'S MESSAGE
TO THE WAR DEPARTMENT

The following is a paraphrase of a message transmitted to the War Department in two parts on November 20, 1945, from the Commanding General of the China Theater. Information copies of this cable were sent to the Supreme Commander Allied Powers in Tokyo, Commander-in-Chief of the Pacific Theater at Pearl Harbor, Commander of the U. S. Seventh Fleet, Commanding General of the Third Amphibious Corps at Tientsin, and to the Commanding General of the Chungking Liaison Group.

Part One: This message is a summary of the problems introduced by developments in China and is intended to assist in solving these problems. The message has been seen by Walter Robertson, the American Minister, and he heartily concurs.

I have intentionally withheld this evaluation of the overall situation in the China Theater until contact could be made with sources of information and until the implications of developments in China could be subjected to objective and careful analysis. The situation has been discussed with Major General Rockey, the Marine Corps Commander, and with Major General Shepherd, the Commander of a Marine Division now located at Tsingtao. These discussions were held during a visit to the Peking area. In addition, many Dutch, British, Chinese, French and other national leaders earnestly desired to talk, most especially about the present and future situation in the Provinces of North China. I have talked to numerous Nationals, including Chinese leaders (in Shanghai), and the situation has been reviewed with members of the staff of the United States China Theater, all of whom are located in Shanghai. Several conferences were held in Chungking during a five-day period with the Generalissimo, the Minister of Finance, the Minister of War, Doctor T. V. Soong, General Ho Ying Chin, with American Minister Robertson, the Ambassadors of France and Great Britain and with United States

447

liaison officers to the Chinese Government. I submit herewith, based on that background, the following information, analyses, and recommendations which may be of assistance in the formulation of future policy and in arriving at decisions on the matter of United States Forces in the China Theater.

It is my belief that Generalissimo Chiang Kai-shek sincerely desires to achieve stability in China, to unify the country, to institute democratic procedures and to implement social reforms of a wide and sweeping character. By American standards, his approach to the problems that are presented probably would be incomprehensible, inefficient and unethical, but one must consider his Oriental philosophy, and his background, experience and training as a war lord and as a politician. It is beyond the capabilities of one man to perform the task. Not only is the required organization lacking, but the Generalissimo is in need of competent assistants and advisors. He is selfless in his approach to the situation. However, surrounding him are men without scruples who are primarily interested in self-aggrandizement. Chiang is extremely loyal to those officials and war lords who in the past have supported him. As a consequence, they have been appointed to positions of responsibility in the Government even though they are incompetent and/or unscrupulous. The opportunities thus presented are exploited by these officials. In addition, worthless subordinates are appointed to lesser positions by these officials. Many of those so appointed are from the same families or in the past have connived in chicanery.

In further clarification it may be appropriate to contrast the integrity of Chinese business men and political leaders with that of Americans in positions that are similar. Whereas the politician in China seeks to enrich himself through machination and chicanery, the Chinese business man has a code of ethics that is exemplary and he usually conforms to this code. In China, it is generally acknowledged that positions in government are a normal and lucrative method to amass a great fortune. In the United States it is accepted that business men are a class that may achieve great wealth. However, the means used will not always bear close examination. On the other hand, Americans in governmental positions uniformly follow a course that is ethical, and it is in isolated cases only that great wealth is acquired through dishonesty in the processes of government or by political manipulation that is unscrupulous.

Confronting me daily are the problems created by Chinese officials of the type just indicated, officials who are constantly dealing in machinations and intrigue. A senior Chinese General, for example, has been unilaterally and surreptitiously dealing with Okamura, a Japanese General, on the use of Japanese ships that are available in Chinese waters. The

Chinese General had been given a careful explanation of why these ships had to be pooled by the Allies to achieve repatriation and rehabilitation in the Far East. This case is only one of many where persons in high office have operated surreptitiously, unilaterally, and corruptly and have made it difficult, if not impossible, to achieve coordination and effective results. These circumstances have been reported to the Generalissimo by me, but cases of a similar character are so numerous that it is very evident and understandable that he is confused and powerless to achieve a solution.

Uniformly, Southern Chinese have been appointed by the Generalissimo to key posts in the Northern Provinces—mayors, governors, and so forth. It seems apparent that he has no confidence in the Northern Chinese. The people of the North have been embittered by these appointments, and the political, economic, and military stability of North China has thus further been retarded.

Some evidence is at hand to indicate that China is determined to restrict and/or exclude foreign business interests, particularly the French, British, Russians and Dutch. Prior to the war most of the industrial establishments, utilities, and lines of communication were operated and financed by non-Chinese. At the present time there are insufficient Chinese technicians or executives to assume the responsibility for operating these facilities. Even in the areas where the forces of the Central Government are in undisputed control, stabilization of the economy is impracticable and the effort of industry is now stultified. Unless foreigners are allowed to operate with reasonable authority and initiative, the measures needed for revival will not be possible.

These observations have been pointed out very clearly to the Generalissimo. I have urged strongly that foreigners be retained to aid in economic recovery, pointing out that this seemed essential at least until China produced sufficient trained technicians and executives from among their own nationals to assume the inherent responsibilities. I have also recommended that the people be allowed to vote for the magistrates of districts and that the appointees for mayors and governors of the Northern Provinces be Northern Chinese. I have suggested, further, that consideration be given to appointing civilians to these important posts in the hope of thus eliminating the military hierarchy now so disastrously entrenched.

The Central Government of China apparently exercises some control in the area commonly referred to as South China—that is, the valley of the Yangtze and the area south of the Yangtze. With assistance from outside China, as earlier indicated, a stable economy can probably be achieved, especially if small industries can be created and efficiently operated.

In the area referred to as North China—that is, most of the area to the north of the valley of the Yangtze and extending to the Great Wall —the Chinese Communists are strongly disputing and, at the present time, effectively disputing control by the Central Government. It is my opinion that the typical Chinese in the North are in a quandary regarding the political implications of control by the Central Government as against the Chinese Communists. The Communists have brought strong propaganda pressure to bear, emphasizing the inefficiency and the corruption of the officials of the Central Government. The Communists intimidate Northern Chinese who lean toward supporting the Generalissimo.

The Generalissimo has been advised that emphasis should be given to establishing control of the Central Government in North China and to initiate promptly political and social reforms intended to eliminate official corruption and prohibitive taxes. I have repeated the suggestion that the services of technicians and executives—foreigners who had operated in the area before the Japanese occupation—should be retained for at least the period of China's political and economic growth to maturity.

A complex situation has developed with reference to Manchuria. The economic and psychological importance of Manchuria to China is recognized by the Generalissimo as well as by both the Chinese Communists and the Soviets. That area was quickly overrun by the military forces of the Soviet Union in August. These forces reportedly indulged in looting, pilferage and rape. According to reports, their program called for the destruction of property that could not be moved or that the Soviets did not want. Also, the Generalissimo has informed me that the Soviets secretly, and often openly, collaborated with the Chinese Communists by making Japanese equipment and arms available and by placing strong obstacles in the way of the troops of the Central Government when an effort was made to move them to Manchuria by sea and/or air. Under existing conditions, the Central Government do not have resources that are sufficient or appropriate to recover North China and at the same time to launch successfully a political and military campaign to recover Manchuria. The resources of the Gimo will be taxed further in South China in the maintenance of order and in facilitating economic recovery.

In my considered opinion the Central Government does not have the ability at least for many months, possibly years, to gain and retain control of North China due to lack of sufficient forces, vastness of area, dearth of communications and doubtful loyalty of people. If present activities are criteria, the Communist guerrillas and saboteurs can and probably will restrict and harass movements of the Central Government forces to a prohibitive degree, thereby resulting in a costly campaign.

Recently the Gimo urged that I provide US air transport to facilitate movement of two Armies to Manchuria from the Tientsin-Peking area. There was a lack of appreciation on the part of the Generalissimo and his Chinese Staff concerning the logistical support required for these forces as well as the necessary measures for their security in the heart of Manchuria. These factors as well as the lack of appropriate forces and transport facilities caused me to advise the Generalissimo that he concentrate his efforts on the recovery of North China and consolidate his political and military positions in that area prior to attempting to occupy Manchuria. The impression I received was that he agreed with this concept.

To disarm and facilitate the repatriation of the Japanese, I pointed out to the Gimo, was the sole reason the Americans had assisted the Central Government in moving sufficient Chinese forces into North China, North FIC and Formosa. With reference to entrance into Manchuria, sufficient armies were moved to occupy that area but its accomplishment had been prevented by the Chinese Communists and the Soviets. Further, I pointed out that under existing directives I am not authorized to employ American forces and resources to move additional Chinese Central Government troops and/or equipment because, such action would irrefutably provide direct assistance to the Central Government forces vis-à-vis the Chinese Communists in their operations.

Apropos of foregoing incident to present developments in China, are my duties as American Commander of China Theater and concurrently the Generalissimo's Chief of Staff. Rightfully in my latter position the Gimo expects advice concerning procuring assistance and formulating of plans for the solution of his internal repeat internal problems, all of which would entail full scale operations against the Chinese Communists. I feel certain that, when the President authorized an American as the Generalissimo's Chief of Staff, he did not visualize that I, or any officer on active duty in the service, should serve in an advisory capacity on matters involving internal and political affairs and especially to internecine or fratricidal warfare. For this reason when in Washington recently I recommended that the officer heading up the Military Advisory Group should be directed not to serve in any capacity on the Generalissimo's staff or in the Chinese Government. Pertinent example: The French Consul General in Shanghai only recently solicited assistance in connection with the disarming of several hundred Frenchmen by the Japanese in the Shanghai area. The French equipment was recovered by the Chinese; however, they refused to return it to the French. I informed the French

Consul General that this matter should be taken up with the Chinese Government direct. In reply he stated that he was appealing to me as the Chief of Staff to the Generalissimo. Another example: In order to secure shipping for the movement of additional forces to the North, the Gimo asked that I contact the British in Chungking. I contacted the British and they were most sympathetic; however, they recounted several British grievances including discriminatory acts and restrictions against their subjects who have heavy financial and commercial interests and who desire to resume their various activities in China. I was strongly urged by the British to ask for remedial action on the part of the Generalissimo. To insure that the British Ambassador will do some scratching along the tortuous spine of the Chinese Dragon, paradoxically I am asked to scratch the back of the British Lion.

The Generalissimo is determined to retain in their present areas the Marines in North China. As a matter of fact he desires the Marines to expose long lines of communications in their occupational areas. He visualizes utilizing the Marines as a base of maneuver. The Gimo would like to concentrate plans based on conducting a campaign against the Chinese Communists instead of repatriating the Japanese. Such a campaign may require several months or years as indicated above. In the interim the Marines are subject to unavoidable incidents which may involve the United States in very serious commitments and difficulties. Careful consideration has been given to the implications of suggesting that we withdraw all of our American forces including the Marines from China. It is impossible to avoid involvement in political strife or fratricidal warfare under present circumstances, yet I am admonished to do so by my directive. The presence of American troops in the Far East as I view it, is for the expressed purpose of insuring continued peace and accomplishing world order. Under the provisions of the lofty aims of the United Nations Charter, however, I doubt that the American people are prepared to accept the role inherent in world leadership. We can justifiably be accused, by removing our forces at this critical time, of deserting an Ally. It is readily discernible that China is incapable of solving her political and economic problems and also repatriate the millions of enemy troops and civilians within her borders.

Conclusions:

a. To stabilize the situation in South China the Generalissimo would have to accept the assistance of foreign technicians and administrators and institute reforms through employment of honest, competent civilian officials in the economic, social and political fields.

b. Unless a satisfactory settlement is accomplished with the Chinese

Communists in North China followed up realistically by action indicated in subparagraph a. above, the Generalissimo will not be able to stabilize the situation in North China for several months, perhaps years.

c. He will be unable for many years to recover Manchuria unless satisfactory agreements again are concluded with the Soviet Government and the Chinese Communists.

d. It appears remote that the Chinese Communists and the Chinese Central Government will come to a satisfactory agreement.

e. In direct contravention to recent Sino-Soviet agreements, the Soviets are in effect creating favorable conditions for the realization of Chinese Communist aims and possibly their own plans in Manchuria and North China.

f. To continue American Forces in China Theater particularly in the North China area might possibly develop a tense and dangerous situation with the Soviet Government and will inevitably lead to serious involvement in fratricidal warfare.

g. No longer tenable are the dual capacities of Chief of Staff to the Generalissimo and American Commander of China Theater.

h. In consonance with existing Theater directive to disarm and repatriate the Japanese in North China, appropriate and full assistance has been provided to the movement of Chinese Central Government forces by American air and sea transport. However, these Chinese forces are largely being deployed for employment against dissident groups and/or Chinese Communists.

Recommendations:

The Chinese Government be notified by the US Government—

a. That the position of the American Commander as Generalissimo's Chief of Staff was approved during the war for the purpose of coordinating Sino-American combat activities against the common enemy, the Japanese, and that this position can be immediately absolved.

b. Confirm my decision as early as practicable to remove all American Forces including Marines in China Theater, or justify under US policies their employment and retention in the area by effecting changes to existing directives.

c. Continued implementation of plans for the projected American Military Advisory Group, however, withhold actual consummation until appropriate military and political stabilization is accomplished to the complete satisfaction of the United States Government.

PART II

The strategic implications and the broader aspects of the situation depicted in Part I are included in the following considerations. To attain the policy goals of China as so often stressed by Chiang, i.e., the establishment of a unified, strong, democratic China will definitely be effected, if not actually determined, by the policies of and the degree and form of assistance provided by foreign countries including the United States, France, Britain, Holland and Soviet Russia, particularly the latter named nation.

China is neither capable of implementing nor is she prepared psychologically, in my considered opinion, to establish democratic procedures in government. The difficulties China is experiencing history accurately depicts in Western Europe when in that area countries were elevated to a more homogeneous monarchies and republics from an amorphous mass of feudalistic dynasties. China should be able to transcend from a medieval state to a democratic form of government by processes of evolution, as opposed to bloody and chaotic revolution for the best interests of World Peace and Advancement.

Accepting the following premises that: China's resurgence will be contingent upon policies and assistance from world powers; that China and Russia are in close juxtaposition geographically with a common border of several thousand miles; and further that certain facilities exist in China which are of paramount interest to Russia both militarily and commercially—it is most certainly fitting, therefore, that we examine Soviet Russia's possible policies for it would appear logical that she may pursue one of the following two courses of action.

1. The Soviets may become strongly nationalistic and further promote the program of establishing a strong industrial and political structure, thus continuing the policy that has characterized the past few years under Stalin. At the same time Russia may create buffer zones on her borders, and maintain the initiative in these areas. This she has already accomplished in Western Europe, for she maintains a paramount sphere of influence in Eastern Poland, throughout the Balkans and in the Baltic States. That such buffer areas will also be established by Russia in the Far East and Middle East is a reasonable assumption. There are indications of powerful Soviet military forces in the Caucasus at the present time, forces which can intimidate Iran, Turkey, and Iraq. Russian actions in Manchuria, Korea, Inner and Outer Mongolia, Sinkiang, Jehol and Chahar Provinces are suggestive of the pattern for the Far East, where the Soviets may create conditions not unlike those that now exist on Russia's European frontiers.

2. The Russian policies just described may have been adopted as a matter of expediency in an effort to cope with a war-created situation, thus permitting a de-emphasis of the revolutionary features of international Communism. Now, Russia may decide upon an aggressive policy, utilizing the buffer areas referred to earlier as spring boards for ideological penetration and, by employing military force, for territorial expansion. The Soviet intention to pursue such a policy is suggested by the establishment of Communist cells in the Arab states, Afghanistan and South America, by overt activities in North China, Manchuria and Korea, by world-wide invidious propaganda and by the more-than-normal interest Russia has shown in General MacArthur's program to stabilize Japan.

In my considered opinion, the Soviets are not prepared to successfully implement the policy outlined in subparagraph 1, above. Thousands of Russian villages, towns and cities must be rehabilitated. Even prewar, Russian industries were not operating effectively, even though they were strongly permeated by British, American, and German technicians. Russian soldiers in large numbers have been in contact with Allied armed forces and have acquired knowledge of democratic processes and living standards outside of the Soviet Union that refute strongly the disparaging Soviet propaganda to the contrary. Also, the evidence is increasing that in many ways the primary Communist principles of Marx and Lenin are being abrogated and that Soviet Russia is following bureaucratic procedures. Probably, many years will pass before the Soviets are sufficiently strong to successfully embark on the international program related above in subparagraph 2. Prior to the 22nd of June 1941, for many years the radio and press of most nations in the world assailed Communism bitterly, with its attendant regimentation, purges, atheism, restriction on human liberty, and stultification of freedom of enterprise. There was a complete about-face after the Nazi attack and the Allied press found justification for a military alliance and an ameliorated public opinion. Today, our motives are suspect, which is only natural, and the Soviets are building defenses against the possibility of interference with whatever policy they pursue. In addition to these factors, when one considers that by far the biggest proportion of the people of Russia are not real Communists, but actually are under the control of a few with powers equalling or possibly surpassing the powers of the Czars, it is a logical assumption that the stratagems of defense pointed out in subparagraph 1 will characterize the policy of the Soviets.

Another vital factor, should the spread of Communism accelerate effectively throughout the Far East, that may effect the future policy of the United States and other foreign nations interested in democratic or capitalistic forms of government. In the world today there is a total of approximately one billion 40 million persons who might embrace Communism in various forms including an estimated 450 million people in China, 100 million in Korea and Japan, 100 million throughout the Philippine Archipelago, the Melanesian and Micronesian Islands, Netherland East Indies, Malay, Indo-China and Burma and 390 million in India. To add to this number the several million scattered throughout Western Europe and in other parts of the world to include the approximate 190 million in Soviet Russia, strategic implications of which must be clearly discernible concerning the dangerous position and/or impotency of the democratic and capitalistic nations.

The aspirations of China to develop a unified democratic form of government has always been supported by the policies of the American Government. However, the present complex situation might indicate that several million Chinese are thwarting the attainment of that goal. Not only would it be distasteful to interfere with China's internal affairs as recently set forth in the President's Navy Day talk on U. S. foreign policy wherein he reaffirmed the principle of self-determination, but also the U. S. might become involved in a serious dispute with Soviet Russia that might possibly lead to an armed conflict.

U. S. policy has always opposed the domination of China and concomitantly insisted upon her territorial integrity to the exclusion of any one power. Our efforts have been to encourage western economic, religious, political and cultural influences as opposed to colonization in the Far East.

The axis between the East and West is China. With the emergence of a strong Soviet Russia, China today is the political and economic arena of the world's two greatest powers, Soviet Russia and the United States. With a Chinese Communist victory, China would become a satellite of the Soviet, which is just what it would mean, and the continents of Europe and Asia would practically be under the control of Soviet Russia. Rule of so large an area, especially by a totalitarian nation, would endanger the peace of the world. Great sacrifices were made to prevent China from becoming a Puppet of the Japanese. If we are to realize our objectives in China it is believed of utmost importance that we preclude the Soviets from gaining control of that area.

A proper question may be posed—are we supporting the wrong horse or is there realistic justification for the hope that China may emerge from her present tribulations? Before the Marco Polo incident the Generalissimo was striving to effect social reforms including the freedom of the coolies and peasants by undertaking an industrial and political revolution to achieve self-government and unity and to provide obstacles against foreign economic domination. Splendid progress was being made and this is often referred to as the real reason for the attack on China in 1937 by the Japanese. The Japanese military leaders felt that this posed a realistic threat to their program of aggression in the Far East and accordingly decided to strike before China became a strong and unified nation.

The resultant progress achieved in unifying China is attested by the fact that she absorbed the loss of all her newly developed industries, her communication and port facilities with the outside world. Though divested of weapons and industrial support and in addition a totally blockaded nation, China under the present government waged war stoically for eight long years under the leadership of Chiang-Kai-shek. To retain confidence in China's ability to solve her internal problems, therefore, would seem to be a sound conclusion. Continued material aid and encouragement to the recognized government of China would be in accord with present U. S. policy of non-interference with internal matters. We should not, however, participate militarily unless world peace is definitely jeopardized thereby during the process of evolution or revolution within the Chinese Government.

Moreover, to avoid any possibility of being involved in the internal affairs of China, it would appear sound to remove all U. S. military forces from China proper. To continue support of China's newly created and revitalized small industries, could be accomplished by furnishing arms and equipment, as well as raw and processed materials.

The racial aspects and legal rights of China to Manchuria are recognized by Soviet Russia, the British and the United States. Therefore, is it not practicable to protect those rights by invoking their combined aid? From the U. S. viewpoint it would seem sound to prevent that area from becoming a puppet or satellite of the Soviet Government. Pending China developing sufficiently strong and stabilized to assume responsibility of full control, the United States could initiate steps for an immediate trusteeship over Manchuria and Korea, inviting Great Britain, China and Russia to participate. Self-government in Korea could be decided after the people themselves had indicated their ability to do so.

Recommendations:

1. Remove from China Theater all U. S. military forces as early as practicable and concomitantly furnish continued and accelerated economic assistance to the existing recognized China Government; or, until China has developed adequate internal power to assume her rightful role in the family of nations and until the repatriation of all Japanese both civilian and military has been accomplished, proclaim a U. S. policy embodying the determination to continue military and economic support

to the Chinese Central Government (this latter course would entail a change in my directive).

2. A trusteeship over Korea and Manchuria be established immediately under the aegis of the United States, China, Great Britain and Russia. This trusteeship to last until China gives evidence to these four nations of her ability to assume responsibilities for control of Manchuria and that the Korean people are prepared to govern themselves.

APPENDIX V

DIRECTIVE TO LIEUTENANT GENERAL WEDEMEYER

You will proceed to China without delay for the purpose of making an appraisal of the political, economic, psychological and military situations —current and projected. In the course of your survey you will maintain liaison with American diplomatic and military officials in the area. In your discussions with Chinese officials and leaders in positions of responsibility you will make it clear that you are on a fact-finding mission and that the United States Government can consider assistance in a program of rehabilitation only if the Chinese Government presents satisfactory evidence of effective measures looking towards Chinese recovery and provided further that any aid which may be made available shall be subject to the supervision of representatives of the United States Government.

In making your appraisal it is desired that you proceed with detachment from any feeling of prior obligation to support or to further official Chinese programs which do not conform to sound American policy with regard to China. In presenting the findings of your mission you should endeavor to state as concisely as possible your estimate of the character, extent, and probable consequences of assistance which you may recommend, and the probable consequences in the event that assistance is not given.

When your mission in China is completed you will proceed on a brief trip to Korea to make an appraisal of the situation there with particular reference to an economic aid program in Korea and its relation to general political and economic conditions throughout the country. Before going to Korea you will communicate with General MacArthur to ascertain whether he desires you to proceed via Tokyo.

You will take with you such experts, advisers and assistants as you deem necessary to the effectiveness of your mission.

Approved

Harry Truman

July 9, 1947

APPENDIX VI

REPORT TO THE PRESIDENT, 1947, PARTS I-V

19 September 1947.

MEMORANDUM FOR THE PRESIDENT:

My dear Mr. President:

In compliance with your directive to me of 9 July 1947, the attached "REPORT ON CHINA-KOREA" is respectfully submitted.

In consonance with your instructions, advisers from State, Treasury, War and Navy Departments accompanied me on a two months fact-finding mission in the Far East. The principal cities and some rural areas in China and Korea were visited. Successful efforts were made to reach all categories of people as measured by economic position, intellectual attainment and divergent political viewpoints. Conferences were held with public officials and with private citizens in all walks of life. Approximately 1,200 memoranda from individuals and groups were received and considered.

The report includes pertinent data in appendices which may be of interest and assistance to appropriate government departments and agencies. The report presents against a global background my estimates of the situations, current and projected, in both China and Korea, and recommends what I deem to be sound courses of action for achievement of United States objectives in the Far East.

Respectfully yours,

A. C. WEDEMEYER,
Lieutenant General, U. S. Army.

461

MEMBERS OF MISSION

16 July-18 September 1947

Captain James J. Boyle . . .	Aide-de-Camp—Secretary, War Department.
Captain Horace Eng	Aide-de-Camp—Interpreter War Department.
Lt. Colonel Claire E. Hutchin, Jr. .	Military Advisor, War Department.
Mr. David R. Jenkins	Fiscal Advisor, Treasury Department.
Mr. Philip D. Sprouse . . .	Political Advisor, State Department.
Rear Admiral Carl A. Trexel . .	Engineering Advisor, Navy Department.
Mr. Melville H. Walker . . .	Economic Advisor, State Department.
Mr. Mark S. Watson	Press and Public Affairs Advisor, *Baltimore Sun*, Baltimore, Md.
Lt. General A. C. Wedemeyer . .	Special Representative of the President of the United States.

CHINA—KOREA

Part I—General Statement

China's history is replete with examples of encroachment, arbitrary action, special privilege, exploitation, and usurpation of territory on the part of foreign powers. Continued foreign infiltration, penetration or efforts to obtain spheres of influence in China, including Manchuria and Taiwan (Formosa), could be interpreted only as a direct infringement and violation of China's sovereignty and a contravention of the principles of the Charter of the United Nations. It is mandatory that the United States and those other nations subscribing to the principles of the Charter of the United Nations should combine their efforts to insure the unimpeded march of all peoples toward goals that recognize the dignity of man and his civil rights and, further, definitely provide the opportunity to express freely how and by whom they will be governed.

Those goals and the lofty aims of freedom-loving peoples are jeopardized today by forces as sinister as those that operated in Europe and Asia during the ten years leading to World War II. The pattern is familiar—employment of subversive agents; infiltration tactics; incitement of disorder and chaos to disrupt normal economy and thereby to undermine popular confidence in government and leaders; seizure of authority without reference to the will of the people—all the techniques skillfully designed and ruthlessly implemented in order to create favorable conditions for the imposition of totalitarian ideologies. This pattern is present in the Far East, particularly in the areas contiguous to Siberia.

If the United Nations is to have real effect in establishing economic stability and in maintaining world peace, these developments merit high priority on the United Nations' agenda for study and action. Events of the past two years demonstrate the futility of appeasement based on the hope that the strongly consolidated forces of the Soviet Union will adopt either a conciliatory or a cooperative attitude, except as tactical expedients. Soviet practice in the countries already occupied or dominated completes the mosaic of aggressive expansion through ruthless secret police methods and through an increasing political and economic enslavement of peoples. Soviet literature, confirmed repeatedly by Communist leaders, reveals a definite plan for expansion far exceeding that of Nazism in its ambitious scope and dangerous implications. Therefore in attempting a solution to the problem presented in the Far East, as well as in other troubled areas of the world, every possible opportunity must be used to seize the initiative in order to create and maintain bulwarks of freedom.

Notwithstanding all the corruption and incompetence that one notes in China, it is a certainty that the bulk of the people are not disposed to a Communist political and economic structure. Some have become affiliated with Communism in indignant protest against oppressive police measures, corrupt practices and mal-administration of National Government officials. Some have lost all hope for China under existing leadership and turn to the Communists in despair. Some accept a new leadership by mere inertia.

Indirectly, the United States facilitated the Soviet program in the Far East by agreeing at the Yalta Conference to Russian re-entry into Manchuria, and later by withholding aid from the National Government. There were justifiable reasons for these policies. In the one case we were concentrating maximum Allied strength against Japanese in order to accelerate crushing defeat and thus save Allied lives. In the other, we were withholding unqualified support from a government within which corruption and incompetence were so prevalent that it was losing the support of its own people. Further, the United States had not yet realized that the Soviet Union would fail to cooperate in the accomplishment of world-wide plans for post-war rehabilitation. Our own participation in those plans has already afforded assistance to other nations and peoples, friends and former foes alike, to a degree unparalleled in humanitarian history.

Gradually it has become apparent that the World War II objectives for which we and others made tremendous sacrifices are not being fully attained, and that there remains in the world a force presenting even greater dangers to world peace than did the Nazi militarists and the Japanese jingoists. Consequently the United States made the decision in the Spring of 1947 to assist Greece and Turkey with a view to protecting their sovereignties, which were threatened by the direct or inspired activities of the Soviet Union. Charges of unilateral action and circumvention of the United Nations were made by members of that organization. In the light of its purposes and principles such criticisms seemed plausible. The United States promptly declared its intention of referring the matter to the United Nations when that organization would be ready to assume responsibility.

It follows that the United Nations should be informed of contemplated action with regard to China. If the recommendations of this report are approved, the United States should suggest to China that she inform the United Nations officially of her request to the United States for material assistance and advisory aid in order to facilitate China's post-war rehabilitation and economic recovery. This will demonstrate that the United Nations is not being circumvented, and that the United States is not infringing upon China's sovereignty, but contrariwise is cooperating constructively in the interest of peace and stability in the Far East, concomitantly in the world.

The situation in Manchuria has deteriorated to such a degree that prompt action is necessary to prevent that area from becoming a Soviet satellite. The Chinese Communists may soon gain military control of Manchuria and announce the establishment of a government. Outer Mongolia, already a Soviet satellite, may then recognize Manchuria and conclude a "mutual support agreement" with a *de facto* Manchurian government of the Chinese Communists. In that event, the Soviet Union might accomplish a mutual support agreement with Communist-dominated Manchuria, because of her current similar agreement with Outer Mongolia. This would create a difficult situation for China, the United States and the United Nations. Ultimately it could lead to a Communist-dominated China.

The United Nations might take immediate action to bring about cessation of hostilities in Manchuria as a prelude to the establishment of a Guardianship or Trusteeship. The Guardianship might consist of China, Soviet Russia, the United States, Great Britain and France. This should be attempted *promptly* and could be initiated only by China. Should one of the nations refuse to participate in Manchurian Guardianship, China might then request the General Assembly of the United Nations to establish a Trusteeship, under the provisions of the Charter.

Initially China might interpret Guardianship or Trusteeship as an infringement upon her sovereignty. But the urgency of the matter should encourage a realistic view of the situation. If these steps are not taken by China, Manchuria may be drawn into the Soviet orbit, despite United States aid, and lost, perhaps permanently, to China.

The economic deterioration and the incompetence and corruption in the political and military organizations in China should be considered against an all-inclusive background lest there be disproportionate emphasis upon defects. Comity requires that cognizance be taken of the following:

Unlike other Powers since V-J Day, China has never been free to devote full attention to internal problems that were greatly confounded by eight years of war. The current civil war has imposed an overwhelming financial and economic burden at a time when resources and energies have been dissipated and when, in any event, they would have been strained to the utmost to meet the problems of recovery.

The National Government has consistently, since 1927, opposed Communism. Today the same political leader and same civil and military officials are determined to prevent their country from becoming a Communist-dominated State or Soviet satellite.

Although the Japanese offered increasingly favorable surrender terms during the course of the war, China elected to remain steadfast with her Allies. If China had accepted surrender terms, approximately a million Japanese would have been released for employment against American forces in the Pacific.

I was assured by the Generalissimo that China would support to the limit of her ability an American program for the stabilization of the Far East. He stated categorically that, regardless of moral encouragement or material aid received from the United States, he is determined to oppose Communism and to create a democratic form of government in consonance with Doctor Sun Yat-sen's principles. He stated further that he plans to make sweeping reforms in the government including the removal of incompetent and corrupt officials. He stated that some progress has been made along these lines but, with spiraling inflation, economic distress and civil war, it has been difficult to accomplish fully these objectives. He emphasized that, when the Communist problem is solved, he could drastically reduce the Army and concentrate upon political and economic reforms. I retain the conviction that the Generalissimo is sincere in his desire to attain these objectives. I am not certain that he has today sufficient determination to do so if this requires absolute overruling of the political and military cliques surrounding him. Yet, if realistic United States aid is to prove effective in stabilizing the situation in China and in coping with the dangerous expansion of Communism, that determination must be established.

Adoption by the United States of a policy motivated solely toward stopping the expansion of Communism without regard to the continued existence of an unpopular repressive government would render any aid ineffective. Further, United States prestige in the Far East would suffer heavily, and wavering elements might turn away from the existing government to Communism.

In China and Korea, the political, economic and psychological problems are inextricably mingled. All of them are complex and are becoming increasingly difficult of solution. Each has been studied assiduously in compliance with your directive. Each will be discussed in the course of this report. However, it is recognized that a continued global appraisal is mandatory in order to preclude disproportionate or untimely assistance to any specific area.

The following three postulates of United States foreign policy are pertinent to indicate the background of my investigations, analyses and report:

> The United States will continue support of the United Nations in the attainment of its lofty aims, accepting the possible development that the Soviet Union or other nations may not actively participate.

> Moral support will be given to nations and peoples that have established political and economic structures compatible with our own, or that give convincing evidence of their desire to do so.

> Material aid may be given to those same nations and peoples in order to accelerate post-war rehabilitation and to develop economic stability, provided:

> That such aid shall be used for the purposes intended.

> That there is continuing evidence that they are taking effective steps to help themselves, or are firmly committed to do so.

> That such aid shall not jeopardize American economy and shall conform to an integrated program that involves other international commitments and contributes to the attainment of political, economic and psychological objectives of the United States.

Part II—China

POLITICAL

Although the Chinese people are unanimous in their desire for peace at almost any cost, there seems to be no possibility of its realization under existing circumstances. On one side is the Kuomintang, whose reactionary leadership, repression and corruption have caused a loss of popular faith in the Government. On the other side, bound ideologically to the Soviet Union, are the Chinese Communists, whose eventual aim is admittedly a Communist state in China. Some reports indicate that Communist measures of land reform have gained for them the support of the majority of peasants in areas under their control, while others indicate that their ruthless tactics of land distribution and terrorism have alienated the majority of such peasants. They have, however, successfully organized many rural areas against the National Government. Moderate groups are caught between Kuomintang misrule and repression and ruthless Communist totalitarianism. Minority parties lack dynamic leadership and sizable following. Neither the moderates, many of whom are in the Kuomintang, nor the minority parties are able to make their influence felt because of National Government repression. Existing provincial opposition leading to possible separatist movements would probably crystallize only if collapse of the Government were imminent.

Soviet actions, contrary to the letter and spirit of the Sino-Soviet Treaty of 1945 and its related documents, have strengthened the Chinese Communist position in Manchuria, with political, economic and military repercussions on the National Government's position both in Manchuria and in China proper, and have made more difficult peace and stability in China. The present trend points toward a gradual disintegration of the National Government's control, with the ultimate possibility of a Communist-dominated China.

Steps taken by the Chinese Government toward governmental reorganization in mid-April 1947 aroused hopes of improvement in the political situation. However, the reorganization resulted in little change. Reactionary influences continue to mold important policies even though the Generalissimo remains the principal determinative force in the government. Since the April reorganization, the most significant change has been the appointment of General Chen Cheng to head the civil and military administration in Manchuria. Projected steps include elections in the Fall for the formation of a constitutional government, but, under present conditions, they are not expected to result in a government more representative than the present regime.

ECONOMIC

Under the impact of civil strife and inflation, the Chinese economy is disintegrating. The most probable outcome of present trends would be, not sudden collapse, but a continued and creeping paralysis and consequent decline in the authority and power of the National Government. The past ten years of war have caused serious deterioration of transportation and communication facilities, mines, utilities and industries. Notwithstanding some commendable efforts and large amounts of economic aid, their overall capabilities are scarcely half those of the pre-war period. With disruption of transportation facilities and the loss of much of North

China and Manchuria, important resources of those rich areas are no longer available for the rehabilitation and support of China's economy.

Inflation in China has been diffused slowly through an enormous population without causing the immediate dislocation which would have occurred in a highly industrialized economy. The rural people, 80 per cent of the total Chinese population of 450 million, barter foodstuffs for local handicraft products without suffering a drastic cut in living standards. Thus, local economies exist in many parts of China, largely insulated from the disruption of urban industry. Some local economies are under the control of Communists, and some are loosely under the control of provincial authorities.

The principal cause of the hyper-inflation is the long-continued deficit in the national budget. Present revenue collections, plus the profits of nationalized enterprises, cover only one-third of governmental expenditures, which are approximately 70 per cent military, and an increasing proportion of the budget is financed by the issuance of new currency. In the first six months of 1947 note-issue was tripled but rice prices increased seven-fold. Thus prices and governmental expenditures spiral upwards, with price increases occurring faster than new currency can be printed. With further price increases, budget revisions will undoubtedly be necessary. The most urgent economic need of Nationalist China is a reduction of the military budget.

China's external official assets amounted to $327 million (US) on July 30, 1947. Privately-held foreign exchange assets are at least $600 million and may total $1500 million, but no serious attempt has been made to mobilize these private resources for rehabilitation purposes. Private Chinese assets located in China include probably $200 million in gold, and about $75 million in U.S. currency notes. Although China has not exhausted her foreign official assets, and probably will not do so at the present rates of imports and exports until early 1949, the continuing deficit in her external balance of payments is a serious problem.

Disparity between the prices of export goods in China and in world markets at unrealistic official exchange rates has greatly penalized exports, as have disproportionate increases in wages and other costs. Despite rigorous trade and exchange controls, imports have greatly exceeded exports, and there consistently has been a heavy adverse trade balance.

China's food harvests this year are expected to be significantly larger than last year's fairly good returns. This moderately encouraging situation with regard to crops is among the few favorable factors which can be found in China's current economic situation.

Under inflationary conditions, long-term investment is unattractive for both Chinese and foreign capital. Private Chinese funds tend to go into short-term advances, hoarding of commodities, and capital flight. The entire psychology is speculative and inflationary, preventing ordinary business planning and handicapping industrial recovery.

Foreign business enterprises in China are adversely affected by the inefficient and corrupt administration of exchange and import controls, discriminatory application of tax laws, the increasing role of government trading agencies and the trend towards state ownership of industries. The Chinese Government has taken some steps toward improvement but generally has been apathetic in its efforts. Between 1944 and 1947, the anti-inflationary measure on which the Chinese Government placed most reliance was the public sale of gold borrowed from the United States. The intention was to absorb paper currency, and thus reduce the effective demand for goods. Under the circumstance of continued large deficits, however, the only effect of the gold sales program was to retard slightly the price inflation and dissipate dollar assets.

A program to stabilize the economic situation was undertaken in February 1947. The measures included a wage freeze, a system of limited rationing to essential workers in a few cities, and the sale of government bonds. The effect of this program has been slight, and the wage freeze has been abandoned. In August 1947, the unrealistic official rate of exchange was replaced, for proceeds of exports and remittances, by a free market in foreign exchange. This step is expected to stimulate exports, but it is too early to determine whether it will be effective.

The issuance of a new silver currency has been proposed as a future measure to combat inflation. If the government continued to finance budgetary deficits by unbacked note issue, the silver would probably go into hoards and the price inflation would continue. The effect would be no more than that of the gold sales in 1944–1947, namely, a slight and temporary retardation of the inflationary spiral. The proposal could be carried out, moreover, only through a loan from the United States of at least $200 million in silver.

In the construction field, China has prepared expansive plans for reconstruction of communications, mines and industries. Some progress has been made in implementing them, notably in the partial rehabilitation of certain railroads and in the textile industry. Constructive results have been handicapped by a lack of funds, equipment and experienced management, supervisory and technical personnel.

On August 1, 1947, the State Council approved a "Plan for Economic Reform." This appears to be an omnibus of plans covering all phases of Chinese economic reconstruction but its effectiveness cannot yet be determined.

SOCIAL–CULTURAL

Public education has been one of the chief victims of war and social and economic disruption. Schoolhouses, textbooks and other equipment have been destroyed and the cost of replacing any considerable portion cannot now be met. Teachers, like other public servants, have seen the purchasing power of a month's salary shrink to the market value of a few days' rice ration. This applies to the entire educational system, from primary schools, which provide a medium to combat the nation's grievous illiteracy, to universities, from which must come the nation's professional men, technicians and administrators. The universities have suffered in an additional and no less serious respect—traditional academic freedom. Students participating in protest demonstrations have been severely and at times brutally punished by National Government agents without pretense of trial or public evidence of the sedition charged. Faculty members have often been dismissed or refused employment with no evidence of professional unfitness, patently because they were politically objectionable to government officials. Somewhat similarly, periodicals have been closed down "for reasons of military security" without stated charges, and permitted to reopen only after new managements have been imposed. Resumption of educational and other public welfare activities on anything like the desired scale can be accomplished only by restraint of officialdom's abuses, and when the nation's economy is stabilized sufficiently to defray the cost of such vital activities.

MILITARY

The overall military position of the National Government has deteriorated in the past several months and the current military situation favors Communist forces. The Generalissimo has never wavered in his contention that he is fighting for national independence against forces of an armed rebellion nor has he been completely convinced that the Communist problem can be resolved except by force of arms. Although the Nationalist Army has a preponderance of force, the tactical initiative rests with the Communists. Their hit-and-run tactics, adapted to their mission of destruction at points or in areas of their own selection, give them a decided advantage over Nationalists, who must defend many critical areas including connecting lines of communication. Obviously large numbers of Nationalist troops involved in such defensive roles are immobilized whereas Communist tactics permit almost complete freedom of action. The Nationalists' position is precarious in Manchuria, where they occupy only a slender finger of territory. Their control is strongly disputed in Shantung and Hopei Provinces where the Communists make frequent dislocating attacks against isolated garrisons.

In order to improve materially the current military situation, the Nationalist forces must first stabilize the fronts and then regain the initiative. Further, since the Government is supporting the civil war with approximately seventy per cent of its national budget, it is evident that steps taken to alleviate the situation must point toward an improvement in the effectiveness of the armed forces with a concomitant program of social, political and economic reforms, including a decrease in the size of the military establishment. Whereas some rather ineffective steps have been taken to reorganize and revitalize the command structure, and more sweeping reforms are projected, the effectiveness of the Nationalist Army requires a sound program of equipment and improved logistical support. The present industrial potential of China is inadequate to support military forces effectively. Chinese forces under present conditions cannot cope successfully with internal strife or fulfill China's obligations as a member of the family of nations. Hence outside aid, in the form of munitions (most urgently ammunition) and technical assistance, is essential before any plan of operations can be undertaken with a reasonable prospect of success. Military advice is now available to the Nationalists on a General Staff level through American military advisory groups. The Generalissimo expressed to me repeatedly a strong desire to have this advice and supervision extended in scope to include field forces, training centers and particularly logistical agencies.

Extension of military aid by the United States to the National Government might possibly be followed by similar aid from the Soviet Union to the Chinese Communists, either openly or covertly—the latter course seems more likely. An arena of conflicting ideologies might be created as in 1935 in Spain. There is always the possibility that such developments in this area, as in Europe and the Middle East, might precipitate a third world war.

Part III—Korea

POLITICAL

The major political problem in Korea is that of carrying out the Moscow Agreement of December 1945 for the formation of a Provisional Korean Government to be followed by a Four-Power Trusteeship over Korea. The United States-Soviet Joint Commission, established in accordance with that Agreement, reached a deadlock in 1946 in the effort to implement the Moscow Agreement due to Soviet opposition to consultations with the Commission by all Korean democratic parties and social organizations, as provided for in that Agreement. Soviet motives have been to eliminate the extreme rightist groups in theUnited States zone from consultations and subsequently from participation in the new government, thus ensuring a Communist-dominated government in Korea. Soviet objections to such consultations have been based on the rightist groups' openly expressed opposition to trusteeship, while the United States has taken the position that to disqualify these groups would deprive a large section of the Korean people of an opportunity to express views regarding their government.

A resumption of the Joint Commission meetings in May 1947, following an exchange of notes between Secretary Marshall and Foreign Minister Molotov, resulted in a further deadlock on the same issue, although these notes had established a formula which would have permitted participation in consultation by the rightist groups in question. After the Soviet Government failed to reply to Secretary Marshall's note of August 12 requesting the submission by the Commission of a joint status report or separate reports by each Delegation, the United States Delegation on August 20 transmitted a unilateral report to Washington. An American proposal then made to China, the United Kingdom and the Soviet Union for a Four-Power Conference to discuss Korea has been agreed to by China and the United Kingdom but has been rejected by the Soviet Union.

Internally, the Korean problem has been complicated by the Soviet establishment of a Communist regime in North Korea and by the machinations in South Korea of Communist groups, openly hostile to the United States. The terrorist activities of extreme rightists, who have strongly opposed trusteeship, have continually obstructed the efforts of United States authorities. The latter, in accordance with their Directives, are endeavoring to turn over to Koreans as rapidly as possible full administrative responsibility in governmental departments. In consonance with this plan they have organized an interim Korean legislative assembly and in general, are striving to carry out a policy of "Koreanization" of government in South Korea.

Economic

South Korea, basically an agricultural area, does not have the overall economic resources to sustain its economy without external assistance. The soil is depleted, and imports of food as well as fertilizer are required. The latter has normally come from North Korea, as have most of the electric power, timber, anthracite and other basic products.

The economic dependence of South Korea upon North Korea, and of Korea as a whole, in pre-war years, upon trade with Japan and Manchuria, cannot be too strongly emphasized. Division of the country at the 38° North parallel and prevention of all except smuggling trade between North and South Korea have reduced the Korean economy to its lowest level in many years. Prospects for developing sizable exports are slight. Food exports cannot be anticipated on any scale for several years, and then only with increased use of artificial fertilizer. South Korea's few manufacturing industries, which have been operating at possibly 20 per cent of pre-war production, are now reducing their output or closing down. In part this is a natural result of ten years of deferred maintenance and war-time abuse, but lack of raw materials and essential repair parts, and a gross deficiency of competent management and technical personnel are the principal factors.

A runaway inflation has not yet occurred in South Korea, because the Military Government has restrained the issuance of currency by keeping governmental expenditures and local occupation costs at reasonable levels; because cannibalization and the use of Japanese stocks have kept some industries going; and because the forcible collection of rice at harvest time has brought in sufficient food to maintain—with imports provided by the United States—an adequate official ration in the cities. Highly inflationary factors such as the exhaustion of raw material stocks, cumulative breakdowns in public services and transportation, and the cutting of power supply from the North might occur simultaneously. The South Korean economic outlook is, therefore, most grave.

A five-year rehabilitation program starting in July 1948, and requiring United States financing at a cost of $647 million, has been proposed by the Military Government. A review of preliminary estimates indicates that the proposed annual rehabilitation cost would be substantially greater than the relief program of $137 million which was tentatively approved for fiscal 1948 but later reduced to $92.7 million. These preliminary estimates of costs and the merits of individual projects need careful review. It is not considered feasible to make South Korea self-sustaining. If the United States elects to remain in South Korea support of that area should be on a relief basis.

SOCIAL—CULTURAL

Since the Japanese were expelled, the Korean people have vehemently and unceasingly pressed for restoration of their ancient culture. There is particular zeal for public education. Individual and collective efforts to reduce illiteracy have produced results meeting the praise of American Military Government officials. There will be materially better results when there are more school buildings, more trained teachers and advisors, and many more textbooks in the Korean language. Current American activities aim at adult visual education on a modest but reasonably effective scale. South Korea's health and public welfare work are at present fully as effective as under Japanese administration and considerably more so in the prevention of serious diseases. Even the Koreans' eagerness for improvement cannot immediately overcome the unquestionable need for large funds for social betterment.

MILITARY

The military situation in Korea, stemming from political and economic disputes which in turn are accentuated by the artificial barrier along the 38° North parallel, is potentially dangerous to United States strategic interests. Large scale Communist-inspired or abetted riots and revolutionary activities in the South are a constant threat. However, American forces supplemented by quasi-military Korean units are adequate to cope with such trouble or disorder except in the currently improbable event of an outright Soviet-controlled invasion. Whereas American and Soviet forces engaged in occupation duties in South Korea and North Korea respectively are approximately equal, each comprising less than 50,000 troops, the Soviet-equipped and trained North Korean People's (Communist) Army of approximately 125,000 is vastly superior to the United States-organized Constabulary of 16,000 Koreans equipped with Japanese small arms. The North Korean People's Army constitutes a potential military threat to South Korea, since there is strong possibility that the Soviets will withdraw their occupation forces, and thus induce our own withdrawal. This probably will take place just as soon as they can be sure that the North Korean puppet government and its armed forces which they have created, are strong enough and sufficiently well indoctrinated to be relied upon to carry out Soviet objectives without the actual presence of Soviet troops.

It appears advisable that the United States organize, equip and train a South Korean Scout Force, similar to the former Philippine Scouts. This force should be under the control of the United States military commander and, initially should be officered throughout by Americans, with a program for replacement by Korean officers. It should be of sufficient strength to cope with the threat from the North. It would counteract in large measure the North Korean People's Army when American and Soviet forces are withdrawn from Korea, possibly preclude the forcible establishment of a Communist government, and thus contribute toward a free and independent Korea.

Part IV—Conclusions

The peaceful aims of freedom-loving peoples in the world are jeopardized today by developments as portentous as those leading to World War II.

The Soviet Union and her satellites give no evidence of a conciliatory or cooperative attitude in these developments. The United States is compelled, therefore, to initiate realistic lines of action in order to create and maintain bulwarks of freedom, and to protect United States strategic interests.

The bulk of the Chinese and Korean peoples are not disposed to Communism and they are not concerned with ideologies. They desire food, shelter and the opportunity to live in peace.

CHINA

The spreading internecine struggle within China threatens world peace. Repeated American efforts to mediate have proved unavailing. It is apparent that positive steps are required to end hostilities immediately. The most logical approach to this very complex and ominous situation would be to *refer the matter to the United Nations.*

A China dominated by Chinese Communists would be inimical to the interests of the United States, in view of their openly expressed hostility and active opposition to those principles which the United States regards as vital to the peace of the world.

The Communists have the tactical initiative in the overall military situation. The Nationalist position in Manchuria is precarious, and in Shantung and Hopei Provinces strongly disputed. Continued deterioration of the situation may result in the early establishment of a Soviet satellite government in Manchuria and ultimately in the evolution of a Communist-dominated China.

China is suffering increasingly from disintegration. Her requirements for rehabilitation are large. Her most urgent needs include governmental reorganization and reforms, reduction of the military budget and external assistance.

A program of aid, if effectively employed, would bolster opposition to Communist expansion, and would contribute to gradual development of stability in China.

Due to excesses and oppressions by government police agencies basic freedoms of the people are being jeopardized. Maladministration and corruption cause a loss of confidence in the Government. Until drastic political and economic reforms are undertaken United States aid can not accomplish its purpose.

Even so, criticism of results achieved by the National Government in efforts for improvement should be tempered by a recognition of the handicaps imposed on China by eight years of war, the burden of her opposition to Communism, and her sacrifices for the Allied cause.

A United States program of assistance could best be implemented under the supervision of American advisors in specified economic and military fields. Such a program can be undertaken only if China requests advisory aid as well as material assistance.

KOREA

The situation in Korea, in its political, economic and psychological aspects, is strongly and adversely influenced by the artificial barrier of the 38° North parallel separating agricultural South Korea from the more industrialized North Korea.

The South Korean economic position is grave. Agriculture is debilitated and there are few other resources.

The establishment of a self-sustaining economy in South Korea is not feasible. Accordingly, United States aid should include a minimum of capital investment and should consist chiefly of items required for support on a relief basis.

Korean Communist agents are creating unrest and fomenting disorder in South Korea. The terrorist and obstructive activities of extreme rightist groups are further aggravating this situation.

Since the United States-Soviet Joint Commission meetings have twice ended in deadlock, and offer no real hope of success, the United Nations now seems to be the appropriate medium through which a Provisional Korean Government, functioning under a Four-Power Trusteeship, can be established.

The United States may be confronted with a situation requiring decision concerning continued occupation in South Korea should the Soviet Union withdraw her occupation forces. This could reasonably be expected to occur when the Soviet-created puppet government and its armed forces are sufficiently well established to carry out Communist objectives without the presence of Soviet troops.

The creation of an American-controlled and -officered Korean Scout Force, sufficient in strength to cope with the threat from the North, is required to prevent the forcible establishment of a Communist government after the United States and Soviet Union withdraw their occupation forces.

Part V—Recommendations

IT IS RECOMMENDED:

That the United States Government provide as early as practicable moral, advisory, and material support to China and South Korea in order to contribute to the early establishment of peace in the world in consonance with the enunciated principles of the United Nations, and concomitantly to protect United States strategic interests against militant forces which now threaten them.

That United States policies and actions suggested in this report be thoroughly integrated by appropriate government agencies with other international commitments. It is recognized that any foreign assistance extended must avoid jeopardizing the American economy.

CHINA

That China be advised that the United States is favorably disposed to continue aid designed to protect China's territorial integrity and to facilitate her recovery, under agreements to be negotiated by representatives of the two governments, with the following stipulations:

That China inform the United Nations promptly of her request to the United States for increased material and advisory assistance.

That China request the United Nations to take immediate action to bring about a cessation of hostilities in Manchuria and request that Manchuria be placed under a Five-Power Guardianship or, failing that, under a Trusteeship in accordance with the United Nations Charter.

That China make effective use of her own resources in a program for economic reconstruction and initiate sound fiscal policies leading to reduction of budgetary deficits.

That China give continuing evidence that the urgently required political and military reforms are being implemented.

That China accept American advisors as responsible representatives of the United States Government in specified military and economic fields to assist China in utilizing United States aid in the manner for which it is intended.

KOREA

That the United States continue efforts for the early establishment of a Provisional Korean Government in consonance with the Moscow Agreement and meanwhile provide necessary support of the political, economic and military position of South Korea.

It is recommended that:

United States withdrawal from Korea be based upon agreements with the Soviet Union to effect proportional withdrawals, with as many guarantees as possible to safeguard Korean freedom and independence.

Military aid be furnished to South Korea which would support the achievement of such adequate safeguards and which would envisage:

Continuing to furnish arms and equipment to Korean National Police and Korean Coast Guard.

The creation of an American-officered Korean Scout Force to replace the present Constabulary of sufficient strength to cope with the threat from the North.

Continued interim occupation by United States Army forces in Korea.

Advice in training of technical specialists and tactical units.

BIBLIOGRAPHY

NOTE: This list is by no means complete. I gratefully acknowledge the stimulus and inspiration I received from many other books, articles, and documents and regret that space does not permit their inclusion.

Speidel, Hans, *Invasion 1944*. Chicago, Henry Regnery Co., 1950.

Dulles, Allen Welsh, *Germany's Underground*. New York, The Macmillan Co., 1947.

Gisevius, Hans Bernd, *To the Bitter End*. Boston, Houghton Mifflin Co., 1947.

Chennault, Claire Lee, *Way of a Fighter*. New York, G. P. Putnam's Sons, 1949.

Utley, Freda, *Last Chance in China*. [Excerpts used by special permission of the publishers.] New York, The Bobbs-Merrill Co., 1947.

Feis, Herbert, *The China Tangle*. Princeton, Princeton University Press, 1953.

Liu, F. F., *A Military History of Modern China*. Princeton, Princeton University Press, 1956.

Higgins, Trumbull, *Winston Churchill and the Second Front*. New York, Oxford University Press, 1957.

DeJaegher, Raymond J., and Kuhn, Irene Corbally, *The Enemy Within*. New York, Doubleday and Company, Inc., 1952.

Flynn, John T., *While You Slept*. New York, The Devin-Adair Company, 1951.

Stuart, John Leighton, *Fifty Years in China*. New York, Random House, 1954.

White, Theodore H., and Jacoby, Annalee, *Thunder Out of China*. New York, William Sloane Associates, Inc., 1946.

Tong, Hollington K., *Chiang Kai-shek*. Taipei, China Publishing Co., 1953.

William, Maurice, *Sun Yat-sen Versus Communism*. Baltimore, The Williams and Wilkins Co., 1932.

Chiang Kai-shek, *China's Destiny*. New York, The Macmillan Co., 1947.

Eisenhower, Dwight D., *Crusade in Europe*. New York, Doubleday and Co., Inc., 1948.

Clark, Mark W., *Calculated Risk*. New York, Harper and Brothers, 1950.

Leahy, Fleet Admiral William D., *I Was There*. New York, Whittlesey House, 1950.

Baldwin, Hanson W., *Great Mistakes of the War*. New York, Harper and Brothers, 1949.

Lyons, Eugene, *Our Secret Allies*. New York, Duell, Sloan & Pearce, Inc., 1954.

Lohbeck, Donald, *Patrick J. Hurley*. Chicago, Henry Regnery Co., 1956.

Lane, Arthur Bliss, *I Saw Poland Betrayed*. New York, The Bobbs-Merrill Co., 1948.

Burnham, James, *The Coming Defeat*. New York, The John Day Co., 1949.

Churchill, Winston S., *The Unknown War*. New York, Charles Scribner's Sons, 1931.

Churchill, Winston S., *The World Crisis*. London, Thornton Butterworth, Limited, 1929.

Churchill, Winston S., *The Gathering Storm*. Boston, Houghton Mifflin Co., 1948.

Churchill, Winston S., *The Grand Alliance*. Boston, Houghton Mifflin Co., 1951.

Churchill, Winston S., *The Hinge of Fate*. Boston, Houghton Mifflin Co., 1953.

Churchill, Winston S., *Closing the Ring*. Boston, Houghton Mifflin Co., 1951.

Wilmot, Chester, *The Struggle for Europe*. New York, Harper and Brothers, 1952.

Kennedy, Sir John, *The Business of War*. London, Hutchinson and Co., 1957.

Bryant, Sir Arthur, *The Turn of the Tide*. London, Collins, 1957.

Butler, J. R. M., *Grand Strategy*, Volume II. London, Her Majesty's Stationery Office, 1957.

Ehrman, John, *Grand Strategy*, Volumes V and VI. London, Her Majesty's Stationery Office, 1956.

De Wiart, Carton, *Happy Odyssey*. London, Pan Books, Ltd., 1955.

MacLean, Fitzroy, *Escape to Adventure*. Boston, Little, Brown and Co., 1951.

Fuller, Major General J. F. C., *The Second World War 1939–1945*. New York, Duell, Sloan and Pearce, 1949.

Fuller, Major General J. F. C., *A Military History of the Western World*. New York, Funk & Wagnalls Co., 1954.

Slim, Field Marshal Sir William, *Defeat Into Victory*. London, Cassell and Co., Ltd., 1956.

Keynes, J. M., *The Economic Consequences of the Peace*. New York, Harcourt, Brace and Howe, 1920.

Grenfell, Captain Russell, *Unconditional Hatred*. New York, The Devin-Adair Co., 1954.

Toynbee, Arnold J., *A Study of History*. New York, Oxford University Press, 1951.

Bevin, Ernest, *The Balance Sheet of the Future*. New York, Robert M. McBride and Co., 1941.

Grey, Viscount of Fallodon, K.G., *Fallodon Papers*. Boston, Houghton Mifflin Co., 1926.

Spykman, Nicholas John, *America's Strategy in World Politics*. New York, Harcourt, Brace and Co., 1942.

Simonds, Frank H., *The Great Powers in World Politics*. Boston, American Book Co., 1937.

Morley, Felix, *The Foreign Policy of the United States*. New York, Alfred A. Knopf, 1951.

Hart, B. H. Liddell, *Strategy*. New York, Frederick A. Praeger, 1954.

Morison, Samuel Eliot, *Strategy and Compromise*. Boston, Little, Brown and Co., 1958.

Kissinger, Henry A., *Nuclear Weapons and Foreign Policy*. New York, Harper and Brothers, 1957.

Nicolson, Harold, *The Congress of Vienna*. New York, Harcourt, Brace and Co., 1946.

Truman, Harry S., *Memoirs*. New York, Doubleday and Company, Inc., 1955.

Stimson, Henry L., and Bundy, McGeorge, *On Active Service in Peace and War*. New York, Harper and Brothers, 1947.

De Toledano, Ralph, *Spies, Dupes, and Diplomats*. Boston, Little, Brown and Co., 1952.

Lavine, Harold, and Wechsler, James, *War Propaganda and the United States*. New Haven, Yale University Press, 1940.

Reed, Douglas, *Somewhere South of the Suez*. New York, The Devin-Adair Co., 1951.

Tansill, Charles Callan, *Back Door to War*. Chicago, Henry Regnery Co., 1952.

Barnes, Harry Elmer, *Perpetual War for Perpetual Peace*. Caldwell, Idaho, The Caxton Printers, Ltd., 1953.

Dulles, John Foster, *War or Peace*. New York, The Macmillan Co., 1950.

Veale, F. J. P., *Advance to Barbarism*. Appleton, Wisconsin, C. C. Nelson Co., 1953.

Willoughby, Major General Charles A., and Chamberlain, John, *MacArthur 1941–1951*. New York, McGraw-Hill Book Co., 1954.

Whitney, Major General Courtney, *MacArthur*. New York, Alfred A. Knopf, 1956.

Hull, Cordell, *The Memoirs of Cordell Hull*. New York, The Macmillan Co., 1948.

King, Ernest J., and Whitehill, Walter Muir, *Fleet Admiral King*. New York, W. W. Norton and Company, Inc., 1952.

Romanus, Charles F., and Sunderland, Riley, *U.S. Army in World War II —Time Runs Out*. Washington, U.S. Government Printing Office, 1958.

Romanus, Charles F., and Sunderland, Riley, *U.S. Army in World War II, China-Burma-India Theater, Stilwell's Command Problems*. Washington, U.S. Government Printing Office, 1956.

Cline, Ray S., *U.S. Army in World War II, The War Department, Washington Command Post: The Operations Division*. Washington, U.S. Government Printing Office, 1951.

Watson, Mark Skinner, *United States Army in World War II, The War Department, Chief of Staff: Prewar Plans and Preparations*. Washington, U.S. Government Printing Office, 1950.

Matloff, Maurice, and Snell, Edwin M., *United States Army in World War II, The War Department, Strategic Planning for Coalition Warfare, 1941–1942*. Washington, U.S. Government Printing Office.

Eastman, Max, *Reflections on the Failure of Socialism*. New York, The Devin-Adair Co., 1955.

Budenz, Louis F., *The Techniques of Communism*. Chicago, Henry Regnery Co., 1954.

Durant, Will, *The Story of Philosophy*. New York, Simon and Schuster, 1953.

Blackett, P. M. S., *Miltary and Political Consequences of Atomic Energy*. London, Turnstile Press, 1948.

Sherwood, Robert E., *Roosevelt and Hopkins*. New York, Harper and Brothers, 1948.

Feis, Herbert, *Churchill, Roosevelt, Stalin*. Princeton, Princeton University Press, 1957.

Loomis, Louise Ropes, ed., *Aristotle—On Man in the Universe*. New York, Walter J. Black, 1943.

United States Relations with China. Department of State Publication 3573, Division of Publications Office, Office of Public Affairs, 1949.

Nazi-Soviet Relations 1939–1941. Documents from the Archives of the German Foreign Office, Department of State, Washington, U.S. Government Printing Office.

Schoonmaker, Nancy, and Reid, Doris Fielding, eds., *We Testify*. New York, Smith and Durrell, Inc., 1941.

Report by The Supreme Commander to the Combined Chiefs of Staff on the Operations in Europe of the Allied Expeditionary Force, 6 June 1944 to 8 May 1945. Washington, U.S. Government Printing Office.

INDEX